The RoutledgeFalmer Reader in Higher Education

D0224037

The *RoutledgeFalmer Reader in Higher Education* provides a balanced selection of the last few years' writing on the topic, offering anyone with an interest in higher education an essential companion.

The editor uses his experience to present a range of articles, illustrating the variety of methodological approaches and theoretical frameworks that have been applied to the study of higher education. Journal articles from Europe, Australia and Asia cover the following key themes:

- teaching and learning;
- course design;
- student experience;
- quality;
- system policy;
- institutional management;
- academic writing;
- knowledge.

This ground-breaking Reader reflects the range of perspectives that contribute to higher education research. It aims to support the growth of higher education as an emerging field of study.

Malcolm Tight is Professor of Education, University of Warwick, and Editor of *Studies in Higher Education* and *International Perspectives on Higher Education Research*.

Readers in education

The RoutledgeFalmer Reader in Higher Education
Edited by Malcolm Tight

The RoutledgeFalmer Reader in Language and Literacy
Edited by Teresa Grainger

The RoutledgeFalmer Reader in Psychology of Education
Edited by Harry Daniels and Anne Edwards

The RoutledgeFalmer Reader in Sociology of Education
Edited by Stephen J. Ball

The RoutledgeFalmer Reader in Science Education
Edited by John Gilbert

The RoutledgeFalmer Reader in Multicultural Education
Edited by David Gillborn and Gloria Ladson-Billings

The RoutledgeFalmer Reader in Inclusion
Edited by Keith Topping and Sheelagh Maloney

The RoutledgeFalmer Reader in Teaching and Learning
Edited by Ted Wragg

The RoutledgeFalmer Reader in Higher Education

Edited by
Malcolm Tight

RoutledgeFalmer
Taylor & Francis Group

LONDON AND NEW YORK

First published 2004
by RoutledgeFalmer
11 New Fetter Lane, London EC4P 4EE

Simultaneously published in the USA and Canada
by RoutledgeFalmer
29 West 35th Street, New York, NY 10001

RoutledgeFalmer is an imprint of the Taylor & Francis Group

© 2004 Selection and editorial matter: Malcolm Tight

Typeset in Sabon and Futura by
Florence Production Ltd, Stoodleigh, Devon
Printed and bound in Great Britain by
TJ International, Padstow, Cornwall

British Library Cataloguing in Publication Data
A catalogue record for this book is available from the
British Library

Library of Congress Cataloging in Publication Data
A catalog record for this book has been requested

ISBN 0–415–32764–4 (hbk)
ISBN 0–415–32765–2 (pbk)

CONTENTS

ACKNOWLEDGEMENTS

The following articles are reproduced with the kind permission of Kluwer Academic Publishers:

Higher Education, 40 (2000), pp. 99–121, *Misconceptions about Learning Approaches, Motivation and Study Practices of Asian Students*, David Kember.

Higher Education, 42 (2001), pp. 85–105, *The Regulation of Transnational Higher Education in Southeast Asia: case studies of Hong Kong, Malaysia and Australia*, Grant McBurnie and Christopher Ziguras.

Higher Education, 42 (2001), pp. 473–492, *Innovation and Isomorphism: a case-study of university identity struggle*, Bjørn Stensaker and Jorunn Dahl Norgård.

The following article is reproduced with the kind permission of Blackwell Publishing:

European Journal of Education, 35, 2 (2000), pp. 141–156, *Graduate Employment and Work in Selected European Countries*, Ulrich Teichler.

All other articles are reproduced with the kind permission of Taylor & Francis Group, http://www.tandf.co.uk.

HIGHER EDUCATION AS A FIELD OF RESEARCH

Malcolm Tight

The commission

When I was invited by the publishers in April 2002 to edit this *Reader in Higher Education* (as one of a series on different aspects of education), it was immediately clear to me that the most challenging aspect of the project would be the selection of the 18 articles or chapters required.

After all, even if we restrict ourselves to considering English language publications produced outside North America, there are at least 300 books on higher education currently in print. The major publishers involved include the Open University Press (recently taken over by McGraw Hill), Jessica Kingsley (though it has now stopped publishing further books in this area), Kogan Page (which focuses more on the 'how to', practical end of the market) and Taylor & Francis (notably through its Routledge and Falmer imprints).

When we look at academic journals, the amount being published on higher education is even more impressive. By my reckoning (Tight 2003), there are currently 17 established specialist higher education academic journals published in the English language outside North America. These are:

- *Active Learning in Higher Education* (ALHE)
- *Assessment and Evaluation in Higher Education* (AEHE)
- *European Journal of Education* (EJE)
- *Higher Education* (HE)
- *Higher Education in Europe* (HEE)
- *Higher Education Management* (HEM)
- *Higher Education Policy* (HEP)
- *Higher Education Quarterly* (HEQ)
- *Higher Education Research and Development* (HERD)
- *Higher Education Review* (HER)
- *International Journal for Academic Development* (IJAD)
- *Journal of Geography in Higher Education* (JGHE)
- *Journal of Higher Education Policy and Management* (JHEPM)
- *Quality in Higher Education* (QHE)
- *Studies in Higher Education* (SHE)
- *Teaching in Higher Education* (THE)
- *Tertiary Education and Management* (TEAM).

There are, of course, many other education journals – and quite a few journals that do not focus specifically on education – which regularly publish articles on higher education, but do not specialise in it. There are also an increasing number of non-academic journals that focus instead on professional or practitioner audiences and concerns; and, while these will not typically referee articles as carefully as the academic journals, they still contain much interesting material. In addition, stimulated by the growing attention being paid to learning and teaching in higher education, a number of new journals are entering the field. So there was plenty of material to make a selection from.

However, higher education, as an area for study and research, is still an emerging field. There are a number of contemporary overviews of the field of higher education research available (Sadlak and Altbach 1997, Schwartz and Teichler 2000, Teichler and Sadlak 2000). There are also an increasing number of academic courses on higher education (Altbach and Engberg 2001), stimulated by the growing expectation that academic staff should engage in initial and continuing training. But it could not be said that there is a developed and widely shared understanding of what the field of higher education research looks like. With few existing guides, how, then, was I to make a selection?

Possible selection strategies

The publisher's guidance on this matter was commendably brief, being confined to the suggestion that I should 'select the most influential, previously published material'. That immediately posed the question to me of just how influential research and writing on higher education was. After all, very few books on higher education (apart from yearbooks and directories, and a handful of 'how to' publications) ever go to a second edition, or sell more than a few hundred copies. Higher education researchers regularly bemoan the lack of articulation between research findings, policy and practice (e.g. Kogan 2000, Scott 2000). And there are few, if any, Readers like this which attempt to provide an overview of the field of research that are in print, certainly outside of North America.

I could, of course, have selected the 18 articles or chapters on higher education that had most influenced me over the 25 odd years I have been involved in this area, but this would have been a rather odd, personal and partial selection. Alternatively, I could have surveyed a number of leading academics, or even practitioners and policy makers, in the field for their views, conducting a kind of Delphi exercise. But I didn't have the time for such an exercise, and suspected anyway that interpreting and acting upon the responses received would not have been straightforward. I did, though, receive some useful comments from two referees, who had been approached by the publisher, regarding my initial proposal for the Reader, some of which I have tried to take on board.

I was, therefore, in the market for strategies for selecting the Reader's contents. Fortunately, revisiting the literature and a little further thought suggested a series of possible approaches.

First, much research on higher education is carried out in departments that are not focused on higher education (or even on education more generally). Such research is also frequently undertaken by academics with no specialist training in, or over-riding focus on, higher education research. Hence, my selection might seek to reflect the range of disciplines contributing to higher education research (Clark 1984, Teichler 1996). These could include, for example, economics, education, history, law, management, philosophy, politics, psychology and sociology.

Second, a related approach would be to seek to reflect the variety of locations in which higher education researchers are found (Hayden and Parry 1997, Teichler 2000). These would include not just different university departments, as well as research centres or institutes, but, perhaps equally importantly, consultancies based outside of universities, government departments and agencies, and international organisations (Brennan 2000).

Third, the selection might seek to illustrate the range of methodological approaches and/or theoretical frameworks that have been applied to the study of higher education. My own analysis of contemporary higher education research, for a related volume (Tight 2003), suggests that there are two dominant approaches to higher education research. The first, and most prevalent, of these is the relatively small-scale, evaluative case study, typically of a development in teaching, learning or evaluation at the course, departmental or institutional level (many such studies, of course, are never published or circulated outside the institution of origin). The methodology of such studies, whether qualitative or quantitative, is usually fairly explicit, and there is often also something of a theoretical framework present. The other dominant approach to higher education research is policy critique, typically national, and usually with no explicit methodology or theoretical framework given.

As well as seeking to reflect the dominance of these two approaches, it might also be argued that the minority of other studies, using other methodological or theoretical frameworks, including the larger-scale and comparative, the conceptual and philosophical, the critical and feminist, deserve particular attention. A similar case could be made for studies applying methodologies that have been developed particularly within the higher education context, such as phenomenography.

Fourth, another strategy would be to focus on the potential audiences for the Reader, and structure the selection of contents accordingly. Clearly, the audience could include all those having any interest in higher education and higher education research, but two sub-audiences are probably the most significant. One of these comprises, of course, existing higher education researchers, but the largest potential audience for this Reader is, at least in my view, most likely to be the increasing numbers of academics, in the United Kingdom and elsewhere, undergoing initial and continuing training. If the latter were seen as the main target audience, this might then suggest a selection of exemplary, overview or representative articles and chapters.

This final point suggests what may seem to be the most obvious (and fifth) approach to selecting the contents for the Reader, namely in terms of the themes or issues that higher education faces, and that higher education researchers have been, or are currently, researching.

Themes in higher education research

A number of attempts have been made to organise or classify higher education research in terms of themes or issues, of which I will consider three here.

First, we may consider the views of Teichler, clearly a leading, perhaps the leading, contemporary European authority and writer in this area. While recognising the lack of 'a generally accepted "map" of higher education research', he goes on to suggest four categories or 'spheres of knowledge in higher education' (Teichler 1996, pp. 440–441):

- quantitative-structural aspects of higher education;
- knowledge and subject-related aspects of higher education;
- person-related as well as teaching and research-related aspects of higher education;
- aspects of organisation and governance of higher education.

Teichler then suggests typical areas of higher education research for each of these four spheres. Thus, quantitative-structural aspects include studies of access, elite and mass higher education, diversification, institutional types, student employment and income, returns on educational investment and mobility. Knowledge and subject-related aspects include disciplinarity, academic and professional emphases, quality, competences and overqualification. Person and process-related aspects include motivation, counselling, pedagogies, learning styles and assessment. And organisation and governance-related aspects include planning, management, efficiency, funding and resource allocation.

A relationship is also suggested between topics, disciplinary bases and hence method-ologies for research. Thus, quantitative-structural aspects are seen as being addressed most commonly by economists and sociologists; knowledge and subject-related aspects by histo-rians and sociologists; person and process-related aspects by educationalists and psychologists; and organisation and governance-related aspects by political scientists, economists, and academics focusing on business/management and law.

Second, Frackmann, focusing solely on higher education research in Western Europe, has suggested five 'clusters of issues' for research (Frackmann 1997, pp. 125–126):

- role and function of higher education;
- nature of knowledge and learning;
- coordination mechanisms between society and higher education;
- learning and teaching;
- higher education and European integration.

While the last of these seems specific to the European context, the other four appear fairly closely related to the spheres identified by Teichler.

Third, and finally for present purposes, Hayden and Parry (1997), writing from an Australasian perspective, identify two main approaches to higher education research: a focus on higher education policy, and an emphasis on academic practice. This seems very close to the methodological distinction I have already made between two dominant approaches to higher education research: policy critiques and small-scale, evaluative case studies.

The selection strategy adopted

After some further thought, and a number of abortive starts, I approached the commission in the following fashion. To begin with, I set myself three constraints to limit the work involved.

The first of these was to restrict myself to material published outside North America. This was in part a convenience, as it reflected the publisher's strengths, but also gave me a prag-matic challenge. As others have noted, while higher education research is better established in the North American systems than elsewhere (Altbach and Engberg 2001), it also has a tendency to be inward looking (Maassen 2000). It struck me as both more interesting and more useful, therefore, to put together a Reader of articles or chapters by non-North American authors published outside of North America.

The second constraint was to limit myself to articles published in academic journals. I decided on this because, unlike book chapters, journal articles necessarily have to be self-contained and are also typically of a fairly standard length (6,000–8,000 words). They should not, therefore, require any further editing.

My third constraint was also practical, but again, in my view, had positive consequences. The move to put journals online has, for researchers, both reduced the need to make frequent visits to academic libraries (or maintain multiple journal subscriptions) and greatly eased access to a wider range of publications. Higher education journals have typically been available online since the late 1990s, so I deliberately confined my selection to the last four or five years. This had the pleasing effect of giving my selection a very immediate and contempo-rary feel. It does mean, however, that there is little included from those whom we might call the 'grand old men' of higher education research, though their influences may be judged by the number of references to their work.

At this point, you may be thinking that, by adopting these three constraints, I was making the job too easy. I wouldn't agree. I still then had to search not only the 17 specialist academic journals identified earlier, but also several other general education journals I had selected as being of particular interest. Six of these were chosen for special scrutiny:

- *British Educational Research Journal* (BERJ)
- *British Journal of Sociology of Education* (BJSE)
- *Comparative Education* (CE)
- *Gender and Education* (GE)
- *Journal of Education and Work* (JEW)
- *Oxford Review of Education* (ORE).

These 23 journals put out between two and eight issues a year, each containing between four and ten articles of potential interest. In short, then, I had a database of over 4,000 articles to make a selection from!

Within the constraints that I had set myself, my selection strategy proceeded as follows. Adopting the third and fifth of the selection strategies identified earlier, and bearing the fourth in mind, I set out to try and represent:

- the range of methods and methodologies applied to higher education research; and
- the range of themes or issues studied, as best as I could; while
- seeking to make the Reader useful and of interest to the widest possible audience.

I did this by producing a long 'short' list of possible articles for inclusion in the Reader, using quality as my criterion, and then categorised each of them in terms of the methods and methodologies used, and the themes and issues addressed.

This categorisation made use of a simple, two-dimensional matrix that I had been developing for a related research project (see Tight 2003 and next section). For that research project, I had already categorised the 406 articles published in the 17 specialist higher education academic journals identified earlier during the sample year of 2000. With this as an indicative map of the relative frequency of the use of methods to investigate particular issues, I had a framework for whittling down the short-listed articles in a more or less representative fashion to the required 18.

In the whittling process, I allowed three further factors to influence my final selection. On the one hand, I wanted to avoid biasing my selection towards articles by United Kingdom authors on United Kingdom issues – naturally enough, these are the dominant source of articles in English published outside of North America – and ensure that I included voices from other countries in Europe, Australia, Asia and elsewhere. On the other hand, I wanted to try and reflect in my selection the relative numbers of women and men currently researching and writing on higher education. And, finally, I was clear that I couldn't justify, with only 18 choices, including more than one article by any one author (just as I felt I couldn't include anything I had written, as I should have more than sufficient of a voice as the editor).

I would not presume to say, and I trust that the authors concerned will forgive me for not doing so, that the 18 articles I finally selected are the 18 'best' or 'most influential' published in English outside North America during the last four or five years. It's simply too early to judge. I most certainly do think that they are all good articles, that they serve my purposes well, and I'm very happy to include them in this Reader. But I could have selected another 18 of a similar quality, as I hope my introductory comments to each article, and suggestions for further reading, indicate.

Themes and methods

The categorisation of higher education research, against which I assessed my initial short-list of articles for possible inclusion in this Reader, consists of eight key themes or issues that higher education researchers are currently addressing, and eight key methods or methodologies that they apply in their research (Tight 2003). I wasn't consciously aiming for two sets of eight categories, though there was clearly a practical need to limit the number of categories – that's just how it worked out.

The eight key themes identified are as follows:

- *teaching and learning*: including approaches to studying, learning styles, pedagogical styles;
- *course design*: including assessment, competencies, critical thinking, learning technologies, portfolios, postgraduate study, reflection, writing;
- *the student experience*: including access, counselling, diversity, employment, evaluation, motivation, multiculturalism, non-completion;
- *quality*: including evaluation, grading, outcomes, qualifications, standards;
- *system policy*: including economies of scale, funding, globalisation, massification, national policy, returns on investment;
- *institutional management*: including autonomy, departments, governance, management, marketisation, mergers;
- *academic work*: including careers, induction, mobility, professionalism, training, writing;
- *knowledge*: including disciplinarity, forms of knowledge, research.

This cannot, of course, be a definitive listing, and there are also inevitably some overlaps between the categories identified. Others would, no doubt, identify more, less or different categories, and include particular items under different themes. Nevertheless, I would argue that it is both an indicative and useful approach, as I hope this Reader will demonstrate.

This categorisation may be usefully compared with those proposed by Teichler and Frackmann, as outlined earlier. Clearly, what I am proposing is rather more disaggregated than either of theirs. Thus, what Teichler termed quantitative/structural aspects, and what Frackmann labelled as coordination mechanisms, appear in my listing as both system policy and institutional management. Quality, which was subsumed by Teichler under knowledge/subject-related aspects, appears here separately: on the grounds that it has been a major focus for policy and research during the last two decades. What Frackmann calls learning and teaching, and Teichler terms person/process-related aspects, have been split up into three related headings: teaching and learning, course design, and the student experience.

The categorisation used here also has the advantage of being empirically based. My own impression, from being involved for many years in both higher education research and the editing of higher education journals, of the frequency with which different themes were being addressed was rather different from what I found when I categorised the journal articles for the sample year. This caused me to develop a rather different set of categories from those I originally had in mind.

The eight key methods or methodologies identified were as follows:

- *documentary analysis*: including historical studies, literature reviews and most policy analyses;
- *comparative analysis*: international studies comparing two or more national systems;
- *interviews*: including face-to-face and internet-based studies, and focus groups;
- *Surveys/multivariate analysis*: including questionnaires, the analysis of large quantitative databases, and experimental studies;
- *conceptual analysis*: including more theoretical studies;
- *phenomenography*: and related approaches such as phenomenology;
- *critical/feminist perspectives*: including studies that set out to critique established positions;
- *auto/biographical and observational studies*: including accounts based largely on personal experience.

Table 1 Themes and methods in higher education research

Method/ology	Themes and issues							
	Teaching/learning	Course design	Student experience	Quality	System policy	Institutional management	Academic work	Knowledge
Biography	−	+	−	−	−	−	+	−
Critical	−	−	−	−	−	−	−	−
Phenomenography	−	−	−	−	−	−	−	−
Conceptual	−	+	−	−	−	−	−	−
Multivariate	−	+++	+++	+	+	+	+	−
Interviews	+	+++	+	−	−	−	+	−
Comparative	−	−	−	−	+	−	−	−
Documentary	−	+++	−	+	+++	+++	+	−

Key: Many published articles +++; some published articles +; few or no published articles −.

Table 2 The selected articles plotted on Table 1

Method/ology	Themes and issues							
	Teaching/learning	Course design	Student experience	Quality	System policy	Institutional management	Academic work	Knowledge
Biography		Johnson Scott				Jenkins	Grant	
Critical								
Phenomenography								Brew
Conceptual		Barnett Maclellan					Land	
Multivariate			Norton Ball					
Interviews			Teichler	Shevlin			Trowler	
Comparative	Kember				Jongbloed McBurnie			
Documentary					Deem	Stensaker		

Note: The first author only has been named for clarity.

Again, this listing might be questioned or altered, and different methods or methodologies given a particular emphasis. The list does, however, bear a close resemblance to many standard overviews of social and educational research methods (e.g. Blaxter *et al.* 2001, Cohen *et al.* 2000, Punch 1998).

Three other points are worth addressing here. First, the list is a mixture of what would commonly be termed 'methods', such as interviews and surveys, and what would be typically termed 'methodologies', such as conceptual analysis and feminist perspectives. The distinction, of course, is not precise, and many of these terms might be treated as either method or methodology. It is a practical listing, reflecting the tendency of many researchers to focus on the method, the actual tools used for collecting and interpreting data, and of others to emphasise methodology, their underlying philosophical perspective used in seeking to understand what they are studying.

Second, and despite my earlier comments, I have not separately identified 'case study' as a method or methodology. I did try at one point working with an 8 × 9 matrix, but this proved to be problematic. The reason was that most pieces of research could be described as being, in some sense, case studies, so this proved to be a not very useful way for categorising published articles.

Third, some may question why I have chosen to separately identify what are, as will become apparent, relatively specialised or 'minority interest' methodologies such as phenomenography and critical/feminist approaches. My answer would be precisely for that reason. To me, phenomenography appears to be the only methodology which has been particularly, though not exclusively, developed within higher education research (Ashworth and Lucas 2000). Critical and feminist approaches to the analysis of higher education, for their part, while easy to overlook, offer some of the most challenging pieces of research currently being undertaken.

Using these two categorisations – of themes and issues, and methods and methodologies – it was a fairly straightforward process to produce an 8 × 8 matrix, on which the location and relative frequency of published articles could be plotted. Of course, any one article may cover more than one of the themes identified, and may also make use of more than one of the methods or methodologies. It was not difficult, however, for most articles, to identify a dominant theme and method, though in a minority of cases particular articles might have been placed in different cells.

Table 1 shows the matrix produced from the categorisation of the 406 articles published in 17 specialist higher education academic journals in the year 2000 (Tight 2003). In order not to give the impression of precision, and recognising that the analysis was for just one year, the relative frequency of publication has been indicated in a threefold fashion: many, some, and few or none published articles.

Table 1 was used as a guide for making the final selection of articles for inclusion in the Reader from the short-list, so as to enable a representation in rough proportion to the frequency of publication of articles on particular themes and using particular methods. At the same time, I was also concerned to include a few articles from some of the less populated cells of the matrix. The resulting selection, as included in this Reader, is mapped onto the matrix in Table 2. Their selection, positioning on the matrix, themes and methods are further discussed in the individual editorial introductions to each article in the Reader.

An overview of the articles selected

The topics covered by the articles charted in Table 2 and included in this Reader range from:

- academic writing to student writing;
- choice to social class;
- entrepreneurialism to research supervision;

- learning styles to student behaviours; and
- curricular to departmental to institutional change.

The subject of each article was summarised by two or three keywords, before being allocated to a theme. The methods or methodologies used were also summarised in terms of two or three keywords. They include action research, biography, feminist critique and personal reflection, as well as the more common interviews, questionnaires, comparative and multivariate analysis.

As well as illustrating the variety of higher education themes and issues currently being researched, and the range of methodologies and methods applied to that research, the selection of articles in this Reader also shows wide differences in the scale or level of research undertaken. Thus, there are articles that focus on the individual level, on small groups, on departments, on single institutions, on groups of institutions or regions, on nations or systems, and on international patterns. This demonstrates not only that, at one extreme, higher education research (like other forms of social research) can be complex, large-scale, expensive and very time-consuming, but that it may also, at the other extreme, be relatively small-scale and thus eminently 'do-able', while still of high quality.

The 18 articles selected have 37 authors, an average of just over two per article, with a range between a single author (in seven cases) and a maximum of four authors (in three cases). Of these, 15 (41%) are women. Twenty-three (62%) of the authors are United Kingdom based, with the remainder based in Australia (seven authors), the Netherlands and Norway (two authors each), and Germany, Hong Kong and New Zealand (one author each).

The articles chosen come from 11 academic journals, based editorially in the United Kingdom, Australia or Europe. Two journals (*Assessment and Evaluation in Higher Education*, and *Higher Education*) are represented by three articles each, and three others (the *International Journal of Academic Development*, *Studies in Higher Education* and *Teaching in Higher Education*) by two articles. The other six journals, the *British Journal of the Sociology of Education*, *Comparative Education*, the *European Journal of Education*, *Higher Education Research and Development*, the *Journal of Geography in Higher Education*, and the *Journal of Higher Education Policy and Management*, are each represented by one article. All of the articles were originally published in 2000, 2001 or 2002.

The order in which the articles appear is deliberate, though I might have ordered them differently. I decided to start with a series of articles focusing on the student experience, teaching and learning, and course design. I did this in the belief that this would make the Reader more immediate and engaging for most readers. There are then a series of articles about academic work, institutional management and knowledge. Finally, there are a number of articles that focus on higher education institutions, system policy and international issues.

Obviously, with only 18 choices to make, there are gaps (one that particularly struck me was the absence of an article taking an historical approach, though recent history is a focus of two of the articles). A typical reaction to examining the selection for the first time might, therefore, be, 'but where is . . . ?' I would, no doubt, react in the same way to another editor's selection. Another possible objection to the selection strategy I have adopted would be that, in seeking to be representative, I have spread the resources too thinly, and that it might have been better to have chosen three or four articles on each of four or five themes. This I have attempted to respond to in my introductory comments on each of the selected articles, where further reading – particularly books – is suggested.

In the end, though, this is my selection.

Overview of higher education research

But what does this selection, and the analysis upon which it is based, say about the current state of higher education research? Table 1 indicates that the most common higher education issue currently being researched – at least, as this manifests itself in articles published in academic journals – is what I have termed course design; that is, how the higher education experience is organised and delivered to students. This may seem entirely reasonable and sensible, as the delivery of courses to students is arguably a (or the) core function of higher education.

Other important themes for higher education research indicated include:

- system policy (government strategies for higher education and their implementation);
- the student experience (their recruitment, treatment and subsequent destinations);
- institutional management (how higher education institutions are organised and operated); and
- academic work (what lecturers and other members of academic staff actually do, and how this is changing).

As with the focus on course design, these emphases also seem appropriate.

The three other themes identified appear to be less commonly researched, though this is not to say that no research is being undertaken. It must be emphasised at this point that the blank cells in Table 1 do not indicate that nothing is being researched – though that may be so in some cases – but that relatively little is being done. These three, less popular, themes are, in decreasing order of frequency:

- quality (how good higher education institutions are at delivering their various functions, and how we measure this);
- teaching and learning (the pedagogical relationship between students and academics); and
- knowledge (that which we are seeking to understand through higher education).

It may be, then, that the concern with quality, which spawned its own 'sub-industry' within higher education in the 1980s and 1990s, has peaked. Interestingly, what appear to be the least researched themes, teaching and learning and knowledge, also appear to be the most theorised, and hence may be perceived as the most difficult to research.

Looking at the other dimension to Table 1, the methods and methodologies used in researching higher education, a rather clearer pattern emerges. Of the eight methods or methodologies identified, three appear dominant: the use of interviews, multivariate and documentary analyses. Interviews and multivariate analysis, of course, are the mainstays of empirical social research, representing the classic forms of qualitative and quantitative research respectively. The significance of documentary analysis is also not surprising, as documents represent both the most universal and the most accessible approach to research. Virtually all higher education research projects will involve the use of documents to some extent, and virtually all of us can get ready access to at least some documents of relevance to higher education research. It would be strange to see an article published in an academic journal – though this does occur from time to time – that did not include some reference to documentary sources, particularly, perhaps, the author's previous writings.

By comparison, the other five methods or methodologies identified – biography, phenomenography, critical, conceptual and comparative analyses – appear far less common as approaches to higher education research. Much the same comment could probably be made, of course, about their use in most other areas of social research.

Three of these approaches – biographical, conceptual and comparative analyses – are, nevertheless, fairly well established, though largely restricted to the examination of particular themes. Each, therefore, has its own characteristics and challenges:

- biographical studies range from straightforward descriptions of initiatives ('how I did it' or 'how to do it') to highly theorised, reflective accounts of experience ('what we learnt about ourselves from doing it');
- conceptual analyses, with their philosophical and literary roots, have a long tradition; while
- comparative analysis presumes greater expenditure and linguistic facility if it is done well, but has been stimulated in recent years, particularly within the European Union, by the increasing international flow of students and staff.

The application of phenomenography and critical approaches to researching higher education is much less common (indeed, both rows appear completely blank in Table 1). Yet, phenomenography has established itself as what might be called a niche methodology within higher education research during the last two decades (Ashworth and Lucas 2000). Critical and feminist approaches are arguably the most marginal, and least respected, methodological approaches to researching higher education. Partly with this in mind, I have deliberately chosen to include examples of each in this collection.

So far, my discussion of Table 1 has emphasised what is there, but perhaps it is more interesting, at least for a while, to focus on what is not there, or at least is relatively absent (i.e. the blank spaces in the table). Here, to use a geographical analogy, one may sense the thrill of an explorer setting out for some terra incognita on the map.

The limited use made of phenomenographic and critical analyses, and to a lesser extent of biographical and conceptual analyses, may be partly explained in terms of their relative unfamiliarity, and the consequent difficulty of applying them appropriately. But, if you think for a moment about applying these approaches to the study of, for example, quality, system policy or institutional management, other explanations for their relative under-use suggest themselves. Such research projects would be likely to pose considerable challenges and risks, not least to the researchers involved. They might also be relatively difficult to gain funding or other support for. This does not, of course, mean that they would not be worth pursuing.

More specifically, there are a number of other blank cells in Table 1 that it would be interesting to see explored and filled out in greater detail. These blanks include, for example:

- interview-based studies of system policy and institutional management;
- comparative analyses of course design and institutional management;
- multivariate or comparative studies of knowledge;
- conceptual analyses of quality;
- biographical studies of teaching and learning and of the student experience; and
- phenomenographic analyses of system policy and institutional management.

The possibilities seem both wide-ranging and attractive.

Higher education as a field of research

The arguments put forward in this introductory chapter, and the whole experience of putting together this Reader, have led me to a series of interim conclusions about higher education as a field of research. In this section I will explore two such conclusions, one to do with the overall health of the field, the other concerning its characteristics. I don't claim any particular originality for these conclusions, as they do confirm what a number of other authors have argued in the recent past.

First, then, and this is probably the most obvious conclusion, it seems clear that – even though it is the subject of thousands of articles and hundreds of books published every year – higher education remains a relatively under-researched area. The amount of research effort devoted to, for example, health care, employment or schools is far greater. Higher education is, however, an area for study that is developing rapidly. Twenty, or even ten, years ago, the amount of research available for consultation would have been much more limited. So we won't be able to use this excuse for much longer.

The explanation for this state of affairs is not far to seek. It has to do with the recent move in most developed nations from elite to mass systems of higher education. Such mass systems, almost by their very nature, absorb more expenditure, engage wider interest within societies, and raise greater concerns about standards and value for money. They also require the training and development of larger numbers of staff. All of these trends serve as stimuli for further research, and, in the case of the last named, help to produce the researchers needed to carry it out.

The current position for higher education research – and higher education researchers – is, therefore, generally healthy and positive. There is much that is worth researching, and an increasing range of opportunities to be engaged professionally in such research; though most such engagement, even where paid, will tend to be, at least initially, part-time and/or short-term.

Second, in terms of the characteristics of higher education research, I would argue that a number of tendencies may be identified. Thus, higher education research tends to:

- be small-scale rather than large-scale;
- be cross-sectional rather than longitudinal;
- be short-term rather than long-term;
- be positivist rather than critical;
- seek solutions to problems rather than challenges;
- be instrumental rather than theoretical.

These trends are, of course, perfectly understandable, and are probably common to many other areas of applied social research. Long-term, large-scale and longitudinal research is expensive, and most researchers will not have the time, funding or commitment necessary to carry it out. Similarly, the emphasis on research that provides evidence-based and fairly immediate answers to perceived problems seems reasonable in an environment where most higher education staff, and their funders, are working hard (and harder) and are looking to higher education researchers for ready help rather than seemingly abstract speculation. But it would be unhealthy if this were the only, or perhaps even the dominant, kind of research being undertaken.

I would, therefore, like to register a plea for continuing and more critical, challenging and theoretical research into higher education. Such research, by establishing and developing the overall framework for our understanding of higher education, feeds over time into both higher education practice and the more immediate and common forms of higher education research. We need it for the sake of our minds and souls.

Using this book

As this introductory chapter has indicated, I have put together this book with the aim of including a selection of high quality articles dealing with higher education research. The articles have been chosen so as to represent, as far as possible, both the range of themes or issues which higher education researchers have tackled in recent years, and the methods or methodologies they have used in conducting their research. In doing so, my intention has been to produce a Reader that will be of use to as wide an audience as possible.

I would, therefore, anticipate two main audiences and two main uses for this volume. I envisage the main audiences as:

- a larger audience consisting of those working in higher education, particularly those just starting on this career, for whom the Reader should be helpful as an introduction to what is known, in research terms, about higher education, and how it is known; and
- a smaller and more specialised audience comprising those with a continuing research interest in higher education, for whom the Reader might serve as a guide to where the field is at the present time.

In a complementary fashion, I would see the two main uses of the volume as being to provide an overview of the current state of research on higher education as expressed in:

- the main themes or issues currently being researched, so that readers can get an idea of what else might be worth researching; and
- the main methods or methodologies currently being applied to this research, so that readers can get an idea of how higher education research might be undertaken.

For some readers, then, who wish to get an overview of the field of research, the whole Reader may be of interest. For others, with a more specific interest in particular themes or methods, only certain chapters may be of immediate interest. Whatever your interests and values, however, I hope that you do find this Reader enjoyable and of use.

References

Altbach, P. and Engberg, D. (2001) *Higher Education: a worldwide inventory of centers and programs.* Phoenix, Oryx Press.

Ashworth, P. and Lucas, U. (2000) 'Achieving Empathy and Engagement: a practical approach to the design, conduct and reporting of phenomenographic research', *Studies in Higher Education*, 25, 3, pp. 295–308.

Blaxter, L., Hughes, C. and Tight, M. (2001) *How to Research.* Buckingham, Open University Press, second edition.

Brennan, J. (2000) 'Higher Education Research in the UK: a short overview and a case study', pp. 87–97 in Schwartz, S. and Teichler, U. (eds) *The Institutional Basis of Higher Education Research: experiences and perspectives.* Dordrecht, Kluwer Academic Publishers.

Clark, B. (ed.) (1984) *Perspectives on Higher Education: eight disciplinary and comparative views.* Berkeley, University of California Press.

Cohen, L., Manion, L. and Morrison, K. (2000) *Research Methods in Education.* London, RoutledgeFalmer, fifth edition.

Frackmann, E. (1997) 'Research on Higher Education in Western Europe: from policy advice to self-reflection', pp. 105–136 in Sadlak, J. and Altbach, P. (eds) *Higher Education Research at the Turn of the New Century: structures, issues and trends.* New York, Garland.

Hayden, M. and Parry, S. (1997) 'Research on Higher Education in Australia and New Zealand', pp. 163–188 in Sadlak, J. and Altbach, P. (eds) *Higher Education Research at the Turn of the New Century: structures, issues and trends.* New York, Garland.

Kogan, M. (2000) 'Higher Education Research in Europe', pp. 193–209 in Organisation for Economic Co-operation and Development *Knowledge Management in the Learning Society: education and skills.* Paris, OECD.

Maassen, P. (2000) 'Higher Education Research: the hourglass structure and its implications', pp. 59–67 in Teichler, U. and Sadlak, J. (eds) *Higher Education Research: its relationship to policy and practice.* Oxford, Pergamon.

Punch, K. (1998) *Introduction to Social Research: quantitative and qualitative approaches.* London, Sage.

Sadlak, J. and Altbach, P. (eds) (1997) *Higher Education Research at the Turn of the New Century: structures, issues and trends.* New York, Garland.

Schwartz, S. and Teichler, U. (eds) (2000) *The Institutional Basis of Higher Education Research: experiences and perspectives.* Dordrecht, Kluwer.

Scott, P. (2000) 'Higher Education Research in the Light of the Dialogue between Policy-makers and Practitioners', pp. 123–147 in Teichler, U. and Sadlak, J. (eds) *Higher Education Research: its relationship to policy and practice.* Oxford, Pergamon.

Teichler, U. (1996) 'Comparative Higher Education: potentials and limits', *Higher Education*, 32, pp. 431–465.

Teichler, U. (2000) 'Higher Education Research and its Institutional Basis', pp. 13–24 in Schwartz, S. and Teichler, U. (eds) *The Institutional Basis of Higher Education Research: experiences and perspectives*. Dordrecht, Kluwer.

Teichler, U. and Sadlak, J. (eds) (2000) *Higher Education Research: its relationship to policy and practice*. Oxford, Pergamon.

Tight, M. (2003) *Researching Higher Education*. Buckingham, Open University Press.

CHAPTER 1

'CLASSIFICATION' AND 'JUDGEMENT'

Social class and the 'cognitive structures' of choice in higher education

Stephen Ball, Jackie Davies, Miriam David and Diane Reay

British Journal of Sociology of Education, 23, 1, 51–72, 2002

EDITOR'S INTRODUCTION

In this article, Stephen Ball and his co-authors report on the analysis of data collected as part of a research project funded by the UK's Economic and Social Research Council (ESRC). Unusually, for this volume, the article does not come from a specialist higher education journal, but from the *British Journal of Sociology of Education*, and that disciplinary base is evident in the approach and framework adopted.

The focus of the authors is on how prospective students choose – assisted and influenced by their parents, friends and teachers – which higher education institutions to study at, and on the role of social class in such choices. For their theoretical framework, the authors refer to the work of the French sociologist Bourdieu, and, in particular, his concepts of 'classification' and 'judgement'.

Within this framework, a number of themes are developed and stressed:

- the status differentiations evident between UK higher education institutions, and the perceptions of these held by prospective students and others;
- the continuing under-participation of those of working-class origin in higher education, and the influence of previous family experience on this;
- the relation between social class, school attended, school examination performance and participation in higher education, the kind of higher education institution attended, and the kind of course chosen; and
- the notion of the choice of which kind of higher education institution to attend as being a lifestyle choice.

A distinction is made between prospective higher education students who pursue 'normal' and 'choice' biographies. In the former case, prospective students from families with experience of higher education typically see university entry as the normal route to take on completion of school, so their decisions focus on which university and course to attend. In the latter case, prospective students from families with little or no experience of higher education will have to make a very conscious choice to do something different.

The article was categorised in the introductory chapter as adopting an interview-based methodology to researching the student experience. In total, 120 prospective students were interviewed in six schools and colleges in and around London, together with 15 teachers and 40 parents. The study was not wholly interview-based, however, and might more strictly be described as multi-method. Questionnaires were also administered to a larger sample of prospective students, with 502 responses, and a limited amount of observation was carried out within the institutions surveyed.

The article may be placed in relation to a number of literatures, not all of them referred to in the text. First, there is the authors' own previous work on the issue of choice in post-compulsory education (e.g. Ball *et al.* 2000, Gewirtz *et al.* 1995, Reay *et al.* 2002). Then there are related studies by others focusing on young people's choices within post-compulsory education (e.g. Gayle *et al.* 2002, Hodkinson and Sparkes 1997, Moogan *et al.* 1999), the matching literature on how institutions recruit and select students (e.g. Ahola and Kokko 2001, Croot and Chalkley 1999), and analyses of participation rates (e.g. James 2001). But there are at least two other literatures of interest. One consists of longitudinal studies (e.g. Banks *et al.* 1992, Jenkins *et al.* 2001) into young people's experiences and choices, which can be relatively expensive and time-consuming to carry out, and are thus comparatively rare. The other is a kind of parallel literature, which has focused on mature rather than young entrants into higher education, and within which a particular interest in working-class and mature women students is evident (e.g. Edwards 1993, Pascall and Cox 1993, Williams 1997).

References

Ahola, S. and Kokko, A. (2001) 'Finding the Best Possible Students: student selection and its problems in the field of business', *Journal of Higher Education Policy and Management*, 23, 2, pp. 191–203.

Ball, S., Maguire, M. and Macrae, S. (2000) *Choice, Pathways and Transitions Post-16: new youth, new economies in the global city*. London, RoutledgeFalmer.

Banks, M., Bates, I., Breakwell, U., Bynner, J., Euler, N., Jamieson, L. and Roberts, K. (1992) *Careers and Identities*. Buckingham, Open University Press.

Croot, D. and Chalkley, B. (1999) 'Student Recruitment and the Geography of Undergraduate Geographers in England and Wales', *Journal of Geography in Higher Education*, 23, 1, pp. 21–47.

Edwards, R. (1993) *Mature Women Students: separating or connecting family and education*. London, Taylor & Francis.

Gayle, V., Berridge, D. and Davies, R. (2002) 'Young People's Entry into Higher Education: quantifying influential factors', *Oxford Review of Education*, 28, 1, pp. 5–20.

Gewirtz, S., Ball, S. and Bowe, R. (1995) *Markets, Choice and Equity in Education*. Buckingham, Open University Press.

Hodkinson, P. and Sparkes, A. (1997) 'Careership: a sociological theory of career decision making', *British Journal of Sociology of Education*, 18, 1, pp. 29–44.

James, R. (2001) 'Participation Disadvantage in Australian Higher Education: an analysis of some effects of geographical location and socioeconomic status', *Higher Education*, 42, pp. 455–472.

Jenkins, A., Jones, L. and Ward, A. (2001) 'The Long-term Effect of a Degree on Graduate Lives', *Studies in Higher Education*, 26, 2, pp. 147–161.

Moogan, Y., Baron, S. and Harris, K. (1999) 'Decision-making Behaviour of Potential Higher Education Students', *Higher Education Quarterly*, 53, 3, pp. 211–228.

Pascall, O. and Cox, R. (1993) *Women Returning to Higher Education*. Buckingham, Open University Press.

Reay, D., Ball, S. and David, M. (2002) '"It's taking me a long time but I'll get there in the end": mature students on access courses and higher education choice', *British Educational Research Journal*, 28, 1, pp. 5–19.

Williams, J. (ed.) (1997) *Negotiating Access to Higher Education: the discourse of selectivity and equity*. Buckingham, Open University Press.

'CLASSIFICATION' AND 'JUDGEMENT'

Introduction

> ... the cognitive structures which social agents implement in their practical knowledge of the social world are internalized, 'embodied' social structures.
>
> (Bourdieu, 1986, p. 468)

Sociologically speaking choice, the implementation of practical knowledge is a highly problematic concept. It threatens all sorts of theoretical and ontological difficulties and needs to be handled with great care. Used without care, choice can 'smuggle in' an untheorised 'free agent', but also 'The introduction of choice adds an element of indeterminacy into the analysis of individual action ...' (Devine, 1998, p. 27). In many respects, what we address here may be better described as decision-making (see also David *et al.*, 1994). Moogan *et al.* (1999) suggest that Higher Education (HE) choice is a form of 'extensive problem solving'. Where choice suggests openness in relation to a psychology of preferences, decision-making alludes to both power and constraint.

Nonetheless, in this paper we begin to sketch out sociology of choice in relation to the field of HE. Three main theoretical resources are deployed in this sketch. First, there is the work of Bourdieu, and specifically his writing on distinctions (Bourdieu, 1986) and the 'logic of practice' (Bourdieu, 1990). Like many others, we find Bourdieu 'enormously good for thinking with' (Jenkins, 1992, p. 11). We argue that the perceptions, distinctions and choices of HE institutions used and made by students play a part in reconstituting and reproducing the divisions and hierarchies in HE. It is in this way that they 'do' or embody social structures. In effect, this is social class 'in the head'. As Bourdieu explains:

> The division into classes performed by sociology leads to the common root of the classifiable practices which agents produce and of the classificatory judgements they make of other agents' practices and their own [...] It is in the relationship between the two capacities which define the habitus, the capacity to produce classifiable practices and works, and the capacity to differentiate and appreciate these practices and products (taste), that the represented social world, i.e. the space of lifestyles, is constituted.
>
> (Bourdieu, 1986, pp. 169–170)

In this vein, we also draw on Hodkinson & Sparkes' (1997) theory of 'careership' and their notion of 'pragmatically rational decision making'. Second, there is some use made of Beckian work on self-reflexive biographies and the idea that, in the context of high modernism, 'prescribed biography is transformed into biography that is self-produced and continues to be produced' (Beck, 1992, p. 135). In this vein, we draw on Du Bois-Reymond's (1998) use of the ideas of 'choice' and 'normal' biographies. Third, our consideration of class advantage draws generally on the concepts and arguments of social conflict theorists (Parkin, Collins, Brown and Bourdieu again; see later). We relate choice to middle-class fears of 'falling' and the attendant strategies of social closure and credentialism.

This paper arises from an Economic and Social Research Council funded study of choice of HE. It is focused on two cohorts of student 'choosers', their parents and various intermediaries (careers teachers, sixth-form tutors, etc.) in six educational institutions: an 11–18 mixed comprehensive with a large minority ethnic, working-class intake (Creighton Community School); a comprehensive sixth-form consortium that serves a socially diverse community (Maitland Union); a tertiary college with a very large A-level population (Riverway College); a Further Education (FE) College that runs HE Access courses (Fennister FE College); and two prestigious private schools, one single-sex boys (Cosmopolitan Boys) and one single-sex girls (Hemsley Girls). All of the institutions are in or close to London. Our research is institutionally located in this way so that we are able to explore the effects of individual, familial and institutional influences and processes in choice-making. We administered a questionnaire to 502 Years 12 and 13 and FE students, ran focus groups and interviewed a subsample of students in each location (120 interviews in all), interviewed various intermediaries in these institutions (15), and interviewed a subsample of parents (40). A small number of careers advice interviews, HE application preparation sessions, Oxbridge application advice sessions and meetings for parents on HE choice were observed.

Distinctions and judgements

HE choice takes place within two registers of meaning and action. One is cognitive/performative and relates to the matching of performance to the selectivity of institutions and courses. The other is social/cultural and relates to social classifications of self and institutions. Having said that, at least from the point of view of many students, performance is also socially constituted in a nexus of effort, motivations and distractions (see Reay *et al.*, 2001). It is in the empirical examination of the relationships between classifiable practices and classificatory judgements in 'particular fields' that 'habitus', as a 'generative formula', fleetingly comes 'into view'. Choice of higher education is one such field and 'moment'. What we are suggesting, then, is that, in important respects, choice of university is a choice of lifestyle and a matter of 'taste', and further that social class is an important aspect of these subtexts of choice. In other words, this is choice as 'class-matching' and thus also a form of 'social closure' (Parkin, 1974). Indeed, Robbins (1991, p. 6) suggests that 'students have become self-selectively homogenized' and that 'the social ethos of students and institutions are mutually reinforcing' (p. 6) (see also Paterson, 1997; Robertson & Hillman, 1997). However, while our discussion here is organised around the patterns of class difference, we must not give the impression that every working-class student ends up attending a 'new' university (ex-Polytechnic) (exceptions are discussed in another project paper; Reay, 2000). Neither is it the case that choice of a 'new' university is some kind of second best or result of lack of alternatives for all students.

The perceptions and choices of prospective HE students are constructed within a complex interplay of social factors that are underpinned by basic social class and ethnic differences. Of course, given the history of HE in the UK, we should not be very surprised by this. The UK HE market is diverse and highly differentiated in terms of general status and reputation, research activity and income, etc. Various studies have confirmed the continuing, indeed increasing, overall dominance of the middle classes in HE (Metcalf, 1997; Roberts & Allen, 1997; Williams, 1997). As Table 3 indicates, during the major period of expansion in the 1990s, the 'participation gap' between professional and intermediate and the working classes increased, at the extremes, from 62 to 66%. Furthermore, in general terms, the university is very much a 'classed concept'. Archer & Hutchings (2000), in their study of working-class non-participants, describe working-class young people as positioning 'themselves "outside" of HE (e.g. constructing HE as a white, and/or middle-class place), placing

Table 3 Social class participation rates (%) in higher education

	1993–94	1994–95	1995–96	1996–97	1997–98
Professional	73	78	79	82	80
Intermediate	42	45	45	47	49
Skilled/non-manual	29	31	31	31	32
Skilled manual	17	18	18	18	19
Partly unskilled	16	17	17	17	18
Unskilled	11	11	12	13	14
All social classes	30	32	32	33	34

Adapted from *Social Trends*, 1999, Table 3.13

themselves as potentially able to take advantage of the benefits it can offer, but not as owners of it' (p. 25). Thus, it is important to bear in mind that when we write in this paper about class differences, differences between middle-class and working-class students, that the latter are distinctly atypical in relation to their class peers. They are, as Bourdieu (1988) terms them, 'lucky survivors' from social categories 'improbable' for the position they have achieved. In terms of educational trajectories and aspirations, they are already exceptions. Bourdieu & Passeron (1979, p. 26), in their study of French HE, note that among HE students those 'from the disadvantaged strata differ profoundly [in certain respects] from the other individuals of their category'. Bourdieu and Passeron found them much more likely to have a member of their extended family who had been to university compared with those previously eliminated from the education system. They are, as Bourdieu and Passeron put it: 'the least disadvantaged of the most disadvantaged'. For the majority of working-class young people, not going to university is part of a 'normal biography' (see later). It is a 'non-decision'.

However, with the increase in the number of students participating in school sixth forms, in taking A levels, BTech National and GNVQ Advanced courses (General National Vocational Qualification), and in applying for and going to HE, it is important that as well as attending to overall class differences in participation, we begin to understand the social diversities and hierarchies at work within these various fields (see Ball *et al.*, 2000, on 'new' and 'traditional' A-levellers). As suggested by various other studies of educational expansion, as access becomes democratised then internal differentiation and differential rates of completion appear to become more significant in relation to social differentiation. This is certainly a major factor of difference between universities. This is a process, as it affects the working classes, that Duru-Bellat (2000) calls 'excluded from within' (p. 36). Her analyses indicate that 'underlying macro-sociological regularities, actors, with unequal assets, strive to use the system in the way they consider to be in their own interest' (p. 39). We argue here that, alongside the academic and social selectivity of HE institutions themselves, the relative status and social exclusivity of universities and the relationship of this to student 'choice' and choice-making are key factors in generating and reproducing patterns of internal differentiation. That is to say, cultural and social capital, material constraints (see Reay, 2000), social perceptions and distinctions, and forms of self-exclusion (Bourdieu & Passeron, 1990) are all at work in the processes of choice.

Here, we will concentrate, in part perforce, on the effects or outcomes of this interplay, rather than its internal dynamics. Some of these dynamics are well established but continually debated within sociological and educational research – in particular, the nature of the relationship between social class and achievement (for example, Savage & Egerton, 1997; Nash, 1999). In our own work, using multiple regression analysis, social class was found to be the main predictor of the schools attended and GCSE attainment of the students in our sample, which were in turn the main predictors of choosing high-status universities.

Furthermore, and unsurprisingly, high GCSE grades was the main predictor in choosing high-status and professionally-related courses such as medicine. In part, here there is a set of 'objective' differences driving or excluding certain choices. That is to say, some choices are only made possible by certain levels of attainment. Those levels of attainment are more or less available to young people in different contexts and different circumstances and with different capabilities. See Hutchings & Archer (2000) for a review and discussion of the factors associated with the lower levels of participation of working-class young people.

However, as already suggested, the process of choice is a lot more than just a matching of qualifications and attainments to opportunities. Various general social patterns and other effects are evident. This is a complex decision-making process (Hodkinson & Sparkes, 1997). We have attempted to look at and make sense of these patterns and effects in a variety of ways both through our questionnaire data, and focus group, observation and interview materials. We are attempting something like what Nash (1999, p. 123) calls a 'numbers and narratives methodology' but with an emphasis, in contrast to Nash, on the latter. This involves attending to both 'the constraining and enabling aspects of the economic, cultural and political structures that affect families, schools and students' and the 'complex and creative set of responses' (p. 123) that these structures call forth when young people 'make decisions about how to utilise [the exchange value of their educational qualifications] after the completion of schooling' (p. 123). In other words, we certainly do not offer a mechanistic or simple, structural class analysis. We share the view of decision making outlined by Hodkinson & Sparkes (1997, p. 32) that: 'individuals are neither dopes nor pawns, yet the limitations on their decisions are realistically recognised'.

Choices are made within differently delimited 'opportunity structures' (Roberts, 1993) and different 'horizons of action' (Hodkinson & Sparkes, 1997). Ball *et al.* (2000), in their study of choice of FE in London, argue that such horizons are social/perceptual but also spatial and temporal. The importance of and differences in the social, temporal and spatial horizons of our sample of university applicants are both material and perceptual. That is, related to cost on the one hand, and confidence, awareness and expectation, community and tradition on the other. Generally, it is clear from UCAS reports that, as the participation rate in HE has increased, the proportion of young people choosing to study locally and regionally has increased; although this trend will also almost certainly be encouraged by the increasing costs of HE participation. UCAS recently reported a fall-off in applications to HE from under-represented groups, which coincided with the introduction of new financial arrangements (*Times Higher Education Supplement*, 8 October 1999). In Bourdieurian terms, we might view the contrast between cosmopolitan and local choosers as 'the opposition between the tastes of luxury (or freedom) and the tastes of necessity' (Bourdieu, 1986, pp. 177–178) but choices also reflect different kinds of attachments to locality. Pugsley (1998) notes this among working-class families in her study of choice of HE based in South Wales. In this vein, and in contrast, Savage *et al.* (1992) make the point that: 'Embedded in the very notion of the middle-class person is the expectation that the relationship of that individual with place or region or residence is a contingent one'.

Generally, our data offers strong support for Hodkinson & Sparkes' (1997) theory of 'pragmatically rational decision-making'.

> ... decisions were pragmatic, rather than systematic. They were based on partial information located in the familiar and the known. The decision-making was context-related, and could not be separated from the family background, culture and life histories of the (young people). The decisions were opportunistic, being based on fortuitous contacts and experiences [...] Decisions were only partly rational, being also influenced by feelings and emotions. Finally, decisions often involved accepting one option rather than choosing between many. Decisions were neither technically rational nor irrational.
>
> (p. 33)

This is very different from either Nash's Family Resource Theory (see earlier) or Goldthorpe's (1996) weak version of Rational Action Theory (see Hatcher's (1998) critique). In effect, Hodkinson & Sparkes (1997) resocialise the rational within choice. In particular, it is vital to recognise the role of non-rational aspects of choice and strategy; '... agents do not simply weigh courses of action in terms of their efficacy in achieving a desired goal, they evaluate the desired goals themselves in relation to a framework of personal values that is not reducible to personal utility' (Hatcher, 1998, p. 17). In other words, utility is one but not the only criterion for decision-making. Hodkinson & Sparkes' (1997) framework is a useful way of representing choice-making in general terms but within our sample there are very different kinds of contexting, opportunism and non-rationality in play; that is, crudely speaking, different 'class frames of reference' (Lauder *et al.*, 1999, p. 27). One of the things we are trying to do, therefore, within the work of the project as a whole, is to understand how such decision-making is exercised differently and works differently for different groups of young people. A glimpse of one or two aspects of such differences may be useful now. These examples are not representative of our data-sets, neither do they exhaust the differences evident in student choice-making. They are merely illustrative.

> ... I thought that the most important thing would be how respected the degree would be by the architectural community ... And then I actually went to a few open days and I realised the more important thing was the university itself, if I'd enjoy going there. And settled upon Sheffield, basically because of the facilities, and the atmosphere just seemed right, like I would really enjoy three years there, for the degree ... I had to know that I would feel comfortable there and enjoy it.
>
> (*Anthony*, Cosmopolitan Boys School)

> I don't know anybody well, who has completed university ... So I suppose that's maybe why I didn't know about the reputations of the universities or any sort of things like that. Apart from what I was told by the prospectuses, the brochures, computers, what my teachers told me. I sort of worked it out as I went along really, played it by ear. Maybe if I had known some people that had gone to university it might have made my choices different, or maybe not, I don't really know.
>
> (*James*, Creighton Community School)

I did read about the African Caribbean societies and the Asian societies and all the different things they do, and I know there are quite a few people, a few black people and Asian people who do go to Sussex and Manchester Met and stuff like that and that was important that they had those sorts of societies there. It means you know you're not going to be the only black person there . . . I prefer to be somewhere where there is different cultures. And so I did make sure that there was a mix . . .

(*Sarah*, Creighton Community School)

. . . I have this friend who works with me, and basically, he has just come from Bangladesh, he wants to do a masters in International Relations, and he heard about Westminster when he was in Bangladesh, so I thought maybe it's because the University is good for that subject so that I decided to do it.

(*Khalid*, Creighton Community School)

I think the decision was more economical than anything else, because ideally I would like to travel outside London and live away from home, probably rent a place, ideally, but looking at the reality of how likely it is, it is very, very, very unlikely. It is more sense to say, you know studying inside London, somewhere that it close by, so I can cycle there or take the train.

(*Ahmed*, Creighton Community School)

These extracts only begin to scratch the surface of the complexities of choice. They simply represent some key criteria, among many cited, that underpinned student choice. Even so, it is possible to see the ways in which context, opportunity, values and emotion play out very differently. These extracts also indicate the interplay of strategic rational action with non-rational or non-utilitarian goals. As Hatcher (1998, p. 16) puts it: ' "rational choice" . . . is a significant element in many transition decisions, but it is neither a necessary nor a sufficient one'. Anthony, who elsewhere in his interview talked about going to university as 'following in the family foot-steps', uses a combination of institutional status and social opportunities and milieu to frame his choice. There are no clear external constraints acting on his choice. For students like Anthony, financial support from parents, supplemented by a loan, makes for an unproblematic and 'confident' attitude towards the cost of HE – this simply does not become part of the calculus of choice (see Hesketh, 1999). On the contrary, Ahmed is very directly constrained by financial considerations, and other criteria very firmly take second place. Shaun, who lived independently and worked long hours part-time, was decisively influenced by setting and formed his view of universities through his own research. Sarah, who is West African, and also firmly embedded in familial expectations about university attendance, is specifically concerned about the ethnic mix of institutions under consideration. And Khalid chooses subject and insti-tution very much by chance. His view of institutional status is based on a single piece of 'hot knowledge' (Ball & Vincent, 1998). For students like Anthony and Sarah, choice is primarily related to factors internal to universities themselves. These are 'real' places that have different qualities and characteristics. For those like Ahmed and Khalid, as Archer and Hutchings put it, university is viewed from the 'outside' and external/extrinsic concerns predominate in choice-making. University is an 'unreal' place (Bourdieu & Passeron, 1979, p. 53).[1] Even from these brief examples, it is possible to begin to see how, in a straightforward sense, habitus as 'the practical mastery which people possess of their situations' (Robbins, 1991, p. 1) and cultural capital, 'subtle modalities in the relationship to culture and language' (Bourdieu,

1977, p. 82) are at work in the 'immanent decisions which people actually make . . .' (p. 1). That is, within the logics of their practices.

Young people like Anthony are living out what Du Bois-Reymond (1998) calls a 'normal biography'. Normal biographies are linear, anticipated and predictable, unreflexive transitions, often gender and class specific, rooted in well-established lifeworlds. They are often driven by an absence of decisions. Such young people talked of going to university as 'automatic', 'taken for granted', 'always assumed' (see also Pugsley, 1998). 'That was the family plan, that was the expectation of everyone', as Tom from Cosmopolitan Boys put it. The decision to go to university is a non-decision. It is rational and it is not. This is the work of 'class wisdom' (Lauder et al., 1999); 'intentionality without intention' (Bourdieu, 1990, p. 108). These middle-class young people 'move in their world as a fish in water' and 'need not engage in rational computation in order to reach the goals that best suit their interests' (Bourdieu, 1990, p. 108). Decision-making comes into play in relation to 'which university?'. The accounts of these students are rendered in 'closed narrative forms' (Cohen & Hey, 2000) that are typically inscribed within transgenerational family scripts or 'inheritance codes'. They portray a 'continuous dramatic life historical thread' (Cohen & Hey, 2000, p. 4). All of this contrasts with the doubts, ambivalances and very deliberate decision-making of many of the working-class and minority ethnic young people in our sample like James, Ahmed and Kalil, who were the first in their families to contemplate HE. They would fit much more within what Do Bois-Reymond calls a 'choice biography'. 'Choice biographies are by no means purely based on freedom and own choices . . . young people are forced to reflect on the available options and justify their decisions . . . *it is the tension between option/freedom and legitimation/coercion which marks choice biographies*' (p. 65). Such accounts are rendered in open narrative forms and are more fragmentary and discontinuous. HE choice is only weakly articulated with a continuing narrative thread. The future is unimagined or highly generic – 'a good job'. The mature FE students and a small number of the private-school students were the only ones to express their decision to go to university in terms of subject interests or personal and intellectual development.

School, class and choice

In the simplest sense, as indicated already, the status of the HE institutions chosen by the students in our sample is strongly related to their class and ethnicity, and thus also to 'school' attended (see Tables 4 and 5).

Our interview and observation data suggest that the 'school effect', what might be called 'institutional habitus', is an independent variable; perceptions and expectations of choice are constructed over time in relation to school friends and teachers' views and advice and learning experiences (as well as, for some, the views and

Table 4 Social class of questionnaire respondents (%) by institution

Social class	Cosmo-politan Boys	Hemsley Girls	Riverway College	Fennister FE College	Maitland Union	Creighton Community School
1–2	83*	93	44	39	58	23
3 nm	8	4	19	17	8	10
3 m to 4–5	9	4	37	44	34	67

* Under-estimate

Table 5 First choice of university cross-tabulation with type of school (% choosing)*

	Hemsley Girls (%)	Cosmo-politan Boys (%)	Riverway College (%)	Creighton Com-munity School (%)	Maitland Union (%)	Fennister FE College (%)	Total
Oxbridge	41	48	5	12	11		22
Other 'old' pre-1992	48	44	31	20	42	48	40
'New' post-1992	2	1	32	15	15	44	15
Colleges of Higher Education	4	1	9	10	8		6
Not named	5	6	23	44	25	7	18

* This table records the 'first choice' institutions indicated by students who completed the questionnaire and had made up their mind, as well as those who did not name a 'first choice'.

expectations of families). Within all this there is without doubt a relationship between the social composition of intakes and family habituses and the institutional habituses. That is, put simply: 'Schools develop processes that reflect their SES mix' (Thrupp, 1999, p. 125; see Pugsley's (1998) comparison of Argoed College and Bragwyn Hall). Embedded perceptions and expectations make certain choices 'obvious' and others unthinkable, according to where you stand in the overall landscape of choice. In this respect, middle-class students in the private schools are as equally, or perhaps more, constrained as their working-class counterparts in the state sector. As Anthony explains, in his Independent school, certain sorts of choices or considerations take on an obviousness that is difficult to evade. Habitus is evident here in its inexplicitness.

> I thought about would I go to Cambridge or not, because quite a lot of people, you know always think – am I going to Cambridge or not? I don't know why, that just seems to be the question a lot of people ask themselves about higher education.
>
> *(Anthony)*

The organisation of the practical logic at work here is very particular – Cambridge or not? Cambridge is the starting point that has to be reasoned against. There has to be a reason for not going. The 'not', the other, is unspecified; already, perhaps by implication, second best. As a strategy of social distinction, as a 'proper' appreciation, the logic here is clear cut. And Omar (Cosmopolitan Boys) explained: '. . . nine out of ten people applied to these sorts of universities, you know prestigious ones, and you don't really want to feel like . . . they will say "why are you doing that?" "Why don't you join the flow?" We tend to flow . . .'. These different institutional habituses are also evident in the nature of choice-making in another sense. The levels of practical support and 'structuring structures, that is . . . principles which generate and organise practices' (Bourdieu, 1990, p. 53) differ.

Altogether 86% of our total sample wanted to go to HE and, of these, 22% put Oxford or Cambridge (Oxbridge) as their first preference; although a good number of these preferences were certainly unrealistic. When broken down in relation to the social class of parents, the relationships here, following from the argument so far, are fairly predictable. The totals of first choices for different kinds of HE institution are made up of very different combinations of 'class groups'; 78% of the choices to Oxbridge come from groups A and B, whereas only 27% of the choice to 'new universities' (ex-polytechnics) come from these groups, etc. Less than 2% of the private school students name the 'new' universities as their first choice. Obviously, again, it has to be acknowledged that, in part, choice is related to likelihood of acceptance and the applicant's knowledge of the 'points requirements' of different courses in different institutions. Nonetheless, this was certainly not the only factor involved in this choice-making, as we have already tried to indicate. Path analysis work on our data indicated that, alongside a relationship to social class and qualifications, those choosing high-status universities were most likely to nominate a career motive as the basis for their choice. Presumably based on the availability of particular kinds of 'imagined futures' (Ball et al., 1999).[2] In contrast, those students primarily motivated by a wish to go to an institution where there were people who shared their culture and ethnicity, and were inclined to refer to their family and home life as important, were the least likely to apply to high-prestige universities. Of course, many of those choosing high-status universities are also making a choice that ensures they will be with others 'like them' in terms of culture and ethnicity, but this is an implicit rather than explicit aspect of choice[3] and of the 'classed' nature of particular universities.[4] It is taken for granted by these choosers that certain sorts of institutions and courses will be populated by certain sorts of students.

The path analysis of our questionnaire data also demonstrated a strong relationship between career-motivated choice and the influence of gaining information about HE from the family. All of this is suggestive again of middle-class concerns about social advantage and strategies of social reproduction (Bourdieu & Boltanski, 2000).

Table 6 Choice of subject by school*

	Cosmopolitan Boys	Hemsley Girls	Riverway College	Creighton Community School	Maitland Union	Fennister FE College
Social science/ economics	2	6	4	3	6	7
Drama/film/ media			7	1	8	
Education/nursing/ PE/sport			2		10	4
Art	1	1	3		15	
History/humanities/ archaeology	6	6			4	2
Applied sciences/ computing/ earth sciences	10		2	2	4	6
Pure science	3	10	1	2	1	
Accountancy/ business	1	2	21	1	4	
Medicine	10	9	3	1	2	

* This table records the course choices indicated by those students who completed the questionnaire and who were sure, at the time, of their preferred course of study at university.

Various writers have argued that there is a heightened level of such concerns in the current economic context (Jordon *et al.*, 1994; Brown, 1997; Ball & Vincent, 2001). Ehrenreich (1989) posits that part of the middle classes increasingly see themselves as assailed by 'intruders from below' and confront a 'fear of falling'. Collins (1979) takes this further and argues that 'the expansion of higher education represents a conflict between social groups for scarce credentials' (Brown & Scase, 1994, p. 18). It is at this point that the 'practical principles of division' (Bourdieu, 1986, p. 471) and, in particular, 'the distances that need to be kept' (p. 472) begin to take on a structural significance. In this way, perception, expectation and choice all relate to and play their part in reproducing social structures. They constitute what Bourdieu calls 'the objectivity of "second order"' – symbolic templates for practical activities (Bourdieu & Wacquant, 1992, p. 7). The distribution of classes and class fractions across, and within, institutions of HE can be viewed as part of the 'self-production of class collectivities through struggles which simultaneously involve relationships between and within classes and determine the actual demarcation of their frontiers' Wacquant, 1991, p. 52).

We can take this a little further and illuminate other aspects of institutional habitus by looking at the relationship between school and choice of subject. There is, of course, considerable literature here.

In Table 6, we can see that courses like drama, etc., the social sciences, and education, etc. (which are, arguably, attached to certain values and certain labour-market and income opportunities) are relatively popular in the state schools and decidedly unpopular in the private schools. In as much that degrees are related to jobs, demarcations between state and private professions are likely to be reproduced (see Power *et al.*, 1998).

The traditional humanities are popular in the private schools, as is medicine. Interestingly, in relation to science courses, the private schools divide on gender lines; the applied sciences are popular with the boys, and pure science with the girls. These choices are complexly gendered within the institutions, as certain sorts of courses are 'talked-up' by tutors and teachers; another dimension of 'institutional habitus'. Business and accountancy is particularly popular in the Tertiary College, and art most popular with the Maitland Union girls. Generally, traditional 'academic' subjects are predominant in the private schools and 'new' subjects more in evidence in the state schools. Again, there may be class fractional difference reflected here, in particular between the 'new middle-class' of Maitland Union, as against the 'old middle-class' of Cosmopolitan Boys and Hemsley Girls. Indeed, within such differences, there may be a great deal more embedded meaning. In a paper on the curricula of elite, American private schools, Goodson *et al.* (1997, p. 177) argue that: 'The elite school student is treated as a recipient of class culture, but also the legitimate heir and possible creator of further expressions of class culture.'

Perception and ranking

A good deal of our discussion so far rests on the assumption that a ranking in terms of status of universities exists, and that it is known to and used by at least some of the young people in our study. We tested this in part of our questionnaire to students (see later) and also in the interviews. However, we were not simply testing the idea that students 'know' that universities are 'ranked' differently, but also whether their perceptions or understanding of these rankings would be more or less 'accurate'. We used *The Times* Universities League Table (*The Times*, 15 May 1998) and asked the students to rank the top, middle and bottom four institutions from *The Times* League

Table 7 League table positions and histories of ranking test universities

Position		Score	Historical ranking
Top third			
1st	Cambridge	938	(1) Elite
2nd	Oxford	910	(1) Elite
3rd	Imperial	907	(2) Russell group, turn of century
4th	London School of Economics	890	(2) Russell group, turn of century
Middle third			
47th	Aston	675	(4) Robbins, 1963, CATS
48th	Aberystwyth	668	(2) Russell group
49th	Kent	664	(3) New university, post-war 1950s/60s
50th	Brunel	633	(4) Robbins, 1963, CATS
Bottom third			
93rd	East London	491	(5) Poly in 1966
94th	Luton	489	(6) 2nd-generation Polys, 1992
95th	Lincoln & Humberside	472	(6) 2nd-generation Polys, 1992
96th (and last)	Bournemouth	449	(6) 2nd-generation Polys, 1992

Table in order (see Table 7). In interviews, it was clear that awareness and use of rankings varied between students. With some simplification, the students can be described as either 'ranking unaware', 'ranking aware' (aware of but not attending to or using the rankings as a factor in their choice-making), and 'ranking active' (aware of and using the rankings as part of their choice-making). There are similarities here with McDonough *et al.*'s (1997) US study (see also later).

This exercise offers another perspective on social class/institutional-related differences in market behaviour and market skills. As might be expected, those students from families who are previous users of HE and from the schools that 'specialise' in HE entry tend to be the most 'accurate' in their rankings.

In the case of the top four institutions (Table 8), Oxford and Cambridge are located accurately by almost all students, underlining their 'elite' status position in the public imagination. When it comes to Imperial College, however, accuracy falls off dramatically in all the four state institutions, with the Fennister FE college students and Creighton Community School students down to just 50% accuracy. The same is true for the London School of Economics, with the Tertiary College students most inaccurate. In three of the four cases here, the private-school girls are more accurate than the private-school boys.

In the middle four institutions (Table 9), Creighton Community School students are the most inaccurate in three of the four cases. Dramatically so for Aston, Aberystwyth and Brunel, but only two schools get above 50% accuracy for Aston and Aberystwyth. Generally, again, either the private-school girls or the boys are most accurate in each case but there is more variability here in the middle reaches of the universities' pecking order, as one might expect.

What we find in looking at the bottom four institutions (Table 10) is that, in the case of UEL and Luton, it is the Creighton Community School students who are most often wrong in their ratings. In the case of Lincoln, Maitland Union students are most wrong, just more so than those of Creighton Community School. Bournemouth

Table 8 Student rankings of top four universities in questionnaire (%)

University/ position	Hemsley Girls	Cosmo- politan Boys	Riverway College	Creighton Community School	Maitland Union	Fennister FE College
Cambridge						
1st	73	75	33	29	49	41
Top four	99	100	90	91	98	100
Oxford						
1st	33	21	64	60	51	67
2nd	55	57	27	23	46	25
Top four	100	97	99	97	99	96
Imperial						
1st	7	3		17		
2nd	19	19	6	27	4	8
3rd	53	40	35	23	25	21
Top four	95	86	56	50	57	50
London School of Economics						
3rd	21	34	21	21	35	52
4th	52	40	22	29	15	13
Top four	84	80	50	61	53	70

Table 9 Student rankings of middle four universities in questionnaire (%)

University/ position	Hemsley Girls	Cosmo- politan Boys	Riverway College	Creighton Community School	Maitland Union	Fennister FE College
Aston						
Top four	3	5	18	22	9	5
Middle four	42	55	46	30	48	54
Bottom four	54	40	33	48	43	32
Aberystwyth						
Top four	2	8	4	15	10	5
Middle four	64	52	45	26	45	45
Bottom four	34	39	50	58	43	50
Kent						
Top four	6	11	15	36	13	5
Middle four	61	53	63	57	56	73
Bottom four	32	45	32	8	27	21
Brunel						
Top four	6	12	30	29	25	70
Middle four	62	63	39	21	45	26
Bottom four	30	25	31	50	30	4

Table 10 Student rankings of bottom four universities in questionnaire (%)

University/ position	Hemsley Girls	Cosmo-politan Boys	Riverway College	Creighton Community School	Maitland Union	Fennister FE College
East London						
Top four	2	8	5	38	9	17
Middle four	25	28	40	21	22	26
Bottom four	64	64	56	42	69	56
Luton						
Top four	1	8	11	12	11	5
Middle four	33	31	30	56	40	27
Bottom four	65	60	58	32	38	68
Lincolnshire and Humberside						
Top four	0	5	4	12	13	0
Middle four	22	35	40	48	42	42
Bottom four	78	61	56	50	48	57
Bournemouth						
Top four	5	2	17	15	11	10
Middle four	59	46	47	23	50	55
Bottom four	36	64	37	62	39	35

creates confusion for many students, with the Creighton Community School students doing relatively well. There may well be interesting confusions here between the town and the university in many students' class-related status perceptions. Overall, Creighton Community School students are most inaccurate, six times out of 12, the FE Access students three times, Tertiary College students twice; the private-school boys once (in the case of Kent), and Maitland Union students once (Lincoln). There was one tie. In part, what we are seeing here, as has been found to be the case in studies of educational choice in other settings, is that in a real sense the capacity for choice is unevenly distributed across the social classes (David *et al.*, 1994; Gewirtz *et al.*, 1995; Reay, 1998).

Again there are similarities here with the McDonough *et al.* (1997) US study. They also found 'higher proportions of students with college-educated parents among students who find rankings important ... [and] higher proportions of low-income students that do not use rankings compared to those who do' (p. 14); also, students attending 'private schools are significantly more likely to have consulted national rankings' (p. 22). All this is true of our sample too. We would also suggest that the accuracy indicators reflect again the differences in institutional habitus. First, in the relative prominence given to university entrance and choice in each of the institutions; second, in the importance given to making the 'right' choice in the independent schools; and third, in terms of the knowledge and 'know-how' of university educated parents. For many middle-class parents, these resources ensure 'their tacit decoding of the rhetoric of equality which accompanied the dissolution of the binary divide between universities and polytechnics in 1992' (Pugsley, 1998, p. 76). And finally, fourth, in the different amounts of time, energy and expertise, and levels of support devoted to entry and choice in different institutions. McDonough *et al.* (1997, p. 25) go on to suggest that 'newsmagazine college rankings are heightening an obsession with reputations in a widespread, accessible way'.

Narratives of choice and reasons for rejection

We want now to look at a different way of exploring the 'classificatory judgements' that students use in relation to HE institutions, other actors and themselves. To do this we will use some further extracts from the narratives of choice elicited in interviews. We will focus in particular on those moments in interviews at which a firm and clear rejection of some institution(s) is articulated. In the coding of the transcripts, all such instances were noted. Bagley *et al.* (2000) argue that rejection within choice-making 'may often be more powerful than positive choice . . . [and] is important because it broadens our understanding of the choice process' (p. 2). Our suggestion here is that 'classificatory judgements' come into view perhaps most clearly in relation to perceptions of what is unacceptable or inconceivable. And what is unacceptable 'works both ways' in social-class terms, as we shall see. Here, we offer six examples of such judgements at work.

One clear example of such rejection came up in a number of transcripts where the use of advertising by certain universities was mentioned. Sarah, a Creighton Community School student, explained:

> I mean, to me, it is like, that university must be really desperate to be advertising on the Northern Line underground and stuff like that, so I wouldn't go, no way.

Answering the same question Arlia, a mature FE College student, offered a similar reaction.

> Well, it's usually for North London and Westminster, isn't it? Neither of those two universities I've applied to; and to be honest if I've noticed adverts at all it has been to put me off. I think I don't want to go somewhere that's pleading for me to go there.

In both cases, advertising conveys the idea that entry to the universities in question is too easy, they are 'desperate' or 'pleading' and, by implication, are undiscriminating. In effect, the students place and classify themselves in relation to the status and reputation of these universities as indicated by the students who are able to attend and the degree of selectivity involved in access. Indeed, in almost all the examples of rejection in our transcripts, the universities are represented or evaluated in one way or another in terms of their student intakes.

Universities have other opportunities to present themselves to potential choosers, like at Open Days. Decisions about what to emphasise to visiting students can have unintended effects. Elisabeth, a Creighton Community School student explained:

> Manchester University, the main one, the first thing they spoke to us was education, they talked about the courses, they talked about the university and education and also they divided us into groups, those of us who wanted to see the law section, those who wanted to see the medical section and so on. So I went, obviously, with the law representative and she showed me the law libraries and stuff like that. It was really good, and they spoke at length on education, and then

they spoke on the social life. When we went to Manchester Met that was very different . . . the first thing they showed us was a video about the social life of Manchester Met. And it was just such a contrast, and I sat there and I was thinking – what are these people doing, are they trying to get us to go to this university? And they showed us the social life and we saw people drinking. I know university students do that anyway, but I just think it was a good way of, you know, of putting us off some of the things the students were doing on the video was just not very nice, and then they took us to the gyms, sport gyms and that and then sat down and we had like a 20 minute discussion on education and the type of courses they offer and how good they were and stuff like that, so very different . . . It put me off, it put me off a great deal . . .

Elisabeth is unimpressed by Manchester Met's portrayal of drinking and social life as the mainstays of student life, and this goes against the strong thread of instrumentalism that runs through the school student interviews.[5] Elisabeth does not see herself as the student to whom Manchester Met aims its marketing and is 'put off a great deal'; she identifies more with the seriousness of Manchester University.

Sheila's account of the rejection of City University emphasises the social dimension of reputation and its relation to recognition.

> . . . yeah I think it's a lot to do with the status of the uni as well. Not just, I mean, going there and studying. Not just going there and studying. Not just going to uni for the sakes of it. But going to a decent uni and so when you say – I went to blah blah somebody actually recognises it. They know it's a good uni with a good reputation. Instead of saying – where's that? Because when I say City everybody says – where's that? But when you say LSE everyone's heard of it. And when you say UCL everyone's heard of it. So it is a lot to do with status as well, definitely.

As Sheila indicates, underlining again the instrumentalism of many of the school students, for her the intrinsic worth of a university experience and a degree is set over and against a field of social judgement in which the reputation and status of a university defines the worth of the experience. Sheila wants to go to a 'decent' university. City fails to meet this requirement.

Deborah, a black student from Creighton Community School was 'put off' Huddersfield by a friend's account of 'so many Asian people'. Deborah is keen to find an institution that is ethnically mixed and 'where people mix in':

> That's the last thing I want, you know, I don't want to go to a university that is dominated by, I don't want, you know, Asians in the cafe here, and everyone else over there, sort of thing. I want somewhere where people mix in. So that put me off a bit, but it wouldn't really bother me, it is not my prime objective. I am not going there because there's lots of Asians in the cafeteria and everyone is divided, but ideally I would like it to be a good mix and everyone is friends and everything.

As this indicates, 'mix' works both ways; institutions or localities can be 'too black' or 'too white' (this is an issue we take further in another project paper; Ball *et al.*, 2002). London provided a 'comfortable' multi-cultural environment for a significant number of the minority ethnic students and some were distinctly wary of provincial locations or 'white highlands'. Oxbridge elicited a particular version of this kind of rejection from several students. Indeed, Oxbridge carries a clear excess of classificatory meanings. Ong, a Chinese student from the sixth form consortium, attended an interview at a Cambridge College.

> It was a complete shock, it was different from anywhere else I have ever been, it was too traditional, too old fashioned, from another time altogether. I didn't like it at all. It was like going through a medieval castle when you were going down the corridors. The dining room was giant long tables, pictures, it was like a proper castle, and I was thinking – where's the moat, where's the armour? Save me from this. You know, you expect little pictures with eyes moving around, watching you all the time. And I just didn't like the atmosphere, not one bit . . . All typical private school, posh people . . . posh and white.

This was not a place for 'people like us'. While acknowledging the other constraints on and possibilities for Oxbridge choice, Table 5 also suggests a pattern of this kind of 'class aversion' among state-school students. Here again there is an aspect of social-class self-reproduction and the maintenance of class demarcations by 'self-exclusion'. In looking from the other side of the class division, or at least the state/private school divide, the picture is somewhat different. In the private-school transcripts, we might expect perhaps to find rejection of the New Universities as not a place for 'people like us'. This is not the case. The New Universities are not rejected as possibilities, they do not even enter into consideration. They are inconceivable (see Table 5). Again, very different 'frames of reference' or 'class wisdoms' – 'rules, norms, tacit assumptions and horizons' (Lauder *et al.*, 1999, p. 43) are at work.

Commentary

Our research indicates some of the ways that choices are 'made', or perhaps 'made up', within the relationship between institution (school), attainment, habitus and circumstance. Habitus rests, in good part, on class differences in knowledge and disposition/position, but in this 'field' gender and ethnicity are also important in various ways (we discuss these and the inter-relationships more fully in other project papers).

Different kinds of practical knowledge are at work in choice-making. Knowledge about and use of status hierarchies and reputations is uneven and varies systematically between schools and families. Social and cultural classifications and distinctions run through and underpin the process of choice in such a way as to combine individualist and collectivist modes of social exclusion (Parkin, 1974, p. 9). Individual attributes are important in a variety of ways; not the least those related to attainment. However, the class-related patterns of social and cultural capital sketched in, as well as the deployment of generalised social attributes based on ethnic or class categories, indicate the continuation of strategies of closure based on vestiges of 'reproduction' rather than pure 'nomination', in Parkin's terms. The latter are evident at key moments of 'choice rejection'.

Furthermore, choice as self-exclusion is an aspect of closure both in the form of aversion to particular HE settings (in terms of class and ethnic 'fit') or more generally, as Archer & Hutchings' (2000) research suggests, in seeing HE as too 'risky' both financially and in terms of 'personal identity benefits'. Beck's (1992, p. 90) notion of 'biography itself acquiring a reflexive project' comes to mind here and, in particular, his suggestion that within 'new modernity': 'one has to choose and change one's social identity, as well as take the risks in doing so' (p. 88). The difference between those who take and those who refuse such risks here may rest on differences between individualist and solidarist fractions or versions of the working class. Beck goes on to suggest 'a new inequality'; that is, 'the inequality of dealing with insecurity and reflex-ivity' (p. 98). We would suggest that this new inequality differs between classes and class fractions. However, this is not a simple story of 'reflexive modernity'. The 'transgenerational family scripts' (Cohen & Hey, 2000, p. 5) of the middle-class and private-school students remain embedded within deeply normalised grammars of aspiration that 'exert a prospective and regulative influence on actual life chances and choices' (Cohen & Hey, 2000, p. 5). In some respects, within the context of expan-sion of HE participation, we might expect these scripts and grammars to be instilled or supervised with ever greater vigilance (see also Pugsley, 1998; Allat, 1996). As Bourdieu (1988, p. 163) suggests, for the privileged classes the hiatus arising between expectation and opportunity, and the concomitant threat of 'downclassing', is 'par-ticularly intolerable'. Given this, it is important to make the point that the 'normal' biographies of middle-class students are neither without risk nor without reflexivity (Brown & Scase, 1994; Brown, 1997). The differences here are a matter of degree. The risks and reflexivity of the middle classes are about staying as they are and who they are. Those of the working classes are about being different people in different places, about who they might become and what they must give up.

The unevenly distributed 'capacity to differentiate and appreciate' is also clearly at work in judgements about the quality and exchange and symbolic value (Lee, 1993) of different university educations. Choice is heavily imbued with meaning-giving perceptions, but most heavily and particularly in the choice-making of those students and families seeking to achieve or maintain (with varying success) middle-class social positions and lifestyles. HE access and choice is a key arena of social reproduction struggles, but these struggles cannot be reduced to the emotionless and acultural deployment of 'rational action' – wherein education is viewed simply as an investment good. Non-choice, and aversion, and the non-rational and culturalist bases of choice are also important here; perhaps particularly for those students from families who have no previous experience of HE.

HE is a delimited field. Such fields may be said to have their own structures of information and communication, which are embodied in forms of social capital, degrees of embeddedness, and positioning in relation to information flows, which generate 'taste categories' and judgements. The social ordering of a field is very much a reflection of this cultural ordering – the meaning of categories and access to them are inter-twined. The different logics of consciousness within a field, as sets of routine assumptions and activities, produce (and are produced through) different logics of practice – although these are subject to constant re-invention. In relation to HE, the very idea of choice assumes a kind of formal equality that in fact, as we have tried to indicate, legitimates and obscures 'the effects of real inequality' (Bourdieu, 2000, p. 76). The operation of choice, or decision-making, 'imposes the same demands' on all 'without any concern for universally distributing the means of satisfying them' (p. 76).

Recent debates about increasing participation in HE and opening up access to 'elite' institutions have focused on 'barriers' to application or entry, and while these are important they tell only part of the story of patterns of access. The distribution of classes and minority ethnic groups within HE and across HE institutions has to be understood as the outcome of several stages of decision-making in which choices and constraints or barriers inter-weave. Many students, especially working-class students, never get to a position where they can contemplate HE. Others are qualified to do so but exclude themselves (Archer & Hutchings, 2000). Others who do apply avoid certain institutions. Conversely, for working-class and minority ethnic students, for a combination of negative and positive factors, other institutions are attractive (Ball *et al.*, 2002; Reay, 2000). Entrenched inequalities in 'participation' in and across HE, if they are to be properly addressed and systematically dismantled, need first to be understood in all their sociological complexity and indeterminacy, as issues of process and structure, and exclusion and 'choice'.

Acknowledgements

The constructive comments of the UNL research team, the Parental Choice and Market Forces Seminar group and BERA symposium participants on earlier versions of this paper are much appreciated. This study was sponsored by Award Number R000237431 'An Exploration of the Processes involved in Students' choice of Higher Education' from the ESRC.

Notes

1   Pugsley (1998, p. 79), writing about the working-class families in her South Wales study, notes that: 'The parents feel that they are out of their depth, that this is an alien environment and one in which their perceived incompetence will hamper rather than facilitate the progress of their child'. Interestingly and importantly, despite the very different location, Pugsley's research identifies almost exactly the same class divisions and differences in HE choice-making as our study.
2   The work of Archer & Hutchings (2000) suggests that working-class non-participants also view the risks and benefits of HE in instrumental terms, but have no repertoire of 'imagined futures' that would ground their risk assessments either in university life or the post-graduate labour market.
3   Anthony was one of the few white, middle-class interviewees to articulate assumptions about commonality and exclusivity. He explained: 'I tend to think that people doing architecture will be, I mean, reasonably cultured . . . You kind of try and absorb yourself into architecture as a sort of, you are studying a lot, and so I don't know about [social] classes, but probably people on the course would be equal to me intellectually'.
4   Working-class students are concentrated within less prestigious institutions (Reid, 1989; Paterson, 1997; Robertson & Hillman, 1997).
5   The mature FE Access students were, on the whole, less instrumental than the younger students.

References

Allat, P. (1996) Consuming schooling, in: S. Edgell, K. Hetherington & A. Warde (Eds) *Consumption Matters* (Oxford, Blackwell).
Archer, L. & Hutchings, M. (2000) 'Bettering yourself?'. *Discourses of Risk, Cost and Benefit in Young Working Class Non-participants' Constructions of HE* (London, STORM, University of North London).
Bagley, C., Woods, P.A. & Glatter, R. (2000) Rejecting Schools: towards a fuller understanding of the process of parental choice. Paper presented at the *BEMAS Conference*, Robinson College, Cambridge.
Ball, S.J. & Vincent, C. (1998) 'I heard it on the grapevine': 'Hot' Knowledge and school choice, *British Journal of Sociology of Education*, 19(3), pp. 377–400.
Ball, S.J., & Vincent, C. (2001) New class relations in education, in: J. Demaine (Ed.) *Sociology of Education Today* (London, Palgrave).
Ball, S.J., Macrae, S. & Maguire, M. (1999) Young lives, diverse choices and imagined futures in an education and training market, *International Journal of Inclusive Education*, 3(3), pp. 195–224.

Ball, S.J., Maguire, M.M. & Macrae, S. (2000) *Choice, Pathways and Transitions Post-16: New Youth, New Economies in the Global City* (London, Routledge/Falmer).

Ball, S.J., Reay, D. & David, M. (2002) 'Ethnic Choosing': Minority Ethnic Students and Higher Education Choice, *Race, Ethnicity and Education*, 15(4), pp. 333–357.

Beck, U. (1992) *Risk Society: towards a new modernity* (Newbury Park, CA, Sage).

Bourdieu, P. (1977) Cultural reproduction and social reproduction, in: J. Karabel & A.H. Halsey (Eds) *Power and Ideology in Education* (New York, Oxford University Press).

Bourdieu, P. (1986) *Distinction: a social critique of the judgement of taste* (London, Routledge).

Bourdieu, P. (1988) *Homo Academicus* (Cambridge, Polity Press).

Bourdieu, P. (1990) *The Logic of Practice* (Cambridge, Polity Press).

Bourdieu, P. (2000) *Pascalian Meditations* (Cambridge, Polity Press).

Bourdieu, P. & Boltanski, L. (2000) Changes in social structure and changes in the demand for education, in: S.J. Ball (Ed.) *Sociology of Education: major themes, volume 2, inequalities and oppressions* (London, RoutledgeFalmer).

Bourdieu, P. & Passeron, J.C. (1979) *The Inheritors: French students and their relation to culture* (London, Chicago University Press).

Bourdieu, P. & Passeron, J.C. (1990) *Reproduction* (London, Sage).

Bourdieu, P. & Wacquant, L.J.D. (1992) *An Invitation to Reflexive Sociology* (Chicago, IL, University of Chicago Press).

Brown, P. (1997) Cultural capital and social exclusion: some observations on recent trends in education, employment and the labour market, in: A.H. Halsey, H. Lauder, P. Brown & A. Stuart Wells (Eds) *Education: culture, economy and society* (Oxford, Oxford University Press).

Brown, P. & Scase, R. (1994) *Higher Education and Corporate Realities; class, culture and the decline of graduate careers* (London, UCL Press).

Cohen, P. & Hey, V. (2000) *Studies in Learning Regeneration: consultation document* (London, University of East London and Brunel University).

Collins, H. (1979) *The Credential Society* (New York, The Free Press).

David, M., West, A. & Ribbens, J. (1994) *Mothers' Intuition: choosing secondary schools* (London, Falmer Press).

Devine, F. (1998) Class analysis and the stability of class relations, *Sociology*, 32(1), pp. 23–42.

Du Bois-Reymond, M. (1998) 'I don't want to commit myself yet': young people's life concepts, *Journal of Youth Studies*, 1(1), pp. 63–79.

Duru-Bellat, M. (2000) Social inequalities in the French education system: the joint effect of individual and contextual factors, *Journal of Education Policy*, 15(1), pp. 33–40.

Ehrenreich, B. (1989) *Fear of Failing: the inner life of the middle class* (New York, Pantheon).

Gewirtz, S., Ball, S.J. & Bowe, R. (1995) *Markets, Choice and Equity in Education* (Buckingham, Open University Press).

Goldthorpe, J. (1996) Class analysis and the reorientation of class theory: the case of persisting differentials in educational attainment, *British Journal of Sociology*, 47(3), pp. 481–505.

Goodson, L., Cookson Jr, P. & Persell, C. (1997) Distinction and destiny: the importance of curriculum form in elite American private schools, *Discourse* 18(2), pp. 173–183.

Hatcher, R. (1998) Class differentiation in education: rational choices?, *British Journal of Sociology of Education*, 19(1), pp. 5–24.

Hesketh, A.J. (1999) Towards an economic sociology of the student financial experience of higher education, *Journal of Education Policy*, 14(4), pp. 385–410.

Hodkinson, P. & Sparkes, A. (1997) Careership: a sociological theory of career decision making, *British Journal of Sociology of Education*, 18(1), pp. 29–44.

Hutchings, M. & Archer, L. (2000) *'Higher than Einstein': constructions of going to university among working class non-participants* (London University of North London, Centre for Higher Education and Access Development).

Jenkins, R. (1992) *Pierre Bourdieu* (London, Routledge).

Jordon, B., Redley, M. & James, S. (1994) *Putting the Family First: identities, decisions and citizenship* (London, UCL Press).

Lauder, H., Hughes, D., *et al.* (1999) *Trading in Figures: why markets in education don't work* (Buckingham, Open University Press).

Lee, M.J. (1993) *Consumer Culture Reborn* (London, Routledge).

McDonough, P.M., Antonio, A.L., Walpole, M. & Perez, L. (1997) College rankings: who uses them and with what impact. Paper presented at the *AERA Annual Meeting*, Chicago, IL.

Metcalf, H. (1997) *Class and Higher Education: the participation of young people from lower social classes* (London, CIHE).

Moogan, Y.J., Baron, S. & Harris, K. (1999) Decision-making behaviour of potential higher education students, *Higher Education Quarterly*, 53(3), pp. 211–228.

Nash, R. (1999) Realism in the sociology of education: 'explaining' social differences in attainment, *British Journal of Sociology Education*, 20(1), pp. 107–125.

Parkin, F. (Ed.) (1974) Strategies of social closure in class formation, in: *The Social Analysis of Class Structure* (London, Tavistock).

Paterson, L. (1997) Trends in Higher Education in Scotland, *Higher Education Quarterly*, 51(1), pp. 29–48.

Power, S., Whitty, G., Edwards, T. & Wigfall, V. (1998) Education and the formation of middle class identities. Paper presented at the *European Conference on Educational Research*, University of Ljubljana, Slovenia, 17–20 September.

Pugsley, L. (1998) Throwing your brains at it: higher education, markets and choice, *International Studies in Sociology of Education*, 8(1), pp. 71–90.

Reay, D. (1998) *Class Work: mothers' involvement in their children's primary schooling* (London, UCL Press).

Reay, D. (2000) 'It's Taking Me a Long Time But I'll Get There in the End': mature students on access courses and higher education choice, ESRC HE Choice Project Paper 4: CPPR (London, King's College London).

Reay, D., Davies, J., David, M. & Ball, S.J. (2001) Choices of degree and degrees of choice, *Sociology*, 35(4), pp. 855–874.

Reid, I. (1989) *Social Class Differences in Britain: life-chances and life-styles*, 3rd edn (Glasgow, Fontana Press).

Robbins, D. (1991) *The Work of Pierre Bourdieu: recognising society* (Milton Keynes, Open University Press).

Roberts, D. & Allen, A. (1997) *Young Applicants' Perception of HE* (Leeds, HEIST).

Roberts, K. (1993) Career trajectories and the mirage of increased social mobility, in: I. Bates & G. Riseborough (Eds) *Youth and Inequality* (Buckingham, Open University Press).

Robertson, D. & Hillman, J. (1997) *Widening Participation in Higher Education for Students from Lower Socio-Economic Groups and Students with Disabilities*. National Committee of Inquiry into Higher Education (London, HMSO).

Savage, M. & Egerton, M. (1997) Social mobility, individual ability and the inheritance of class inequality, *Sociology*, 31(4), pp. 645–672.

Savage, M., Barlow, J., Dickens, P. & Fielding, A.J. (1992) *Property, Bureaucracy and Culture: middle class formation in contemporary Britain* (London, Routledge).

Social Trends (1999) Vol. 29 (London, HMSO),

Thrupp, M. (1999) *Schools Making a Difference: Let's be Realistic!* (Buckingham, Open University Press).

Wacquant, L.J.D. (1991) Making class(es): the middle classes in social theory and social structure, in: S. McNall, R. Levine & R. Fantasia (Eds) *Bringing Class Back In: contemporary and historical respectives* (Boulder, CO, West View Press).

Williams, J. (Ed.) (1997) *Negotiating Access to HE* (Buckingham, SRHE/Open University Press).

CHAPTER 2

MISCONCEPTIONS ABOUT THE LEARNING APPROACHES, MOTIVATION AND STUDY PRACTICES OF ASIAN STUDENTS

David Kember

Higher Education, 40, 99–121, 2000

EDITOR'S INTRODUCTION

In this article, David Kember, who moved to Hong Kong in the late 1980s, marshals his experience of working on 90 action research projects in his own and other local universities to dispel a series of myths about Asian higher education students. These, somewhat contradictory, myths are that such students are relatively passive learners, are fond of rote learning, and are also high achievers motivated by their future career prospects.

Kember argues instead that matters are rather more complex than that. Asian students may appear as relatively passive and make much use of memorisation as an aid to learning, but that has much to do with the ways in which they have been taught at school, and with underlying socio-cultural patterns of behaviour. Memorisation may be used as a means to developing understanding, leading to deep learning, rather than the surface forms of learning it seems to imply. Similarly, Asian students are not simply motivated by the desire to achieve good marks and qualifications in order to get better jobs, but may combine this with both intrinisic motivation and more collective behaviours.

Two related areas of theory are used to provide a framework for the article and its argument. One has to do with different forms of motivation, variously categorised as achieving, career, intrinsic and collective. The other has to do with approaches to learning and teaching, in particular the distinction that has been made between surface and deep approaches to learning, as well as what have been called strategic or achieving approaches.

One of the key messages of the article has to do with the close relationship between the higher education curriculum, teaching and learning. Courses may be taught or delivered in different ways, but time needs to be allowed for the students on these courses – whether Asian or otherwise – to adapt to changed ways of learning in order for them to get the greatest benefit.

This article was categorised in the introductory chapter as adopting a comparative methodological approach to researching teaching and learning. It was called comparative because its key focus is on comparing the experience of Asian students with the predominantly Western research literature on teaching and learning in higher education. While Kember himself labels his methodological approach as action research (see, for example, Atweh *et al.* 1998, Greenwood and Levin 1998, Griffiths 1998), the methods used included questionnaires – including the widely applied Study Process Questionnaire (SPQ) – and interviews.

The key literature within which Kember locates his research is that on approaches to learning and teaching, an area to which both multivariate and phenomenographical methods have been extensively applied (e.g. Biggs 1999, McLean 2001, Marton *et al.* 1984, Prosser and Trigwell 1999, Ramsden 1992, Richardson 2000, Severiens *et al.* 2001), and in which there have been a few other comparative studies (e.g. Ramburuth and McCormick 2001). There is another related literature, however, having to do with the experience and treatment of overseas or international students in higher education; that is, students studying outside their native country (e.g. Campbell 2000, Grey 2002, Kinnell 1990, Littlemore 2001, McNamara and Harris 1997), to which the Richardson article (1994) referred to by Kember provides a link.

References

Atweh, B., Kemmis, S. and Weeks, P. (1998) *Action Research in Practice: partnerships for social justice in education.* London, Sage.

Biggs, J. (1999) *Teaching for Quality Learning at University: what the student does.* Buckingham, Open University Press.

Campbell, A. (2000) 'Cultural Diversity: practising what we preach in higher education', *Teaching in Higher Education*, 5, 3, pp. 373–384.

Greenwood, D. and Levin, M. (1998) *Introduction to Action Research: social research for social change.* Thousand Oaks, CA, Sage.

Grey, M. (2002) 'Drawing with Difference: challenges faced by international students in an undergraduate business degree', *Teaching in Higher Education*, 7, 2, pp. 153–166.

Griffiths, M. (1998) *Educational Research for Social Justice: getting off the fence.* Buckingham, Open University Press.

Kinnell, M. (ed.) (1990) *The Learning Experiences of Overseas Students.* Buckingham, Open University Press.

Littlemore, J. (2001) 'The Use of Metaphor in University Lectures and the Problems that it causes for Overseas Students', *Teaching in Higher Education*, 6, 3, pp. 333–349.

McLean, M. (2001) 'Can we Relate Conceptions of Learning to Student Academic Achievement?' *Teaching in Higher Education*, 6, 3, pp. 399–413.

McNamara, D. and Harris, R. (eds) (1997) *Overseas Students in Higher Education: issues in teaching and learning.* London, Routledge.

Marton, F., Hounsell, D. and Entwistle, N. (eds) (1984) *The Experience of Learning.* Edinburgh, Scottish Academic Press.

Prosser, M. and Trigwell, K. (1999) *Understanding Learning and Teaching: the experience in higher education.* Buckingham, Open University Press.

Ramburuth, P. and McCormick, J. (2001) 'Learning Diversity in Higher Education: a comparative study of Asian international and Australian students', *Higher Education*, 42, pp. 333–350.

Ramsden, P. (1992) *Learning to Teach in Higher Education.* London, Routledge.

Richardson, J. (1994) 'Cultural Specificity of Approaches to Studying in Higher Education: a literature review'. *Higher Education*, 27, pp. 449–468.

Richardson, J. (2000) *Researching Student Learning: approaches to studying in campus-based and distance education.* Buckingham, Open University Press.

Severiens, S., Ten Dam, G. and van Hout Walters, B. (2001) 'Stability of Processing and Regulation Strategies: two longitudinal studies on student learning', *Higher Education*, 42, pp. 437–453.

MISCONCEPTIONS ABOUT THE LEARNING APPROACHES, MOTIVATION AND STUDY PRACTICES OF ASIAN STUDENTS

Introduction

When I first went to work in Hong Kong, over twelve years ago, I talked to many people about the students. I was given a list of characteristics with a high level of consensus. I was informed that the students:

Rely on rote-learning
Are passive
Resist teaching innovations
Are largely extrinsically motivated, which is usually regarded negatively
Have high levels of achievement motivation
Are high achievers
Are good at project work
Are willing to invest in education.

The characteristics were not perceived as unique to Hong Kong students. Representatives of many universities from round the world passed through Hong Kong on missions to recruit students from the Asian region. It was common to hear them talk of Asian students, in general, in a similar way. It was also evident that similar views were informing teaching practice. The following quotation is taken from the minutes of a Course Planning Committee in my (then) new university. It appeared to be quite typical of attitudes prevailing at the time. The fact that it appeared, without question, in an official curriculum development document shows that the views were influencing programme planning and teaching.

> Students in Hong Kong . . . expect lecturers to teach them everything that they are expected to know. They have little desire to discover for themselves or avail themselves of the facilities which are available to them within the teaching insti-tution. They wish to be spoon fed and in turn they are spoon fed. Lecturers are under pressure to feed the student with a certain amount of academic and community needs information and the simplest way to do it is to adopt the old and traditional approaches to teaching.
> (Minutes of the [. . .] Course Planning Committee 1989, p. 13)

Though similar perceptions were widespread, the characteristics were puzzling. The students were portrayed as rote learners, which is associated with poor academic outcomes in Western universities (Biggs 1987; Watkins and Hattie 1981). A prefer-ence for passive over active learning methods also tends to be associated with low level outcomes. Yet the students were recognised as high academic achievers by my new colleagues in Hong Kong.

The achievements of Asian, and particularly Chinese, students are well docu-mented. For comparative international studies, mathematics is the easiest subject to devise tests for, so it is the subject with the greatest number of studies. Stevenson and Lee (1996) reviewed these studies and concluded that students from China, Hong Kong, Singapore and Taiwan performed consistently well. Comparative studies of language and science are more difficult to conduct because of language differences, but Stevenson and Lee concluded that the evidence there also pointed to impressive performances by Asian and particularly Chinese students.

There are also comparisons of the performance of ethnic groups within Western countries. Siu (1992) reviewed the performance of Asian Americans and came to the following conclusion (1992, p. 5), which is in marked contrast to the quotation above.

> The consistent finding is that Asian Americans start school earlier, stay in school longer, drop-out less often, have larger percentages of high school graduates, are over-represented in gifted student programs, and under-represented in programs for learning disabled, manifest fewer disciplinary problems, and are better prepared for college than candidates overall.

There was, then, ample evidence to confirm the impression that students from Hong Kong and other parts of Asia tended to be high academic achievers. Yet there was a widespread view that Asian students commonly employed study methods which inevitably resulted in low-level academic outcomes. There appeared to be a dichotomy between the perceived learning methods and the achievements of these students.

At that time there was little or no research in the literature which addressed this issue. It was possible to find descriptions of Asian students which conformed to the above list. These, though, appeared to be impressionistic rather than informed by research. In view of the conclusion of this article it seems better not to cite such papers.

The purpose of this article is to give an account of subsequent research on these characteristics. The research provides two explanations for the apparent dichotomy between perceived rote learning and high achievement. There has been quite extensive research into this paradox about the learning approaches of Asian students, to the extent that a large part of a book (Watkins and Biggs 1996) has been devoted to the topic.

There has been less written about the other characteristics of Asian students, so what is relatively new about this article is that it also challenges the other rather negative perceptions of Asian students. It is shown that Asian students can and do adjust to active forms of learning if given the opportunity. Characterisations of the motivation of the students as predominantly extrinsic are also drawn into question, as evidence is presented which shows that the students could be motivated by courses which provide a good preparation for a future career, while also being intrinsically motivated by them. The nature of achieving motivation, which is normally seen as individualistic and competitive, is also called into question. Evidence is presented of a communal nature to achievement motive, which fits well with Confucian tradition.

Much of the cited research is into Chinese students, and of this a significant amount is from Hong Kong. For most of the points made, though, there is sufficient research in other Asian countries to make intelligent speculations as to how generalisable the results are throughout the Asian region. In view of widespread misperceptions an understanding of Asian students is of value to the many academics who have to teach Asian students. This includes those teaching in universities in Asia, staff in universities which recruit students from Asia and those who have, in their classes, students from the substantial Asian communities in Western countries.

Approaches to learning

The initial research, into the apparent dichotomy between achievement and learning approach, used the student approaches to learning framework. Extensive work on approaches to learning was reviewed by Richardson (1994) who concluded that:

In short, both qualitative and quantitative research procedures have produced evidence from a reasonable variety of national systems of higher education for the broad distinction between two fundamental approaches to studying: first an orientation towards comprehending the meaning of the materials to be learned; and, second, an orientation towards merely being able to reproduce those materials for the purposes of academic assessment. (p. 463)

The framework was appropriate for investigating Asian students since it identified an approach which relied upon learning material by heart so that it could be reproduced in examinations, which was what Asian students were commonly perceived to do. The contrasting orientation towards trying to understand, which Asian students were thought not to employ, was normally associated with high academic achievement. An instrument designed to measure approaches to learning is the Study Process Questionnaire (SPQ) (Biggs 1987). The questionnaire contains main scales for three approaches: deep, surface and achieving. The first two correspond to the meaning and reproducing orientations respectively. Achieving approach is a conventional measure of achieving motive, so is based on competition and ego-enhancement. Students aim to obtain the highest grades, whether or not the material is interesting.

Figure 1 shows results from a survey, with the SPQ, of 4863 students from over half the departments of a university in Hong Kong. The data was collected by collaborating lecturers, but the sampling was sufficiently extensive to be reasonably representative of types of discipline and course and year of study. Figure 1 compares the mean scores for deep, surface and achieving approaches with similar mean scores from a large sample of students in similar Australian institutions by Biggs (1987).

The differences between the mean Hong Kong and Australian scores are significant, though statistical results are not given as the samples were not necessarily matched on the arts and sciences division. The Hong Kong university concentrates upon applied sciences and professional courses so the best comparison is with the Australian science results, which did include applied sciences.

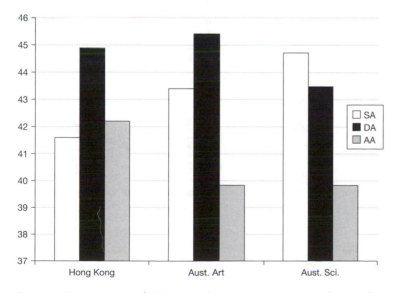

Figure 1 A comparison of SPQ scores between Hong Kong and Australian students

It can be seen that the mean score for achieving approach is higher in the Hong Kong sample than Australian arts and science students, as might be anticipated from the common perceptions of Asian students. However, the deep approach score is about the same level as those in Australia and the surface approach score is lower. If the common perception of Asian students were to be believed, it would be expected that Hong Kong students would have lower deep approach and higher surface approach scores and that the difference would be substantial.

At first it was thought that results like these were some form of experimental artefact, but all conceivable ones were explored and eliminated (Kember and Gow 1991). A wide range of similar data was gathered from other universities and colleges in Hong Kong, which was eventually compiled in Biggs (1992). Collectively this pool of data also challenged the view of Asian students as rote-learners by revealing surface approach scores which were lower than had been found in other countries, rather than considerably higher, which would have been expected from the reported perceptions.

Understanding and memorising

One explanation for these initially puzzling results came from clarifying the nature of approaches to learning of Hong Kong students. A combination of comparing factor structures of the SPQ data with those from elsewhere (Kember and Gow 1990) and interviews with students about their approaches to tackling specific academic tasks suggested that memorisation might be occurring in conjunction with attempts to reach understanding.

Kember and Gow (1990) initially characterised a 'narrow approach' which involved the students working systematically through material section-by-section. The students attempted to understand each new concept and then commit it to memory before proceeding to the next. The following quotation, from an interview with a Hong Kong student, illustrates the approach.

Table 11 Approaches to learning characterised by an intention and a strategy (adapted from Kember 1996)

Approach	Intention	Strategy
Surface	Memorising without understanding	Rote-learning
Intermediate 1	Primarily memorising	Strategic attempt to reach limited understanding as an aid to memorisation
Understanding and memorising	Understanding and memorising	Seeking comprehension then committing to memory
		Repetition and memorising to reach understanding
Intermediate 2	Primarily understanding	Strategic memorisation for examination or task after understanding reached
Deep	Understanding	Seeking comprehension

I read in detail section by section. If I find any difficulties I try my best to solve the problem before I go onto the next section. . . . If you don't memorise important ideas when you come across them then you will be stuck when you go on. You must memorise and then go on – understand, memorise and then go on – understand, memorise and then go on. That is my way of studying.

(Kember and Gow 1990, p. 361)

Others have subsequently reported observations of memorisation occurring in conjunction with understanding (Biggs 1996; Gow, Balla, Kember and Hau 1996; Marton, Dall'Alba and Kun 1996; Watkins 1996). The combination can take different forms to the narrow approach described above. Marton, Dall'Alba and Kun (1996) reported that memorisation could be used as an attempt to reach understanding in addition to understanding preceding memorisation. Evidence of the intention to both understand and memorise has also been found in mainland China (Marton, Dall'Alba and Kurt 1996) and Japan (Hess and Azuma 1992), so it may be quite widespread among Asian students.

Kember (1996) suggested that the various forms of combining memorisation and understanding meant that approaches to learning might be better characterised as a continuum rather than dichotomous deep and surface approaches. The positions upon the continuum are characterised by the intention and the strategy employed. Table 11 shows the main positions observed so far.

The intermediate position closer to the deep end of the spectrum arises from students who have a preference for seeking understanding, but recognise that their examinations normally require them to reproduce material. They, therefore, try to understand the concepts and then make sure the material is learnt so that they can get a good grade in the examination.

The intermediate position towards the surface end of the spectrum arose because students, who initially intend to memorise, found the memory load became such that some selection became necessary as they progressed through the school. Watkins (1996) interpreted interviews with Hong Kong secondary school students as showing that students developed through a sequence of three or four stages. Initially their intention was to achieve through reproduction, by rote-learning everything. The students then passed to the next stage of rote-learning things perceived as more important. In the subsequent developmental stage, the students started to see the benefit of trying to understand material before committing it to memory.

The first explanation for the apparent dichotomy between the high achievement of Asian students and the perceptions of rote-learning lies in a misunderstanding of observed memorisation. Teachers have observed their students trying to memorise material and have assumed the students were rote-learning or learning by heart. This may have been a common occurrence as the signs of this can be quite visible. For example, students can often be seen, before an examination, reading through flash cards containing key material. Students who have to do presentations in seminars can also be observed rehearsing their speech out loud.

The evidence of memorisation occurring in conjunction with attempts to reach understanding suggests that the assumption that these students were rote-learning could well be false. If the learning involves understanding as well as memorising then it is neither rote-learning nor a surface approach. The combined approach is likely to result in high grades as the students can reach an understanding of underlying concepts so are able to tackle assignments requiring application or problem solving. They are also likely to do well in examinations which require the students to demonstrate that they have absorbed a body of knowledge.

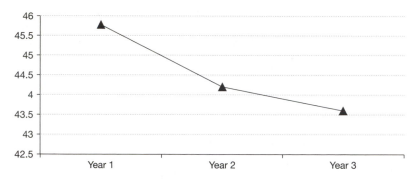

Figure 2 Deep approach by year of study

Surface learning because of curriculum

Evidence for the second explanation for the widespread perception that Asian students rely heavily upon rote-learning occurred from plotting the SPQ data for deep approach, originally shown in Figure 1, by year of study. The graph, shown in Figure 2, exhibits a decline in deep approach scores by year of study. An ANOVA test was performed to test the hypothesis that the mean scores of deep approach for the years of study were equal. A statistically significant F statistic ($F = 21.1$, df1 = 3 and df2 = 4588 with p-value = 0.000) was observed which indicates the population means of deep approach scores are unequal. To pinpoint where the differences were, the Scheffe procedure (SPSS Inc. 1986, pp. 762–764) was used to show which year's scores differed significantly from the others. The result showed that the mean deep approach score of year 1 was statistically greater than that of year 2 and year 3 at the 5% level of significance.

It is true that the decline is small, but the results are incompatible with the normal goals of higher education which stress the development of critical thinking, problem solving skills and the ability to tackle ill-defined issues. If the courses were achieving these aims, deep approach scores would be expected to rise markedly during a degree program as these higher order learning goals can only be achieved if students are aiming to understand course material. Unfortunately the converse appears to be all too common as evidence of deep approach scores declining by year of study are quite normal (Biggs 1987; Watkins and Hattie 1985).

Approaches to learning are not stable psychological characteristics of individuals. It is true that students normally have preferred or predominant approaches. The approach adopted for a particular learning task will, though, be a function of the nature of the task and it is common to observe students switching between surface and deep approaches depending upon the nature of the assignment or learning task (Laurillard 1984; Ramsden 1984). The approach students adopt for a particular course will be affected by factors such as the nature of the course content and assessment, the workload, the teaching method and the students' perception of the relevance and interest of the course (Gibbs 1992; Ramsden 1987).

The curriculum design and the way the course is taught can, therefore, affect the learning approach which students adopt. This means that the attitude and beliefs of the instructors are relevant as these have a marked impact upon the nature of the courses they teach (Gow and Kember 1993; Kember and Gow 1994; Kember 1997). If teachers believe that their students have a predilection for rote-learning they might

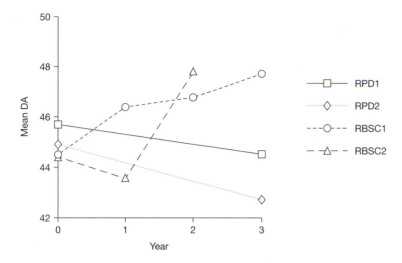

Figure 3 Deep approach scores for the old and new courses

structure their teaching and assessment to cater for this type of learning. When students perceive the demands of the course they adopt a surface response. The instructor observes this and a self-fulfilling prophecy comes home to roost.

A case study showing the effects of believing that students expect to be spoon fed is given in McKay and Kember (1997). The article began with the quotation, from the minutes of a course planning committee, given near the start of this article. The programme for which this course leader was responsible did adopt old and traditional approaches to teaching and spoon fed the students. The influence of the curriculum was monitored by administering the SPQ at intervals to the final two intakes to the programme. The mean deep approach scores for the penultimate (RPD1) and final (RPD2) deep approach scores are shown in Figure 3.

At this point the course leader departed and the department started planning a new programme with a course leader with very different views of students and their learning (McKay 1995). The SPQ was also used to monitor the first (RBSC1) and second (RBSC2) intakes to this new programme. The results are included in Figure 3 for comparison.

The apparent declines in deep approach scores for the final two intakes to the old programme were not statistically significant (F = 1.74 for RPD1 and F = 1.64 for RPD2). These data are, though, quite sufficient to establish that a change occurred between the two programmes, as the multivariate test of the repeated measures analysis of variance showed that mean deep approach scores for the two intakes to the new programme did have a statistically significant increase (F = 5.3, DF = 41, p < 0.01 for RBSC1 and F = 7.7, DF = 38, p < 0.01 for RBSC2).

The results show that a curriculum designed according to a different philosophy had a markedly different effect upon the learning approaches adopted by the students. The didactic spoon-feeding approach did not encourage students to adopt a deep approach or think critically as they proceeded through their programme. Whereas a programme designed to stress independent learning and student-centred approaches (McKay and Kember 1997) obviously had some measure of success in this respect as deep approach scores rose by year of study.

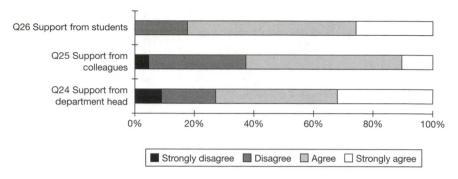

Figure 4 Level of support for innovation from students, colleagues and department heads

The second explanation for observations of Asian students' rote-learning is that they could be doing it because they perceive that this is what their teachers and their courses expect them to do, or if it is what the assessment requires. This is particularly likely to happen if their teachers believe that this is all they are capable of.

This particular explanation for observations of rote-learning is certainly not a phenomenon peculiar to Hong Kong. It is, rather, a universal phenomenon. Students will adopt a surface approach if they perceive that is what the course and assessment requires or if that approach best enables them to deal with the demands of the course. Teachers, wherever, must expect that if they design curricula or courses of this type, that student behaviour will be consistent with their perceptions of the course design.

Attitudes to teaching innovation

Returning to the list of beliefs about Asian students cited at the start, this article will now deal with the widespread beliefs that the students prefer to be passive learners and resist the introduction of forms of teaching which are not didactic and require them to play an active role in their own learning.

The case cited above is one of the first action research projects in which I was involved, in which the participants aim to improve the quality of student learning in courses they teach (Kember and Gow 1992; Kember and McKay 1996). Academics within my university had become concerned about evaluation data like that in Figure 2 and found the action research approach to be appropriate for tackling identified problems and introducing more innovative forms of teaching and learning.

This work eventually led to an initiative known as the Action Learning Project which has supported 90 action research projects within eight universities and colleges in Hong Kong (Kember 2000). These projects have introduced a wide variety of innovative forms of teaching and learning using almost anything other than didactic lecturing to passive students. Examples of the types of alternative teaching and learning methods are problem-based learning, group projects, peer teaching, games and simulations, learning from multimedia packages and using reflective journals as a precursor to group discussion.

The first phase of the Action Learning Project, which supported 50 projects, was evaluated with a multiple-method, multiple-voice approach. This included a questionnaire to all project participants. Three of the questions in the questionnaire asked respondents to indicate the level of support received from (1) students, (2) departmental colleagues and (3) heads of department. Figure 4 indicates the proportion of the 72 respondents who disagreed or agreed with the statement that they had received support from each of the three sectors.

It can be seen clearly that few respondents did not feel that the students had supported their initiative. The level of support from students was greater than that from departmental colleagues and at least as great as that from department heads. This is hardly indicative of a student body resistant to innovative forms of teaching and learning.

Other facets of the evaluation agreed with this conclusion. Perhaps the most relevant, in terms of this point, were the evaluations conducted on each individual project by the participants (Kember, Lam, Yan, Yum and Liu, 1997). All of these evaluations sought feedback from students through questionnaires and/or interviews. It is obviously difficult to generalise across 50 projects and their individual evaluations. Perhaps the most appropriate way to seek an overall evaluation is to quote the final paragraph from report by a panel of independent evaluators (Biggs and Lam 1997, p. 171).

> Given all the above, that valuable outcomes can be reliably associated with probably most projects (and less reliably with all completed projects), the positive outcomes are in fact considerable. If, as seems likely, most participants got something of value as far as their teaching was concerned, then it follows that the teaching of at least one hundred teachers, and the learning of thousands of students, were improved at a cost of . . . This seems pretty good value for money.

The projects could only have achieved valuable outcomes and the learning of thousands of students improved if the students exhibited at least reasonable levels of cooperation with the initiatives, came to appreciate the forms of teaching and learning introduced and participated fully in them. If this conclusion can be drawn from such a substantial set of innovative teaching projects, the impression that Hong Kong students prefer passive learning and resist teaching innovations can have little or no foundation. There seems no reason to suppose that this is a mis-perception only in Hong Kong, but is also likely to apply elsewhere in Asia.

The need for adaptation

A possible explanation for the widespread perception of the conservative nature of Asian students lies in the need to allow them to adapt to new forms of teaching and learning. In a number of the Action Learning Project initiatives, students initially found the new course formats taxing, but eventually came to appreciate them.

To illustrate this effect evidence is taken from a project which investigated in some detail the affective dimension of the introduction of students to a new form of teaching (Kember, Jones, Loke, McKay, Sinclair, Tse, Webb, Wong, Wong and Yeung, 2001, ch. 10). The nursing course aimed to promote awareness, exploration and critical analysis of current professional issues. The approach was to encourage the students to reflect upon their daily encounters by writing reflective journals. The reflective writings formed the starting point for small group discussion of selected issues.

For most of the students, their previous educational experiences could largely be summed up as didactic teaching and passive learning. They were used to tightly structured courses in which the teacher defined the content and delivered it. The written assignments they had been required to do were accomplished by transposing material from textbooks.

Many of the students found the new course format difficult or uncomfortable. They found it hard to adjust to the seeming lack of structure in the course. Reflective writing was quite different to other forms of writing they had undertaken. Most initially distrusted the notion that their own reflections and materials they had to search for could supply much of the content for the course.

> In the past I was quite inflexible in my method of study. I only revised what the teachers said was important. Now I have to read books and find (relevant) material for myself. Of course they are different . . . very different, so I am not able to cope with this (learning approach). . . . I could not decide what was right or wrong, the feeling was so insecure. Through journal writing and sharing in the learning process, I found that writing papers is very difficult. Maybe I am still not familiar with the learning approach in tertiary education.

The above quotation was taken from an interview in the early stages of the course. By the end of the course most of the students had not only overcome these initial difficulties but had come to see the value of learning from the experiences of themselves and their fellow students, as shown by the typical quotation below.

> When we discussed it further, some of them even agreed with me, so there was an integration of our thoughts . . . Small group discussion helped me a lot. The other students are from different hospitals, different clinical units. Sometimes, they talked about their experiences which I have never heard before.

Those who formed the impression that Asian students resist innovation may not have allowed the students time to adapt. They also might not have taken steps to ease the transition process. In the project used as an example, the teachers provided a structured introduction to reflective writing and students making the transition received support from tutors and fellow students (Kember *et al.*, 2001). Most people find change of any sort can be difficult to adapt to, so when new forms of teaching are introduced it is important to address the issue of implementing the change and allow the students time to make the transition.

Again it seems possible to generalise this explanation for perceptions of resistance to innovation to a wider context. Most people find it difficult to adapt from well established practices and beliefs. It is common for any form of major change to meet initial resistance. Successful integration of an innovation requires strategies to deal with the initial resistance. (See e.g. Hunkin 1980, ch. 2, for a general treatment of curriculum change, innovation, resistance and planning change.)

Career motivation

In psychology textbooks motivation is most commonly characterised as either intrinsic or extrinsic. Anecdotal evidence suggested that the students in Hong Kong were motivated to succeed at university by the prospect of well-paid career on graduation. Motivation of this type would normally be classified as extrinsic and viewed in a negative light.

Kember, Wong and Leung (1999) question both the anecdotal observations and their interpretation in terms of the categorisation scheme commonly applied to motivation. In an extensive series of interviews with Hong Kong students there were many statements about career preparation and career relevance of courses, which were hard to classify as extrinsic motivation.

There were numerous positive comments about courses which provided a good preparation for a future career. For example, a student studying textiles and clothing felt that the breadth of the course widened career opportunities. The student was motivated to study the double major in spite of the heavier workload.

> The best feature is that the course covers textile technology and the skills of marketing which can actually be used after our study. Otherwise, it would be hardly used if we just acquired the knowledge of textile and clothing. Also, we can have a wider range of choices of career because we have also acquired marketing skills which are related to the field of business. The worst is that it is too hard for us to study both areas. The workload is very heavy as there are many assignments and projects to do.
>
> (Kember, Wong and Leung 1999, p. 326)

A further feature of the career motivation was that it often occurred in conjunction with intrinsic motivation. Students expected their courses to provide both intrinsic and career motivation. They wanted them to be both interesting and provide an appropriate preparation for their future career. Courses which failed to do this were rated in a negative way on one or both of these aspects. The student quoted above is a good example.

> I think the best is that our course is combining the study of textiles and that of business. You can have some knowledge on both aspects. But it's also the worst because you only learn it superficially. For example, we won't study textiles as deeply as those who study only textiles and won't learn as much business as business students. It's diverse but it is quite superficial. . . . But the question is you only know it superficially. You don't know how to do it or how it works practically. You just know it a little bit and don't know it clearly. Although I think it's not good, I think it's not so important. Because I think the course not only give me some knowledge in this field, but also give me a chance to train my thinking, working ability and presentation skills, etc., which is very important.
>
> (Kember, Wong and Leung 1999, p. 328)

The student appreciated the career preparation resulting from the combined majors. Yet, the student was still dissatisfied with the fact that each subject in this curriculum was superficially taught. There was a desire for greater knowledge which is surely a sign of unfulfilled intrinsic interest. The student has a very intelligent perception of the perennial dilemma in curriculum development over breadth versus depth.

Overall about 40% of the interviewed students commented on both intrinsic and career motivation. The students were asked open questions about curriculum issues, rather than questions about motivation, let alone specific questions about types of motivation. In this light the number of students feeling that a course should both stimulate intrinsic interest and display a relevance to future career needs is considerable.

The above discussion suggests that this career related form of extrinsic motivation should not be seen in a negative light. A course which provides a good preparation for a future career appears to motivate students to study and to study for understanding.

Further, the transcripts did not show evidence of incompatibility between intrinsic interest and career motivation. It does not appear that the presence of career motivation detracted from intrinsic interest. Rather, the data suggested that students expected their courses to be both interesting and career relevant. A course which did provide a good preparation could also be perceived as interesting and in many cases one form of motivation seemed to enhance the other.

This observation, though, is contrary to the assertion in many standard psychology textbooks that the presence of extrinsic motivation decreases the level of intrinsic motivation. This position is not universal, though, as some researchers claim to have produced evidence that praise or rewards did not diminish intrinsic motivation. Deci and Ryan (1985) attempted to rationalise this position with their cognitive evaluation theory. They asserted that it is the perception of the subject which is important in determining whether intrinsic motivation is depressed. It depends whether the extrinsic factor is perceived as providing information or feedback, in which case intrinsic motivation can increase through an increased perception of self-determination or competence.

From both the interview transcripts and knowledge of common beliefs of Hong Kong society, it seems reasonable to argue the case that it could be common for Hong Kong students to have internalised a value for high-status well-paid careers. Stevenson and Lee (1996) note that there has been traditional value placed upon education for personal improvement and social advancement throughout Chinese societies. In developing societies material success is widely admired. It is, therefore, reasonable to assume that the students interviewed in our study could have internalised a prevailing society belief that it is appropriate to work hard to gain entry to a lucrative career. A course which boosted career prospects would, therefore, be seen as enhancing self-regulation so would not diminish intrinsic motivation and might well increase it. There seems no reason to doubt that the same would apply to other parts of Asia too.

Achieving motive

To examine the assertions that Asian students have high levels of achieving motive, it is first necessary to look at a definition of achieving motive. The definition of the achieving motive scale incorporated within the SPQ is given by Biggs (1987, p. 11) as follows:

> Achieving Motive is based on competition and ego-enhancement: obtain highest grades, whether or not material is interesting.

Other definitions of achieving motive would agree with the main points of this definition. For the purposes of this article it is salient to note the stress on the individual, and his or her ego, and the competitive nature of the motivation.

The evidence of many Asian students performing so well suggests that they do display some form of achieving motive. Whether the conventional definition, from Western textbooks, adequately describes the form of motivation is questionable.

Firstly there is considerable evidence of students in Hong Kong working collaboratively. In a study of out-of-class learning activities, Yan (1996) found a wide range of activities tackled in groups. Some students and groups were placed in a category labelled 'avoiders' as the underlying reason for the joint activity was minimising the amount of work each student had to do. Typical activities under this category were copying notes, sharing material, sharing assignments and working out likely examination questions together.

Other students were classified as 'engagers' since the joint activities aimed towards achieving a better understanding of the course material. Typical activities within this category were discussing subject matter in a study group, helping each other understand difficult points and discussing how to approach questions.

Whether the groups adopted avoider or engager behaviour was again influenced by the broad curriculum design and the teaching and learning environment. There is a close parallel with the way individual students tend to adopt either deep or surface approaches to learning according to their perception of the course demands. What is most pertinent for the argument of this article is that neither type of group displays evidence of individualistic competitive ideals.

Tang (1993) also found evidence of a range of collaborative activities focused on assessment tasks. Furthermore, the collaborating students tended to exhibit both better performance and deeper approaches than those studying individually.

Salili (1996) reviewed the literature on achievement motivation among Chinese students. She noted the cultural impact of a strong sense of collectivism manifest in loyalty to the family and other social groups. Academic success would be seen as a source of pride for the entire family unit. Yang (1986) pointed out that the influence of Confucian philosophy meant that Chinese culture values hard work, effort and endurance. Learning and education are valued implicitly as well as for social advancement (Ho 1981).

Taken together the evidence of group activity and the nature of achievement motivation suggest that, within countries influenced by a Confucian tradition, characterising achievement motivation primarily as an individual drive and a competitive force may not be appropriate. Achievement motivation with a collective emphasis should not be confined to countries with a Confucian tradition. There are other cultures in the Asian and Pacific regions which have strong affiliations to extended families, villages or tribal groupings.

Remaining characteristics

The two remaining characteristics derived from popular beliefs about Asian students will not be questioned. The observation that students in Hong Kong did well in projects can be explained in terms of the Confucian tradition, so should also apply to other countries with similar traditions.

For group projects the main influence is the collective affiliation referred to above. When students have been taught to value communal goals, they should find it easier to form a coherent and committed team than those who have only been exposed to an individual competitive ethos.

The observation that individuals work hard on projects, other assignments and school work in general owes much to the respect paid to scholars and education by Chinese society. There is a long history, going back thousands of years, of scholars studying for entry to the civil service through an examination system which aimed to select a small proportion of citizens with a rounded education (Stephenson and Lee 1996). From these traditions the society has developed a considerable respect for scholars and education, which is rarely matched by other societies.

Chinese students are also brought up to see the importance of working hard at their studies (Wu 1996). Salili and Hau (1994) showed that Chinese students saw effort and academic ability as closely related. American students in higher grades expressed a strong negative relationship between ability and effort, suggesting that hard work was only necessary if students lacked ability.

The value placed on education itself and social and economic advancement through education explain the reasons why Chinese and other Asian societies are willing to invest in education. As achievement motivation can have a collective nature, there is often a willingness for family or extended family members to contribute to educational costs. This no doubt puts pressure upon those benefiting from these investments to work hard and succeed with their studies.

Conclusion

I will now return to the original list of characteristics commonly attributed to Asian students.

Rely on rote-learning
Are passive
Resist teaching innovations
Are largely extrinsically motivated, which is usually regarded negatively
Have high levels of achievement motivation
Are high achievers
Are good at project work
Are willing to invest in education.

The apparent dichotomy between the characteristics towards the top of the list with the lower ones can now be explained as a set of common mis-perceptions about Asian students. The perception that students rely upon rote-learning can be explained as a failure to realise that memorisation could be accompanied by an intention to seek understanding. Alternatively, students attempting to learn material by heart could be following a logical strategy because they perceive that the course and assessment require them to reproduce bodies of material. In many cases it is likely that these two explanations act in concert as academics who perceive their students as only capable of rote-learning design curricula accordingly.

There is also ample evidence that Asian students are not inherently resistant to innovative teaching strategies so are perfectly capable of participating actively in their own learning. Perceptions that they resist forms of teaching, other than traditional didactic ones, probably arose because the students were not given time and support to adapt from teaching styles they had experienced a great deal towards others which they were fresh to.

Asian students are motivated by the prospect of a good career. This is frequently not the negative form of extrinsic motivation in which the aim is to do the minimum amount of work to achieve a degree certificate as the passport to a well paid job. Rather, it is commonly accompanied by an interest in the course material indicating that the students expect their course to be both interesting and provide a good preparation for their future career.

It is true that Asian students display high levels of achievement motivation but it is a mistake to assume this can be directly equated to Western characterisations which see achievement motive being derived from an individual's need for ego enhancement and competitive drive. There is evidence that Asian achievement motivation has a more collective nature, which accords with observations of high levels of out-of-class learning in groups and good performance in group projects.

The evidence of high achievement by Asian students has not been questioned. Indeed there may well be a potential for better performance still. It is clear that common mis-perceptions of the learning approaches and preferences of Asian students have resulted in the adoption of didactic teaching methods and assessment and examinations which test recall. If the academics concerned realise that Asian students are capable of more active forms of learning and benefit from curricula which demand higher forms of learning, the performance could be better still.

Implications

The original rationale for much of this research was trying to reach an understanding of the learning approaches and study habits of Chinese and Asian students. It is now possible to describe and explain these fully. There must be a high level of confidence that the explanation is correct as there is agreement from a wide range of studies. Furthermore there is a logical consistency within the aspects of the description of the study habits of typical Asian students, whereas the previous anecdotal picture was internally inconsistent.

It is now possible to provide a coherent and comprehensive account of the learning and study behaviours of Chinese and Asian students, though there is some uncertainty as to the regions for which some of the characteristics are applicable. This better understanding should be helpful to those who have to teach Asian students. As these students are now studying in many parts of the world in numerous universities, this better understanding should be of wide benefit.

There are clear implications from this work in how to design curricula and teaching for Asian students. The first is to design teaching, curricula and assessment to foster a deep approach. Reasonably short lists of factors which promote a deep approach can be found in Biggs (1992), Gibbs (1992) and McKay and Kember (1997), Two books which provide detailed treatments are Biggs (1999) and Ramsden (1992).

It is desirable that courses make use of teaching and learning methods which require active participation of the students. When introducing these be mindful, though, that the students may not be familiar with such forms of learning so will need help and time for adaptation. Initial guidance and explanation is important and teachers should be prepared to provide support. Arranging the students into groups so that they can support each other is also conducive to successful implementation.

Motivation for study comes from courses which are relevant to and provide a good preparation for future careers. Stimulation through this career motivation will not diminish intrinsic interest and is more likely to enhance it. To benefit from the high levels of achievement motive, group learning should be encouraged rather than encouraging competition between individuals.

It would not matter if these teaching and curriculum implications were put into practice in mixed classrooms because they are consistent with good practice with all students.

Acknowledgement

The results cited in this article come from a number of projects funded by the University Grants Committee of Hong Kong.

References

Biggs, J. (1987). *Student Approaches to Learning and Studying*. Melbourne: Australian Council for Educational Research.
Biggs, J. (1992). *Why and How Do Hong Kong Students Learn? Using the Learning and Study Process Questionnaires*. Hong Kong: Hong Kong University.
Biggs, J. (1996). 'Western misperceptions of the Confucian-heritage learning culture', in Watkins, D. and Biggs, J.B. (eds), *The Chinese Learner: Cultural, Psychological and*

Contextual Influences. Melbourne and Hong Kong: Australian Council for Educational Research and the Comparative Education Research Centre, University of Hong Kong.

Biggs, J. and Lam, R. (1997). *Action Learning Project: Final Evaluation Report*. In D. Kember with T.S. Ha, B. H. Lam, A. Lee, S. Ng, L. Yan and J.C.K. Yum. Hong Kong: Action Learning Project.

Biggs, J.B. (1999). *Teaching for Quality Learning at University: What the Student Does*. Buckingham. SRHE: Open University Press.

Deci, E.L. and Ryan, R.M. (1985). *Intrinsic Motivation and Self-determination in Human Behavior*. New York and London: Plenum Press.

Gibbs, G. (1992). *Improving the Quality of Student Learning*. Bristol: Technical and Educational Services.

Gow, L. and Kember, D. (1993). 'Conceptions of teaching and their relationship to student learning', *British Journal of Educational Psychology* 63, 20–33.

Gow, L., Balla, J., Kember, D. and Hau, K.T. (1996). 'Learning approaches of Chinese people: A function of socialisation processes and the context of learning?', in Bond, M.H. (ed.), *The Handbook of Chinese Psychology*. Hong Kong: Oxford University Press.

Hess, R.D. and Azuma, M. (1991). 'Cultural support for schooling: Contrasts between Japan and the United States', *Educational Researcher* 20(9), 2–8.

Ho, D.Y.F. (1981). 'Traditional patterns of socialisation in Chinese society', *Acta Psychologica Taiwanica* 23(2), 81–95.

Hunkin, F.P. (1980). *Curriculum Development: Program Improvement*. Columbus, OH: Charles E. Merrill.

Kember, D. (1996). 'The intention to both memorise and understand: Another approach to learning?', *Higher Education* 31, 341–351.

Kember, D. (1997). 'A reconceptualisation of the research into university academics' conceptions of teaching', *Learning and Instruction* 7(3), 255–275.

Kember, D. (2000). *Action Learning and Action Research: Improving the Quality of Teaching and Learning*. London: Kogan Page.

Kember, D. and Gow, L. (1990). 'Cultural specificity of approaches to study', *British Journal of Educational Psychology* 60, 356–363.

Kember, D. and Gow, L. (1991). 'A challenge to the anecdotal stereotype of the Asian student', *Studies in Higher Education* 16(2), 117–128.

Kember, D. and Gow, L. (1992). 'Action research as a form of staff development in higher education', *Higher Education* 23(3), 297–310.

Kember, D. and Gow, L. (1994). 'Orientations to teaching and their effect on the quality of student learning', *Journal of Higher Education* 65(1), 58–74.

Kember, D. with Jones, A., Loke, A.Y., McKay, J., Sinclair, K., Tse, H., Webb, C., Wong, F.K.Y., Wong, M.W.L. and Yeung, E. (2001). *Reflective Teaching and Learning in the Health Professions*. Oxford: Blackwell Science.

Kember, D. and McKay, J. (1996). 'Action research into the quality of student learning: A paradigm for faculty development', *Journal of Higher Education* 67(5), 528–554.

Kember, D., Lam, B.H., Yan, L., Yum, J.C.K. and Liu, S.B. (1997). *Case Studies of Improving Teaching and Learning from the Action Learning Project*. Hong Kong: Action Learning Project.

Kember, D., Wong, A. and Leung, D.Y.P. (1999). 'Reconsidering the dimensions of approaches to learning', *British Journal of Educational Psychology* 69, 323–343.

Laurillard, D. (1984). 'Learning from problem solving', in Marton, F., Hounsell, D. and Entwistle, N. (eds), *The Experience of Learning*. Edinburgh: Scottish Academic Press.

Marton, F., Dall'Alba, G. and Kun, T.L. (1996). 'Memorising and understanding: the keys to the paradox?', in Watkins, D. and Biggs, J.B. (eds), *The Chinese Learner: Cultural, Psychological and Contextual Influences*. Melbourne and Hong Kong: Australian Council for Educational Research and the Comparative Education Research Centre, University of Hong Kong.

McKay, J. (1995). Promoting reflection within teaching: A case study in educational change within a department. Unpublished Ph.D. Dissertation, Hong Kong Polytechnic University.

McKay, J. and Kember, D. (1997). 'Spoonfeeding leads to regurgitation: A better diet can result in more digestible learning outcomes', *Higher Education Research and Development* 16(1), 55–67.

Ramsden, P. (1984). 'The context of learning', in Marton, F., Hounsell, D. and Entwistle, N. (eds), *The Experience of Learning*. Edinburgh: Scottish Academic Press.

Ramsden, P. (1987). 'Improving teaching and learning in higher education: the case for a relational perspective', *Studies in Higher Education* 12(3), 275–286.

Ramsden, P. (1992). *Learning to Teach in Higher Education*. London: Kogan Page.

Richardson, J.T.E. (1994). 'Cultural specificity of approaches to studying in higher education: A literature survey', *Higher Education* 27, 449–468.

Salili, F. (1996). 'Accepting personal responsibility for learning', in Watkins, D. and Biggs, J.B. (eds), *The Chinese Learner: Cultural, Psychological and Contextual Influences*. Melbourne and Hong Kong: Australian Council for Educational Research and the Comparative Education Research Centre, University of Hong Kong.

Salili, F. and Hau, K.T. (1994). 'The effect of teachers' evaluative feedback on Chinese students' perception of ability: A cultural and situational analysis', *Educational Studies* 20, 223–236.

Siu, S.F. (1992). *Towards an Understanding of Chinese-American Educational Achievement: A Literature Review*. Boston, MA: Center for Families, Communities, Schools and Children's Learning.

SPSS Inc. (1986). *SPSS-X Users Guide*. Chicago: SPSS Inc.

Stevenson, H.W. and Lee, S.Y. (1996). 'The academic achievement of Chinese students', in Bond, M.H. (ed.), *The Handbook of Chinese Psychology*. Hong Kong: Oxford University Press.

Tang, K.C.C. (1993). 'Spontaneous collaborative learning: A new dimension in student learning experience?', *Higher Education Research and Development* 12(2), 115–130.

Watkins, D. (1996). 'Hong Kong secondary school learners: a developmental perspective', in Watkins, D. and Biggs, J.B. (eds), *The Chinese Learner: Cultural, Psychological and Contextual Influences*. Melbourne and Hong Kong: Australian Council for Educational Research and the Comparative Education Research Centre, University of Hong Kong.

Watkins, D. and Biggs, J.B. (eds) (1996). *The Chinese Learner: Cultural, Psychological and Contextual Influences*. Melbourne and Hong Kong: Australian Council for Educational Research and the Comparative Education Research Centre, University of Hong Kong.

Watkins, D. and Hattie, J. (1981). 'The learning processes of Australian university students: investigations of contextual and personological factors', *British Journal of Educational Psychology* 51, 384–393.

Watkins, D. and Hattie, J. (1985). 'A longitudinal study of the approaches to learning of Australian tertiary students', *Human Learning* 4, 127–141.

Wu, D.Y.H. (1996). 'Chinese childhood socialisation', in Bond, M.H. (ed.), *The Handbook of Chinese Psychology*. Hong Kong: Oxford University Press.

Yan, L. (1996). 'Learning outside the classroom: Students' involvement in peer group work', in James, R. and McInnis, C. (eds), *Transition to Active Learning: Proceedings of the 2nd Pacific Rim Conference on the First Year in Higher Education, Centre for the Study of Higher Education, University of Melbourne*.

Yang, K.S. (1986). 'Chinese personality and its change', in Bond, M.H. (ed.), *The Psychology of the Chinese People*. Hong Kong: Oxford University Press.

CHAPTER 3

STUDENT, CRITIC AND LITERARY TEXT
A discussion of 'critical thinking' in a student essay

Mary Scott

Teaching in Higher Education, 5, 3, 277–288, 2000

EDITOR'S INTRODUCTION

In this article, Mary Scott provides a detailed analysis of one essay by one student of English literature – a student she has never met. It is an example of how a small-scale, focused piece of research can nevertheless yield much of interest and use, provided it is harnessed to theory and/or practice, and handled with clarity and reflection.

Scott's concern is with the notion of critical thinking, a commonplace expectation in the evaluation of student essays in the humanities and social sciences, yet one that is rarely explained by lecturers with clarity. She explores one student's understanding of critical thinking through an examination of one of her essays. She notes that the student's tutor judged that this essay was not sufficiently critical, and thus awarded it a poor mark. Scott argues, however, that it does display critical thinking of a sort, but that it could not have satisfied the tutor's expectations because of the student's evident lack of knowledge of a significant literature.

Scott provides a theoretical framework for her analysis of critical thinking through her use of Bakhtin's concept of dialogic text. Trends in literary criticism are referred to in the text, in particular what is called modern theory, as well as feminist critiques. Scott concludes her article by indicating some of the pedagogical implications of her argument for tutors, and by offering some self-reflexive comments.

The main higher education literature which offers a context for Scott's analysis is clearly, as she indicates, that focusing on student writing (e.g. Campbell *et al.* 1998, Cook 2000, Lea and Stierer 2000, Lea and Street 1998, Lillis 2001, Read *et al.* 2001, Torrance *et al.* 2000). There is a more practical, 'how to', element of this literature (e.g. Fairbairn and Winch 1996, Thomson 1996). There is also a parallel literature, however, on academic writing, of which the article by Grant and Knowles (2000) included in this Reader is an example.

This article was categorised in the introductory chapter as adopting a critical perspective on course design, though it also clearly includes elements of biographical analysis.

References

Campbell, J., Smith, D. and Brooker, R. (1998) 'From Conception to Performance: how undergraduate students conceptualise and construct essays', *Higher Education*, 36, pp. 449–469.

Cook, I. (2000) 'Nothing can ever be the case of "us and them again": exploring the politics of difference through border pedagogy and student journal writing', *Journal of Geography in Higher Education*, 24, 1, pp. 13–27.

Fairbairn, G. and Winch, C. (1996) *Reading, Writing and Reasoning: a guide for students.* Buckingham, Open University Press.

Grant, B. and Knowles, S. (2000) 'Flights of Imagination: academic women be(com)ing writers', *The International Journal for Academic Development,* 5, 1, pp. 6–19.

Lea, M. and Stierer, B. (eds) (2000) *Student Writing in Higher Education: new contexts.* Buckingham, Open University Press.

Lea, M. and Street, B. (1998) 'Student Writing in Higher Education: an academic literacies approach', *Studies in Higher Education,* 23, 2, pp. 157–172.

Lillis, T. (2001) *Student Writing: access, regulation, desire.* London, Routledge.

Read, B., Francis, B. and Robson, J. (2001) '"Playing Safe": undergraduate essay writing and the presentation of the student "voice"', *British Journal of Sociology of Education,* 22, 3, pp. 387–399.

Thomson, A. (1996) *Critical Reasoning: a practical introduction.* London, Routledge.

Torrance, M., Thomas, G. and Robinson, E. (2000) 'Individual Differences in Undergraduate Essay-writing Strategies: a longitudinal study', *Higher Education,* 39, pp. 181–200.

STUDENT, CRITIC AND LITERARY TEXT

Introduction

Students in higher education tend to be aware that evidence of 'critical thinking' is the primary criterion of a 'good essay' in many fields of study (Scott, 1996). However, as Barnett (1997) points out, 'critical thinking' can carry a number of different meanings. Barnett's observation is true, too, of the synonymous terms which cluster around 'critical thinking' – terms such as 'analyse', 'argue', 'discuss' and 'evaluate'. These terms frequent essay titles where they serve to encode particular modes of enquiry within particular fields of study. However, the problem is that students often fail to decipher these codes, or to grasp the meaning and implications of tutor feedback or guidance which uses one or another of the sets of terms that call for the adoption of a critical stance in a student essay (Hounsell, 1987; Ballard & Clanchy, 1988; Lea & Street, 1998).

The need to address this problem is now widely recognised. It is reflected, for example, in the Quality Assurance Agency's emphasis on the explicit statement of course aims and anticipated outcomes as essential requirements for student success. This emphasis on explicitness has also led to a number of projects which aim to provide students with descriptions of the characteristics of essays which demonstrate critical thinking. The most notable of these projects are, perhaps, those currently located at Middlesex University where researchers and practitioners seek to improve the learning and teaching of 'argument', which they, like many colleagues elsewhere, regard as the primary expression of critical thinking in higher education (Riddle, 1994; Mitchell, 1994a; Andrews, 1995).

I, too, am eager to improve students' ability to produce essays which give evidence of 'critical thinking'. I am also conscious that 'critical thinking' (or its absence) is a quality I have difficulty in conceptualising let alone describing. This paper thus represents an attempt on my part to enlarge my own awareness in ways which might benefit student essay writers. My focus is different, though, from that adopted at Middlesex University. In fact, as I indicate below, my theoretical orientation seeks to remedy what I see as a narrowing of perspective in Mitchell (1994a, 1997) and Riddle (1997) – a narrowing which derives from the high level of generality in their approach to making argument explicit, the consequence of which is a tightly circum-scribed view of pedagogy, In other words, it is not the need to aim at explicitness regarding critical thinking in relation to essay writing which I question, but rather a particular exemplar of explicitness together with the pedagogic consequences which it is likely to generate.

Explicitness as a problem: the case of 'argument'

Mitchell (1994a) places the following question at the centre of her research: 'What is this thing called argument?' In pursuing that question, Mitchell (1994a, 1997) and also Riddle (1997) arrive at a set of elements which can function as a deep structure into which they and colleagues from diverse fields of study can then slot 'argument'. This underlying structure is largely derived from Toulmin *et al.* (1979, 1984). It is a structure which has the following as its main components: 'claim' (i.e. an assertion being made which is open to questioning), 'grounds' (i.e. evidence to support the claim) and 'warrant' (the principles within the field of study which legitimate the status of the grounds as grounds). Mitchell and Riddle have added some refinements to this basic frame, but as with all models, their description of argument subordinates the specifi-city of particular instances to the pursuit of something 'abstract enough to remain relatively stable across and between contexts' (Mitchell, 1997, p. 26).

In thus setting out the 'ground rules' of argument Mitchell and Riddle seek to provide university teachers with understandings which they can apply in their own classrooms. This has, however, inevitably meant that Mitchell's earlier focus on the student (1994a,b) has now disappeared. In fact, the student has become an empty theoretical category. In other words, a transmission model of pedagogy now lurks within Mitchell's (1997) and Riddle's (1997) writing about argument. It is a model of pedagogy which invites a view of the student as simply the recipient of knowledge – whatever past experience or understandings she might bring with her are outside the focus of attention. In short, the emphasis is exclusively on teaching, but teaching is considered in isolation from learning and from the specificities of particular instances of critical thinking within particular fields of study. It is precisely these neglected aspects of the pedagogic situation to which I aim to draw attention in this paper. The pursuit of this goal has led me to peg out a theoretical context which can help me to engage with 'critical thinking' in all the specificity which it assumes in a student essay. I outline this context below – a context which has offered me a new perception of 'critical thinking'.

Critical thinking in the student essay: a theoretical context

The essay which I will be discussing was written by a novice undergraduate who was following a course on literature in English. To put it another way, the essay was the work of a student still in the process of making the transition from school to university. When confronted with the uncertainties of their transitional condition, new undergraduates tend, naturally, to rely on the familiar. To be more precise: they draw on the only resources they possess, namely assumptions and understandings deriving from their past learning. They then attempt, consciously or intuitively, to remake those resources in the light of their perceptions of what is now required. What they learned in the past may, however, no longer be appropriate and their assumptions regarding what is expected may fail to match their teachers' expecta-tions. The pedagogic relevance of this focus is clear: if our students are to move on from what they could successfully do in their final school examinations to what they need to do now in the university, our interventions as teachers are crucially important.

This Vygotskian focus on pedagogy (see Vygotsky, 1962) does, of course, prompt the question: what should we be trying to move students on to? It is here that I have come to supplement my expectation of 'critical thinking' on the part of the student with an awareness of my own need to make 'critical thinking' a defining characteristic of my role as a tutor. Underlying that statement is my perception of the existence of competing and developing theoretical perspectives in any field of study – perspectives which should make me alive to a range of possible interpretations in my students' responses to the essay titles which I provide. However, my emphasis on critical thinking in relation to the role of the tutor has taken me further than that. It has led me to read a student essay, especially the unsuccessful student essay, as evidence of the student's assumptions about essay-writing in a particular field of study. In other words, I attempt to identify why a student's essay might be as it is – or, to put that another way, I approach a student essay as being like any other text (oral or written) in that it is a 'motivated sign' (Kress, 1995). This is not to suggest that the student is necessarily conscious of the many possible reasons why her essay is as it is and not otherwise; nor does it mean that I can identify all those reasons. In fact, the accuracy or completeness of my reading is not actually the issue. What is important is the style of pedagogy which is suggested by the idea of a text as motivated. It is a pedagogy which emphasises self reflexivity on the part of the student and the tutor; a reflexivity that is promoted by tutor–student dialogue – a dialogue which needs, however, to be preceded by the tutor's careful attempt to identify the assumptions and meanings in the student's essay, and to consider their possible source.

In accordance with the reservations which I expressed earlier concerning the research into argument, I do not attempt to relate the essay I discuss to any conception of argument or critical thinking as an abstract category. Instead, I focus on a concrete feature of essays in many fields of study, but particularly in the Humanities and Social Sciences, a feature which abstract categories in their generality edit out, namely, the fact that an essay which is judged to demonstrate 'critical thinking' reflects an engagement with relevant literature. That literature itself represents particular theoretical perspectives in their engagement with other perspectives. This is a focus which Bakhtin (1981) helps me to amplify. Insisting that the word cannot be abstracted from the contexts in which it is and has been used, Bakhtin (1981, pp. 293–294) wrote:

> The life of the word is contained in its transfer from one mouth to another; from one context to another context, from one social collective to another, from one generation to another generation. In this process the word does not forget its own path and completely free itself from the power of those concrete contexts into which it has entered.

This quotation elaborates Bakhtin's key concept of the 'dialogic' text: every text cannot but speak to, hear and understand other meanings deriving from past contexts.

In adopting this Bakhtinian perspective, I include in the texts that are entwined with other texts all the understandings and assumptions which the student writer brings to her attempt to be critical in an essay. To put it another way, I assume that a student essay contains within it traces of the preconceptions which influenced the student's reading of the relevant literature and of the essay question. As I hope to show shortly, 'critical thinking' is then a concept with a broad sweep; it reveals itself in an essay (as elsewhere) as a text's transformation of other texts – a process in which the writer is involved both intuitively and consciously.

The student's essay

I will now attempt to give substance to the focus outlined above by discussing an essay written by an undergraduate student of literature. I begin by considering the essay in relation to the critical text which had been recommended to the students as highly relevant to the given essay title. I concentrate on how that critical text is transformed in the student's essay. My focus at this point reflects the tutor's expectation that the novice undergraduate would use the critical text as a key to the meaning of both the essay title and the literary work which she had chosen to discuss. Finally, however, in keeping with my emphasis on self-reflexivity, I do a *volte-face*. I suggest that within the student's essay there are the hints of an approach which would call in question the assumptions on which I had been basing my idea of what is appropriate in an essay – assumptions which actually run counter to my wish to give the student a central place in my refocusing of 'critical thinking'. I thus conclude the paper by keeping criticism in play.

Like her fellow students, Jessica, as I shall call her, had been asked to discuss the 'psychological or social meaning of an early crime fiction text' and to 'include in the analysis some close analysis of both form and meaning'. There is an obvious attempt at explicitness in this essay title with its repetitive 'analysis . . . close analysis'. This suggests a deliberate intention on the part of the tutor to ease the students into writing literary criticism at university by carefully guiding their approach to the early crime fiction texts they chose to discuss. Further direction was provided for those who, like Jessica, decided to concentrate on the 'social meaning' of *The Woman in White*. Tamar Heller's (1992) *Dead Secrets* was recommended to them. It is a text which has a direct bearing on the essay title, as I shall show shortly. Consequently, how the tutor expected the students to interpret the meaning, and the implications for critique, of 'social meaning' and of 'close analysis of form and meaning' might justifiably be assumed to be very clear in this instance. However, this is not what Jessica's essay suggests. From the evidence of her text it would seem that Jessica lacked the knowledge of trends in literary criticism which would have enabled her to perceive the relevance of *Dead Secrets* to the given essay title – and then, perhaps to critique it. Such a conclusion needs justification, however, so I preface my discussion of the student's essay with a brief account of Heller's critical approach in *Dead Secrets*.

Heller's approach: a demonstration of 'modern theory'

Dead Secrets is subtitled: *Wilkie Collins and the Female Gothic*. The blurb on the dust jacket glosses this subtitle by informing the reader that Heller 'makes use of modern theory, fusing Gothic, gender, marketplace and class issues'. *Dead Secrets* thus departs from the conventions of New Criticism in that Collins' novels are not treated as autonomous linguistic artefacts removed from the contexts of their author's life and times. Instead, and in keeping with certain trends in 'modern theory', namely, feminist literary theory with its social and political concerns, *Dead Secrets* blurs the distinctions between the writer, the social environment, and the text. This is evident in Heller's statement of her focus:

> I am concerned . . . with Collins' gender politics. But I place my analysis of Collins' representations of gender in a more fully historicized context. In examining

Collins' representations of gender through the female Gothic plot I link the relation of Collins' generic choices to his position as a male writer in the Victorian literary market.

(p. 4)

Concentrated into these few lines are the cornerstones of the theory which plays a central role in shaping Heller's approach to *The Woman in White*. As 'gender politics' suggests, Collins' novel is viewed as a signifying practice with a political purpose and not as an exploration of moral complexities such as is to be found in 'intrinsic criticism' (Birch, 1989). 'Representation' signals the breaking down of boundaries between text and context while 'gender' links the text to its ideological context, that is, to the attitudes and beliefs which can be related to the unequal social positioning of men and women in Victorian society. In other words, Heller's critique is based on a view of texts as dealing in discourses which reflect differences in power that are socially constructed and legitimated (Foucault, 1981). Consequently, Heller does not connect Collins' 'generic choices' in *The Woman in White* (i.e. his particular use of female Gothic conventions such as female victimisation and subversiveness as primary themes) to aesthetic or moral criteria but approaches them instead as indices of Collins' 'position as a male writer in the Victorian literary market'. From this perspective, literary modes of textualisation become a political rather than a linguistic or structural issue; they carry contestable meanings relating to differences in social identities and so in power.

A corollary of the critical focus outlined above is that a literary text is viewed as a polemic that seeks to persuade. To put it another way, such a text can be said to present a critical stance either by naturalising a socially constructed difference in power or by challenging the taken for granted with the aim of making a difference beyond the confines of the page. Heller chooses to emphasise the ideological challenge which Collins mounts. She gives detailed attention to his 'liberal views' and shows how he uses the female Gothic to draw his readers' attention to the iniquitous position and plight of women in Victorian society. She concludes, however, that Collins presents a flawed critique in that he finally breaks with the Gothic novel's support for female subversiveness. Like most of Collins' novels, *The Woman in White* ends with the 'containment of female power and subversion' (p. 8).

Heller is, of course, also seeking to make a difference beyond the pages of her text – and not only in the form of a contribution to knowledge-making (MacDonald, 1994) within academia. She, too, is engaged in gender politics as she analyses Collins' views on the plight of women. She writes from a particular ideological position which she does not, however, hold up to reader scrutiny. That position is evident not only in her criticism of Collins' containment of women's subversiveness but also in her choices within the genre of literary criticism. Through her citations, for example, she locates herself in a body of feminist writing, that is, in a particular committed discourse community, which seeks to encourage resistance to the representation of gender and its social meanings as they pertain to women. The citations refer to writing from different periods in history (e.g. Wollstonecraft, 1790; Showalter, 1985). In this way, Collins' representation of women's inequality in Victorian England is given a historical continuity and drawn into an alliance with late twentieth century gender politics and a commitment to female subversiveness. This alliance between then and now is also indicated by the significance Heller attaches to the role of writing in *The Woman in White*. The control of the signifier and the silencing of women's voices are central feminist issues (see, for example, Olsen, 1978; Miller, 1990). Heller also takes up those issues. She points to the fact that, while the story is written by several of the characters, it is a man, Walter Hartright, who edits the text, and who finally has the last word in which he describes the active and potentially subversive Marian Halcombe as 'our good angel'. Feminist crticism is also woven into the lexis of Heller's text, most notably in the reference to women as blank pages to be 'inscribed' by men, and in nouns which – to borrow Bakhtin's (1981) metaphor – carry the 'voices' of their use in other contexts, for example, 'resistance', 'subversiveness' and 'identity'.

Jessica's approach: a demonstration of transformations

Jessica was not one of my students. I have, in fact, never met her. She was a student at another university and made her essay available for the purpose of research. It is thus not possible to include her 'voice' in the form of comments by her on her essay – nor would I wish to do so at this stage given that my focus is on texts as motivated signs (Kress, 1995). From that theoretical perspective a student's comment is another motivated sign which should thus not be taken at face value. In other words, like Lensmire (1995), I regard the use of 'voice' as misleading when it is taken to denote the 'real' or 'authentic'.

Jessica's essay refers explicitly to *Dead Secrets*. However, while Jessica focuses on gender inequalities in *The Woman in White*, she does so from a theoretical perspective that is very different from Heller's. To some extent her essay fits MacDonald's (1994) description of New Criticism's mode of textualisation as generalisations supported by particularities. In keeping with that approach, Jessica begins with the statement that 'the primary theme [of *The Woman in White*] is the gender theme'. She then breaks that theme down into other themes or rather into other versions of the same theme: she refers to women's 'lack of power' in Victorian England; to 'the helplessness of women'; and to 'the greater social power of the male'. These abstractions are made concrete and particular by being linked to details of the plot. For example:

> Throughout the novel the lack of power women have over their own destiny is constantly conveyed to the reader. Laura has no legal power over her marriage to Sir Perceval. She must submit herself to him in order to obey another male, her father, who the reader discovers has committed his daughter on his deathbed to the marriage with Sir Perceval. Thus Laura must dismiss her true love for another man, Walter Hartright.

As these lines indicate, Jessica intends the particularities which she lists to serve as illustrations of literary method; she shifts quickly from statement of theme to how the theme is 'conveyed'. This kind of transition is, in fact, a typical feature of the essay. However, the essay suggests that Jessica has at her disposal only a narrow conception of literary devices. This seems evident in her treatment of plot as the only relevant aspect of the novel's 'how'. Furthermore, the details of the plot tend to become the primary focus of attention, so obscuring their role as the concrete signifiers of a literary device. For example, in the lines quoted above, Jessica is dramatically retelling events, thus creating a narrative of her own that is analogous to *The Woman in White*. She does this effectively and with insight. Although the sentence structures which she uses are simple, they indicate a not unsophisticated, even if largely intuitive, appreciation of the women characters' situation and of the melodrama in *The Woman in White*. For example, Laura's only possession is seen to consist ironically in non-possession: 'she has no legal power'. This statement is followed by a further irony: the only action open to Laura represents the absence of spontaneous or willed action, and thus scarcely qualifies as action. 'She must submit . . .'; 'she must dismiss . . .'. This theatrical dramatisation of powerlessness is intensified by the contrast between the grammatical agent, Laura, and the 'real' agent, the man whose authority in forcing her to submission and obedience is reinforced by the law. By this point, however, story has ousted plot.

In her discussion of students writing about literature, Mitchell (1994b) provides examples which are similar in kind to Jessica's text as I have described it in the paragraph above. Mitchell concludes that such writing represents an empathic or interpretative response which does not prise apart reader, text and world. Consequently, Mitchell judges it to be exclusive of the critical stance which she identifies with argument. However, in terms of my theorising, Jessica's essay is a demonstration of critical thinking (both conscious and intuitive), since it offers a theoretical perspective which is in dialogue with other perspectives. In other words I treat 'critical thinking' as first of all a function or process in a text, and not as a norm. However, within the university system of assessment Jessica's essay was viewed very differently. It was given a low mark on the grounds that it was 'uncritical'.

I hope, however, that my reading has shown that such a judgement bypasses what it is that Jessica has done in her text. To put it another way, the blanket judgement, 'uncritical', edits out a dimension of critical thinking to which I have already referred – critical thinking as a process of transformation in which the student writer engages past learnings and current perceptions. In my reading of Jessica's essay as an exemplar of that view of critical thinking Jessica can be seen to draw on a number of aspects of her 'interest' (Kress, 1995, 1996), including her assumptions about fictional texts, literary criticism and what is required in student essays about literature – assumptions that reflect approaches which are rooted in New Criticism, and which Andrews (1995) and Mitchell (1994b) have shown to be dominant in the secondary school. These assumptions shape the way in which Jessica transforms both *The Woman in White* and Heller's critique as she places them in dialogue with each other. From this perspective her problem is not that she is without the ability to think critically. Her fundamental difficulty needs to be viewed rather as the failure of her text to deploy certain other kinds of 'text' in dialogue with Collins' novel and with Heller's approach to it. In short, on the evidence of her essay, Jessica's resources do not appear to include a knowledge of 'modern theory' and the way in which it challenges the approaches with which she is familiar,

However, while Jessica's essay imposes a particular, school-learned, kind of coherence on *The Woman in White* – the coherence of theme with illustrations – there are ruptures and ambiguities in her approach which suggest a 'zone of proximal development' (Vygotsky, 1962); that is, there are places in Jessica's text where tutor intervention might enable Jessica to gain access to Heller's text and also to critique it, i.e. to meet the tutor's criteria regarding being critical. These places are marked by a change of modality, by a movement from an assertion of what is the case to the suggestion of what might be the case. For example, 'Collins does show through Anne the social invisibility of women and their rights' contrasts with the sentence which immediately follows it: 'Marian Halcombe's outburst after her sister's marriage may embody Collins' beliefs upon the subject of female inequality within his society'. Behind both sentences there lies a concern with evidence. The first sentence implies that there is reliable evidence in the text that Anne is an effective means of developing one of the novel's central themes: the social invisibility of women. At this point 'Collins' is primarily an authorial function, an intention which the text realises. The second sentence, on the other hand, presents Collins as a person inhabiting the world beyond the text. The tentativeness of 'may is echoed by Collins' beliefs' [...] can be read in several ways. First, and especially in view of the fact that the essay refers frequently to 'Collins' beliefs', it can imply that the novel cannot be read as evidence of its author's views. The change of modality may thus denote the hold on Jessica's thinking of a school-learned focus on texts as separate from their writers; a focus in which 'close analysis of form and meaning' means treating the text as a linguistic object. However, since in this particular instance the sentence concerns Marian Halcombe, whom Heller presents as the embodiment of female subversiveness, which Collins' finally seeks to contain, 'may' and 'beliefs' could mean that Jessica is pointing to Collins' ambivalence towards the qualities and attitudes which Marian represents.

There is a third possible reading, too. As in other parts of the essay where Jessica refers to what Heller 'believes', the tentativeness here might indicate a resistance to the authority of Heller's text – a resistance which could be developed into a critique of Heller's argument and the feminist ideology which it unquestioningly reflects. In other words, tutor intervention at this point could help Jessica both to understand Heller and to separate from her. This separation should enable her to arrive at a clearer understanding of her own theory and its sources. It should also help her to appreciate that literary criticism is characterised by a diversity of approaches and that essay titles rest on trends in literary criticism.

What I have tried to show in my discussion of Jessica's essay is that her failure to indicate the relevance of Heller's analysis to the given essay title was not an irremedial failure, but rather evidence of transformations based on a very different dominant conception of literary criticism – a conception which was probably held intuitively, rather than explicitly and derived no doubt primarily from Jessica's prior school experience of being critical about texts.

Pedagogic implications

Since my view of critical thinking sets out to accommodate the specificities of a student's text, I can only express its pedagogic implications as broad principles, or a general orientation, which would take on different particularities and nuances of meaning in relation to other essay titles especially in other fields of study. Of particular significance within my theoretical framework is the fact that my reading of Jessica's essay, as of any text, is a motivated sign. As a teacher, my response to a student's essay should ideally be followed by a discussion with the student concerned – a discussion in which the two motivated signs – the student's text and my reading of it – are brought into dialogue. This would not require my denial of the asymmetry which inevitably exists between tutor and student (Scott, 1994), but neither would I seek to reinforce that asymmetry. Instead, in accordance with the Vygotskian perception of pedagogy outlined earlier, I would seek to lend the student my consciousness, while at the same time being open to how the student's essay and her comments might challenge and change the shape of my consciousness.

It could be argued at this point that I am evading the realities of the current situation in higher education in the UK where there is little if any time on many undergraduate courses for one-to-one tutorials. Time is not in itself the major issue, however. More important is the disposition of tutors towards 'critical thinking', and its relationship to teaching and learning. Thus, though I personally regard the individual tutorial as indispensable, I recognise that there are, fortunately, other ways in which a dialogic view of 'critical thinking' could be demonstrated in pedagogic practice. I would give priority to a change in the self perception of many tutors – a change in which all tutors came to regard themselves as playing a role in the teaching, rather than just in the assessment, of essay writing. It would be a role which would involve tutors in thinking beyond the current research into 'argument', that is it would take them along an intellectual route which would lead them to consider as 'motivated signs' (i.e. signs with a history both personal and social) the essay questions they set, the critical works which they recommend, the discourses they use in feedback and assessment, and so on. This route would also have the rethinking of the curriculum of English studies in higher education as one of its primary destinations, a rethinking that would result in more attention being given to the examination and discussion of writing about literature – both critics' and students' writing – as texts that transform other texts.

These comments may sound like the reiteration of pedagogic cliches. I could be accused, too, of ignoring distinctions between, for example, creativity and critique; distinctions which others have found useful. In a sense, though, the erasure of such boundaries is my point. What I offer is actually a common core of meaning at the heart of widely used pedagogic terms. An awareness of that core, which houses a dynamic view of any text, seems to me to be essential since without it there is the danger of settled definitions which encourage their mechanical application. In other words, I offer a focus which would challenge a technicist approach to teaching like that reflected in the research on argument to which I referred earlier. Such research which seeks neat answers is actually at odds with my perception of critical thinking as an ongoing activity involving the perception of a student essay as not simply something to be pigeonholed and graded, but rather as a spur to self reflexivity on the part of the student and the reader.

Self reflexivity – that is the theme which I take up in this my concluding paragraph. I return to Jessica's essay and how I read its transformation of Heller's text. I now note an irony at the centre of my discussion so far. I have concentrated on how Jessica's essay fails to use Heller's text in the way that the tutor expected. What I have ignored is how this focus has resulted in my offering a reading which finally runs counter to my explicit intention to bring the student into the picture, something which I accused Mitchell (1997) of not doing in her recent work on argument. This is doubly ironic in that Heller's feminist criticism places the writer (i.e. Collins) in a social and political context, whereas I implicitly treat Jessica as primarily the representative of a particular view of how to write about a literary text and I measure her against what I (in an attempt to identify with her tutor) think she should have written. This realisation leads me to look critically at my failure up to this point to comment on the fact that Jessica is a woman writing about a novel which deals with social injustice to women. The movement from plot into the 'theatrical dramatisation' of character and event, on which I commented earlier, now takes on a new significance. It becomes a reminder that modes of criticism have been seen as involving gender issues, in discussions not only of literary criticism, but also of academic writing in general. The empathic writing which Jessica demonstrates, and which Mitchell (1994b) would exclude from 'argument' is one of the forms of writing (autobiography is another) which some women academics (e.g. Miller, 1990; Ivanic, 1998) would introduce into the university. In short, female subversiveness now seeks to escape the containment of the modes of criticism which are dominant in UK universities. So I conclude with another 'text' that I need to enter into dialogue with in considering student writing: the text of gender as difference – a text which trails other texts to do with identity, power and authorship. However, critical voices have to fade into silence at some point and so this is where I pause, with an agenda for the future: 'to make an end is to make a beginning' (Eliot, 1942).

References

Andrews, R. (1995) *Teaching and Learning Argument* (London, Cassell).

Bakhtin, M.M. (1981) Discourse in the novel, in: M. Holquist (Ed.) *The Dialogic Imagination: four essays*, Trans. C. Emerson & M. Holquist (Austin, TX, University of Texas Press).

Ballard, B. & Clanchy, C. (1988) Literacy in the university: an anthropological approach, in: G. Taylor, B. Ballard, V. Beasley, H.B. Bock, J. Clanchy and P. Nightingale (Eds) *Literacy by Degrees* (Buckingham, SHRE, and Open University Press).

Barnett, R. (1997) *Higher Education: a critical business* (Buckingham, SHRE and Open University Press).

Birch, D. (1989) *Language, Literature and Critical practice: ways of analysing text* (London, Routledge).

Collins, W.W. [1861] (1973) *The Woman in White*, H.P. Sucksmith (Ed.) (Oxford, Oxford University Press).

Eliot, T.S. [1942] (1963) Little Gidding, in: T.S. Eliot (Ed.) *Collected Poems 1909–1962* (London, Faber and Faber).

Foucault, M. (1981) The order of discourse, in: R. Young (Ed.) *Untying the Text: a post-structuralist reader* (Boston, MA, Routledge and Kegan Paul).

Heller, T. (1992) *Dead Secrets: Wilkie Collins and the female gothic* (New Haven, CT, Yale University Press).

Hounsell, D. (1987) Essay writing and the quality of feedback, in: J.T.E. Richardson, M.W. Eysenck & D. Warren Piper (Eds) *Student Learning: research in education and cognitive psychology* (Buckingham, SHRE and Open University Press).

Ivanic, R. (1998) *Writing and Identity: the discoursal construction of identity in academic writing* (Amsterdam, John Benjamins).

Kress, G. (1995) *Making Signs and Making Subjects: the English curriculum and social futures* (London, Institute of Education).

Kress, G. (1996) *Before Writing: rethinking paths into literacy* (London, Routledge).

Lea, M.R. & Street, B. (1998) Student writing in higher education: an academic literacies approach, *Studies in Higher Education*, 23(2), pp. 157–172.

Lensmire, T.-J. (1995) Rewriting student voice, paper presented at the annual meeting of the American Educational Research Association, San Francisco, CA, April, 18–22.

MacDonald, S.P. (1994) *Professional Academic Writing: in the humanities and social sciences* (Carbondale, IL, Southern Illinois University Press).

Miller, J. (1990) *Seductions: studies in reading and culture* (London, Virago Press).

Mitchell, S. (1994a) *The Teaching and Learning of Argument in Sixth Forms and Higher Education*, a project funded by the Leverhulme Trust: Final Report (Hull, University of Hull).

Mitchell, S. (1994b) A level and beyond: a case study, *English in Education*, 28(2), pp. 36–47.

Mitchell, S. (1997) Quality in argument: why we should spell out the ground rules, in: M. Riddle (Ed.) *The Quality of Argument: a colloquium on issues of teaching and learning in higher education* (London, Middlesex University).

Olsen, T. (1978) *Silences* (London, Virago).

Riddle, M. (1994) *Report of an Enquiry into Staff Practice in Setting and Marking Coursework Essays* (London, Middlesex University).

Riddle, M. (1997) Introducing the colloquium, in: M. Riddle (Ed.) *The Quality of Argument: a colloquium on issues of teaching and learning in higher education* (London, Middlesex University).

Scott, M. (1994) The 'pedagogic relation' in accounts of student writers' needs and difficulties, in: G. Gibbs (Ed.) *Improving Student Learning: theory and practice* (Oxford, Oxford Centre for Staff Development).

Scott, M. (1996) Context as text: a course for student writers in higher education, in: G. Rijlaarsdam, H. Van Den Bergh & M. Couzijn (Eds) *Effective Teaching and Learning of Writing: current trends in research* (Amsterdam, University of Amsterdam Press).

Showalter, E. (1985) *The Female Malady: women, madness and English culture*, 1830–1980 (New York, Penguin).

Toulmin, S., Rieke, R. & Janik, A. (1978, 1984, 1st and 2nd edn) *An Introduction to Reasoning* (London, Collier Macmillan Publishers).

Vygotsky, L.S. (1962) *Thought and Language*, E. Hanfmann & G. Vakar (Eds) (Cambridge, MA, MIT Press).

Wollstonecraft, M. (1995) *A Vindication of the Rights of Woman* (1790) edited and introduced by A. Tauchert (London, J.M. Dent).

CHAPTER 4

THE PRESSURES OF ASSESSMENT IN UNDERGRADUATE COURSES AND THEIR EFFECT ON STUDENT BEHAVIOURS

Lin Norton, Alice Tilley, Stephen Newstead and
Arlene Franklyn-Stokes

Assessment and Evaluation in Higher Education, 26, 3, 269–284, 2001

EDITOR'S INTRODUCTION

This article may be read as the coming together of the research interests of two groups of researchers based in two different higher education institutions. As such, it builds upon their earlier, independent researches (Newstead *et al.* 1996, Norton *et al.* 1996).

The authors have a general interest in the relations between approaches to studying and assessment practices, and in exploring how the latter influence students' strategies for the former. In this article, they focus in particular on students' essay writing tactics and cheating behaviours, examining how these are correlated (this is a quantitative piece of work) with approaches to studying.

This article was categorised in the introductory chapter as adopting a multivariate approach to researching the student experience. It presents the results of a survey of 267 third-year undergraduate psychology students in four UK higher education institutions. Each student was required to complete three separate questionnaires:

- a 'rules of the game' questionnaire (Norton *et al.* 1996), devised to assess students' essay writing tactics, in particular how these are adapted with a view to impressing the academics who will assess them;
- a cheating questionnaire (Newstead *et al.* 1996), listing '21 behaviours which might be considered to be cheating', and asking whether the student had ever made use of them; and
- the Approaches to Studying Inventory (ASI), devised by Entwistle and his colleagues (Entwistle *et al.* 1979), and subsequently much used and modified, in a version devised by Richardson (1990).

The analysis proceeds by, first, presenting the results from the three questionnaires separately, detailing frequencies of responses, means and standard deviations. Then, after converting the responses to the three questionnaires into indexes, correlations were calculated between all three questionnaires, in pairs, to explore whether the students' behaviours they measure are related.

The authors found evidence that many of the students surveyed were using essay writing tactics and cheating behaviours, findings that they link with the assessment pressures faced by these students. However, their analysis of studying approaches produced 'rather disappointing' results, with many students adopting surface or strategic, rather than deep, approaches to studying. Correlations between approaches to studying and essay tactics and cheating were mostly small.

The main literature within which this study may be located (as for the article by Kember (2000) also included in this Reader) is clearly that on approaches to learning and teaching (e.g. Biggs 1999, Marton *et al.* 1984, Prosser and Trigwell 1999, Ramsden 1992, Richardson 2000). There is a related literature on students' academic performance, and the reasons for variations in this (e.g. Cantwell *et al.* 2001, McKenzie and Schweitzer 2001), and another on student non-completion (e.g. Yorke 1999, 2000). The literature specifically focusing on students' assessment tactics and cheating behaviours is more limited, but growing (e.g. Ashworth *et al.* 1997: see also the article by Shevlin *et al.* (2000) included in this Reader).

References

Ashworth, P., Bannister, P. and Thorne, P. (1997) 'Guilty in Whose Eyes? University students' perceptions of cheating and plagiarism in academic work and assessment', *Studies in Higher Education*, 22, 2, pp. 187–203.

Biggs, J. (1999) *Teaching for Quality Learning at University: what the student does*. Buckingham, Open University Press.

Cantwell, R., Archer, J. and Bourke, S. (2001) 'A Comparison of the Academic Experiences and Achievement of University Students entering by Traditional and Non-traditional Means', *Assessment and Evaluation in Higher Education*, 26, 3, pp. 221–234.

Entwistle, N., Hanley, M. and Hounsell, D. (1979) 'Identifying Distinctive Approaches to Studying', *Higher Education*, 8, pp. 365–380.

Kember, D. (2000) 'Misconceptions about the Learning Approaches, Motivation and Study Practices of Asian Students', *Higher Education*, 40, pp. 99–121.

McKenzie, K. and Schweitzer, R. (2001) 'Who Succeeds at University? Factors predicting academic performance in first year Australian university students', *Higher Education Research and Development*, 20, 1, pp. 21–33.

Marton, F., Hounsell, D. and Entwistle, N. (eds) (1984) *The Experience of Learning*. Edinburgh, Scottish Academic Press.

Newstead, S., Franklyn-Stokes, A. and Armstead, P. (1996) 'Individual Differences in Student Cheating', *Journal of Educational Psychology*, 88, 2, pp. 229–241.

Norton, L., Dickins, T. and McLaughlin Cook, N. (1996) 'Rules of the Game in Essay Writing', *Psychology Teaching Review*, 5, 1, pp. 1–14.

Prosser, M. and Trigwell, K. (1999) *Understanding Learning and Teaching: the experience in higher education*. Buckingham, Open University Press.

Ramsden, P. (1992) *Learning to Teach in Higher Education*. London, Routledge.

Richardson, J. (1990) 'Reliability and Replicability of the Approaches to Studying Questionnaire', *Studies in Higher Education*, 15, pp. 155–168.

Richardson, J. (2000) *Researching Student Learning: approaches to studying in campus-based and distance education*. Buckingham, Open University Press.

Shevlin, M., Banyard, P., Davies, M. and Griffiths, M. (2000) 'The Validity of Student Evaluation of Teaching in Higher Education: love me, love my lectures?' *Assessment and Evaluation in Higher Education*, 25, 4, pp. 397–405.

Yorke, M. (1999) *Leaving Early: undergraduate non-completion in higher education*. London, Falmer Press.

Yorke, M. (2000) 'The Quality of the Student Experience: what can institutions learn from data relating to non-completion?' *Quality in Higher Education*, 6, 1, pp. 61–75.

THE PRESSURES OF ASSESSMENT IN UNDERGRADUATE COURSES AND THEIR EFFECT ON STUDENT BEHAVIOURS

Introduction

Since Marton and Saljo's (1976) original distinction of deep and surface approaches to learning, there has been a concerted attempt throughout higher education to encourage students to take a deep approach to their studies. Indeed, seven volumes reporting on research from the Improving Student Learning Symposia bear witness to the power and influence of this distinction on the thinking of lecturers, researchers and staff developers in many countries throughout the world including Australia, the USA, South Africa, Sweden and the UK (Gibbs, 1994, 1995, 1996; Rust, 1998, 1999, 2000; Rust & Gibbs, 1997).

Much of the research has been carried out using the Approaches to Studying Inventory (ASI) devised by Entwistle and his colleagues which has been developed in many different versions (Entwistle *et al.*, 1979; Entwistle & Ramsden, 1983; Entwistle & Tait, 1990; Ramsden & Entwistle, 1981, Tait & Entwistle, 1996). The items and constructs for the original ASI came from interviews with students and consisted of 64 statements to which students responded on a Likert-type scale measuring the strength of agreement. One of the most consistently reliable versions has been a 32-item inventory recommended by Richardson (1990, 1995). This consists of two studying orientations: a Meaning Orientation (incorporating sub-scales of 'a deep approach', 'comprehension learning', 'interrelating ideas' and 'use of evidence and logic') and a Reproducing Orientation (incorporating sub-scales of 'a surface approach', 'improvidence', 'fear of failure' and 'syllabus-boundness'). The ASI questionnaire has been used by researchers and teaching staff in higher education to evaluate the effectiveness of teaching innovations as well as more routine teaching, and to identify students who were having trouble studying. Research reporting on initiatives to actively help students change from taking a surface to a deep approach have met with only limited success (for example, Cuthbert, 1995; Norton & Crowley, 1995; Solomonides & Swannell, 1995). Marton and Saljo (1997) have suggested that this is because students work out the demands of the learning situation and 'technify' their learning, by adopting a mechanistic, artificial type of deep learning rather than genuinely engaging with and understanding the issues, concepts and principles of what they are being asked to learn.

Fundamental to this concept of the demands of a learning situation is the role played by assessment, well documented amongst others, in Biggs (1996), Brown (1997), Entwistle (1995), and Ramsden (1992). In an interesting study to investigate what effect the method of assessment might have on students' approaches, Scouller (1998) found that students were more likely to take a deep approach when preparing for essay assignments and a surface approach when preparing for a multiple choice examination. From the research literature, it would be expected not only that assessment would be used by lecturers to improve student learning but also that students who take a deep approach should do better on measures of academic performance. Yet this does not appear to always be the case. Boud (1990, 1995a, b) in commenting on traditional assessment in higher education has argued that lecturers often assess students on easily assessable matters such as memorisation of large bodies of factual material (a surface approach) rather than on how students use, interpret or criticise that material to do something further with it (a deep approach). In addition, Newstead

(1992) has indicated that the link between meaning orientation scores and academic grades is not very strong. Norton *et al.* (1999) found some evidence to support this view. In two departments (psychology and theology), students' ASI scores were correlated with the marks they obtained on their coursework essays. The findings showed the expected negative correlation with reproducing orientation scores but not the expected positive correlation with meaning orientation scores. This may mean that tutors are not rewarding students when they do take a deep approach in their academic work, or it may be that since the ASI is based on an attitude scale it might not be fine grained enough to relate to specific assignment tasks. Perhaps it is an indication that lecturers sometimes award marks for things other than a deep approach, a belief that seems to be widely held among students. In essence then, students may be picking up on hidden messages that operate in higher education by working out how to be strategic. Entwistle (1987) has described such students as being achievement-orientated, alert to assessment requirements and gearing work to the preferences of lecturers. This is similar to the earlier identification of such students by Miller & Parlett (1974) who used the term 'cue-seekers'.

Such student perceptions may well account for strategies that lecturers have not explicitly set out to encourage but which nevertheless seem to exist. Norton *et al.* (1996a, b) looked at these strategies in two studies concerned with essays and called them 'rules of the game', by which they meant tactics that students used when producing coursework essays in the hopes that they would get them better marks. Norton and her colleagues argued that the essential point about these tactics and the reason they were called 'rules of the game' was that they were not what lecturers told students to do to get a good mark; they were what students believed would influence lecturers to give them a good mark. In order to investigate this, Norton asked a cohort of second-year students to generate as many 'tactics' as they could think of that they had used themselves or that they knew other students had used. From this original 'trawl', 25 items were generated which formed the basis of the questionnaire for both studies. This questionnaire was in no way designed to deceive students that it was measuring something else. Psychology students in particular are very familiar with being participants in all types of research and because of their knowledge of research methodologies could easily 'see through' any attempt to make the questionnaire appear to be something that it was not. The purpose of the 'rules of the game' questionnaire was quite openly stated in the instructions where a definition was given. It was hoped that honest responses would be given because all questionnaires were anonymously completed. The first study investigated first and third-year psychology students in a university college and found not only that 'rules of the game' were widely used but also that third-year students used significantly more of these tactics than first-year students (Norton *et al.*, 1996a). In the second study, 254 third-year students took part in three different departments at the same institution representing the sciences, the social sciences and the arts. Students from another institution in the same social science department also took part. Broadly, the findings not only confirmed but extended those of the first study showing that their use was not confined to psychology students in one department in one institution, but was also common among psychology students in another institution. It was also widespread over different departments in the same institution which suggests it was not exclusively a feature of the essay-writing strategies of psychology students (Norton *et al.*, 1996b). In a further study conducted by Norton *et al.* (1999) investigating third-year psychology students' strategies when undertaking work for a specified final year essay assignment, it was found that similar 'rules of the game' were used but there was no correlation between the number of 'rules of the game' used and the obtained essay mark. Such a finding would suggest that despite what the students themselves believed, using a number of 'rules of the game' was not a very effective strategy for maximising marks.

Another consequence of the unwanted yet sometimes potent effects of assessment on student learning is that students can view it as inauthentic, pointless and another hurdle to jump over, something that is unconnected with real learning (McDowell & Mowl, 1995; Ramsden, 1997). This might account for the widespread occurrence of actual cheating behaviours found in undergraduates in the UK. The literature on student cheating is considerable but comes mainly from North America, where findings have consistently shown that more than half of university students engage in some sort of cheating behaviour. Franklyn-Stokes and Newstead have carried out a number of studies in Britain which have confirmed the American findings (Franklyn-Stokes & Newstead, 1995; Newstead *et al.*, 1996). In their first study they asked 128 students from two science departments in a British university about cheating. They found that over half the students had used a range of cheating behaviours. Since so many students do appear to cheat, the question that has to be asked is: why? Once again the findings in the US and Britain have been consistent. The two main reasons given have been time pressure and the desire to get a better mark.

In their second study involving 943 students from 19 disciplines in a British university, Newstead and his colleagues looked at individual differences as a way of explaining why students cheat. They found that students who were male, younger, less able and less intrinsically motivated tended to cheat more. Interestingly, when they looked to see if students who cheat had 'inferior' moral judgement, the evidence for it was rather weak. They also found differences in cheating between the different disciplines. They argue that cheating is not a unitary concept, students are not 'cheaters' or 'non-cheaters' – it is a matter of gradation.

Individual differences are, though, only one part of the story and if, as Newstead *et al.* suggest, there are differences between different subject areas then maybe departmental culture and demands are also a determining factor. A study by Poltorak (1995) looked at cheating in four Moscow institutes and found that the main reason given for cheating was that it was the fault of the educational system. Students felt it was justifiable to cheat on courses that they perceived to be of little use either intellectually or in terms of preparing them for a career. Supporting evidence for this interpretation has come from a recent interview study by Bannister and Ashworth (1998), where one of the reasons given by students for cheating was an alienation from the education system and from the assessment system in particular. One of their interviewees talked critically about the same assignment being set year after year with virtually no change. The implications from this research suggest cheating may be some sort of adaptation to academic demands as students perceive them. They may, therefore, be influenced by the institutional context, which might be a possible explanation as to why Newstead and his colleagues found differences across different subject disciplines within the same university.

The research literature discussed here suggests that assessment is a powerful influence which does not always encourage students to take the desired deep approach but may actually do the opposite or, in some cases, lead them to use even less desirable strategies in their efforts to get good grades. The main aim of the research reported here was to investigate the relationship between approaches to studying and two examples of undesirable strategies: 'rules of the game' (essay writing tactics), and cheating behaviours.

The specific aims were:

(1) To find out how widespread was the reported use of 'rules of the game' and cheating behaviours among psychology students in four different institutions of higher education in the UK.
(2) To see whether there were any age or sex differences in these behaviours.
(3) To investigate whether there was any relationship between using 'rules of the game,' cheating behaviours and approaches to studying.

Method

A volunteer sample of 267 third-year psychology students took part from four institutions:

(1) a university college (North-West England) $(N = 108)$
(2) a 'traditional' university (North-West England) $(N = 49)$
(3) a 'new' university (North-West England) $(N = 55)$
(4) a 'new' university (South-West England) $(N = 55)$

The three questionnaires that were used in this study were:

(1) The 'rules of the game' questionnaire devised by Norton *et al.* (1996a). This consisted of 25 items representing essay writing tactics (a complete list of items used in this questionnaire is shown in the Results section in Table 13). Students were asked to indicate whether or not they had used any of these tactics when preparing for a psychology essay during the course of their undergraduate degree. An example of the format of the questionnaire with a couple of items is:

> In this questionnaire there are listed a number of 'tactics' that undergraduates have been known to adopt in the past in the belief that it may favourably influence their tutor when s/he is marking their essays. These tactics have been called 'Rules of the Game'. Please read each statement carefully and indicate by circling either 'Yes' or 'No', whether you have *ever* (meaning at least once) used any of these tactics.

> As an undergraduate, have you ever? ...   *Please circle*
>   Put your greatest effort into getting a high mark
>   for the first submitted essay in a course
>   (because of the 'halo' effect)   Yes   No
>   Tried to reflect your tutor's opinions/views/style as
>   closely as possible   Yes   No

Responses scored 1 for 'Yes' and 0 for 'No' giving a possible maximum overall score of 25 and a minimum overall score of 0.

(2) The cheating questionnaire devised by Newstead *et al.* (1996). This consisted of 21 items (a complete list of the items is presented in the Results section, in Table 15). The format of this questionnaire was very similar to the 'rules of the game' as described here:

> In the questionnaire which follows there are listed 21 behaviours which might be considered to be cheating. We are interested in whether or not you have carried out any of these behaviours as an undergraduate ...

... Each behaviour is listed separately, and beneath each one there are two boxes, labelled 'Yes' and 'No'. Ticking the 'Yes' box indicates that you have carried out that behaviour *at least once* during your *undergraduate career*; ticking the 'No' box would indicate that you had never done this during your undergraduate career.

Copying another student's coursework without their knowledge

Yes ☐   No ☐

Lying about medical or other circumstances to get an extended deadline or exemption from a piece of work

Yes ☐   No ☐

Students were simply asked to indicate if they had ever used any of the cheating behaviours in the course of their undergraduate study. Again, the responses were scored 1 for 'Yes', and 0 for 'No'; therefore the maximum possible score was 21 and the minimum score was 0,

(3)   The Approaches to Studying Inventory (ASI). For this study, Richardson's (1990) abbreviated version of the ASI was used in preference to later versions. This was partly because it was considerably shorter than other versions which is an important consideration in a study of this kind where questionnaire fatigue is a problem. The main reason however was that Richardson (1995) has made a convincing case for this version as being a consistent and reliable measure of both the meaning orientation and the reproducing orientation which was the particular focus of interest in this study.

The ASI used in this research consisted of 32 items structured as follows (the numbers in brackets indicate the highest possible scores obtainable):

(64) MEANING ORIENTATION
(16) Deep approach: active questioning in learning
(16) Comprehension learning: readiness to map out subject area and think divergently
(16) Interrelating ideas: relating to other part of the course
(16) Use of evidence and logic: relating evidence to conclusions

(64) REPRODUCING ORIENTATION
(24) Surface approach: preoccupation with memorisation
(12) Fear of failure: pessimism and anxiety about academic ability
(16) Improvidence: over-cautious reliance on details
(12) Syllabus-boundness: relying on staff to define learning tasks

The questionnaire asks students to circle the number beside each statement that most closely conforms with their view:

4 means that you definitely agree
3 means that you agree with reservations
1 means that you disagree with some reservations
0 means that you definitely disagree
2 is only to be used if the item does not apply to you or if you find it impossible to give a definite answer

Table 12 Means and standard deviations for 'rules of the game'

Institution	N	Mean	SD	Min.	Max.
All data	264	8.2	3.7	0	19
University college (NW)	106	8.6	3.6	2	19
Traditional university (NW)	49	8.7	3.9	2	19
New university (NW)	55	8.3	3.8	1	18
New university (SW)	54	6.8	3.5	0	16

A couple of examples of items are:

> The best way for me to understand what technical terms mean is to remember the textbook definitions (Surface approach item).
> I generally put a lot of effort into trying to understand things that initially seem difficult (Deep approach item).

Students were asked by a research assistant in the North-West institution and by another student in the South-West institution to complete a pack of the three questionnaires in formal lecture time and return them directly to them and not to the lecturers. The packs presented the questionnaires in different orders to minimise any possible order effects. Attached to each pack was a cover sheet which simply asked students to indicate whether they were under 21 or 21 and over as well as their sex. Students were told they did not have to take part in the research if they did not want to. They were also assured of confidentiality – the questionnaires were anonymous and would be scored and analysed by the research assistant. In this way, their lecturers would not see actual completed response sheets, and could not, therefore identify any individual student.

Results

'Rules of the game'

Looking at Table 12, it can be seen that using such tactics was widespread across the four institutions. The mean number of 'rules of the game' for all the data was 8, which represented nearly a third of the possible total on the questionnaire. In each of the four institutions some students admitted to more than 16 'rules of the game' and only in one institution, the new university (South-West) were there any students who claimed not to have used any of these strategies.

An Analysis of Variance showed that there was a significant difference overall between institutions, $F (3,260) = 3.14$, $p < 0.05$. A *post hoc* Tukey HSD (Honestly Significantly Different) test showed that students in the new university (South-West) used significantly fewer 'rules of the game' than students in the university college (North-West). There were no other significant differences between the four institutions, nor were there any main effects for age or sex on the incidence of 'rules of the game' usage. It would appear then that this study confirms previous findings reported by Norton *et al.* (1996a; 1996b) and Norton *et al.* (1999) that 'rules of the game' are strategies widely used by students in higher education, although there may be some small institutional variations.

A more detailed breakdown of which individual 'rules of the game' were most widely used is shown in Table 13 where the responses from the overall sample are presented in descending order of frequency. Looking at these it can be seen that five of these 'rules of the game' are more dishonest than lecturer-impressing strategies, they are clearly cheating behaviours. These 'cheating' items are identified in this Table. Although the order is slightly different, the same three most frequently admitted 'rules of the game' in this study were also found in the study by Norton *et al.* (1996b), a pattern that was repeated when looking at each of the four institutions separately.

It is interesting to note that of the five strategies identified as cheating, three were reported by 16% or less of the students. This shows perhaps, that fewer students

Table 13 Table showing rank ordered percentage of students overall who have engaged in individual rules of the game

'Rules of the game' items (total N = 267)	%
Chosen the easiest title to give you a good chance of getting a high mark	79
Tried to include information not covered in the lectures/obscure references	79
Used up-to-date/interesting references /lots of references/contradictory references in your essay	75
Played the role of a good student	55
Used big words/technical terms/jargon to impress your lecturer	49
Wrote a lot/wrote big/made the essay look longer/exceeded word limit	41
*Presented a false bibliography	39
Tried to reflect your lecturer's opinions/views/style as closely as possible	38
Made your essay visually exciting	36
Put your greatest effort into getting a high mark for the first submitted essay in a course	34
Asked lecturer for help so s/he will approve of you and think you are a keen student	31
When feeling confident, argued a position regardless of your lecturer's views in order to appear insightful /clever etc.	29
Avoided criticising your marker's views and/or research in the essay	28
*Avoided putting simple/basic textbooks in the bibliography even though you have used them	28
Acted extra 'nice'/asked for sympathy to get an extension for your essay	26
Chosen an essay title nearest to the lecturer's subject or research area	24
*Put a theorist's name against your own point/criticism/comment to make it look erudite	16
Avoided writing anything controversial in the essay	15
Found out who would mark the essays so that you could choose the title set by the easiest marker, or the lecturer you get on best with	14
*Invented studies/research/articles to include in the essay	14
Handed the essay in before the deadline to create the impression that the assignment was mastered without difficulty/to show eagerness	14
Chosen an unpopular essay title so that your answer is distinctive	13
Chosen a difficult title in the hope of being given extra credit	12
Got to know the lecturers socially in order to favourably influence them	7
*Changed dates of old research to make it look like up-to-date research	5

Note: * indicates items described as cheating behaviours.

are likely to cheat rather than indulge in what they might consider to be 'acceptable' lecturer-impressing strategies. Interestingly, the two cheating behaviours that were more commonly reported were both concerned with altering the bibliography (i.e. 'presented a false bibliography' – 39%; 'avoided putting simple/basic textbooks in the bibliography even though you have used them' – 28%). This might indicate a perception among some students that falsifying a bibliography is not as serious as the other dishonest tactics that involve altering the text of the essay itself.

Cheating

The incidence of cheating behaviours also appears to be widespread across all participating institutions, the mean for all data being 4, which is about a fifth of the possible total on the cheating questionnaire (see Table 14). In addition when the institutions are looked at separately, it can be seen that there were some students who admitted to no cheating at all, although other individuals reported high levels of between 14 and 18 such behaviours. The lower incidence of cheating as opposed to using 'rules of the game' is not surprising given the nature of the items which most students would presumably regard as more serious than the essay tactics. No significant differences were found between institutions on cheating behaviours, so the picture appears fairly consistent in this study and supports the findings by Newstead *et al.* (1996) that cheating strategies are also widespread.

Since there was no difference between institutions on the number of cheating behaviours, a two-way Analysis of Variance was carried out using age and sex as the independent variables, This showed significant main effects for sex only F $(1,246) = 10.1$, $p < 0.01$, with male students scoring higher on cheating behaviours than female students. There were no significant interactions between sex and age. These findings also confirm those of Newstead *et al.* (1996) who suggested that male students generally appear to report cheating more than female students. As with the 'rules of the game' data, the cheating behaviours were also examined in terms of each individual item to see how common they were. These are shown in Table 15.

This pattern of results is very similar to that obtained in both the Franklyn-Stokes and Newstead (1995) and the Newstead *et al.* (1996) studies. The only real difference was that in this study no student in any of the four institutions admitted to taking an exam for someone else or having someone else take an exam for them. This may be because this behaviour is rated as the most serious by students (Newstead *et al.*, 1996). The relative seriousness of different types of cheating was discussed by Abouserie (1997) who showed that students tended to see exam cheating as more serious than coursework cheating. The findings from the current study regarding the occurrence of exam cheating behaviours supports this view. Looking at Table 15, it can be seen that no kind of exam cheating was admitted to by more than 6% of the students.

Table 14 Means and standard deviations for cheating behaviours

Institution	N	Mean	SD	Min.	Max.
All data	267	4.3	3.5	0	18
University college (NW)	108	4.3	3.5	0	16
Traditional university (NW)	49	4.8	2.9	0	14
New university (NW)	55	4.6	3.5	0	14
New university (SW)	55	3.8	3.8	0	18

Table 15 Table showing rank ordered percentage of students overall who have engaged in individual cheating behaviours

Cheating items (total N = 267)	%
Paraphrasing material from another source without acknowledging the original author	61
Inventing data	51
Copying material for coursework from a book or other publication without acknowledging the source	45
Allowing own coursework to be copied by another student	42
Fabricating references or a bibliography	39
Altering data (e.g. adjusting data to obtain a significant result)	35
Ensuring availability of books/journals by deliberately mis-shelving them or by cutting out the relevant article/chapter	34
Copying another student's coursework with their knowledge	22
In a situation where students mark each other's work, coming to an agreement to mark it more generously than it deserves	20
Lying about medical or other circumstances to get an extended deadline or exemption for a piece of work	16
Submitting a piece of coursework as an individual piece of work when it has actually been written jointly with another student	11
Doing another student's coursework for them	8
Copying another student's coursework without their knowledge	7
Taking unauthorised material into an examination (e.g. 'cribs')	6
Copying from a neighbour during an exam without them realising	6
Lying about medical or other circumstances to get special consideration by examiners	5
Submitting coursework from an outside source (e.g. 'essay banks')	5
Illicitly gaining advance information about the contents of an exam paper	4
Premeditated collusion between two or more students to communicate answers to each other during an exam	3
Attempting to obtain special consideration by offering or receiving favours through, for example, bribery, seduction, corruption	0.4
Taking an exam for someone else or having someone else take an exam for you	0

Approaches to studying

The scores from the ASI were analysed first in descriptive terms which are presented in Table 16 where it can be seen that overall, students scored just over the midpoint for both meaning and reproducing orientation. A two-way Analysis of Variance with repeated measures showed no significant differences between institutions in either meaning or reproducing orientation scores.

Both meaning orientation and reproducing orientation scores were lower than those found by Norton & Dickins (1995) on a small sample of 37 first-year psychology students and also lower than the scores from two more small samples of 24 found in the study by Norton *et al.* (1999). This may be nothing more than an artefact of the methodology in Norton's studies where the ASI was used to evaluate the

Table 16 Approaches to studying inventory scores compared to normative data

ASI measures	Current study (N = 265)		Norms for psychology students (Entwistle & Ramsden, 1983)	
Overall orientation scores	*Mean*	*SD*		
Meaning orientation	38.7	9.2		
Reproducing orientation	38.9	9.6		
Sub-scales	*Mean*	*SD*	*Mean*	*Range*
Deep approach	10.8	3.0	10.8	9.9–12.4
Comprehension learning	8.1	3.8	9.0	7.9–10.1
Relating ideas	11.0	2.6	10.9	10.1–12.0
Use of evidence	8.9	2.9	9.6	8.5–11.0
Surface approach	14.5	4.5	12.8	11.7–14.1
Improvidence	8.2	3.2	7.4	6.2–8.7
Fear of failure	7.8	2.9	5.9	4.8–7.0
Syllabus-boundness	8.3	2.6	7.7	6.4–8.6

effectiveness of learning interventions. A comparison of the sub-scales in both orientations with norms provided by Entwistle and Ramsden (1983) shows a reasonably consistent similarity but with some evidence that the reproducing orientation sub-scales are higher in this study than the norms produced nearly 20 years ago. Could this perhaps be an indication that students in higher education nowadays are becoming more strategic? To look at this question more closely, scores from the three questionnaires were correlated.

Links between 'rules of the game', cheating and approaches to studying

In order to carry out correlations, the responses to both the 'rules of the game' and the cheating questionnaires were converted into indexes. This was done according to the method recommended by Newstead and his colleagues (1996). A detailed description of the procedure and rationale for its use is presented in their paper, but briefly, for this study it involved calculating the mean percentage of 'Yes' responses given by each student over all 25 'rules of the game' to give a 'rules of the game' index, and over all 21 cheating behaviours to give a cheating index. Thus both indexes are essentially a measure of the range of behaviours rather than a measure of whether or not the behaviours actually occurred.

The first analysis was to correlate scores on the 'rules of the game' index and the cheating index. This showed a moderate link between the two measures ($r = 0.37$, $p < 0.0001$). Perhaps this result is not surprising given the fact that five of the items on the 'rules of the game' questionnaire were actually cheating rather than lecturer-impressing strategies. To check, therefore, that the 'rules of the game' questionnaire and the cheating questionnaire were not both measuring the same behaviours, the five items (identified in Table 13) that overlapped with cheating behaviours were removed from the 'rules of the game' questionnaire. The amended total score for 'rules of the game' was converted to a 'rules of the game' index and then correlated with the cheating index. The results still indicated a significant positive correlation

Table 17 Correlation matrix for 'rules of the game', cheating and ASI (*N* = 259)

ASI items	'Rules of the game' index	Cheating index
Meaning orientation	0.10	−0.10
Reproducing orientation	0.11	0.08
Deep approach	0.13*	−0.10
Comprehension learning	0.09	0.03
Relating information	0.05	−0.11
Use of evidence	0.01	−0.16**
Surface approach	0.04	0.07
Improvidence	0.09	−0.02
Fear of failure	0.17**	0.02
Syllabus boundness	0.06	0.18**

Note: *$p < 0.05$, **$p < 0.01$.

($r = 0.25$, $p < 0.0001$) but the size of the effect is quite small and accounts for only 6.25% of the relationship.

The second analysis (shown in Table 17) was to correlate scores on the original 'rules of the game' index and the cheating index with the two main factors in the ASI as well as the eight sub-factors from which they were constructed. Since so few differences were found on any of the measures between the four institutions in this study, all correlations were carried out using the overall data.

Looking first at the relationship between scores on the 'rules of the game' index and the ASI it can be seen that there was no overall correlation with either of the meaning orientation or reproducing orientation factors. However, when the individual sub-factors were looked at, two significant but very small correlations emerged: 'rules of the game' with deep approach ($r = 0.13$, $p < 0.05$) and 'rules of the game' with fear of failure ($r = 0.17$, $p < 0.01$). Such small correlations although statistically significant actually only account for 1.69% and 2.89% of the relationships, so a rigorous interpretation might conclude that they were negligible. Perhaps though this is an area that future researchers might like to look at more closely to see whether students who are anxious about their academic performance do follow what they perceive to be the demands of the learning task by taking a deep approach, but at the same time play safe by using essay tactics which they hope will impress their lecturers.

Correlating scores on the cheating index with the ASI scores also showed no overall correlations with either of the two main ASI factors. Again, however, the analysis of the sub-factors showed an interesting picture. Scores on the cheating index were found to correlate negatively with use of evidence ($r = -0.16$, $p < 0.01$) but positively with syllabus-boundness ($r = 0.18$, $p < 0.01$). Again it must be pointed out that statistical significance does not necessarily mean a relationship of any practical importance, accounting in these two cases for only 2.56% and 3.24% of these respective relationships. Nevertheless, it might be an area of interest for future investigators suggesting that perhaps students who cheat and who are tied to the syllabus do not seek out evidence and may be more inclined to make it up. Such interpretations can only be speculative with these findings but would lend support to Newstead's view that cheating is not a unitary concept, but is a range of different behaviours carried out for different reasons.

The correlations discussed here are very weak, but what they might suggest is some sort of link between anxiety about academic performance (characterised by fear of failure or by being syllabus-bound) which results in either trying to comply with learning requirements by taking a deep approach and impressing the lecturer, or by not looking for evidence and trying to deceive the lecturer. A stepwise forward multiple regression analysis using the 'rules of the game' index as the dependent variable and the ASI scores as the independent variables showed fear of failure (beta = 0.17, $p < 0.05$) and deep approach (beta = 0.17, $p < 0.01$) to both be significant predictors of using 'rules of the game'. A further forward stepwise multiple regression using the cheating index as the dependent variable and the ASI sub-factors as independent variables showed syllabus-boundness to be a significant positive predictor (beta = 0.19, $p < 0.01$) and use of evidence as a significant negative predictor (beta = −0.16, $p < 0.01$) of cheating behaviours.

Conclusions

Looking at the reported incidence of 'rules of the game' in the four participating institutions, it seems that there is a widespread tendency to use such essay tactics to try to impress lecturers. This confirms the findings of Norton and her colleagues (1996a, b, 1999). Furthermore, these tactics were reported equally by students regardless of age or gender. Why 'rules of the game' should be used by so many students cannot be determined from this study alone. However, since the definition of a 'rule of the game' is that it is a tactic used to impress the lecturer marking the essay and therefore by implication influence her or him to give the student a higher mark than the essay truly deserves, it seems reasonable to suppose that students who use many 'rules of the game' are being driven by the pressure of assessment instead of using the task as a real learning opportunity. Indeed, this study showed that use of 'rules of the game' correlated weakly with fear of failure. This supports findings by Sarros and Densten (1989) who found the most frequently mentioned stressors for undergraduates were the assessment workload. Perhaps it is not surprising then that Brown (1997), in reviewing the literature on the effects of assessment on student learning, concludes that much of the traditional type of assessment carried out in higher education promotes poor quality learning and a surface approach. While not wanting to argue that essays should not form part of students' coursework, the widespread existence of 'rules of the game' for coursework essays suggests that lecturers might be advised to consider other types of assessment as well as reducing the assessment load, a point made by McDowell & Mowl (1995).

While the use of 'rules of the game' can be seen as a strategy designed to cope 'legitimately' with the demands of assessment, cheating behaviours show a definite intention to break the rules. The findings from this research confirm those of other recent studies that show cheating behaviours are common among undergraduates in the UK and reported by more males than females (see Franklyn-Stokes & Newstead, 1995 and Newstead *et al.*, 1996). The fact that this study shows that they are less common than 'rules of the game' and that some of the most frequent ones may seem to be less serious to some students might support Abouserie's (1997) conclusion that perhaps students do not think of such behaviours in such stark terms as breaking the rules or indeed cheating. Such an interpretation is also supported by the current study's finding that there is a small positive correlation between cheating behaviours and use of 'rules of the game', which shows that students employ a wide variety of tactics which range from lawful through to dishonest. Hence it has been suggested by Franklyn-Stokes & Newstead (1995) and again by Bannister and Ashworth (1998) that academic staff may need to be more explicit in actually conveying to students what is viewed as cheating by departments and institutions in higher education, so students who proceed to break the rules do so in full knowledge of what they are doing and the likely consequences of their actions.

The results from the analysis of the ASI scores in this study were rather disappointing. Since most educators in higher education are in agreement that encouraging students to take a deep approach is one of the major goals of higher education, it can be argued that students should be taking a deep rather than a surface approach in their studying. After two years of being in the academic system, it would be expected that students would have picked up this message from their lecturers but students in this research appeared not to be taking the desired approach. Again any explanations must be speculative, but a recent piece of research might throw some light on this finding. Brunas-Wagstaff & Norton (1998) asked second-year psychology students, among other things, if they thought that at their institution the assessment system as a whole rewarded ability over effort or effort over ability. What they found was that students who took a meaning orientation approach believed that the system rewarded ability over effort whereas students who took a reproducing orientation approach believed that the system rewarded effort over ability. This would seem to suggest that some students tend to adopt a strategic approach according to how they perceive the demands of the learning task, so they may not actually believe lecturers when they say they want a deep approach. This might have been what was happening with the students in our study. Perhaps future research might test this out using the latest adaptation of the ASI by Tait *et al.* (1998) called ASSIST, which actually measures a strategic approach as well as factors such as motivation and studying styles.

The findings from this research suggest that psychology students do feel under pressure by the assessment system and respond by using a variety of stratagems such as cheating, and using 'rules of the game'. Clearly more detailed research would have to be carried out looking at individual strategies, before generalising to the entire undergraduate population. Nevertheless, given this caution, if these results are an indication that students actually are affected by assessment demands in this way, the implications for lecturers are profound. Knapper (1995) among other academics, and indeed the UK government, has argued that higher education should be about life-long learning, so lecturers need to design courses that prepare students for life beyond the university and not just teach them how to jump through academic hoops. Marton and Saljo (1997) have described this process as the technification of learning where the perceived demands are so predictable that students use this knowledge to economise their efforts. Such a strategy may give short-term benefits of a good class of degree, but it may also leave graduates ill-prepared for the learning challenges that face them in today's rapidly changing society.

References

Abouserie, R. (1997) Students' academic dishonesty: locus of control and approaches to studying, *The Welsh Journal of Education*, 6(2), pp. 43–59.

Bannister, P. & Ashworth, P. (1998) Four good reasons for cheating and plagiarism, in: C. Rust (Ed.) *Improving Student Learning. Improving Students as Learners* (Oxford, The Oxford Centre for Staff and Learning Development).

Biggs, J. (1996) Enhancing teaching through constructive alignment, *Higher Education*, 32, pp. 347–364.

Boud, D. (1990) Assessment and the promotion of academic values, *Studies in Higher Education*, 15(1), pp. 101–111.

Boud, D. (1995a) Assessment and learning: contradictory or complementary? in: P. Knight (Ed.) *Assessment for Learning in Higher Education* (London, Kogan Page).

Boud, D. (1995b) *Enhancing Learning through Self Assessment* (London, Kogan Page).

Brown, G. (1997) Teaching psychology: a vade mecum, *Psychology Teaching Review*, 6(2), pp. 112–126.

Brunas-Wagstaff, J. & Norton, L. (1998) Perceptions of justice in assessment: a neglected factor in improving students as learners, in: C. Rust (Ed.) *Improving Student Learning. Improving Students as Learners* (Oxford, The Oxford Centre for Staff and Learning Development).

Cuthbert, K. (1995) Student project work in relation to a meaning oriented approach to learning, in: G. Gibbs (Ed.) *Improving Student Learning. Through Assessment and Evaluation* (Oxford, The Oxford Centre for Staff Development).

Entwistle, N. (1987) A model of the teaching-learning process, in: J. T. E. Richardson, M. W. Eysenck & D. Warren Piper (Eds) *Student Learning. Research in Education and Cognitive Psychology* (Milton Keynes, Open University Press & SRHE).

Entwistle, N. (1995) The use of research on student learning in quality assessment, in: G. Gibbs (Ed.) *Improving Student Learning. Through Assessment and Evaluation* (Oxford, The Oxford Centre for Staff Development).

Entwistle, N., Hanley, M. & Hounsell, D. (1979) Identifying distinctive approaches to studying, *Higher Education*, 8, pp. 365–380.

Entwistle, N. J. & Ramsden, P. (1983) *Understanding Student Learning* (London, Croom Helm).

Entwistle, N. & Tait, H. (1990) Approaches to learning, evaluations of teaching, and preferences for contrasting academic environments, *Higher Education*, 19, pp. 169–194.

Franklyn-Stokes, A. & Newstead, S. E. (1995) Undergraduate cheating; who does what and why? *Studies in Higher Education*, 20(2), pp. 39–52.

Gibbs, G. (Ed.) (1994) *Improving Student Learning. Theory and Practice* (Oxford, The Oxford Centre for Staff Development).

Gibbs, G. (Ed.) (1995) *Improving Student Learning. Through Assessment and Evaluation* (Oxford, The Oxford Centre for Staff Development).

Gibbs, G. (Ed.) (1996) *Improving Student Learning. Using Research to Improve Student Learning* (Oxford, The Oxford Centre for Staff Development).

Knapper, C. (1995) Approaches to study and lifelong learning; some Canadian initiatives, in: G. Gibbs (Ed.) *Improving Student Learning. Through Assessment and Evaluation* (Oxford, The Oxford Centre for Staff Development).

McDowell, L. & Mowl, G. (1995) Innovative assessment: its impact on students, in: G. Gibbs (Ed.) *Improving Student Learning. Through Assessment and Evaluation* (Oxford, The Oxford Centre for Staff Development).

Marton, F. & Saljo, R. (1976) On qualitative differences in learning: 1. Outcome and process, *British Journal of Educational Psychology*, 46, pp. 4–11.

Marton, F. & Saljo, R. (1997) Approaches to learning, in: F. Marton, D. Hounsell & N. Entwistle (Eds) *The Experience of Learning, Implications for Teaching and Studying in Higher Education*, 2nd edn (Edinburgh, Scottish Academic Press).

Miller, C. M. L. & Parlett, M. (1974) *Up to the Mark. A Study of the Examination Game* (London, Society for Research into Higher Education).

Newstead, S. E. (1992) A study of two 'quick and easy' methods of assessing individual differences in student learning, *British Journal of Educational Psychology*, 62(3), pp. 299–312.

Newstead, S., Franklyn-Stokes, A. & Armstead, P. (1996) Individual differences in student cheating, *Journal of Educational Psychology*, 88(2), pp. 229–241.

Norton, L. S. & Crowley, C. M. (1995) Can students be helped to learn how to learn? An evaluation of an Approaches to Learning programme for first year degree students, *Higher Education*, 29, pp. 307–328.

Norton, L. S. & Dickins, T. E. (1995) Do Approaches to Learning courses improve students' learning strategies? in: G. Gibbs (Ed.) *Improving Student Learning. Through Assessment and Evaluation* (Oxford, The Oxford Centre for Staff Development).

Norton, L. S., Dickins, T. F. & McLaughlin Cook, A. N. (1996a) Rules of the Game in essay writing, *Psychology Teaching Review*, 5(1), pp. 1–14.

Norton, L. S., Dickins, T. E. & McLaughlin Cook, N. (1996b) Coursework assessment: what are lecturers really looking for? in: G. Gibbs (Ed.) *Improving Student Learning. Using Research to Improve Student Learning* (Oxford, The Oxford Centre for Staff Development).

Norton, L., Brunas-Wagstaff, J. & Lockley, S. (1999) Learning outcomes in the traditional coursework essay: do students and lecturers agree? in: C. Rust (Ed.) *Improving Student Learning. Improving Student Learning Outcomes* (Oxford, The Oxford Centre for Staff and Learning Development).

Norton, L. S., Scantlebury, E. & Dickins, T. E. (1999) Helping undergraduates to become more effective learners: an evaluation of two learning interventions, *Innovations in Education and Training International*, 36(4), pp. 273–284.

Poltorak, Y. (1995) Cheating behavior among students of four Moscow universities, *Higher Education*, 30(2), pp. 225–246.

Ramsden, P. (1992) *Learning to Teach in Higher Education* (London, Routledge).

Ramsden, P. (1997) The context of learning in academic departments, in: F. Marton, D. Hounsell & N. Entwistle (Eds) *The Experience of Learning. Implications for Teaching and Studying in Higher Education*, 2nd edn (Edinburgh, Scottish Academic Press).

Ramsden, P. & Entwistle, N. J. (1981) Effects of academic departments on students' approaches to studying, *British Journal of Educational Psychology*, 51, pp. 368–383.

Richardson, J. T. E. (1990) Reliability and replicability of the Approaches to Studying Questionnaire, *Studies in Higher Education*, 15, pp. 155–168.

Richardson, J. T. E. (1995) Using questionnaires to evaluate student learning, in: G. Gibbs (Ed.) *Improving Student Learning. Through Assessment and Evaluation* (Oxford, Oxford Centre for Staff Development).

Rust, C. (1998) (Ed.) *Improving Student Learning. Improving Student Learning Outcomes* (Oxford, The Oxford Centre for Staff and Learning Development).

Rust, C. (1999) (Ed.) *Improving Student Learning. Improving Students as Learners* (Oxford, The Oxford Centre for Staff and Learning Development).

Rust, C. (2000) (Ed.) *Improving Student Learning. Improving Student Learning Through the Disciplines* (Oxford, The Oxford Centre for Staff and Learning Development).

Rust, C. & Gibbs, G. (1997) (Eds) *Improving Student Learning. Improving Student Learning through Course Design* (Oxford, The Oxford Centre for Staff and Learning Development).

Sarros, J. C. & Densten, I. L. (1989) Undergraduate student stress and coping strategies, *Higher Education Research and Development*, 8(1), pp. 47–57.

Scouller, K. M. (1998) The influence of assessment method on student's learning approaches: multiple choice question examination versus assignment essay, *Higher Education*, 35, pp. 453–472.

Solomonides, I. & Swannell, M. (1995) Can students learn to change their approach to study? in: G. Gibbs (Ed.) *Improving Student Learning. Through Assessment and Evaluation* (Oxford, The Oxford Centre for Staff Development).

Tait, H. & Entwistle, N. J. (1996) Identifying students at risk through ineffective study strategies, *Higher Education*, 31, pp. 97–116.

Tait, H., Entwistle, N. & McCune, V. (1998) ASSIST: a reconceptualisation of the *Approaches to Studying Inventory*, in: C. Rust (Ed.) *Improving Student Learning. Improving Students as Learners* (Oxford, The Oxford Centre for Staff and Learning Development).

CHAPTER 5

ASSESSMENT FOR LEARNING
The differing perceptions of tutors and students

Effie Maclellan

Assessment and Evaluation in Higher Education, 26, 4, 307–318, 2001

EDITOR'S INTRODUCTION

This article reports on a study of the theory and practice of assessment in one UK higher education institution, and reflects upon the relationship between this and students' learning strategies. It focuses on the differences between perceptions and practices, and between lecturers' beliefs and students' experiences.

This article was categorised in the introductory chapter as adopting a multivariate approach to researching course design. It makes use of a 40-item questionnaire, and analyses the responses of 80 lecturers and 130 third-year undergraduates. The questionnaire asked respondents to place their answers on a four-point scale: 'frequently', 'sometimes', 'never' and 'don't know'.

The author – possibly in response to one of the comments of a referee who reviewed the article in draft form – acknowledges that the questionnaire was a fairly blunt instrument, but justifies this in terms of efficient use of time. The findings are reported in straightforward fashion in terms of frequencies of response along the scale. Nevertheless, the article is an example of a very practical and achievable piece of research, and one that raises lots of important questions about higher education practices.

The findings reveal some contradictions, and form the basis for an interesting discussion. While staff reported that they favour assessment which is formative (i.e. developmental, diagnostic and motivating, and so enabling further learning) and authentic (i.e. assesses the full range of learning undertaken on a course), their students found that this was not reflected in practice. They felt that assessment was primarily summative (i.e. about grading and ranking their achievements), and was frequently not authentic. However, the students' understanding of assessment was seen as being less well developed than that of their lecturers, in part because the latter's portrayal of its practice and purposes was confusing.

Maclellan concludes by arguing in favour of a particular model of assessment, the 'standards model' which 'attempts to reflect *what has been learned* in criterion referenced terms' (Biggs 1999), and against the 'measurement model' which has been dominant historically, and remains so in higher education today.

Clearly, the key literature providing the context for Maclellan's article is that focusing on assessment practices in higher education. This is quite a substantive literature (e.g. Bridges *et al.* 2002, Brown *et al.* 1997, Brown and Glasner 1999, Brown and Knight 1994, Greer 2001, Heywood 2000, Holroyd 2000, Klenowski 2002, Leach *et al.* 2001, Mutch 2002, Stewart and Richardson 2000, Warren Piper 1994, Yorke *et al.* 2002). It evidences a concern with not only demonstrating the wide range of forms of assessment that may be used, but also with encouraging users (i.e. lecturers *and* students) to make use of formative and authentic as well as summative approaches. There is also a book specifically focusing on researching assessment in colleges and universities (Ashcroft and Palacio 1996).

References

Ashcroft, K. and Palacio, D. (1996) *Researching into Assessment and Evaluation in Colleges and Universities*. London, Kogan Page.

Biggs, J. (1999) *Teaching for Quality Learning at University: what the student does*. Buckingham, Open University Press.

Bridges, P., Cooper, A., Evanson, P., Haines, C., Jenkins, D., Scurry, D., Woolf, H. and Yorke, M. (2002) Coursework Marks High, Examination Marks Low: discuss, *Assessment and Evaluation in Higher Education*, 27, 1, pp. 35–48.

Brown, G., Bull, J. and Pendlebury, M. (1997) *Assessing Student Learning in Higher Education*. London, Routledge.

Brown, S. and Glasner, A. (eds) (1999) *Assessment Matters in Higher Education: choosing and using diverse approaches*. Buckingham, Open University Press.

Brown, S. and Knight, P. (1994) *Assessing Learners in Higher Education*. London, Kogan Page.

Greer, L. (2001) 'Does Changing the Method of Assessment of a Module Improve the Performance of a Student?' *Assessment and Evaluation in Higher Education*, 26, 2, pp. 127–138.

Heywood, J. (2000) *Assessment in Higher Education: student learning, teaching, programmes and institutions*. London, Jessica Kingsley.

Holroyd, C. (2000) 'Are Assessors Professional? Student assessment and the professionalism of academics', *Active Learning in Higher Education*, 1, 1, pp. 28–44.

Klenowski, V. (2002) *Developing Portfolios for Learning and Assessment*. London, RoutledgeFalmer.

Leach, L., Neutze, U. and Zepke, N. (2001) 'Assessment and Empowerment: some critical questions', *Assessment and Evaluation in Higher Education*, 26, 4, pp. 293–305.

Mutch, A. (2002) 'Thinking Strategically about Assessment', *Assessment and Evaluation in Higher Education*, 27, 2, pp. 163–174.

Stewart, S. and Richardson, B. (2000) 'Reflection and its Place in the Curriculum on an Undergraduate Course: should it be assessed?' *Assessment and Evaluation in Higher Education*, 25, 4, pp. 369–380.

Warren Piper, D. (1994) *Are Professors Professional? The organisation of university examinations*. London, Jessica Kingsley.

Yorke, M., Barnett, G., Bridges, P., Evanson, P., Haines, C., Jenkins, D., Knight, P., Scurry, D., Stowell, M. and Woolf, H. (2002) 'Does Grading Method Influence Honours Degree Classification?' *Assessment and Evaluation in Higher Education*, 27, 3, pp. 269–279.

ASSESSMENT FOR LEARNING

Introduction

The power of assessment to determine the quality of learning has been established for quite some time (Ramsden, 1997), with the evidence clearly concluding that the quality of student learning is as high (or as low) as the cognitive demand level of the assessment tasks (Crooks, 1988; Gibbs, 1999). In other words, if students perceive a need to understand the material in order to successfully negotiate the assessment task, they will engage in deep learning but if they perceive the assessment instrument to require rote learning of information, they will be unlikely to engage with the higher level objectives which may well have been intended by the programme of study. While a powerful determinant of learning outcome, students' experiences of assessment do not occur in a vacuum but are contextualised in their overall perceptions of the goals they have to achieve, the workload they carry, the teaching they experience and the autonomy they have to direct their own learning (Prosser & Trigwell, 1999). More than that, however, since students' perceptions of their learning environment will *vary* within any one group or class of students (Prosser & Miller, 1989), so the quality of learning will vary, not only through perceptions of the learning environment but also through what the students do or do not do in response to their perceptions. Assessment practices, then, play a subtle, complex, and enormously important role in the students' experiences of learning.

Assessment itself, however, is undergoing a paradigm shift (Gipps, 1994) with a movement from the measurement model to a standards model (Taylor, 1994). Such a movement comes from an increasing recognition that the assumptions of traditional learning theory are now very questionable. Learning is now more commonly recognised as a process of knowledge construction (rather than of knowledge reproduction), as being situated in particular contexts (and therefore not necessarily transferable to other contexts) and as being knowledge dependent (Resnick, 1989). The realisation that learning is not linear and atomistic and that it is not decontextualised, has led to the desire that assessment should represent meaningful, significant and worthwhile forms of human endeavour and accomplishment. In other words, assessment tasks should reflect the ways in which knowledge and skills are used in real world contexts (Newmann & Archbald, 1992).

But while moving to a standards model of assessment may be seen as desirable, it is not automatic since the assumptions which underpin the measurement and standards models are very different. The measurement model is concerned with the relative, reliable performance of individuals on decontextualised, standardised tasks that are deemed to be valid indicators of the domain being assessed. This model seeks to emphasise individual differences. The standards model, on the other hand, is concerned with the level to which knowledge is embedded in deep (and possibly new) understanding, and can be demonstrated in authentic tasks. This model seeks to emphasise the value of education as a means of promoting the development of individuals (Taylor, 1994).

The study reported here had the aim of trying to discern what model underpinned extant in-faculty assessment practices. It was assumed that the model could be inferred from descriptions of assessment practices as these were perceived by students and staff most immediately involved in assessment.

Method

Since the purpose of the study was to describe the student and staff perceptions of assessment, an actuarial survey was deemed appropriate. Data on perceptions of in-faculty assessment were collected from staff and students by means of a questionnaire. While a questionnaire can be rightly criticised for yielding only superficial information, the questionnaire in this study was seen as being an efficient use of time, as allowing academic peers and students to respond anonymously and as gleaning hitherto unknown information on a range of practices which ultimately shape the assessment 'events' that staff and students experience. Of primary importance were views on the extent to which assessment is concerned to enable learning rather than merely measure learning. Since assessment which is explicitly designed to promote learning is probably one of the most powerful tools that we have in higher education, it was considered important to solicit views on *why* assessment was taking place and on *how useful* the assessment process was. Also of importance were views on how judgements are made, since educational assessment is essentially a matter of making valid judgements about the incidence of learning, so *who* makes the judgement, *when* the judgements are made and what the *rules or procedures* are for making the judgements are important matters on which to gain some clarity. Finally it was of importance to capture views on the learning being assessed. What is considered important to assess will strongly determine what is considered important to learn. Moreover, since any mode of assessment has its inherent limitations the mode that is used will underscore the actual learning that is being focused on. It was therefore important to be aware of the *assessment instruments* used and of the *cognitive demand level* of the learning. All of these issues were incorporated into the questionnaire which was devised by the author but which was influenced by the theoretical ideas of Biggs (1999), Bowden and Marton (1998) and Prosser and Trigwell (1999) together with McDowell's (1998) account of old and new assessment practices. The 40-item questionnaire was clustered in eight variables: the purpose (4 items), content (6 items), timing (4 items), mode (9 items) and marking of assessment (10 items), feedback on assessment (4 items), the assessor (2 items) and the identity of the participant (1 item). All items, with the exception of the item on participant identity, reflected the range of assessment issues that are documented in the literature. Small-scale piloting of the questionnaire was conducted with five members of faculty staff and five undergraduate students.

A 4-point itemised rating scale of 'frequently', 'sometimes', 'never', 'don't know' was used for collecting responses. Faculty staff members were issued with the questionnaire forms and asked to complete them within 10 days. The students were issued with the questionnaire during class time at the start of a module on assessment. Eighty members of faculty staff (80% return) and 130 3rd-year undergraduates (100% return) completed a 40-item questionnaire on their experiences of assessment. Faculty staff members were all experienced in teaching and assessment practices. The undergraduates were following a B.Ed. (Hons) Programme and were selected because:

(1) they were a sufficiently large and collectively accessible sample;
(2) they represented a degree course which is a major part of the faculty's teaching;
(3) they were deemed to have had a range of assessment experiences within the faculty.

Participants were asked to think about their experiences to date of assessment practices within the faculty and to draw on the totality of that experience when responding to the questions. Staff and students were asked not to include the assessment of field experience/placement in their considerations.

Results

Summary of questionnaire findings

The essential purpose of this study was to describe assessment practices as these were perceived by staff and students. Each item in the questionnaire was endorsed in terms of the frequency with which the participant had experienced the practice under consideration. The modal preferences are summarised in Table 18.

The most frequently endorsed purpose of assessment, as perceived by both students and staff, was to grade/rank student achievement. A second important purpose for staff was the motivation of learning though the students largely perceived assessment to be only sometimes motivating, with 25% of the students claiming that assessment

Table 18 Modal values for students and staff (in percentages to the nearest whole number)

Item	Students	Staff
1 Assessment motivates learning	sometimes (65)	frequently (69)
2 Assessment is used to grade/rank	frequently (82)	frequently (83)
3 Assessment is used for diagnosis	sometimes (50)	frequently (66)
4 Assessment is used to evaluate teaching	sometimes (52)	frequently (41)
5 Development of knowledge is assessed	frequently (64)	frequently (81)
6 Application of knowledge is assessed	sometimes (50)	frequently (76)
7 Presentation of information is assessed	frequently (72)	frequently (66)
8 Analysis of information is assessed	frequently (75)	frequently (86)
9 Synthesis of information is assessed	frequently (52)	frequently (76)
10 Evaluation of information is assessed	frequently (63)	frequently (79)
11 Self-assessment is used	sometimes (59)	sometimes (50)
12 Peer assessment is used	sometimes (55)	sometimes (47)
13 Assessed at the start of a module	never (77)	never (73)
14 Assessed during a module	sometimes (82)	sometimes (53)
15 Assessed at the end of a module	frequently (97)	frequently (86)
16 Assessed when student feels ready	never (88)	never (76)
17 Assessed in tutorials	sometimes (75)	sometimes (48)
18 Assessed through presentations	sometimes (88)	sometimes (59)
19 Assessed by essay	frequently (95)	frequently (79)
20 Assessed by multiple choice questions	sometimes (80)	never (60)
21 Assessed by short answer questions	sometimes (76)	sometimes (45)
22 Assessed through case notes	frequently (77)	sometimes (44)
23 Assessed through reflective diaries	sometimes (51)	sometimes (58)
24 Assessed in labs/workshops	sometimes (65)	never (53)
25 Assessed through audio/video products	never (91)	never (63)
26 Assessed against implicit criteria	sometimes (50)	never (63)
27 Assessed against explicit criteria	frequently (54)	frequently (81)
28 Marking strengthens knowledge	sometimes (60)	sometimes (60)
29 Marking develops thinking	sometimes (57)	frequently (64)
30 Marking improves presentation	sometimes (55)	sometimes (54)
31 Work is given a summative grade	frequently (59)	frequently (85)
32 Work is routinely second marked	sometimes (61)	sometimes (50)
33 Work is second marked if a fail	sometimes (37)	frequently (50)
34 Marking is moderated	sometimes (64)	sometimes (44)
35 Marking is anonymous	never (49)	never (43)
36 Feedback is helpful in detail	sometimes (73)	frequently (49)
37 Feedback prompts discussion with tutor	never (50)	frequently (63)
38 Feedback helps to understand assessment	sometimes (62)	frequently (50)
39 Feedback improves learning	sometimes (72)	frequently (49)
40 Status	student (100)	staff (100)

was never motivating. The diagnosis of strengths and weaknesses was seen as a frequent purpose of assessment by 41% of students and 66% of staff. Staff were divided on the degree to which assessment was used to evaluate teaching, with 41% saying that this happened frequently and 40% saying 'sometimes'. Students, however, were much less convinced that assessment was frequently used to evaluate teaching [see Table 19].

Amongst staff, assessment was frequently used to judge the development of knowledge (81%) and the application of knowledge (76%). Assessment events were frequently designed to assess students' ability to analyse, synthesise and evaluate information (86%, 76% and 79% respectively). Students too (but to a lesser extent than staff) acknowledged that these aspects of development were assessed frequently. This is consistent with Norton's (1990) finding that students put more emphasis on demonstrating knowledge than on constructing an argued position in response to the set task [see Table 20].

Self and peer assessments were not frequent occurrences. Indeed, the staff respondents were fairly evenly divided on whether self and peer assessments never happen (41% endorsing self-assessment and 48% endorsing peer assessment) or happen sometimes (50% endorsing self-assessment and 48% endorsing peer assessment) [see Table 21].

Seventy-seven per cent of students and 73% of staff reported that students were never assessed at the start of a module. Ninety-seven per cent of student responses and 86% of staff responses indicated that assessment typically occurred at the end of a module. Only 12% of students and 24% of staff reported that students' views of their own readiness to be assessed had a bearing on the timing [see Table 22].

Table 19 Purpose of assessment (percentage frequencies to the nearest whole number)

Assessment is used to	Frequently		Sometimes		Never		Don't know	
	•	*	•	*	•	*	•	*
Motivate learning	5	69	65	23	25	9	4	0
Grade/rank achievement	82	83	17	15	1	2	0	0
Diagnose strengths/ weaknesses	41	66	50	23	6	11	3	0
Evaluate teaching	21	41	52	40	20	19	7	0

Note: • = students; * = staff.

Table 20 Content of assessment (percentage frequencies to the nearest whole number)

Assessment focuses on the	Frequently		Sometimes		Never		Don't know	
	•	*	•	*	•	*	•	*
Development of knowledge	64	81	35	15	1	4	0	0
Application of knowledge	49	76	50	23	1	1	1	0
Presentation of knowledge	72	66	28	30	0	4	0	0
Analysis of knowledge	75	86	25	14	1	0	0	0
Synthesis of knowledge	52	76	45	23	0	1	5	0
Evaluation of knowledge	63	79	36	18	0	4	1	0

Note: • = students; * = staff.

Table 21 Assessors (percentage frequencies to the nearest whole number)

Assessment is carried out by	Frequently		Sometimes		Never		Don't know	
	•	*	•	*	•	*	•	*
Self	25	9	59	50	15	41	2	0
Peers	6	5	55	48	39	48	1	0

Note: • = students; * = staff.

Table 22 Timing of assessment (percentage frequencies to the nearest whole number)

Assessment is carried out	Frequently		Sometimes		Never		Don't know	
	•	*	•	*	•	*	•	*
At the start of the module	0	4	19	24	77	73	4	0
During the module	3	29	82	53	14	19	1	0
At the end of the module	97	86	3	8	0	6	0	0
When the student is ready	2	10	10	14	88	76	1	0

Note: • = students; * = staff.

The most frequent mode of assessment was the essay (95% of students and 79% of staff). Other forms of written assessment were variously perceived. Eighty per cent of students thought multiple choice questions were sometimes used while 60% of the staff thought the self same mode was never used. Seventy-seven per cent of students thought case/fieldwork notes were frequently assessed while 41% of staff thought these were never assessed. Short answer questions (76% of students and 45% of staff) and reflective logs/diaries (51% of students and 58% of staff) were used sometimes.

In the non-written mode students perceived assessment to be sometimes through seminar contributions, presentation to peers and participation in workshops/labs (75%, 88% and 65% respectively), and while staff respondents also acknowledged these modes of assessment (48%, 59% and 38% respectively), 40% of staff said seminar contributions were never assessed and 53% said participation in workshops/labs was never assessed. Ninety-one per cent of students and 63% of staff reported that students were never assessed through audio/video recordings [see Table 23].

Amongst staff, marking was most frequently against explicit criteria (81%) and focused on knowledge (60%), thinking (64%) and presentation (54%). As a result of marking, a summative grade was frequently awarded, according to 85% of the staff. Only in 18% of the staff sample was there the view that assessed work is marked by second assessors as a matter of routine, although this number increased to 50% of the sample when considering 'fails'. Alarmingly, perhaps, 18% of the staff reported that the second marking of 'fails' never happened. Internal consistency was checked frequently (38%) or sometimes (44%) according to respondents, and while work for assessment was frequently submitted anonymously, according to 39% of the staff, another 43% maintained that anonymous marking never happened [see Table 24].

Amongst students, marking was also most frequently against explicit criteria (54%), although 50% of the students thought that marking was sometimes against implicit

92   *Effie Maclellan*

Table 23 Mode of assessment (percentage frequencies to the nearest whole number)

Assessment is through	Frequently		Sometimes		Never		Don't know	
	•	*	•	*	•	*	•	*
Seminar contributions	6	13	75	48	15	40	4	0
Presentations to peers	6	10	88	59	6	31	0	0
Essay	95	79	5	16	0	5	0	0
Multiple choice questions	9	5	80	35	10	60	1	0
Short answer questions	12	13	76	45	12	43	1	0
Case/fieldwork notes	77	15	17	44	5	41	1	0
Reflective logs/diaries	21	19	51	58	28	24	1	0
Participation in labs	3	10	65	38	30	53	2	0
Audio/video recordings	0	6	7	31	91	63	2	0

Note: • = students; * = staff.

Table 24 Marking of assessment (percentage frequencies to the nearest whole number)

Marking is	Frequently		Sometimes		Never		Don't know	
	•	*	•	*	•	*	•	*
Against implicit criteria	28	9	50	29	15	63	7	0
Against explicit criteria	54	81	39	15	4	2	3	0
To assess knowledge	25	60	60	31	12	9	2	0
To assess thinking	27	64	57	29	13	5	3	0
To assess presentation	23	54	55	31	20	15	2	0
Given a summative grade	59	85	25	11	12	4	3	0
Routinely second marked	6	18	61	50	22	33	12	0
Second marked if a fail	24	50	37	33	14	18	25	0
Sampled by a moderator	10	38	64	44	14	19	12	0
Anonymous	12	39	26	19	49	43	13	0

Note: • = students; * = staff.

Table 25 Value of feedback (percentage frequencies to the nearest whole number)

Feedback	Frequently		Sometimes		Never		Don't know	
	•	*	•	*	•	*	•	*
Is helpful in its detail	12	49	73	44	13	8	2	0
Prompts discussion	2	63	46	30	50	8	2	0
Enables understanding of assessment	5	50	62	40	30	10	2	0
Improves learning	15	49	72	45	9	6	4	0

Note: • = students; * = staff.

criteria. Marking sometimes focused on knowledge (60%), thinking (57%) and presentation (55%), and as a result a summative grade was frequently awarded according to 59% of the students. Sixty-one per cent of students thought that work is sometimes marked by a second assessor, while 25% of the students did not know if 'failing' work is marked by anyone else. Internal consistency was sometimes checked (64%) and almost half of the sample (49%) reported that anonymous marking never happened.

The majority of staff respondents considered feedback to be helpful in its detail (93%) and to improve learning (94%) either sometimes or frequently. Most of the students too recognised the value of feedback although they did not consider the value to be as frequent as staff claimed. Differences in student and staff perceptions were noted in the role played by feedback in prompting discussion between staff and student(s) and in enabling students to understand assessment [see Table 25].

Although the modal responses summarised in Table 18 might suggest a fair degree of correspondence in the perceptions of staff and students, this apparent agreement between staff and students is more likely to be an artefact of the somewhat crude rating scale. Statistically, there were considerable differences between staff and students. On a Mann-Whitney U Test, perceptions of assessment were significantly different on 32 out of the 39 items [see Table 26].

Discussion

In discussing assessment practices as these were perceived by staff and students, there will be an attempt to deduce the respective 'views' of the two groups. These views will be in very general terms since the measuring instrument could access fairly blunt perceptions only.

The staff view of assessment

For staff the primary purpose of assessment was to grade or rank students, but the more developmental purposes of motivating students, diagnosing learning and evaluating teaching were not discounted. The importance given to grading/ranking achievement (confirmed in a number of the items concerned with the marking of students' work) is perhaps not misplaced given the need for universities to be able to establish students' levels of achievements and to communicate these with professional regulating bodies and potential employers (Atkins *et al.*, 1993). That staff perceive the developmental function of assessment to be important seems to be corroborated in the valuable role they see being played by feedback in strengthening the students' knowledge base, in developing student thinking and in improving presentation. However, the importance allegedly placed on the developmental or formative function of assessment is not internally consistent with other views endorsed by staff. For example, staff reported that assessment neither took place at the beginning of a module nor could students be assessed when they themselves felt ready. Furthermore, staff reported that self and peer assessment were infrequent occurrences. There are at least three important educational implications arising from this. First, the practice of not assessing at the start of a module precludes the opportunity to modify/design teaching in response to student understanding (Prosser & Trigwell, 1999). Second, the practice of not allowing students to be assessed when they feel ready for assessment denies that students may need differential amounts of time to achieve desired learning outcomes (Boud, 1995). Third, to discount students' judgements is to fail to appreciate that effective learning is in large measure a function of strategic metacognitive behaviour (Biggs,

Table 26 Differences in staff and student perceptions of assessment

Item	Mean rank for students	Mean rank for staff	$p < 0.05$ (two-tailed)
1 Assessment motivates learning	131.32	63.54	significant
2 Assessment is used to grade/rank	105.81	105.00	n/s
3 Assessment is used for diagnosis	114.41	91.02	significant
4 Assessment is used to evaluate teaching	114.60	90.72	significant
5 Development of knowledge is assessed	111.98	94.97	significant
6 Application of knowledge is assessed	116.51	87.61	significant
7 Presentation of information is assessed	102.66	110.11	n/s
8 Analysis of information is assessed	110.20	97.87	significant
9 Synthesis of information is assessed	115.53	89.21	significant
10 Evaluation of information is assessed	111.29	96.09	significant
11 Self-assessment is used	92.68	126.32	significant
12 Peer assessment is used	102.26	110.76	n/s
13 Assessed at the start of a module	109.99	98.21	n/s
14 Assessed during a module	112.72	93.76	significant
15 Assessed at the end of a module	101.15	112.56	significant
16 Assessed when student feels ready	110.93	96.67	significant
17 Assessed in tutorials	100.10	114.28	n/s
18 Assessed through oral presentations	97.52	118.46	significant
19 Assessed by essay	99.05	115.99	significant
20 Assessed by multiple choice questions	86.30	136.70	significant
21 Assessed by short answer questions	95.28	122.10	significant
22 Assessed through case notes	79.14	148.33	significant
23 Assessed through reflective diaries	106.49	103.89	n/s
24 Assessed in labs/workshops	99.59	115.10	significant
25 Assessed through audio/video products	118.48	84.41	significant
26 Assessed against implicit criteria	89.72	131.14	significant
27 Assessed against explicit criteria	116.33	87.89	significant
28 Marking strengthens knowledge base	119.15	83.31	significant
29 Marking develops thinking	120.47	81.17	significant
30 Marking improves presentation	117.42	86.13	significant
31 Work is given a summative grade	116.17	88.17	significant
32 Work is routinely second marked	110.25	97.78	n/s
33 Work is second marked only if a fail	120.25	81.53	significant
34 Marking is moderated	117.21	86.47	significant
35 Marking is anonymous	118.83	83.83	significant
36 Feedback is helpful in detail	120.49	81.14	significant
37 Feedback prompts discussion with tutor	134.42	58.50	significant
38 Feedback helps to understand assessment	126.12	72.00	significant
39 Feedback improves learning	119.80	82.27	significant

1999). All three practices, which discount the status of the students' learning, are inconsistent with a constructivist view of learning and, by extension, with a standards model of assessment.

Amongst staff, assessment was frequently used to judge the development and application of knowledge together with the skills of analysis, synthesis and the evaluation of information. This finding is reflected in the perceptions of both the content and marking of assessment. That declarative knowledge *per se* was not the sole focus of assessment suggests that students were being assessed on their ability to assemble and interpret information, formulate ideas, construct a defensible argument and critique a line of reasoning, an emphasis which Norton (1990) also found among staff. Being able to engage in these particular types of cognitive tasks is important because they have the potential to be generalisable to other learning and problem solving situations in the real world (Messick, 1994). In other words, in being assessed on their ability to engage in these various cognitive tasks the students were being required to demonstrate authentic academic achievement (Newmann & Archbald, 1992). However, the extent to which assessment genuinely focused on students' capacity to apply, transform or evaluate the relevance of declarative knowledge in new situations could be viewed as questionable when considering the processes through which the assessment information was gathered. Initial perusal of the different 'instruments' suggested some to more obviously mirror real life than others. For example, tutorial contributions and oral presentations might be seen as manifestations of the practical, real world skills of group interaction and problem solving (Taylor, 1997). Similarly, reflective diaries are promoted as evidencing continuing professional development (Brockbank & McGill, 1998). Finally, the creation of videotapes, the maintenance of case notes and participation in labs/workshops can directly map on to real life activity. The extent to which these real life modes of assessment were used was, by staff's own admission, not frequent. Conversely, while the essay mode and short answer mode may well assess the use of cogent argument and the expression of complex ideas, writing about one's ideas is somewhat removed from actively demonstrating one's knowledge. The extent to which assessment tasks made authentic demands of students is then questionable. Staff believed that they were assessing a full range of learning, but the heavy emphasis on one particular mode suggests a more limited range of learning was actually being assessed. This would not be fully consistent with the standards model.

The student view of assessment

Students agreed that a frequent purpose of assessment was to make a summative judgement in the form of grading or ranking student performance. However, students claimed that formative purposes were served only some of the time. For example, most students did not view feedback on their learning as either routinely helpful in itself or as a catalyst for discussion. That students primarily perceived assessment to be about judging levels of achievement rather than about enabling learning may be partly a function of what formative assessment can mean. Its most essential meaning is that it provides the teacher with information that can be fed back into the teaching/learning process (Crooks, 1988; Gipps, 1994). However, a conception of formative assessment that focuses on the teacher's role but discounts that of the learner is increasingly being understood as incomplete. Sadler (1989) noted that even when learners are given valid and reliable information about the quality of their work, there is no necessary improvement in the work. Sadler's analysis has led to the realisation that assessment can only have a formative influence if learners are involved in the process (Pryor & Torrance, 1996; Tunstall & Gipps, 1996; Wiliam & Black,

1996). The implication of this is that if students are not actually monitoring and regulating the quality of their own learning, feedback of itself, regardless of its degree of detail, will not cause improvement in learning. That students did not view assessment as offering them opportunities within which to advance their own learning is further evidenced in the perception by almost 80% of the students that assessment was frequently or sometimes carried out using implicit criteria. The dangers of this do not need to be exaggerated. If they believe the criteria are implicit, students will, by definition, be unclear as to what to do to achieve the desired standard. Further, if students believe the criteria to be implicit, then they may see assessment as some sort of lottery in which they experience inequable treatment from idiosyncratic staff. Such a perception is not impossible given the subjectivity of staff in the marking process (Norton, 1990). In not recognising their own role in formative assessment, students see staff as having the power to determine either the veracity of student performance *per se* or the validity of the evidence from which performance is inferred. Such a view is consistent with the measurement model of assessment.

Like staff, students perceived a range of learning to be assessed although they were of the view that the full range was assessed only some of the time rather than frequently. Unlike staff, the students considered this learning to be assessed through various modes. Although the essay mode was the most frequently endorsed, seminar contributions, presentations to peers, case/fieldwork notes and multiple-choice questions were acknowledged by large numbers of students as being modes of assessment that they experienced. Quite at odds with the staff perception, students seemed to perceive assessment as being ubiquitous. Furthermore, that large numbers of students saw themselves engaging in self-assessment at least some of the time while 41% of the staff denied student self-assessment, suggests that there was a lack of shared meaning between students and staff as to the status of assessment. This is perhaps an example of the general finding that there are varied conceptions of learning and teaching amongst university staff and student populations (Prosser & Trigwell, 1999), and may be partly attributed to the students' lack of appreciation of the distinction between learning *activities* and learning *goals* (Dwyer, 1998) and partly to a failure to align learning goals, learning activities and the assessment of learning outcomes (Biggs, 1999). Given that (albeit small numbers of) students were unaware of marking and moderation procedures and given that the students appear not to have any real grasp of the power or value of formative assessment, it does seem likely that the student conception of assessment was somewhat primitive. This is not to suggest that the student view was wrong, merely that it was underdeveloped. But this is perhaps not surprising since, by dint of professional power, the staff view of assessment will influence the students' attitudes towards, and perceptions of, assessment (Sadler, 1998). Since the staff view of assessment did not fully espouse the philosophy of the standards model, thereby presenting a somewhat confusing picture of assessment, it should not be surprising that the student view of assessment was somewhat incoherent.

Conclusion

The standards model of assessment is the desirable model in formal education (Biggs, 1999) because it attempts to reflect *what has been learned* in criterion referenced terms. However, the historical dominance of the measurement model together with the difficulties of implementing assessment which is premised on a standards model means that extant practices in educational assessment may not be consistent with a standards model (Taylor, 1994). In this study such inconsistency was indeed evidenced.

Staff declared a commitment to the formative purposes of assessment but engaged in practices that militated against formative assessment being fully realised. Similarly, staff maintained that the full range of learning was frequently assessed yet the dominant mode of assessment was the traditional, academic essay, thereby attenuating the idea that students were engaging in authentic assessment which could enhance their learning. In other words, the staff view suggested aspirations towards the standards model of assessment but these aspirations have yet to be fully realised.

Overall the student view of assessment is a depressing one. The students do not exploit assessment to improve their learning and, furthermore, appear to have a very underdeveloped conception of what assessment is. Given that assessment practices may or may not precipitate powerful or transformative learning it seems important to appreciate the central involvement of students themselves in the assessment process. Such understanding may well have to be developed in staff who in turn could identify the changes which they need to make in their practice in order to help students take greater responsibility for their own learning. Only when all assessment tasks can be fully authentic and only when staff and students can put the students' learning at the very centre of the educational enterprise, can the assessment practices be consistent with the standards model.

References

Atkins, M., Beattie, J. & Dockrell, W. (1993) *Assessment Issues in Higher Education* (Great Britain, Employment Department).

Biggs, J. (1999) *Teaching for Quality Learning at University* (Buckingham, The Society for Research into Higher Education & The Open University Press).

Boud, D. (1995) *Enhancing Learning through Self Assessment* (London, Kogan Page).

Bowden, J. & Marton, F. (1998) *The University of Learning* (London, Kogan Page).

Brockbank, A. & McGill, I. (1998) *Facilitating Reflective Learning in Higher Education* (Buckingham, The Society for Research into Higher Education & The Open University Press).

Crooks, T. (1988) The impact of classroom evaluation practices on students, *Review of Educational Research*, 58(4), pp. 438–481.

Dwyer, C. (1998) Assessment and classroom learning: theory and practice, *Assessment in Education*, 5(1), pp. 131–137.

Gibbs, G. (1999) Using assessment strategically to change the way students learn, in: S. Brown & A. Glasner (Eds) *Assessment Matters in Higher Education* (Buckingham, The Society for Research into Higher Education & The Open University Press).

Gipps, C. (1994) *Beyond Testing* (London, The Palmer Press).

McDowell, L. (1998) Editorial, *Assessment and Evaluation in Higher Education*, 23(4), pp. 335–338.

Messick, S. (1994) The interplay of evidence and consequences in the validation of performance assessments, *Educational Researcher*, 23(2), pp. 13–23.

Newmann, F. & Archibald, D. (1992) The nature of authentic academic achievement, in: H. Berlak, F. Newmann, E. Adams, D. Archibald, T. Burgess, J. Raven & T. Romberg (Eds) *Towards a New Science of Educational Testing and Assessment* (New York, State University of New York Press).

Norton, L. (1990) Essay-writing: what really counts? *Higher Education*, 20, pp. 411–442.

Prosser, M. & Miller, R. (1989) The 'how' and 'what' of learning physics, *European Journal of Psychology of Education*, 4(4), pp. 513–528.

Prosser, M. & Trigwell, K. (1999) *Understanding Learning and Teaching* (Buckingham, The Society for Research into Higher Education & The Open University Press).

Pryor, J. & Torrance, H. (1996) Teacher-pupil interaction in formative assessment: assessing the work or protecting the child? *The Curriculum Journal*, 7(2), pp. 205–226.

Ramsden, P. (1997) The context of learning in academic departments, in: F. Marton, D. Hounsell & N. Entwistle (Eds) *The Experience of Learning*, pp. 198–216 (Edinburgh, Scottish Academic Press).

Resnick, L. (1989) Introduction, in: L. Resnick (Ed.) *Knowing Learning and Instruction* (New Jersey, Lawrence Erlbaum Associates).

Sadler, R. (1989) Formative assessment and the design of instructional systems, *Instructional Science*, 18, pp. 119–144.

Sadler, R. (1998) Formative assessment: revisiting the territory, *Assessment in Education*, 5(1), pp. 77–84.

Taylor, C. (1994) Assessment for measurement or standards: the peril and the promise of large-scale assessment reform, *American Educational Research Journal*, 31(2), pp. 231–262.

Taylor, I. (1997) *Developing Learning in Professional Education* (Buckingham, The Society for Research into Higher Education & The Open University Press).

Tunstall, P. & Gipps, C. (1996) 'How does your teacher help you to make your work better?' Children's understanding of formative assessment, *The Curriculum Journal*, 7(2), pp. 185–203.

Wiliam, D. & Black, P. (1996) Meanings and consequences: a basis for distinguishing formative and summative functions of assessment? *British Educational Research Journal*, 22(5), pp. 537–548.

CHAPTER 6

THE VALIDITY OF STUDENT EVALUATION OF TEACHING IN HIGHER EDUCATION

Love me, love my lectures?

Mark Shevlin, Philip Banyard, Mark Davies and Mark Griffiths

Assessment and Evaluation in Higher Education, 25, 4, 397–405, 2000

EDITOR'S INTRODUCTION

Student evaluation of teaching is a mainstay of most higher education institutions' quality assurance practices, and it would be an unusual institution, department or course team nowadays that did not pay some attention to the results of such evaluations. In some cases, decisions on lecturers' employment and promotion may be, in part, based on such evaluations. But just how accurate or valid are they? And what constitutes effective teaching? Those are the questions posed in this article by Shevlin and his colleagues.

This article was categorised in the introductory chapter as adopting a multivariate approach to researching quality issues. The research involved administering a questionnaire to 213 undergraduate students at one UK higher education institution. The questionnaire asked the students to rate their lecturer in terms of twelve items: six to do with the lecturer's ability, five concerning the attributes of the module or course they were studying, and a final item assessing whether their lecturer had charisma. The data collected was then subjected to factor analysis, and a model produced of teaching effectiveness and charisma.

The authors locate their study within the context of previous research that:

- tried to identify the key characteristics of effective teaching: here little consensus was apparent;
- indicated a relationship between expected assessment grades and reported evaluations of teacher effectiveness.

To this they add, from the business/management literature, the concept of charismatic or transformative leadership. In the business/management literature, perceptions of charisma have been shown to positively affect employees' perceptions of their managers and employers. The authors' hypothesis, then, is that students' perceptions of their lecturers as charismatic will have a positive affect on their assessment of those lecturers.

The model that the authors produce from their factor analysis does indeed suggest that there is a 'halo effect' in students' evaluations of their lecturers produced by the former's perception of the latter as charismatic. They then, naturally enough, raise the issue of how much reliance should then be placed upon student evaluations.

There are two literatures to which this interesting study may be related. One is the general literature on teaching in higher education, how to teach, what works and how to assess and evaluate teaching (e.g. Aylett and Gregory 1996, Biggs 1999, Brown and Atkins 2002, Johnson 2000, Knight 2002, Laurillard 2002, Nicholls 2002, Ramsden 1992, Walker 2001). The other is the developing literature on student behaviours, of which the article in this Reader by Norton *et al.* (2001) is an example.

References

Aylett, R. and Gregory, K. (eds) (1996) *Evaluating Teacher Quality in Higher Education*. London, Falmer.
Biggs, J. (1999) *Teaching for Quality Learning at University: what the student does*. Buckingham, Open University Press.
Brown, G. and Atkins, M. (2002) *Effective Teaching in Higher Education*. London, Routledge.
Johnson, R. (2000) 'The Authority of the Student Evaluation Questionnaire', *Teaching in Higher Education*, 5, 4, pp. 419–434.
Knight, P. (2002) *Being a Teacher in Higher Education*. Buckingham, Open University Press.
Laurillard, D. (2002) *Rethinking University Teaching: a conversational framework for the effective use of learning technologies*. London, RoutledgeFalmer.
Nicholls, G. (2002) *Developing Teaching and Learning in Higher Education*. London, RoutledgeFalmer.
Norton, L., Tilley, A., Newstcad, S. and Franklyn-Stokes, A. (2001) 'The Pressures of Assessment in Undergraduate Courses and their Effect on Student Behaviours', *Assessment and Evaluation in Higher Education*, 26, 3, pp. 269–284.
Ramsden, P. (1992) *Learning to Teach in Higher Education*. London, Routledge.
Walker, M. (ed.) (2001) *Reconstructing Professionalism in University Teaching: teachers and learners in action*. Buckingham, Open University Press.

THE VALIDITY OF STUDENT EVALUATION OF TEACHING IN HIGHER EDUCATION

Introduction

What makes a good teacher and how can we recognise him or her? First we might value a teacher by their ability to effect personal change and development in their students. This is a long-term outcome and problematic if we attempt to quantify it. Second we might value a teacher by their effectiveness in facilitating good academic work in their students. This is more measurable and it is currently the subject of debate in the UK as the British Government considers incentives for teachers based on examination results. A third way of evaluating teachers is to ask their students to rate them. This is the most immediate and the most widely used of the three strategies and is commonly measured by questionnaire at the end of courses. One of the issues to consider is whether we are measuring the most important variables of teaching effectiveness or whether some variables are becoming more important just because they are measurable. A further issue to consider, and the one that is addressed in this paper, is the validity of measures of teaching effectiveness gathered from student evaluations.

The practice of student evaluation of teaching (SET) in universities is ubiquitous in the UK and the US. In the UK, information from SET is considered as important evaluative information, but also as a guide for potential changes in course material and method of delivery. The significance of SET is noted by the Quality Assurance

Agency for Higher Education (QAA) in the documentation regarding subject review practices, in particular quality assessment and management (QAA, 1997). In the US, information from SET can be used for faculty decisions about conditions of employment such as salary and promotion. In short, SET is an integral part of higher education practices.

Despite the perceived importance of SET there are theoretical and psychometric issues related to the assessment of teaching effectiveness that are yet unresolved. First, there appears to be little agreement on the nature and number of dimensions that represent teaching effectiveness (Patrick & Smart, 1998). Studies predominantly use questionnaires and factor analysis to derive the dimensions of effective teaching. For example, Swartz *et al.* (1990) identify the two factors of effective teaching as (1) clear instructional presentation, and (2) management of student behaviour, whereas Lowman and Mathie (1993) identify them as (1) intellectual excitement, and (2) interpersonal rapport. There is no obvious mapping between these two pairs of dimensions. Further studies identify more and different factors of teaching effectiveness. For example Brown and Atkins (1993) identify the three factors of effective teachers as (1) caring, (2) systematic, and (3) stimulating, whereas Patrick and Smart (1998) identify the three factors of teaching effectiveness as (1) respect for students, (2) organisation and presentation skills, and (3) ability to challenge students. Other researchers have suggested as many as seven factors (Ramsden, 1991) or nine factors of effective teaching (Marsh & Dunkin, 1992),

In terms of the psychometric properties of evaluation instruments the primary issue of concern is validity. A number of extraneous variables have been examined that may confound the measurement of teaching effectiveness. The relationships between ratings of teaching effectiveness and variables related to student characteristics, lecturer behaviour, and the course administration have been examined (d'Apollonia & Abrami, 1997). For example, in relation to student characteristics, Marsh (1987) and Feldman (1976) reported a positive association between expected grades and ratings of teaching effectiveness. Further to this, Marsh & Roche (1997) reported similar relationships between ratings and the prior subject interest of the student and the reason for taking the course. The variable related to the lecturer behaviour that has received the greatest research interest is that of grading leniency. Using a large sample of American students, Greenwald and Gillmore (1997) demonstrated that grading leniency had a strong positive relationship with ratings of teaching effectiveness. With regard to the effect of course administration, there is, for example, a weak relationship between class size and student ratings with the largest and the smallest classes giving the most positive ratings (Fernàndez *et al.*, 1998). A further problem concerns the validity of the conclusions that are drawn from SET data due to the lack of statistical sophistication in the personnel committees that may use the information (McKeachie, 1997). Overall, research on the effects of extraneous variables on the validity of SET suggests the need for caution in the interpretation of this data.

It would appear, then, that consensus on the characteristics of effective teaching is low, and there are a number of factors that challenge the validity of the data. There is also disagreement on whether the different dimensions are discrete or are representative of a single higher-order teaching effectiveness dimension (Abrami *et al.*, 1997; Marsh & Roche, 1997). It is argued here that if students have a positive personal and/or social view of the lecturer this may lead to more positive ratings irrespective of the actual level of teaching effectiveness. Support for this idea comes from the classic work of Asch on implicit personality theories (Asch, 1946; Bruner & Tagiuri, 1954). Studies found that manipulation of bi-polar attributes such as warm-cold (e.g. Kelly, 1950) produced a large effect in student judgements of lecturers. So-called halo and horns effects (Vernon, 1964) can also be argued to have an impact. These studies illustrate how single attributes are generalised to other judgements of the individual.

Students may respond to a central quality of leadership that then influences their evaluations of teachers. One approach to leadership that offers parallels to teaching is charismatic leadership. For example, House's (1977) theory of charismatic leadership emphasises the relationship between the leader and the follower. According to this approach the principal behavioural features of a charismatic leader are: (1) impression management, by which the leader creates the impression of competence; (2) setting an example, by which followers are encouraged to identify with the leader's beliefs and values; (3) setting high expectations about the followers' performance; (4) providing an attractive vision for the future; and (5) arousing motivation in the followers to be productive. A development of this approach can be seen in Bass's model of transformational leadership (Bass, 1990). This model has four components (the four I's), (1) individual consideration, or leadership by developing people; (2) intellectual stimulation; (3) inspirational motivation; and (4) idealised influence. This last point is often seen as the charismatic component of transformational leadership. The distinctions between transformational leadership and charismatic leadership are not clear (Shackleton, 1995), and even if we make the distinction then the feature of Bass's model that has been found to have the greatest effect on satisfaction ratings is idealised influence (or charisma) (Bryman, 1992). The features of charismatic leadership and transformational leadership resemble the features of teaching effectiveness identified above (Patrick & Smart, 1998). It is argued here that the quality of charisma affects judgements including that of teaching effectiveness. Charisma has been shown to affect voter judgements of politicians (Pillai *et al.*, 1997), as well as leadership at work (Fuller *et al.*, 1996). Distinctions are drawn between expert power, referent power and charisma, though it has been shown in a study of public sector workers, that the only characteristic which influenced workers' ratings of satisfaction with their supervision was charisma (Kudisch *et al.*, 1995).

The impact of charisma in student evaluations of teachers is further enhanced because of the special features of the teacher's role as a 'critical other', in which they challenge students, assess students and attempt to motivate students (Woods, 1993). It is argued that charisma is such a salient trait in students' perceptions of teachers that it affects assessment of teacher effectiveness. From these various literatures, a study was devised to examine the relationship between charisma and teaching effectiveness. It was predicted that the student's perception of the lecturer would significantly predict teaching effectiveness ratings.

Method

Sample

The sample consisted of 213 undergraduate students at a UK university in the Midlands. They were all enrolled full-time on courses within a department of social sciences. Due to the anonymous nature of the evaluation no details of demographic variables are available, although there is no apparent reason why the profile of the students at the university would significantly differ from other institutions in the area. The sample size after listwise deletion of missing data was 199. The participants were required to rate their lecturer. In total eight lecturers (four males and four females) were rated during this study.

Measurements

An 11-item teaching effectiveness self-report scale was administered (Appendix 1) to students by a member of lecturing staff. The scale was designed to measure two dimensions of teaching effectiveness. Six items related to lecturer attributes (items 1, 2, 3, 4, 5, 11) measure the 'lecturer ability' factor, and five items related to aspects of the particular module (items 6, 7, 8, 9, 10) measure the 'module attributes' factor. Responses to the items were made on a 5-point Likert scale anchored with 'strongly agree' and 'strongly disagree'. An addition item was included, 'The lecturer has charisma', which used the same response format as the other items.

Analysis

The model presented in Figure 5 was specified and estimated using LISREL8 (Jöreskog & Sörbom, 1993).

Figure 5 specifies a two-factor measurement model for the 11 items ($y_1 - y_{11}$) measuring student evaluations. The two factors, lecturer ability (η_1) and module attributes (η_2) are measured by their respective items in the self-report teaching evaluation scale. The factor loadings are given the symbol λ, and the error variances for each item the symbol ε. The lecturer ability (η_1) and module attributes (η_2) factors are regressed on the charisma factor (η_3). The regression coefficients are symbolised as β. As the charisma factor is measured by a single item (y_{12}) the reliability was specified at 0.478, which was the average reliability of the other 11 items in the scale. The model estimates can be used to determine the percentage of variation in the lecturer ability and module attributes factor that is attributable to the charisma factor.

From the sample data a covariance matrix was computed using PRELIS2 (Jöreskog & Sörbom, 1993) and the model was estimated using maximum likelihood.

Results

The fit indices show that the model is a reasonable description of the data (χ^2 = 114, df = 52, $p < 0.05$; RMSEA = 0.075; SRMR = 0.049; GFI = 0.92; CFI = 0.94; IFI = 0.94). The standardised parameter estimates are reported in Table 27.

The factor loading s indicates that the items used in the teaching effectiveness self-report scale are good indicators of the lecturer ability and module attributes factors. All the factor loadings are positive, high and statistically significant. The standardised regression coefficients from the charisma factor to the lecturer ability (β_{13}) and module attributes factors (β_{23}) are 0.83 and 0.61 respectively. These effects are statistically significant ($p < 0.05$). Therefore the charisma factor accounts for 69% of the variation of the lecturer ability factor and 37% of the module attributes factor.

Discussion

The results of this study raise issues regarding the interpretation and utility of SET ratings. The SET ratings were demonstrated to be significantly affected by the students' perception of the lecturer thereby questioning the validity of this particular scale. Further, they raise questions about how the effect of confounding variables can be minimised thereby increasing the validity of SET ratings.

The main aim of this study was to determine whether a halo effect occurs in the completion of SET ratings and to estimate the magnitude of this effect. The results

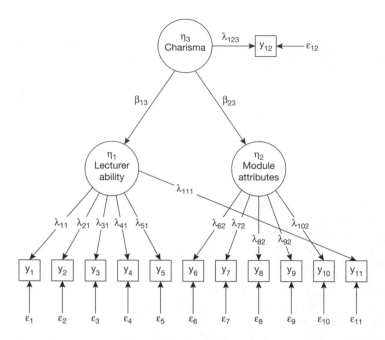

Figure 5 Model of teaching effectiveness and charisma factors

Table 27 Standardised parameter
estimates for teaching
effectiveness ratings model

Parameter	Estimate
λ_{11}	0.60*
λ_{21}	0.76*
λ_{31}	0.82*
λ_{41}	0.77*
λ_{51}	0.77*
λ_{62}	0.53*
λ_{72}	0.54*
λ_{82}	0.56*
λ_{92}	0.74*
λ_{102}	0.85*
λ_{111}	0.67*
β_{13}	0.53*
β_{23}	0.61*

Note: *$p < 0.05$.

indicate that a halo effect does indeed operate during the measurement of teaching effectiveness as the relationships between the charisma factor and the lecturer ability and module attributes were statistically significant. Indeed, the effect is large with the charisma factor accounting for 69% and 37% of the variation in the lecturer ability and module attributes factors respectively. This means that a significant proportion of the scale's variation is reflecting a personal view of the lecturer in terms of their charisma rather than lecturing ability and module attributes. The authors acknowledge that alternative specifications of the model are possible, but on the basis of substantive psychological theory and previous research we have specified this particular model. For example, an alternative model could be specified where the direction of influence is from the SET factors to the charisma factor. This specification would suggest that lecturers are attributed a level of charisma based on their level of 'lecturer ability' and 'model attributes', that is, the better the lecturer the more charismatic they are rated. In addition, cross-lagged designs or models with reciprocal effects between the charisma and teaching effectiveness factors are interesting alternatives that may be examined in future research.

These results of this study raise issues regarding the interpretation and utility of SET ratings. The SET ratings were demonstrated to be significantly affected by the students' perception of the lecturer on a variable that should be unrelated to assessments of teaching ability, thereby questioning the validity of this particular scale. However, the findings could be argued to be likely to generalise to most teaching assessment instruments on the basis of the prevalence of the halo effect. In addition, the results raise questions about how the effect of confounding variables can be minimised thereby increasing the validity of SET ratings.

The two-factor structure of the scale, with high factor loadings, would appear to suggest that meaningful and useful variables related to teaching quality were being measured. However, this is not the case. The two factors are reflecting a positive halo effect as well as variance attributable to teaching quality. This raises questions regarding the utility of using information from such scales since the attribute of charisma is having a central trait effect on student evaluations.

The wide discrepancy in the factors of effective teaching identified above (Brown & Atkins, 1993; Marsh & Roche, 1997; Patrick & Smart, 1998; Ramsden, 1991) can be partly attributed to the existence of an underlying variable. It is argued that this underlying attribute is the personal quality of leadership commonly described as charisma. An alternative explanation is that the effectiveness of a teacher affects the ratings of charisma, though this explanation still implies a single underlying trait that accounts for SET scores.

It is not argued that good and effective teaching is a one-dimensional skill. Teaching is shown to be multi-dimensional, as are the well-designed SET forms. The issue is about how students approach the evaluation of teaching and how they use the SET forms. They are not trained in rating or psychometrics, and it is argued here and elsewhere (for example, d'Apollonia & Abrami, 1997), that they rate specific features of teaching on the basis of a global evaluation. That global factor is lecturer charisma.

This study presents a challenge to the use of SET in higher education and, in particular, raises questions of fairness if such ratings are to be used in decisions relating to employment issues.

References

Abrami, P. C., d'Apollonia, S. & Rosenfield, S. (1997) The dimensionality of student ratings of instruction: what we know and what we do not, in: R. P. Perry & J. C. Smart (Eds) *Effective Teaching in Higher Education: research and practice*, pp. 321–367 (New York, Agathon Press).

Asch, S. E. (1946) Forming impressions of personality, *Journal of Abnormal and Social Psychology*, 41(2), pp. 258–290.

Bass, B. M. (1990) *Boss and Stodgdill's Handbook of Leadership*, 3rd edn. (New York, Free Press).

Brown, G. & Atkins, M. (1993) *Effective Teaching in Higher Education* (London, Routledge).

Bruner, J. S. & Tagiuri, R. (1954) The perception of people, in: G. Lindzey (Ed.) *Handbook of Social Psychology*, Vol. 2 (London, Addison Wesley).

Bryman, A. (1992) *Charisma and Leadership in Organizations* (London, Sage).

d'Apollonia, S. & Abrami, P. C. (1997) Navigating student ratings of instruction, *American Psychologist*, 52(11), pp. 1198–1208.

Feldman, K. A. (1976) Grades and college students' evaluations of their courses and teachers, *Research in Higher Education*, 18(1), pp. 3–124.

Fernàndez, J., Mateo, M. A. & Mu-iz, J. (1998) Is there a relationship between class size and student ratings of teaching quality? *Educational and Psychological Measurement*, 58(4), pp. 596–604.

Fuller, J. B., Patterson, C. E. P., Hester, K. & Stringer, D. Y. (1996) A quantitative review of research on charismatic leadership, *Psychological Reports*, 78(1), pp. 271–287.

Greenwald, A. G. & Gillmore, G. M. (1997) Grading leniency is a removable contaminant of student ratings, *American Psychologist*, 52(11), pp. 1209–1217.

House, R. J. (1977) A 1976 theory of charismatic leadership, in: J. G. Hunt & L. L. Larson (Eds) *Leadership: the cutting edge*, pp. 189–207 (Carbondale, IL, Southern Illinois University Press).

Jöreskog, K. G. & Sörbom, D. (1993) *LISREL 8: Structural equation modeling with the SIMPLIS Command Language* (Chicago, Scientific Software International).

Kelley, H. H. (1950) The warm-cold variable in first impressions of persons, *Journal of Personality and Social Psychology*, 18(3), pp. 431–439.

Kudisch, J. D., Poteet, M. L., Dobbins, G. H., Rush, M. C. et al. (1995) Expert power, referent power, and charisma: toward the resolution of a theoretical debate, *Journal of Business and Psychology*, 10(2), pp. 177–195.

Lowman, J. & Mathie, V. A. (1993) What should graduate teaching assistants know about teaching? *Teaching of Psychology*, 20(2), pp. 84–88.

Marsh, H. W. (1987) Students' evaluations of university teaching: research findings, methodological issues, and directions for future research, *International Journal of Educational Research*, 11(3), pp. 253–388.

Marsh, H. W. & Dunkin, M. (1992) Students' evaluations of university teaching: a multidimensional perspective, in: J. C. Smart (Ed.) *Higher Education: handbook on theory and research*, Vol. 8, pp. 143–234 (New York, Agathon Press).

Marsh, H. W. & Roche, L. A. (1997) Making students' evaluations of teaching effectiveness effective, *American Psychologist*, 52(11), pp. 1187–1197.

McKeachie, W. J. (1997) Student ratings: the validity of use, *American Psychologist*, 52(11), pp. 1218–1225.

Patrick, J. & Smart, R. M. (1998) An empirical evaluation of teacher effectiveness: the emergence of three critical factors, *Assessment and Evaluation in Higher Education*, 23(2), pp. 165–178.

Pillai, R., Stites Doe, S., Grewal, D. & Meindl, J. R. (1997) Winning charisma and losing the presidential election, *Journal of Applied Social Psychology*, 27(19), pp. 1716–1726.

Quality Assurance Agency For Higher Education (1997) *Subject Review Handbook: October 1998 to September 2000 (QAA 1/97)* (London, Quality Assurance Agency for Higher Education).

Ramsden, P. (1991) A performance indicator of teaching quality in higher education: the course experience questionnaire, *Studies in Higher Education*, 16(2), pp. 129–150.

Shackleton, V. (1995) *Business Leadership* (London, Routledge).

Swartz, C. W., White, K. P. & Stuck, G. B. (1990) The factorial structure of the North Carolina Teacher Performance Appraisal Instrument, *Educational and Psychological Measurement*, 50(1), pp. 175–185.

Vernon, P. E. (1964) *Personality Assessment: a critical survey* (London, Methuen).

Woods, P. (1993) The charisma of the critical other: enhancing the role of the teacher, *Teaching and Teacher Education*, 9(8), pp. 545–557.

Appendix 1. Student evaluation questionnaire

1   The lecturer speaks clearly.
2   The lecturer presents material in a well-organised and coherent way.
3   The lecturer is able to explain difficult concepts in a clear and straightforward way.
4   The lecturer makes effective use of examples and illustrations in his or her explanations.
5   The lecturer is successful in presenting the subject matter in an interesting way.
6   The lecturer is successful in encouraging students to think independently and do supplementary reading on the subject matter of the module.
7   The module was what I expected.
8   The references were very useful.
9   In this module I learned a lot.
10   In my opinion this module was enjoyable and worthwhile.
11   The lecturer was very approachable.
12   The lecturer has charisma.

CHAPTER 7

GRADUATE EMPLOYMENT AND WORK IN SELECTED EUROPEAN COUNTRIES

Ulrich Teichler

European Journal of Education, 35, 2, 141–156, 2000

EDITOR'S INTRODUCTION

This article stems from a project funded by the European Commission, and examines the quality of the available international statistics on graduate employment in nine western European countries. It comments on the difficulties of comparative analyses, the usefulness of surveys of this kind, and what might be done to improve matters in the future.

As a piece of research, the article offers an evaluation of two sets of secondary data, the term social scientists commonly use to refer to previously collected information that they haven't gathered themselves. Teichler focuses in particular on two existing data sets published each year: that compiled by EURYDICE, the European Commission agency responsible for collecting educational data, and that compiled by the Organisation for Economic Co-operation and Development (OECD).

The key statistics examined include: enrolment rates in higher education, the proportion of graduates in their age group, the percentage of adults who have completed higher education, and the variations in these statistics in terms of age, gender and field of study. Teichler then goes on to look at key employment statistics, including unemployment and labour force participation rates, and the relative earnings of those who have completed higher education.

Throughout his analysis, Teichler points out problems with the available data and their interpretation: varying definitions of what it means to be a student, differences in the age group typically in initial full-time higher education, what is and is not included within higher education in different countries. In the final third of the article, he goes on to consider some more generic issues, including the relevance of the graduation rate in an era of mass higher education, and recent graduate employment problems. He ends the article with some suggestions for improving international, and particularly European, higher education statistics.

This article was categorised in the introductory chapter as adopting a comparative approach to researching the student experience. The facet of the student experience being considered is primarily its outcome: what students do after they have finished being students.

The main literature to which this article relates is that substantial body of work dealing with the relation between the worlds of higher education and work. In recent years, Teichler and his colleagues have been responsible for a significant amount of research and publication in this area themselves (e.g. Maiworm and Teichler 1996, Teichler 1999a, 1999b, 2000, Teichler and Maiworm 1994), though others, of course, have contributed as well (e.g. Brennan *et al.* 1993, Egerton 2001a, 2001b, Harvey 2000). Two other literatures of interest here are those which deal with making the higher education experience more relevant to the world of work (e.g. Bennett *et al.* 2000, Boud and Solomon 2001, van Ernst *et al.* 2001), and with general evaluations of changing national policy (e.g. Kogan and Hanney 2000).

The extension of European Union policy and funding into higher education has also stimulated comparative research into other aspects of higher education policy and practice within western Europe (e.g. Sullivan 2002).

References

Bennett, N., Dunne, E. and Carre, C. (2000) *Skills Development in Higher Education and Employment.* Buckingham, Open University Press.

Boud, D. and Solomon, N. (eds) (2001) *Work-based Learning: a new higher education?* Buckingham, Open University Press.

Brennan, J., Lyon, E., McGeevor, P. and Murray, K. (1993) *Students, Courses and Jobs.* London, Jessica Kingsley.

Egerton, M. (2001a) 'Mature Graduates I: occupational attainment and the effects of labour market duration', *Oxford Review of Education*, 27, 1, pp. 135–150.

Egerton, M. (2001b) 'Mature Graduates II: occupational attainment and the effects of social class', *Oxford Review of Education*, 27, 2, pp. 271–286.

van Ernst, B., Paterson, H., Langworthy, A., Costello, B. and Jones, M. (2001) 'Of Boxes and Bridges: a quality experience in the interface of higher education and the workplace', *Assessment and Evaluation in Higher Education*, 26, 5, pp. 437–448.

Harvey, L. (2000) 'New Realities: the relationship between higher education and employment', *Tertiary Education and Management*, 6, 1, pp. 3–17.

Kogan, M. and Hanney, S. (2000) *Reforming Higher Education.* London, Jessica Kingsley.

Maiworm, F. and Teichler, U. (1996) *Study Abroad and Early Career: experiences of former ERASMUS students.* London, Jessica Kingsley.

Sullivan, K. (2002) 'Credit and Grade Transfer within the European Union's SOCRATES Programme: unity in diversity or head in the sand?' *Assessment and Evaluation in Higher Education*, 27, 1, pp. 65–74.

Teichler, U. (1999a) 'Higher Education Policy and the World of Work: changing conditions and challenges', *Higher Education Policy*, 12, pp. 285–312.

Teichler, U. (1999b) 'Research on the Relationships between Higher Education and the World of Work: past achievements, problems and new challenges', *Higher Education*, 38, pp. 169–190.

Teichler, U. (2000) 'New Perspectives of the Relationship between Higher Education and Employment', *Tertiary Education and Management*, 6, pp. 76–92.

Teichler, U. and Maiworm, F. (1994) *Transition to Work: the experiences of former ERASMUS students.* London, Jessica Kingsley.

GRADUATE EMPLOYMENT AND WORK IN SELECTED EUROPEAN COUNTRIES

Introduction

It is very difficult to compare the employment and work situation of higher education graduates and the relationships between higher education and the world of work in the various European countries. The educational systems differ so considerably that we are not certain which institutions and programmes should be included in a comparative analysis. Most available statistics give the stocks of students and of the labour force, but not the transitions, i.e. the number of graduates, recent employees, etc. The definitions in the national statistics often vary as regards employment status, occupational categories, etc., and the comparative statistics of EUROSTAT (Eurostat,

1995), OECD (OECD, 1997a), UNESCO (UNESCO, 1997), or other agencies only reproduce national statistics. More in-depth information, such as on the period of search and transition, the work assignment or the use of knowledge on the job are collected in national surveys and the results cannot be compared internationally.

The aim of this article is to illustrate the major statistical information provided by OECD and EURYDICE, the agency of the European Commission in charge of educational information. Then, the limitations of these statistics will be discussed, as well as the potentials of graduate surveys to fill the gaps left by available statistics.

The account of available statistics was compiled in the framework of the research project Higher Education and Graduate Employment in Europe, sponsored by the European Commission's Targeted Socio-Economic Research (TSER) programme. Data are provided on only the nine countries for which country reports were also written, analysing the available statistics and surveys. The countries are Austria, Finland, France, Germany, Italy, the Netherlands, Norway, Spain and the UK.

Ratio of new entrant students

Statistics on the total number of students are always presented in educational statistics, but these absolute figures are strongly determined just by the size of the total population. It does not come as a surprise to find that the absolute number of students varies from somewhat less than 200,000 in Norway to over 2 million in France in 1995, since the total population ranges from just over 4 million in Norway and 5 million in Finland to almost 60 million in France and the UK and over 80 million in Germany.

All major comparisons on the relationships between higher education and work show that the ratio of those studying and graduating among the respective age groups is more indicative. However, there are no generally agreed upon statistical measures for establishing the proportion of those beginning their studies, those studying and those graduating from higher education. On the one hand, we find different definitions of new entry students, first year students, etc. We observe varying definitions of university, higher, tertiary and post-secondary education and statistics on the number or quota of graduates can be misleading because, for varying proportions of graduates, a diploma or degree might be viewed as an interim stage of pre-career education. On the other hand, major statistical agencies abandoned the idea of considering a certain 'age group' as the one corresponding to entry into higher education, period of study or graduation and thus defining a 'ratio of the respective age group' as they did in the past.

Table 28 provides data which can be understood as an approximation of the ratio of the new entrant students among the respective age group:

–   Among the nine EU countries included in the project, the rate of the 20-year-olds enrolled in some kind of (post-secondary) education varied in 1995 according to OECD statistics from about 26% in Austria to about 60% in the Netherlands.
–   The 'net entry rate' calculated by OECD predicts, with the help of the age distribution of new entrant students, the proportion of the current cohort of secondary leavers likely to take up study in the course of their life. The net entry rate for university-level education varies among the five countries for which it provides information from 26% in Austria to 43% in the UK.
–   The peak enrolment rate, i.e. the single age cohort with the highest proportion of students enrolled in higher education (the peak age ranged from 19 years in the UK to 23 years in Germany), varied in 1994/95 according to a chart provided by EURYDICE from about 15% in Austria to about 40% in France.

Table 28 Approximations to enrolment rates (percentages)

Country	Net enrol- ment rate in education, age 20 (1995)[1]	Net entry rates for university- level education (1995)[2]	Peak enrolment rate (1994/95)[3]		Percentage of age groups enrolled (1995)[4]		
			Min.	Max.	18–21	22–25	26–29
Austria	25.8	26	15	16	.	.	.
Finland	42.9	.	29	37	17.5	27.4	12.9
France	55.7	33	35	45	34.2	17.7	4.6
Germany	45.2	27	20	20	10.6	12.0	11.4
Netherlands	59.6	34	28	28	23.2	18.7	5.6
Norway	43.0	.	26	31	17.5	23.6	10.0
Spain	49.7	.	25	33	25.6	17.5	5.5
UK	39.2	43	28	30	25.8	9.3	4.8

Sources: [1]OECD, 1997b, p. 98; [2]OECD, 1997a, p. 165, [3]EURYDICE, 1997, pp. 90–91; [4]OECD, 1997b, p. 114

–   According to four-year groups of age cohorts (18–21, 22–25 and 26–29) aggregated in OECD statistics, the highest proportion of students in one of these groups varied in 1995 from about 12% in Germany (data on Austria were not presented) to 34% in France.

It should be taken into consideration that the statistics on new entrant students differ in various respects:

–   In some countries a distinction is made between students at universities and similar institutions or programmes and other ('non-university') institutions of higher education or programmes. These national demarcations often do not match the distinction made by OECD between university-level and non-university programmes because OECD includes in the former programmes of non-university institutions of higher education leading to a bachelor degree or an even more demanding degree (e.g. the German and Austrian *Fachhochschule* programmes or the Dutch HBO programmes).

–   The distinction often made between a university sector and a non-university sector is becoming more and more blurred in many countries. In some countries, it is seen in types of institution, curricular thrusts and levels of programmes, in others only according to one or two of these dimensions, and in others it is hardly visible or was officially discontinued through an upgrading of former non-university institutions.

–   The distinction between non-university higher education and post-secondary education (sometimes including elements of upper secondary or vocational education) officially not viewed as higher education is also becoming increasingly blurred. The international agencies that collect statistics are inclined to include post-secondary institutions in the presentations of higher education, often at the request of national governments, even if these continue to define them in their national analyses as being outside higher education (EURYDICE, 1997, p. 77, mentions the German *Schulen des Gesundheitswesen* as a case, and OECD, 1996, pp. 389–402, the training of *Techniker* in Germany or the Swiss *Fachausweis*).

–   Also, the length of study in post-secondary or higher education cannot be considered a consistent criterion. The suggestion made by the EU in December 1988 to define a higher education qualification as successful completion of three years' study might still not be satisfactory in international comparisons where, for example, the DUT awarded in France after two years of study by an IUT seems to be as well accepted by the labour market as a three-year degree in some other countries.

Graduation statistics

Ratio of graduates in the age group

(a) This ratio is cited in various country reports of the TSER project as well as in international statistics. One must bear in mind that the definitions vary in the calculation of these ratios. First, OECD calculated the ratio of tertiary graduates to the population of the 'typical' age (i.e. the graduation age of an educational course without any delay). It comes to the conclusion, as Table 29 shows, that the total number of graduations corresponds to more than 50% of the age group in the UK and to less than 20% in Austria. One must bear in mind, however, that a substantial proportion of persons takes more than one degree in a stage system of degrees (notably in the UK).

(b) Second, OECD calculated the 'net' ratio of graduates from university-level education, where the dispersion of age at the time of graduation is taken into consideration. Data are presented for only six countries, whereby the graduation ratios vary from 42% in the UK to 9% in Austria.

As the proportions of the graduations among the respective age groups include multiple degrees (e.g. a bachelor and a master or a *licence* and a *maîtrise* in a stage system), the number of higher education-trained persons among persons who are about 30 years of age could provide a more precise picture of the degree holders. But here some time has elapsed since graduation and therefore the proportion of recent graduates among the respective age group is likely to have increased in the meantime.

Table 29 Graduation ratios 1995 (percentages)

Country	Non-university certification	Short first university degree		Long first university degree		Second university degree		Ph.D.		Total	
	A	A	B	A	B	A	B	A	B	A	B
Austria	5	–	–	10	8	–	–	1.2	1.2	15	(9)
Finland	22	8	7	13	12	–	–	2.0	1.9	45	(21)
Germany	12	–	.	16	–	–	1.6	.	–	30	.
Italy	7	1	.	11	11	–	–	1.6	.	21	(11)
Netherlands	–	–	–	19	20	–	–	1.9	1.8	21	(32)
Spain	2	10	9	14	10	–	–	0.9	–	27	(19)
UK	17	31	30	–	–	11	11	0.9	1.0	60	(42)

A: Ratio of tertiary graduates to population at the typical age of graduation.
B: Net graduation rate.

Source: OECD 1997a, pp. 333–334

Table 30 Percentage of persons having completed higher education in 1995

Country	25–34-year-olds[1] having completed tertiary education	30–34-year-olds[2] with a higher education qualification	25–64-year-olds[3] having completed tertiary education		
			Non-univ.	Univ.	Total
Austria	9	10	2	6	(8)
Finland	23	25	9	12	(21)
France	25	22	8	11	(19)
Germany	21	24	10	13	(23)
Italy	8	9	–	8	(8)
Netherlands	25	24	–	22	(22)
Norway	32	.	11	18	(29)
Spain	27	23	4	12	(16)
UK	23	24	9	12	(21)

Source: [1]OECD 1997a, p. 40; [2] EURYDICE 1997, p. 172; [3]OECD 1997a, p. 38

(c) According to OECD statistics, the proportion of 25–34-year-olds having completed tertiary education was over 30% in Norway (32%); between 20% and 30% in the majority of countries included in the project, but only 9% in Austria and 8% in Italy (see Table 30).

(d) According to the EUROSTAT labour force survey, the proportion of 30–34-year-olds who were awarded a higher education qualification was between 20% and 30% in most EU countries included in the project: 25% in Finland, 24% each in Germany, the Netherlands and the UK, 23% in Spain, 22% in France, and 10% or less in Austria (10%) and Italy (9%).

The available data suggest that the proportion of recent graduates of the respective age group with at least a three-year degree varied in the early 1990s from about one quarter to less than 10% in the countries surveyed. One should take into consideration, however, that in some countries various programmes that were not formally recognised as higher education or that are shorter than three years were recently upgraded and new institutions were established. Thus, this proportion might increase substantially in some countries in the near future.

The proportion of young higher education-trained persons is greater in all countries surveyed than the ratio of higher education-trained persons in the total labour force. But the actual difference is smaller than one might expect on the basis of higher education statistics. This holds true because the employment statistics may include graduates from institutions which are not yet formally higher education institutions, because not all the expansion of student numbers has translated into a respective expansion of graduates and because the actual expansion of higher education since about the mid-1970s has been moderate in some countries.

The intergenerational differences of graduation quotas become most visible in a comparison between the cohorts of relatively recent graduates and the age groups of the labour force close to retirement. As Table 30 also shows, the proportion of graduates among 30-year-olds is on average almost twice as high as that of higher education-trained persons close to retirement age. This ratio, however, varies according to OECD and EUROSTAT data from about three times in Spain, a country with a relatively late expansion of higher education, to less than one-and-a-half times in Germany where the expansion of higher education started relatively early.

Age at time of graduation

If students pursue an educational career without any interruptions, second-chance options and prolongation, they might be awarded a short university degree (e.g. a British bachelor or a French *licence*) between the ages of 20 and 23 and a long university degree (e.g. an Austrian *Magister*, a French *maîtrise*, a German university *Diplom*, *Magister* or *Staatsexamen*, or an Italian *laurea*) between the ages of 22 and 26.

The OECD statistics, however, show that the average age of graduation is substantially higher. The median age ranges for short university-level degrees from about 22 in the UK to about 26 in Finland and Sweden; for long university degrees between 25 and 28; and for second university degrees (e.g. master subsequent to bachelor) from about 25 to about 30. There is also a substantial difference within the individual countries. For example, the age at which a bachelor degree is awarded in the UK is 21 at the 25th percentile and 25 at the 75th percentile. The respective figures for graduates of long university programmes are 24 and 28 years in the Netherlands and Norway, 25 and 29 years in Italy and 26 and 30 years both in Austria and Finland (OECD, 1997a, p. 335).

Gender

On average, more women than men graduate. In more than half the countries, the number is clearly higher, as EUROSTAT data of 1994–95 graduates suggest: 59.8% in Finland, 57.0% in Spain, 56.1% in Italy, 55.4% in Norway and 53.6% in the UK. In some countries, such as Austria (51.6%), the Czech Republic (51.2%) and the Netherlands (49.9%), approximately the same number of women as men graduate. Only in Germany (45.2%) was the number of women graduates clearly lower than that of men.

The data suggest that the proportion of men is higher when the time to obtain the respective degree is longer. In all countries, the number of men awarded a Ph.D. or equivalent is higher than that of women [see Table 31].

The ratio of women graduates, however, continues to vary substantially according to subject. They were the majority in humanities in all countries for which data are available (from 76% in Italy to 55% in Germany). In most countries, they dominated in medicine (in Spain, 72%). But more men graduated in Germany and Italy. In law/business, women outnumbered men in a few countries, and in the natural sciences, there were almost as many women as men in some countries. In engineering/architecture and mathematics/computer science (the latter except for Italy), women continued to be a clear minority. But again, differences between countries are worth noting. For example, women made up 20% or more of graduates in engineering and architecture in Italy and Norway, whereas they made up only 4% in Spain.

Altogether we note that, in most of the countries surveyed, the proportion of women students and graduates has substantially grown over the last two decades. This has caused a substantial change in the composition of qualified labour according to gender.

Fields of study

The fields of study vary more strikingly than we would expect. According to statistics collected by EUROSTAT:

–   The social sciences (including economics) comprise about 25% on average of the degrees across the countries surveyed. They range from 37% in the Netherlands to 9% in Finland.

Table 31 Proportions of men and women graduating of the typical age group 1995 (percentages)

Country	Non-university certification		Short first university degree		Long first university degree		Second university degree		Ph.D.	
	M	W	M	W	M	W	M	W	M	W
Austria	3	7	–	–	10	9	–	–	1.7	0.7
Finland	14	31	10	6	11	14	–	–	2.2	1.7
Germany	11	14	–	–	18	14	–	–	2.1	1.0
Italy	5	9	1	1	10	12	–	–	1.8	1.7
Netherlands	–	–	–	–	18	20	–	–	2.2	1.5
Norway	42	53	12	23	5	6	9	7	1.2	0.5
Spain	2	2	8	13	12	16	–	–	1.0	0.7
UK	12	22	30	32	–	–	11	11	1.3	0.6

Source: OECD 1997a, p. 333

– The other fields (with teacher training as the largest component) comprise 20%, varying from 38% in Italy to 12% in the UK.
– 16% on average were enrolled in engineering, ranging from 23% in Finland and Germany to 8% in Italy.
– The proportion of medical science graduates was 14% on average, ranging from 30% in Finland to 9% in Norway.
– 13% graduated in humanities and fine arts fields, varying from 22% in Norway to 6% in Finland.
– Only 7% graduated in mathematics, natural sciences and computer sciences, varying from 12% in the UK to 3% in Norway.
– Finally, 5% on average were enrolled in law, ranging from 14% in Spain to 2% in Norway.

This also holds true if we look at major groups of fields. At one extreme, 62% of graduates in Finland but only 21% in Norway were graduates in science and engineering. OECD had already pointed out in its synthesis report of the project *Transition from Higher Education to Employment* (OECD, 1993) that the higher education systems of industrial countries differ strikingly in their quantitative emphasis on the sciences or on the humanities and social sciences.

The figures vary somewhat less, but still to a considerable extent, if we take into account only university-level degrees as reported by OECD (1997a, p. 340). For example, the percentage awarded in humanities and general fields (including teacher training) ranges from 45% in the Netherlands to 25% in Italy, that in medical sciences from 22% in Italy to 5% in Japan, and that in engineering from 26% in Finland to 11% in Spain.

It would be interesting to examine how far differences in the subject composition of graduates reflect corresponding differences in the occupation and economic structure between the European countries or indicate different links between subjects and occupational areas.

Table 32 Unemployment rates one year and five years after graduation in 1995 (percentages)

Country	One year after graduation[1]		Five years after graduation[1]		Total labour force[2]	
	Non-university	University	Non-university	University	Non-university	University
Finland	20	9	11	6	9.7	6.2
France	17	20	6	10	5.9	7.0
Germany	.	5	.	.	5.2	4.7
Italy	.	52	.	.	.	7.3
Spain	58	46	31	17	16.6	13.8

Source: [1]OECD 1997a, p. 276 [2]OECD 1997a, p. 252

Employment statistics

The transition from higher education to employment is not addressed in international statistics. But OECD collected data for some countries on employment rates one year after graduation and five years after graduation, as well as unemployment rates of 25–29-year-olds according to educational level.

Unemployment

The data presented in Table 32 suggest that the speed of transition from higher education to employment varies substantially according to country. One year after graduation, the unemployment rate of university graduates from German universities is no longer higher than that of university-trained persons in the labour force. Similarly, the unemployment quota of university-trained persons who are under 30 in Germany and the UK hardly differs from that of all university-trained persons in these countries. In contrast, early unemployment is far more frequent among recent graduates or young higher education-trained persons than among the average of higher education-trained persons in Italy, Spain and France.

Participation in the labour force

Available statistics show that the participation of higher education-trained persons in the labour force is very high. Even among men, the labour force participation of persons with a university-level degree is on average 8% higher than among all 25–64-year-olds.

Higher education-trained women are much more frequently professionally active than those who did not attend or complete higher education, as Table 33 shows:

– In Spain, we observe the biggest difference: 84% of men as compared to 47% of women. The respective rates for those with a non-university qualification are 94% and 77%, and for those with a university degree 91% and 84%.
– In contrast, the labour force participation of university-trained persons in Finland hardly differs according to gender: the respective ratios are 93% and 89%. This also holds true for those who do not hold a college degree. The overall labour force participation rate was 83% for men and 77% for women.

Table 33 Labour force participation of higher education-trained persons by gender in 1995 (percentages)

Country	Educational attainment					
	Non-university education		University education		All levels of education	
	Men	Women	Men	Women	Men	Women
Austria	88	85	94	86	85	63
Finland	87	84	93	89	83	77
France	94	85	92	81	85	68
Germany	90	82	93	83	86	65
Italy	–	–	92	82	81	45
Netherlands	–	–	91	81	84	58
Norway	91	84	95	91	88	77
Spain	94	77	91	84	84	47
UK	91	82	93	87	87	70

Source: OECD 1997a pp. 266–267

Higher education and income

The statistics also show the income advantages of graduates. They earn on average more than one-and-a-half times as much as those having completed upper secondary education. As Table 34 shows, among those who are between 30 and 44 years of age, those having completed non-university higher education earned between 37% (UK) and 7% (Germany) more than those having completed upper secondary education. British university degree holders earned 90% more and Dutch graduates 29% more than upper secondary school leavers. Women had a slightly higher income than men through participation in higher education. One should bear in mind, though, that in the countries surveyed, they earn on average only about two-thirds as much as men holding the same level credentials.

OECD calculated rates of return to investment in education for some countries (OECD, 1997a, p. 272). High rates are reported for the UK (14% for non-university

Table 34 Relative earnings of higher education-trained persons aged 30–44 by gender in 1995 (upper secondary education = 100)

Country	Relative earnings					
	Non-university tertiary education			University education		
	M	W	Total	M	W	Total
Finland	121	123	121	175	169	175
France	138	139	132	180	170	174
Germany	105	114	107	148	165	159
Italy	–	–	–	139	120	129
Netherlands	121	134	122	148	160	159
Norway	129	131	129	153	147	147
UK	115	159	137	162	210	190

Source: OECD 1997a, pp. 266–267

graduates and 19% for university graduates), France (20% and 13%) and Finland (12% and 14%). Moderate rates are seen in Norway (8% and 13%) and Germany (9% and 8%). They are relatively low in Italy (5% for university graduates). All these calculations refer to higher education-trained persons in general, not to recent graduates.

Other issues

The relevance of the graduation rate

The debate on the relationships between higher education and employment has sometimes been inappropriately overshadowed by the expansion of the number or ratio of new entrant students or the total number of students. When references are made to 'mass higher education' and its possible impacts, one tends to refer to these types of data. Actually, however, the quota of graduates among the corresponding age group is considerably smaller than that of new entrant students. This is only partly due to the fact that increases among new entrant students only affect the graduation rate a few years later. More important, though, a substantial proportion of students complete their studies without obtaining a degree or any other credential. Depending on the country, between less than 20% and over 60% drop out.

In the mid-1990s, the quota of graduates among the corresponding age group varied within the European Union from more than 30% to less than 10%. One has to bear in mind, however, that the international statistics published by OECD, EURO-STAT, etc. often include students and graduates from institutions which are not officially considered 'higher education' in their respective countries. If the statistics followed national definitions of higher education, the quotas would be lower in various countries, and even more diverse across European countries.

In theory, we could explain the different graduation ratios and their links to employment according to three dimensions:

-   the extent to which higher education satisfies a 'hard' demand, i.e. higher education produces graduates for which a demand is undisputedly conceived by most politicians, practitioners and experts: is it now about 10% among recent graduates in most European countries or higher? Does it differ substantially between the European countries?
-   the extent to which and in which way higher education serves the labour market beyond such a 'hard' demand: how many graduates fill jobs for which prior studies are seen as rather useful or at least useful for some of the assignments on the one hand, and, on the other, how many graduates accept jobs where they feel underemployed or face difficulties in finding a job at all?
-   the extent to which countries differ in naming institutions and programmes which fall between university-level education and skill-labour training as 'higher' or 'tertiary'/'post-secondary' education.

One might ask: what are the benefits and what are the drawbacks if the individual member states of the European Union pursue divergent policies in these respects? To what extent is transparency needed and achieved? Would less divergence be beneficial?

Employment problems of recent graduates

Most studies that discuss issues of graduate employment on the basis of education and employment data are guided by a question which has prevailed since about the mid-1970s: what proportion of graduates succeeds in being employed and taking on assignments which match their studies and level of education, and what proportion, in contrast, ends up with a less fortunate link between study and employment? Many politicians, practitioners and experts believe that this question has kept its relevance, whereas others call for a paradigmatic shift at the advent of the 'massification of higher education', the 'knowledge society' or the 'life-long-learning society' (Teichler, 1999).

In discussing the first question, one tries to establish the extent to which graduates face problems in finding employment, taking a first regular and somewhat demanding job, and ending up in a position and with an assignment which can be viewed as appropriate.

More fundamentally, one could raise two questions:

– To what extent do we observe a problem of transition from higher education to employment?
– What do we know, in observing the first years after graduation, about a match or mismatch between higher education and employment/work?

We face a major methodological problem: most of the information available cannot be clearly demarcated according to these dimensions and questions. Thus, it is no surprise that the interpretations of the available data are quite heterogeneous and often lack clarity in terms of their reference to those basic questions.

It is generally assumed, first, that the number of privileged and intellectually highly demanding positions has not grown over the last few decades in line with the expansion of higher education. Second, the perceived threshold between a somewhat appropriate graduate job and 'underemployment' or 'inappropriate' employment certainly has changed as a consequence of the growing supply of graduates. Third, it seems obvious that employment in general – and more especially that of higher education-trained persons – has become more risky in recent years than 'regular employment' for a graduate in the past.

Beyond that, it seems difficult to make generalisations about changes of graduate employment and work in European countries during the 1990s. The situation seems to have improved in the UK. In some countries, we noted ups and downs, for example in France and Norway, and in some countries, prospects for graduates have clearly worsened, e.g. in Austria and Finland.

It is obvious, though, that in the 1990s, the debates on employment and work of higher education graduates tend to remain within the same paradigmatic domain as in about the mid-1990s: there is concern that a certain proportion of graduates will not find employment and work which match the concept of a graduate job, and the question remains as to how grave this concern must be and who are those who are most at risk. There are concurrent debates about a knowledge society, new technologies etc., but they continue to play at most a supplementary role, if currently the employment and work situation of recent graduates is assessed.

Equality of opportunity and graduate employment

Available statistics suggest that parental income and educational attainment continue to be linked to their children's participation in higher education. Less information, however, is available on the relationships between parental background and education and career in recent years than for 1970.

In contrast, women's opportunities for study and subsequent employment are among the best documented themes. The available data show, first, that the total number of women graduating from higher education has surpassed that of men in the majority of countries analysed. There remain some advantages for men, as far as graduation from science and engineering fields, being awarded an advanced degree and entry into the labour force are concerned, but the gap has become smaller. The data also suggest that a higher education degree makes a greater difference for women than for men.

Women clearly have fewer career opportunities than men when child-care begins to absorb them, and only a few catch up on the career ladder at a later stage. The measures needed to counterbalance this career disadvantage are obviously outside the domain of higher education (except for improving opportunities in academic careers).

Limits of statistics and the role surveys can play

Statistics on graduate employment and on the relationships between higher education and employment are often criticised methodologically, but the critique is sound. This indicates a widespread desire to have information at hand and to accept some weaknesses in the data.

Very often, doubts are raised regarding the comparability of education and employment data. Definitions, for example, vary concerning the sector of higher education or tertiary education and the types of institutions as well as levels of programmes and degrees. Therefore the definitions of university-level education and tertiary education used by OECD or the definition used by the European Commission of higher education do not necessarily coincide with the definitions of the sectors by the respective countries which provided the statistical information to these agencies. Four other limitations are worth noting:

–   First, available statistics usually inform on only a very small list of variables.
–   Second, statistics often present a snapshot of the learners and the labour force at a given time, thereby neglecting 'paths', 'passages' and sequences in the life course.
–   Third, statistical data are often provided in isolation. They do not allow us to analyse, for example, whether it is the socio-economic background or the type of course that determines the graduates' career opportunities.
–   Fourth, official statistical data gathering tends to avoid 'subjective' themes. Information is gathered which seems to be factual and 'objective' even if the 'indicator' might be irrelevant for the issue at stake. As will be pointed out below, 'over-education' cannot be measured only by analysing the statistical links between educational attainment and occupation. Ratings by graduates must be taken into consideration, even though they might be somewhat biased.

Statistics and surveys – a dubious juxtaposition

Student and graduate surveys do not differ in essence from statistics, since the information compiled in statistics is often based on surveys. Statistical offices often send questionnaires to companies, educational institutions, households or individuals to gather information that is published as statistics. However, statistics tend to be different from survey studies because they are:

–   official, i.e. undertaken by public agencies which often have the legal right to request certain information,
–   large-scale, i.e. including the whole 'population' or at least a large sample,
–   short as regards the themes addressed by the individual survey,
–   fact-oriented and 'objective', as stated above.

Some graduate surveys could be considered 'statistics' rather than 'surveys' in the way these terms tend to be distinguished in the public debates. For example, a long-lasting tradition exists in the UK of surveying the 'first destinations' of university graduates (bachelor level) six months after graduation. The institutions of higher education help to trace the data. The data set has all the strengths and limitations of a short, fact-oriented inquiry. It includes the name of the higher education institution, the field of study, the employment status and the economic sector.

Some countries have opted for a mix of statistics and surveys in undertaking regular graduate surveys with extended questionnaires which primarily rely on factual information and include some assessments by graduates. This, for example, holds true for Norway and the Dutch HBO sector.

In these countries as well as in others, graduate surveys are undertaken which tend to be broader in the themes addressed. They also tend to trace some elements of the educational and career paths retrospectively and to determine time spans since graduation (instead of age categories predominantly employed in statistical studies). And they include individuals' perceptions and opinions (cf. the examples presented in *Higher Education and Employment*, 1995, and Brennan, Kogan & Teichler, 1995).

Themes addressed in graduate surveys

One of the major themes of graduate surveys is the transition from higher education to employment. They might address:

–   the collection of information about the graduate labour market,
–   the support sought for and provided by employment agencies, institutions of higher education, friends and relatives, etc.,
–   the length of the search,
–   search activities,
–   search criteria as well as perceived recruitment criteria on the part of the employers,
–   transitory activities, such as accepting jobs that are not considered related to one's professional identity,
–   timing of transition to first regular employment,
–   characteristics of first employment, e.g. short-term contract, involuntary part-time contract, etc.

Findings show that the transition process is relatively autonomous where smartness and luck might play a major role. It is not merely a stage where the extent to which education shapes and predetermines subsequent careers becomes manifest, but a stage where decisions are at stake.

Links between study and occupational status and job assignments are a second major theme of graduate surveys. Most seem to be based on the assumption that higher education does not serve the expected useful function for the employment system and students' expectation if it merely helps to secure employment. It is generally expected that study and the kind of work match to a certain extent and that the nature of the employment and work conditions will be assessed as desirable, e.g. in terms of demanding, challenging, relatively autonomous work, etc., and that a relatively privileged status is ensured.

This is clearly the area in which the diversity of theories, socio-political notions, concepts on the part of the graduates and difficulties of measuring and of collecting data lead to great heterogeneity of definitions, measurements and findings. In summarising available research from the late 1970s to the mid-1980s, I showed that the proportion of 'inappropriate employment', 'mismatch', 'underemployment' or similarly defined conditions varied between 3% and over 40% in surveys undertaken in various European countries. The differences were primarily due to the concepts and methods employed (Teichler, 1989).

In the 1990s, the respective concepts and findings do not differ as strikingly as in the past. In the meantime, many graduates, politicians and experts have adjusted to a middle-of-the-road attitude whereby the majority of graduates will no longer be the 'chosen few' but will still expect above-average job assignments and careers. But definitions of 'over-education', etc. still vary substantially, as the following observations underscore.

Some analyses try to infer weak links between higher education and employment in terms of 'under-employment' or 'inappropriate employment' on the basis of occupational categories. Categories such as 'lower white collar', manual worker jobs, etc. are considered from the outside as not matching a higher education degree. They systematically tend to underestimate the variety of job requirements within occupational categories, the emergence of new demanding job assignments and upgrading trends. Therefore, most surveys ask graduates to state whether their status is inappropriate, whether they can use their knowledge on the job, whether their job corresponds to their education, etc. They show that a substantial number of graduates employed in occupational categories that do not necessarily require a degree consider that their studies correspond to the appropriate level of preparation for their career.

Studies combining a factual and 'subjective' approach also found that a substantial proportion of those employed in jobs that do not necessarily require a degree preferred such employment for other reasons, e.g. living with their partner, job security, temporary involvement in child rearing, political motives, etc. Also, a study showed that the utilisation on the job of the knowledge acquired during their studies tends to slightly decline over the years, whereas the proportion of those who consider themselves as holding a position that is appropriate for degree-holders increases over the years after graduation (Schomburg & Teichler, 1993). The study also pointed out that two categories of graduates observe a partial mismatch: those employed in higher education and research lack a certain degree of job security, and many socially and politically engaged graduates accept a lower-paid job if the assignment is viewed as relevant and interesting.

Finally, graduate surveys help us to measure the impact of higher education on graduate employment. Already the employment statistics might show the difference of career patterns according to the type of higher institution or the level of degree and how the field of study influences access to certain occupations. Graduate surveys might go a step further and examine whether the choice of a certain institution was meaningful or whether certain characteristics of study programmes, provisions and conditions put a footprint on graduate employment and work. So far, only a few graduate surveys carry out such complex analyses.

For example, a Dutch analysis on factors determining HBO graduates' employment indicates that, apart from regions and fields of study, the duration of study plays a role: prolonging study leads to protracted entry into the labour market and lower level jobs. The study suggests a relatively moderate impact of gender, if we exclude low monthly wages as a consequence of frequent part-time work.

Improvement of databases and research

As far as the knowledge base is concerned, we note that comparative statistical data for an analysis of higher education and subsequent careers have improved recently. However, problems not only remain as regards the comparability of data, but also the range of themes to be analysed with the help of statistics has remained small. What improvements could be made?

First, one could call for an improvement of the *European education and employment statistics relevant for the relationships between higher education and employment*:

–   an extension of themes for which data are collected and aggregated,
–   an improvement of categories in order to increase the relevance of the statistics,
–   a harmonisation of data in Europe in order to increase their comparability.

Second, *a more ambitious reporting* could be extended. *Key Education Data* by EURYDICE (1997) and *Education at a Glance* by OECD (1997a) both show the achievements reached and the possibilities for improvement.

Graduate surveys can provide information on many important aspects of the relationships between higher education and employment. The variety of the approaches and themes chosen both offers opportunities and sets limits: opportunities, because the multitude of relevant aspects cannot be covered by a single study, and limits, because the comparability of findings is low. Despite the virtue of varied approaches and themes, the survey of the relationships between higher education and employment in a large number of European countries undertaken in 1999 with the help of the TSER programme shows the potentials of regular comparative graduate surveys in Europe.

Finally, one should bear in mind that *substantial financial means are required to undertake regular European surveys*. Very scattered surveys which do not really provide any opportunity for comparison across institutions, fields, countries and over time will continue to prevail if no efforts are made to establish a regular European graduate survey.

References

Brennan, J., Kogan, M. & Teichler, U. (Eds) (1995) *Higher Education and Work* (London and Bristol, PA, Jessica Kingsley Publishers).
EUROSTAT (1995) *Bildung in der europaischen Union: Daten und Kennzahlen* (Luxembourg, Amt für amtliche Veröffentlichungen der europäischen Gemeinschaften).
EURYDICE (1997) *Key Data on Education in the European Union 97* (Luxembourg, Office for Official Publications of the European Communities).
"Higher Education and Employment" (special issues) (1995) *European Journal of Education*, 30, nos. 1 and 2.
OECD (1992) *Transition from Higher Education to Employment*. 4 volumes (Paris, OECD).
OECD (1993) *Transition from Higher Education to Employment: Synthesis Report* (Paris, OECD).
OECD (1997a) *Education at a Glance: OECD Indicators 1997* (Paris, OECD).
OECD (1997b) *Education Policy Analysis 1997* (Paris, OECD).
Schomburg, H. & Teichler, U. (1993) Does the programme matter? Approach and major findings of the Kassel Graduate Survey, *Higher Education in Europe*, 18, pp. 37–58.

Teichler, U. (1989) Research on higher education and work, *European Journal of Education*, 24, pp. 223–247.

Teichler, U. (1999) Higher education policy and the world of work: changing conditions and challenges, *Higher Education Policy*, 12, pp. 285–312.

UNESCO (1997) *UNESCO Statistical Yearbook 1997* (Paris, UNESCO).

CHAPTER 8

THE PhD AND THE AUTONOMOUS SELF
Gender, rationality and postgraduate pedagogy

Lesley Johnson, Alison Lee and Bill Green

Studies in Higher Education, 25, 2, 135–147, 2000

EDITOR'S INTRODUCTION

This article focuses on what has hitherto been an under-researched and essentially 'secret' area of academic life, but which is now being subjected to an increasing amount of research: the supervisory relationship between research students and academics. The nature of this relationship varies significantly between disciplines, with research students in the laboratory sciences typically experiencing much more regular, even day-to-day, supervision as part of a research group. This article, however, examines the experience in the humanities and social sciences, where the supervisory relationship is more typically individualised, and research students often pursue a lonely road, perhaps only meeting their supervisor every month or so.

The authors stress the contested nature of the concepts of autonomy and independence, which underlie many understandings of the supervisory relationship, and highlight its gendered aspect. They present and analyse a number of alternative models for supervision: an 'always-already' independent model involving benign neglect or tough-mindedness from a typically male supervisor; an 'invisible pedagogy' model, involving more subtle forms of regulation; and possible feminist responses to these.

This article was categorised in the introductory chapter as adopting a critical perspective to course design. As the authors indicate, it forms part of a larger project exploring the history of PhD practices in Australia, and is based on oral history interviews with both established academics and contemporary supervisors. The article is very carefully written, contextualising the experiences of selected interviewees, as illustrated through quotations, within existing writing on supervision, changing academic practices and feminist perspectives.

While only three interviewees are directly referred to in the article, a range of issues is raised regarding the supervisory relationship. The article offers an example of how to make the most of your data.

As suggested, a growing number of recent publications have focused on the research student experience and the supervisory relationship. These can be divided into two kinds: the more analytical (e.g. Bartlett and Mercer 2000, Delamont *et al.* 2000, Heath 2002, Hunt 2001, Parry 1998, Tinkler and Jackson 2000) and those adopting a 'how to' approach, offering guidance on good practice (e.g. Cryer 1996, Delamont *et al.* 1997, Murray 2002, Potter 2002, Phillips and Pugh 2000). There are also increasing numbers of studies on postgraduate education – taught as well as research – in general (e.g. Becher *et al.* 1994, Burgess 1994, Knight 1997, Smeby 2002, Taylor 2002).

126   *Lesley Johnson* et al.

References

Bartlett, A. and Mercer, G. (2000) 'Reconceptualising Discourses of Power in Postgraduate Pedagogies', *Teaching in Higher Education*, 5, 2, pp. 195–204.

Becher, T., Henkel, M. and Kogan, M. (1994) *Graduate Education in Britain*. London, Jessica Kingsley.

Burgess, R. (ed.) (1994) *Postgraduate Education and Training in the Social Sciences: processes and products*. London, Jessica Kingsley.

Cryer, P. (1996) *The Research Student's Guide to Success*. Buckingham, Open University Press.

Delamont, S., Atkinson, P. and Parry, O. (1997) *Supervising the PhD: a guide to success*. Buckingham, Open University Press.

Delamont, S., Atkinson, P. and Parry, O. (2000) *The Doctoral Experience: success and failure in Graduate School*. London, Palmer.

Heath, T. (2002) 'A Quantitative Analysis of PhD Students' Views of Supervision', *Higher Education Research and Development*, 21, 1, pp. 41–53.

Hunt, C. (2001) 'Climbing out of the Void: moving from chaos to concepts in the presentation of a thesis', *Teaching in Higher Education*, 6, 3, pp. 351–367.

Knight, P. (1997) *Masterclass: learning, teaching and curriculum in taught master's degrees*. London, Cassell.

Murray, R. (2002) *How to Write a Thesis*. Buckingham, Open University Press.

Parry, S. (1998) 'Disciplinary Discourse in Doctoral Theses', *Higher Education*, 36, pp. 273–299.

Phillips, B. and Pugh, D. (2000) *How to Get a PhD: a handbook for students and their supervisors*. Buckingham, Open University Press, third edition.

Potter, S. (ed.) (2002) *Doing Postgraduate Research*. London, Sage.

Smeby, J.-C. (2002) 'Consequences of Project Organisation in Graduate Education', *Teaching in Higher Education*, 7, 2, pp. 139–151.

Taylor, J. (2002) 'Changes in Teaching and Learning in the Period to 2005: the case of postgraduate higher education in the UK', *Journal of Higher Education Policy and Management*, 24, 1, pp. 53–73.

Tinkler, P. and Jackson, C. (2000) 'Examining the Doctorate: institutional policy and the PhD examination process in Britain', *Studies in Higher Education*, 25, 2, pp. 167–180.

THE PhD AND THE AUTONOMOUS SELF

Introduction

Fundamentally, the department (and indeed the university itself) was unashamedly elitist. Since only a tiny proportion of school-leavers went on to university . . ., academics could persist in the conviction that they were catering for the brightest and most dedicated. That attitude manifested itself in all sorts of ways, not the least in the apparent indifference to students, for which university people were to be so strenuously criticised in later years. There was indeed an icy, magisterial disdain in much of their dealings with us. And yet few of us resented it, because it was recognised by many – certainly by me – as a sign of respect. It was a wonderful liberation to be left to your own devices, without the watchful eye of those in charge. It seemed to mark more surely than any other ceremony our entry into the adult world, our being responsible for ourselves. That independence came at a price, it is true . . . Of course, the examinations in November revealed all: those who failed to meet rigorous standards could expect little mercy. Yet none of us would have imagined that the responsibility was anyone's but ours. Most understood that our teachers equipped us with the means of meeting the standards required of us. To have taken steps to supervise our progress in the way of our contemporary academics would have seemed a breach of good manners – or intolerable intrusion.

(Riemer, 1998, p. 13)

Andrew Riemer here recalls his life as an honours student at Sydney University in the late 1950s. He goes on to describe his experiences as a PhD student in London a few years later with a supervisor who also showed very little interest in his work. The only real opportunity Riemer had of contact with his PhD supervisor, the elusive Mr Brown, during the course of his candidature, was to find him in the local pub just off Tottenham Court Road. Riemer describes himself in the subtitle of his book as an 'accidental academic', yet his account of the years before he became an academic, of his education as an honours and PhD student in English Literature, and of his subsequent life as an academic at Sydney University, include a number of references to the fantasies which clearly led him to undertake these forms of training. He speaks, at various points in the book, of the dream of becoming an academic and of entertaining 'fantasies of the scholar's life', where he imagined himself in 'a handsome panelled library with thick leather-bound folios propped up in front of me' (Riemer, 1998, p. 64). He describes his aspirations to walk 'among dreaming spires' (p. 40) as he prepares to meet his PhD supervisor for the first time after arriving in England. He celebrates the pedagogy of indifference that he experienced at Sydney University and London University in the 1950s, which perversely, perhaps, made him feel part of an elite, but the description of his fantasies of being a scholar also indicates what sustained him as an aspiring academic and enabled him to find encouragement in disdain and neglect.

Understanding the role of such fantasies is important in explaining the deep investments in, and attachments to, the existing structures and processes of the PhD that prevail in the humanities and social sciences today. The strength of these continuing attachments can be seen in the resistance to, and unease caused by, debates about so-called 'professional doctorates', as they can in the relentless search for quality controls on postgraduate education that do not at any stage seek to make either the PhD itself, or its primary pedagogical technology, the supervision relationship, problematic. Remaining substantially unaltered since the introduction of the degree in Australia after the Second World War, and deriving in large part from the practices developed in England in the 40 years prior to that (Simpson, 1983), the supervision relationship is personalised and frequently protracted. Through the pedagogical technologies of 'supervision' and of 'study', an intelligible academic identity is produced, a licensed scholar, a 'doctor', who, appropriately credentialled, is deemed safe to pursue research unsupervised, autonomously. More private than any other scene of teaching and learning, supervision – and more generally, the pedagogic practices of the PhD – in the humanities and social sciences at least, have remained largely unscrutinised and unquestioned.

Yet the supervision relationship is often fraught and unsatisfactory – as much marked by neglect, abandonment and indifference as it is by careful instruction or the positive and proactive exercise of pastoral power. The pedagogy of 'magisterial disdain', which Riemer describes as characterising the university as an elite institution, continues to have a role in the arena of postgraduate research training in the mass higher education system we have today. The experience of isolation and abjection often appears so widespread as to be structural and endemic, a seemingly 'necessary' feature of the doctoral programme for many, rather than an accidental and ameliorable problem. Indeed, it may in some senses be a condition of the production of independence and autonomy, which is the goal of the pedagogy and practice of the PhD. Certainly, Riemer's account of his experiences as an honours and PhD student suggests that for him this was the case. His narrative begins to show how the historically produced relations of power and desire between the academic and student are complexly bound up with the production and experience of, and the investment in, 'independence'. At the same time, we suggest, this production has, until recently, been intimately connected to, and necessarily dependent upon, the preservation of the domain of doctoral education for a tiny 'exemplary elite'. This has, of course, been historically a normatively masculine elite.

As Anna Yeatman (1998) points out, however, the 'traditional' (no matter how recent) personalised and privatised practices of the PhD supervision pedagogy are deeply problematic in the context of the development of a mass higher education system where PhD candidature has become much more frequent. For Yeatman (1998, p. 23) it is:

> simply inadequate to the demands of a situation where many supervisees are barely socialised into the demands and rigours of an academic scholarly and research culture. It is especially inadequate to the needs of many new PhD aspirants who, by historical-cultural positioning, have not been invited to imagine themselves as subjects of genius. These include all those who are marginalised by the dominant academic scholarly culture: women, and men or women who come from the non-dominant class, ethnic or race positions. When PhD candidature was infrequent, the rare one of these could distinguish themselves as an exception to the rule of their particular gender, ethnic or class category, and show that by their highly exceptional qualities, they deserved to be admitted as a disciple. Even then, it was rare that their minority status did not continue to qualify their own belief as the belief of others in their *genius*. Now, however, there is a high proportion of PhD candidates who do not fit the old mould, and whose numbers bely any exceptionalist approach to them.

This article, then, explores the problematic character of ideas of autonomy and the independent scholar that underpin the traditional practices of postgraduate pedagogy. Despite the implication of Yeatman's argument that these practices are no longer appropriate in a mass higher education system, they persist largely unaltered in the current circumstances. Moves to make the training component of the PhD more explicit and more pronounced, in Australia, but more particularly in Britain, do not appear to have challenged in any fundamental way the deep attachment that persists among humanities and social sciences scholars, at least, to the supervisory relationship as being central to the pedagogy of the PhD.

The article is part of a larger research project on the history and practices of the PhD in the humanities and social sciences in Australia. In this project we seek to examine the productivity of current practices of supervision and doctoral education more generally. We are interested in what form of personhood is assumed by the pedagogic practices of the PhD – that is, what do they set out to produce in terms of capacities and forms of subjectivity, whether it be by the pedagogy of indifference that Riemer celebrates, or newer, more bureaucratised approaches in which the progress of the student is more closely monitored, at the same time as the traditional supervisory relationship remains fundamentally intact (see also, Lee & Williams, 1999).

We have begun to see the gender problematics of the PhD as intimately connected to a series of paradoxes arguably at the heart of the enterprise of doctoral education in the late 1990s, but which stem from much older tensions and paradoxes central to modern conceptions of the educational project since the Enlightenment. In this article we focus particularly on the gendered character of the independent, autonomous scholar that lies at the heart of the pedagogic practices and regularity regimes of the PhD, and on the paradoxical nature of the processes of producing the autonomous scholar self that is seen as the goal of doctoral education. We look at some of the arguments of feminists who have addressed the question of the possibility of a feminist pedagogy and the implications for doctoral education. We conclude by suggesting that some of the arguments currently emerging about new modes of knowledge production may provide some fruitful directions for the future, in thinking about how to address some of the problems of doctoral education identified in this article.

The article draws on both oral history interviews of key figures in the formation of several humanities and social sciences disciplines in Australia, as well as interviews of current supervisors in these same disciplines. In this study we have focused primarily on the disciplines of English (and cultural studies), sociology and education. Many of the scholars interviewed for the oral history part of our project continue to supervise students today, but they also emerge as key figures in our interviews with current academic staff, either as models for their own supervisory practices or as central to the formation of the disciplines in which they work. We are not trying to present a detailed empirical account here of the interview work of our study, but to use several exemplary statements to explore the questions outlined earlier. The oral history interviews, as well as Riemer's account of his development as an academic, reveal the importance of the colonial relationship of Australia to Britain in the 1950s in the institutionalisation of these disciplines. This history is apparent, not only in the dominance of the fantasy of Oxbridge in the academic imaginary in Australia, but also in the way Australia adopted the British model of PhD training when it began to provide this form of training in the immediate post-war period. Australian postgraduate research education continues to rely almost solely on the production of a dissertation by the student after a period of extended study. Coursework is limited.

'Always-already' independent

> There was no student whose thesis I read in full. And I told them at the beginning. And I said I'm not going to be reading more than half of this and if you are uneasy about that, I won't supervise you. I will recommend someone else. Because it is more than about . . . it is more than just writing a thesis. It's about learning to be independent. And I think that's one of the great things in scholarship, learning . . . but it's tough, you've got to learn to rely on your own judgement and not to run to the supervisor for every problem that you have. And that's the test in the end. And you can fail it.
>
> (*Oral history interview 1*, April 1998)

In this interview for the oral history part of our study, the interviewee describes her own experience of being a DPhil student in Oxford in the early 1950s as providing the model for the supervisory practices she was later to adopt, on her return to Australia, to ensure her students were independent scholars. It was, she reports, an Oxford rule that no supervisor was to read more than half the thesis. Her own supervisor explained the rule as: 'the reason is that we want to be quite clear in our own minds and we want the student to be quite clear that it is their work'. Oxford students (and, as it would appear from her own account, those of our interviewee) were required to reveal themselves as 'always-already' having the capacities for which they were to be credentialled at the end of the PhD process. They were to find in themselves the capacity to be autonomous, and they were to demonstrate that they could work on their own without supervision, just as they were to respond to assistance when it was made available. Recognising themselves as 'always-already' able to be the independent scholar, such students clearly were expected to be members of an elite whose previous training had produced in them the capacities and the sense of themselves that would secure their entry into this academic world, at the same time as it would enable them to respond positively to the warning that they would only be 'half' supervised.

Although she could not remember exactly why she wanted to go to Oxford, this interviewee reports having had 'a burning desire' to go there: 'I don't know why, I had no idea what it was like, I knew nothing about it, but I had this ambition to go to Oxford'. The 'dreaming spires' of the ancient university, the lure of just the name 'Oxford', or the image of the scholar in 'his' library, all represent continuing group fantasies or social utopias for the aspiring academic, just as the imagined, longed for, community of scholars continues to be a reference point which academics frequently invoke as representing the 'real university' of 'the past'. These fantasies are productive and sustaining of the desire to be a certain figure, the independent scholar. The body of the scholar that frequents these spaces is often the tweed-coated figure conjured up by Riemer's library full of leather-bound tomes (and echoed by many of the women and men who have participated in this and our earlier research). Of course, it is a masculine figure, even though women have managed throughout the history of the PhD to imagine themselves into these spaces, and hence to submit themselves to the pedagogical practices that both rely on and sustain these fantasies.

This is all the more remarkable when we look at the ideas of reason and autonomy that underlie the concept of the independent scholar so central to the PhD, and which the practices of supervision described by the interview with which we began this section were designed to produce. An analysis of these ideas suggests that the masculinity of the figure of the independent scholar invoked in doctoral education is more than simply a matter of PhD students being 'normally male' (Giblett, 1992, p. 137). Genevieve Lloyd's book, *The Man of Reason* first published in 1984, remains a key text in analysing the way in which Western ideals of Reason and Knowledge, and associated assumptions about the scholar or the subject of Knowledge, are profoundly masculine. The 'maleness of the Man of Reason' (Lloyd, 1984, p. ix), as she puts it, is not the result of a superficial linguistic bias, but stems from the way in which, from:

> ... the beginnings of philosophical thought, femaleness was symbolically associated with what Reason supposedly left behind – the dark powers of the earth goddesses, immersion in unknown forces associated with mysterious female powers.
>
> (Lloyd, 1984, p. 2)

'Rational knowledge', she says, 'has been construed as a transcending, transformation or control of natural forces; and the feminine has been associated with what rational knowledge transcends, dominates or simply leaves behind' (Lloyd, 1984, p. 2).

Lloyd examines the writing of figures like Descartes, Hume, Rousseau, Kant and Hegel to trace this tradition throughout the history of Western philosophy. In the seventeenth century, she argues, Reason became not just a distinguishing characteristic of mankind but a set of skills, a distinctive way of thinking to be learned. Descartes provided one of the most elaborated versions of what was understood to be involved in this way of thinking. For him, a precisely ordered mode of abstract thought could be applied to all fields of human endeavour, regardless of subject matter. This mode of reasoning was, according to Descartes, 'simply a systematization of the innate faculty of Reason or "good sense" ', but it demanded a transcending of the body, of the practical activities of everyday life. '[T]he sharpness of his separation of the ultimate requirements of truth-seeking from the practical affairs of everyday life', says Lloyd (1984, pp. 49–50), 'reinforced already existing distinctions between male and female roles, opening the way to the idea of distinctive male and female consciousness'.

But, of the thinkers examined by Lloyd, it is probably the work of Kant that has had the most influence on the university curriculum and that of humanities particularly (see Readings, 1996). According to Kant, Lloyd argues, the Enlightenment required man to emerge from his own 'self-incurred immaturity'. Maturity for man, he proposed, consisted of having the 'courage to use your own understanding' without the guidance of another. Reason was precisely the power to judge autonomously, that is 'freely' (Kant, quoted in Hunter, 1995, p. 67); and access to 'a public space of autonomous speech', Kant believed, was essential for man to be able to exercise this Reason (Lloyd, 1984, pp. 66–67). While he did not develop, in any explicit form, a gendered characterisation of the capacities of humanity to pursue the ability to exercise one's own judgement, his discussion of an immature consciousness under the sway of 'guardians', 'as are the entire fair sex', and his stress on public space as the location of autonomous speech and the exercise of Reason, suggest that Kant necessarily saw women falling short of the humanity required of the subjects of Reason (Lloyd, 1984, pp. 66–70).

Both Kant and Rousseau had distinct notions about the spatial requirements for the exercise of Reason and autonomous judgement. While Kant insisted on the need for access to a public space 'in which men of learning enjoy unlimited freedom to use their own reason and "speak in their own person" ' (Lloyd, 1984, p. 68), Rousseau, according to Lloyd (1984, p. 59), believed that 'a few "learned of the first rank" should be given an "honourable refuge" in the courts of princes, where they might by their influence promote "the happiness of the people they have enlightened by their wisdom" '. According to Bill Readings (1996, p. 58), Kant envisaged the modern university as guided by the concept of Reason and argued that the state had an obligation to protect the university in order to ensure the rule of Reason in public life. Thus, the university becomes one of the essential spaces in which the autonomous subject of Reason is understood to be located (even though Kant had some difficulties with the institutionalisation of Reason that such ideas appeared to imply). Nineteenth-century German ideas about the university, such as those of Schleiermacher and Humboldt, which then played a major role in shaping concepts of the functioning and organisation of modern universities, reworked Kant's arguments, replacing, according to Readings, the idea of Reason as the guiding principle of the university with the idea of Culture. But what certainly remains is the concept of the university as being the protected space of autonomous judgement, of the independent scholar – whether as 'honourable refuge' or as exemplary public sphere. And with these moves, the 'Man of Reason', as analysed by Genevieve Lloyd, is placed at the centre of the university and the role of the personal and the irrational are disavowed in understandings of how this figure is to be produced. The scholar is required to develop a particular ethical comportment or 'relation of the self', as Ian Hunter (1995, pp. 76–78) points out, through which, according to this modern conception of Reason, 'he' learns to purify his will of sensuous inclinations.

Many feminists have now critiqued the long-standing dualisms in Western culture associated with the concept of Reason: rationality and irrationality, subject and object, autonomy and dependence. But while some have argued that the idea of Reason itself should be abandoned (see Harding, 1986), others, like Zoe Sofia (1993, p. 23) (now Sofoulis), however, have proposed that the abstracted mode of thought associated with this concept simply be demoted to just one of the tools of thought to be used in any process of thinking or understanding. At the same time, she adds, we should recognise that Reason is a fantasy. As a fantasy, it invokes both dreams of mastery/domination and dreams of pleasure in being the 'reasonable person – one who is in love with ideas rather than bodies, one who is able to triumph over the contingency of the body and the unreasonableness of the emotions (Sofia, 1993, p. 29). In thus banishing the emotions and the embodiment of the individual, the fantasy of Reason, according to Jessica Benjamin (1990, p. 185), is 'patently linked to the split between the father of autonomy and the mother of dependency'. The rational, autonomous individual establishes his identity by separating off from, and in opposition to, this mother and by 'splitting off certain human capabilities, called feminine' (Benjamin, 1990, p. 189). Autonomy is achieved by rejecting the emotions, embodiment and human dependency.

Traditional practices of PhD supervision, whether they be the neglect and indifference recalled by Andrew Riemer or the tough-minded but more carefully targeted regimes described by oral history interviewee 1, assume 'autonomy' – in the form of the exemplary figure of the independent scholar – to be the desired outcome. Our analysis suggests that this figure is a problematic one for the profoundly gendered character of the assumptions of Reason and autonomy it invokes. Of course, not all supervisors have been neglectful, nor have they necessarily taken the stance of oral history interviewee 1 in explicitly demanding that the PhD student be effectively 'always-already' capable of independent scholarship from the beginning of their candidature. However, in the next section we analyse how even the more pastorally-oriented practices of supervision continue to work unproblematically within the notions of Reason and autonomy from the Enlightenment tradition analysed earlier and, indeed, deploy a regime of person formation, the roots of which can be found in the ideas of Rousseau. Our interest here is in the paradoxical character of the processes of person formation involved in the shaping of the autonomous scholar self.

Invisible pedagogies

So I suppose I've made the assumption that these students have got . . . [pause] any student that I've come in contact with has had an immense amount to offer, is different from the last student that I had, is different from the . . . [pause] who's got different intellectual interests, different abilities and my task as supervisor is to try to find out what they are and help them, challenge them, maybe, but not impose my own personal interests . . . [pause] I guess that's what I mean by trying to get inside their minds, to challenge their mind, to help the person if they needed help if you could, and then when they finished they owned it. They'd written it not me, although I'd influenced it I suppose . . . [pause] my image of what my students would say was that I drove them mad about that and I did but I was . . . [pause] it was part of making them independent.

(*Oral history interview* 2, April 1998)

In *Sentimental Education*, James Donald (1992) traces the historical effects on modern systems of education of the Enlightenment project which sought to produce the

Rational Man. Indeed, for Kant, education was central to the achievement of humanity: 'Man can only become man by education' (Kant, cited in Donald, 1992, p. 4). At the centre of eighteenth-century European conceptions of education, suggests Donald, lies a paradox which, arguably, remains in contemporary educational conceptions and practices and which finds perhaps its most intense formulation in the PhD. This is the paradox of the apparently conflicting demands of liberty and regulation, autonomy and restraint in the educational project. As indicated in the previous section, these demands do not exist independently of the Enlightenment project, but derive from its formulation by thinkers like Kant and Rousseau who, in critiquing the individualistic form this project had taken in German speculative idealist philosophy, sought to assert the demands of both the human soul for freedom and autonomy and the 'higher need' for attention to the moral well-being and happiness of the human species as a whole (Vekley, 1989, pp. 32–39). In the work of Kant, for instance, 'man' can only become independent and rational through the imposition of restraint (Donald, 1992, p. 4). In educational terms, individual autonomy and independence can only be achieved 'through submission to pedagogic norms' (Donald, 1992, p. 4). This apparent paradox attained its most explicit formulation in the work of Rousseau.

For Rousseau, children's natures needed to be educated (protectively) against the harmful influences of society. Their innate psychological and physical patterns needed space to develop from within, but they needed to develop in the direction of rationality and independence. The changes produced by education, then, were, seemingly ironically, both spontaneous and desired. The role of the Tutor was crucial in choreographing these changes while appearing to be benevolently standing by, 'supervising'. Rousseau's injunction to Tutors is worth quoting at some length here:

> Let [your pupil] always think he is master while you are really master. There is no subjection so complete as that which preserves the forms of freedom; it is thus that the will itself is taken captive. Is not this poor child, without knowledge, strength, or wisdom, entirely at your mercy? Are you not master of his whole environment so far as it affects him? Cannot you make of him what you please? His work and play, his pleasure and pain, are they not, unknown to him, under your control? *No doubt he ought only to do what he wants, but he ought to want to do nothing but what you want him to do.*
>
> (Rousseau, cited in Donald, 1992, p. 5, emphasis added)

Rousseau named the pedagogy of the education of Emile, 'well-regulated liberty'. The end of this pedagogy was the identification by Emile with the authoritative position from which he is observed and managed by the Tutor. Upon this identification, he is given 'a mandate to act as a free agent within the intersubjective symbolic network' (Donald, 1992, p. 7).

Such, we want to suggest, is the pedagogy described in oral history interview 2 with which we began this section. It is an 'invisible pedagogy' in the terms outlined by Basil Bernstein (1977), in his analysis of child-centred approaches to education. Unlike the pedagogy described in oral history interview 1, quoted in the previous section of this article, it requires a more subtle exercise of power. The supervisor's task is to arrange the context, to attend to the student's needs and differences, and to observe and monitor. Necessary to the sense of autonomy that is the end-point of this pedagogy for the development of the rational, independent scholar, the student must experience themselves as in control, as author of their intentions, as exercising free will and independence. The goal of a more explicit pedagogy in which the student is told that they will only be half-read, half-supervised, is the same, but in the case of a more invisible pedagogical style, 'regulation', in Valerie Walkerdine's (1985) terms, in her analysis of progressive education, 'has gone underground'. The supervisor is caring, solicitous, not disdainful or indifferent, but nevertheless 'master', in control. He acknowledges that the students go through considerable stress and pain, but this is necessary to the process of development, of attaining maturity.

'Supervision' carries powerful overtones of 'overseeing' (of 'looking over' and 'looking after') production and development with regard to academic knowledge and identity. All research degrees, and especially those associated with doctoral work, are required by formal legislation to be subject to 'supervision', which means that both the student (the 'candidate') and the dissertation are to be constructed under the authorised and authorising gaze of an already-established researcher, standing in, in some sense, for the field of study in question and for the Academy more generally. Elsewhere, in a manner strikingly reminiscent of the tutelory regime of Rousseau's Emile, Evans & Green (1995, p. 7) have noted:

> 'Supervision' in this sense is better grasped as a 'pan-optics' of pedagogic power, with due regard for its productivity in terms of securing the best conditions for postgraduate research and training and hence for the formation of appropriate research(er) subjectivities. Here postgraduate pedagogy might well be better understood as a matter of artfully arranging the educational environment for the novice researcher, with 'environment' conceived here as inclusive of resources, information, accommodation, different or multiple perspectives, expertise, networks, 'direct instruction', and so on.

This regime holds powerful sway in the pedagogies articulated by the oral history participants cited earlier; this is in spite of the fact that often, in relation to their own work, 'the student is more likely to have the over-view (super-view) than the super-visor' (see Brennan & Walker, 1994).

Like the Tutor and the Pupil of Rousseau's pedagogy, the supervisor and the doctoral candidate play out a fantasy in which the student produces 'their own thesis' and, in doing so, is produced as an autonomous and rational scholar. This more-or-less invisible pedagogy of 'super-vision' is one of assuming 'liberty', under a surveillance which is more or less invisible in its normativity. What is disavowed or glossed over is the paradoxical nature of the processes of the production of the autonomous scholar self. The roots of this paradox, as we have indicated, emerged within the Enlightenment tradition in the eighteenth century, as thinkers like Rousseau and Kant sought to reconcile the demands of individual freedom and social integration, and to claim them complementary. The *Bildungsroman* tradition represents a further attempt to establish the legitimacy of these two imperatives and to resolve the seeming conflict between them (see Donald, 1992, p. 8). In the licensing or credentialling practices of doctoral education, the PhD works within the narrative form adopted by the more conservative strand of this literary tradition, in which both demands are reconciled in an apparently harmonious solution. The licensed scholar, the desired outcome of doctoral education, is one who both indicates 'his' deep indebtedness to the masters, to authorities in the field, through the literature review considered fundamental to the standard dissertation format for the PhD, *and* displays 'his' autonomy – 'his' readiness for independent research, through the demand for 'originality' considered axiomatic in institutional specifications of what distinguishes the PhD from other university degrees.

Thus, the centrality of the ideal of the autonomous, independent scholar to post-graduate pedagogy can be seen in a range of possible different scenarios for the practices of supervision. The three that we have looked at by no means necessarily constitute the full range of practices adopted by supervisors until recent times, but they represent significant traditions which continue to have salience today, despite the shift to greater bureaucratic monitoring of the supervisory relationship. That the ideal of the autonomous self is unproblematic in all three scenarios testifies to its centrality to the history of the PhD, at the same time as it indicates how powerfully but silently its assumptions about who has the right to regard themselves as ready to take on the mantle of the subject of Knowledge, the 'one who knows', continue to operate unscrutinised. In the final section of this article we turn to explore briefly how some women have negotiated the supervisory relationship, focusing only here on supervisors. We are interested in the extent to which women have rejected or struggled with the centrality of traditional conceptions of the autonomous scholar to postgraduate pedagogy. We also consider the arguments of a number of feminists who have sought to address the question of the possibility of a feminist pedagogy and the implications of their concerns for doctoral education. Finally, we discuss the extent to which arguments about the emergence of new modes of knowledge production might suggest a new image of the scholar, that takes us beyond the paradoxes and tensions of the Enlightenment project for doctoral education, but potentially, perhaps, also confronts us with new complexities.

A new image of the scholar?

> In a sense it's an incredibly charged relationship and she can be just awful, and she pushes everyone around, and my head of school can't bear to talk to her. But there is obviously something there in that I think it's not anything I've done, I think she's cast me as a sort of [pause] not quite sure, it's not a mother figure but it's something close to that I suppose. It's also an authority figure ...
>
> I think right at the start I'm very sympathetic and I listen, as I'm sure Anne does too, you listen, you're very careful to try and pick up what it is you think they're trying to formulate. Into the bargain you also hear about their private stuff. Jenny tells me the same thing happens with her, that they dump on women a lot of the private stuff and I'm quite sure that's true. And, you know, they'll feel relieved and happy that they've let you know their total picture whereas the male students don't do that. Well, one of them does but it's taken time and he's a practising artist, so he's a bit different. David. Yeah, he's quite different from the other couple of men I've got. The men are very independent and very ... [pause] you know they don't have this kind of ... [pause] it's a very warm relationship but they don't ... the women just want to tell you, especially if they're on the premises.
>
> (*Interview with female supervisor*, June 1998)

In our interviews with current supervisors, we have heard stories of women who, in attempting to move away from the position of 'master' – whether explicitly or implicitly – have felt overwhelmed in their relationships with students. Frequently torn between their students' expectations (and no doubt their own) for someone who is both 'the mother of dependency' and 'the father of autonomy', in Jessica Benjamin's terms, they find it difficult to create a new and satisfactory role for the PhD supervisor. Indeed, the family drama endures as the frame within which even alternative narratives and procedural metaphors are imagined, whether it be by someone trying to be both 'mother' and 'father', simply 'mother', or yet again 'sister' (see, for example, Bartlett & Mercer, 1999).

These are not new problems in the attempt by women to devise feminist pedagogical practices as effective alternatives within higher education more generally. As Lauren Berlant (1997) indicates, feminist teaching has now developed its own fantasies that can be just as troublesome for women as those traditional to the university. The teacher, for example, who is 'infinitely patient, available, confident in her knowledge, an intellectual and sexual role model, who uses her long office hours therapeutically to help students develop subjectivity and self-esteem and to solve personal problems', Berlant (1997, p. 147) suggests, became part of the iconography of women's studies and feminist pedagogy in the 1970s and 1980s. She argues that this fantasy seeks pleasure in the identification between teachers and students just as much as traditional pedagogies of the university based more securely on Enlightenment ideals. It is a fantasy that potentially leaves women exhausted, burnt out. Although not all feminist pedagogies pose the problems that Berlant suggests, her analysis reminds us that an apparently feminist stance does not necessarily solve the issues encountered in higher education, such as those we have outlined in the previous sections of our article. Just as Berlant has pointed to the dangers that can emerge in feminist practices of undergraduate teaching, the feminist graduate student supervisor, endlessly responding to her students' needs and demands, certainly needs to be questioned too as an unsatisfactory alternative to the 'master' Tutor.

Part of the solution to this problem lies in recognising, as Vicki Kirby (1994, p. 19) argues, the conditions of impossibility of a feminist pedagogy. Women need to acknowledge, she says, their 'passion for the power in learning, our delight in the flirtatiousness of intellectual debate, in the game of competing . . . in the sexiness of winning'; a woman's desire for authority, she insists, should not be diagnosed as a moral failing. Pedagogical practices, at whatever level, need to be recognised as deeply implicated, necessarily, in the relationships of power that they are committed to in playing out these desires. A more self-conscious approach to the goal of pedagogical practices too, in terms of the forms of personhood, the capacities and modes of comportment to be produced in students, will also assist supervisors to work with the diversity of students now involved in the mass higher education system. An implicit pedagogy, whether of the more pastoral kind, or in the genre of magisterial disdain or in the form of only 'half-teaching', may work for those who are 'always-already' in part shaped as the form of personhood that these practices seek to produce. But it does not necessarily work so effectively, at least, for a more diverse, mass population – particularly for that group, women, for whom the form of personhood currently required as an independent scholar potentially involves the negation of the values and modes of operating historically associated with their gendered identities. Although individual women have clearly developed desires to be the independent scholar, these desires are likely to be differently inflected as women have sought ways of imagining themselves as such a figure outside those provided by the dominant cultural representations of university life.

But the question remains: is it appropriate to continue to retain the seemingly unproblematic status of autonomy or independence as the goal of postgraduate pedagogy? In part, what seems necessary is a greater acknowledgement of and engagement with the apparently conflicting demands of autonomy and authority, of the way in which autonomy is a question of achieving 'a well-regulated liberty' rather than a matter of untrammeled freedom. The demand for students to be 'original' is not a question of their throwing off or stepping outside the domain of knowledge in which they have been trained, but simply of their achieving a licence to understand themselves as contributing to this domain, as being the subject of Knowledge. As Barry Hindess (1995, p. 41) argues, in considering a different set of issues about the modern university, 'autonomy' involves the internalisation of authority rather than being fundamentally opposed to it.

In understanding the goal of autonomy as learning, in Hindess's (1995, p. 40) terms, 'to identify the appropriate rules for oneself', the apparent intensity of the demands of the PhD can potentially be reduced. The autonomy sought of the student can be recognised as a set of capacities, a mode of conducting oneself, that can be learned – and taught – rather than a capacity which already exists in the individual and has to be revealed in order for him or her to be or become the successful PhD candidate. The supervisor no longer needs to be 'master', in whatever guise, but a teacher of particular skills, ways of thinking and writing. But pursuing such a line of argument, and the possible pedagogical strategies that might flow from it, while important, does not necessarily engage with a central issue addressed in this article – the issue of the way in which the subject of Knowledge assumed by the fantasy of Reason has been understood in masculine terms.

However, other pressures are beginning to occur in and around universities which may undermine the status of this fantasy and its efficacy in the production of know- ledge. These developments, in turn, could precisely bring about the demise of this fantasy, or at least a rethinking, in ways that might be useful in addressing the gendered character of the figure of the independent scholar. According to the work of people like Michael Gibbons and his colleagues (1994), knowledge is no longer necessarily being produced by the independent scholar within the university, and then applied 'outside' in the realms of the economy, business, or policy. They suggest that knowledge is increasingly being produced in collaborations between universities and these other agencies, addressing problems in context, often in interdisciplinary ways.

Gibbons *et al.*'s work has been criticised for exaggerating the differences between traditional and new modes of knowledge production. It has been suggested by Benoit Godin (1998), for example, that Gibbons *et al.* are more involved in writing a perfor- mative history of changes in the organisation of knowledge than looking at the reality of what scientists do and have done. Rather than documenting major shifts in how research is done, they are operating as social analysts interested in influencing govern- ment and university policy. They are wanting to reshape the models of academic research, and the underlying rhetoric about the scholar, so that there is more emphasis in science policy, nationally and internationally, on collaborative research between universities, industry and the community.

But what interests us in this article is precisely the way a certain image of the scholar, a fantasy of how knowledge is produced, shapes current practices of post- graduate pedagogy. The PhD as a form of research training, in the humanities and social sciences at least, is based on the idea of the independent scholar working free from connections with the 'outside world', a disembedded and disembodied figure driven by the love of ideas, of scholarship, alone. With the arguments emerging, as outlined earlier, about new modes of knowledge production, new fantasies could begin at least to coexist with or even undermine those around the romantic figure of 'the scholar'. While continuing to incite and sustain desires around the power of knowledge and the pleasure of demonstrating certain competencies or capacities associated with the subject of Knowledge, a new figure of the scholar would appear to be more appropriate to forms of research training associated with new modes of knowledge production. If the arguments of Gibbons *et al.* gain acceptance in the university context, the collaboration they claim to be emerging as characteristic of new modes of knowledge production will require skills of learning to work with a diverse range of individuals. It will also encourage recognition of the contribution of others rather than a preoccupation with whether or not one is demonstrating the appropriate characteristics of the autonomous self.

These developments could precisely open up a different space for those women in doctoral programmes who, in the past, have found their identities as scholars and gendered beings in conflict. To the extent that universities begin to accept that new modes of producing knowledge are emerging, or should at least be thought about, they will require researchers who are skilled in collaboration, in the recognition of the interdependence of human relations, and in the appreciation of the concrete skills and specific capacities of others. These shifts constitute a potential major challenge to the notion of autonomous judgement as being essential to the subject of Knowledge.

In this context, it would seem that those characteristics historically associated with the feminine could become valued rather than negated in producing the new type of researcher. As we indicated in the second section of this article, autonomy has been conceptualised in terms of the rejection of the emotions, embodiment and human dependency. Yet, the argument that a new mode of the production of knowledge is emerging would appear to require the development of capacities where these oppositions are no longer appropriate. Research training to produce scholars able to work in these new ways will require students to develop sensitivities to the concerns of others, a willingness to work with others, and a capacity to reason or make judgements on the basis of contextual information rather than relying purely on abstract, universalising principles. In the teaching of these skills to PhD students, new forms of pedagogy would need to emerge and the primacy of the supervisory relationship be reviewed. And in reconsidering this central pedagogical technology of the PhD for the sort of research training needed for new modes of the production of knowledge, it may also be possible to go beyond the family drama as the only frame within which to think about the relationships appropriate to managing the challenge of the PhD. Of course, the danger also exists, in very real ways, that the developments that we have outlined may be the occasion simply for new definitions of the Subject of Knowledge to emerge that are just as masculine as those that have gone before. The task for feminist pedagogies will be to attempt to open up the spaces that these developments potentially allow for a more democratic and inclusive definition of this Subject.

References

Bartlett, A. & Mercer, G. (1999) Mud maps and mud cakes – finding metaphors for postgraduate supervision, paper delivered at the *Winds of Change Conference*, University of Technology, Sydney, July.

Benjamin, J. (1990) *The Bonds of Love. Psychoanalysis, feminism and the problem of domination* (New York, Pantheon Books).

Berlant, L. (1997) Feminism and the institutions of intimacy, in: E. A. Kaplan & G. Levine (Eds) *The Politics of Research* (New Brunswick, NJ, Rutgers University Press).

Bernstein, B. (1977) Class and pedagogy: visible and invisible, in: J. Karavel & A. H. Halsey (Eds) *Power and Ideology in Education* (New York, Oxford University Press).

Brennan, M. & Walker, R. (1994) Educational research in the workplace: developing a professional doctorate, in: R. Burgess & M. Schratz (Eds) *Zeitschrift für Hochschuldidaktic: International Perspectives in Postgraduate Education and Training*, 2, pp. 220–233.

Donald, J. (1992) *Sentimental Education, schooling, popular culture and the regulation of liberty* (London, Verso).

Evans, T. & Green, B. (1995) Dancing at a distance? Postgraduate studies, 'supervision', and distance education, paper presented at the *25th Annual National Conference of the Australian Association for Research in Education*, Hobart, 26–30 November.

Gibbons, M. *et al.* (1994) *The New Production of Knowledge. The Dynamic of Science and Research in Contemporary Societies* (London, Sage).

Giblett, R. (1992) The desire for disciples, *Paragraph*, 15, pp. 136–154.

Godin, B. (1998) Writing performative history: the new *New Atlantis? Social Studies of Science*, 28, pp. 465–483.

Harding, S. (1986) *The Science Question in Feminism* (Ithaca, NY, Cornell University Press).

Hindess, B. (1995) Great expectations: freedom and authority, *Oxford Literary Review* 17, pp. 29–49.

Hunter, I. (1995) The regime of reason: Kant's defence of the philosophy faculty, *Oxford Literary Review*, 17, pp. 51–85.

Kirby, V. (1994) Response to Jane Gallop's 'The Teachers' Breasts': bad form, in: J. J. Matthews (Ed.) *Jane Gallop Seminar Papers, Proceedings of the Jane Gallop Seminar and Public Lecture 'The Teachers' Breasts' Held in 1993 by the Humanities Research Centre* (Canberra, The Humanities Research Centre, the Australian National University).

Lee, A. & William, C. (1999) 'Forged in fire': narratives of trauma in PhD supervision pedagogy, *Southern Review* 32, pp. 6–26.

Lloyd, G. (1984) *The Man of Reason. 'Male' and 'Female' in Western Philosophy* (London, Methuen).

Readings, B. (1996) *The University in Ruins* (Cambridge, MA, Harvard University Press).

Riemer, A. (1998) *Sandstone Gothic. Confessions of an Accidental Academic* (Sydney, Allen & Unwin).

Simpson, R. (1983) *How the PhD Came to Britain. A Century of Struggle for Postgraduate Education* (Guildford, Research into Higher Education Monographs).

Sofia, Z. (1993) *Whose Second Self? Gender and (IR)rationality in Computer Culture* (Geelong, Deakin University Press).

Vekley, R. L. (1989) *Freedom and the End of Reason. On the Moral Foundations of Kant's Critical Philosophy* (Chicago, IL, Chicago University Press).

Walkerdine, V. (1985) On the regulation of speaking and silence: subjectivity, class and gender, in: C. Steedman, C. Urwin & V. Walkerdine (Eds) *Language, Gender and Childhood* (London, Routledge, Kegan & Paul).

Yeatman, A. (1998) Making research relationships accountable: graduate student logs, in: A. Lee & B. Green (Eds) *Postgraduate Studies. Postgraduate Pedagogy* (Sydney, Centre for Language and Literacy, University Graduate School, University of Technology, Sydney).

CHAPTER 9

CONCEPTUALISING CURRICULUM CHANGE

Ronald Barnett, Gareth Parry and Kelly Coate

Teaching in Higher Education, 6, 4, 435–449, 2001

EDITOR'S INTRODUCTION

This article was categorised in the introductory chapter as adopting a conceptual approach to the analysis of course design. It relates, however, to a larger research project, funded by the Economic and Social Research Council (ESRC), which explored changing patterns in the undergraduate curricula by interviewing academic staff in five subject areas in six British higher education institutions. While the data collected by that project is used to illustrate the argument of the authors, the focus of the article is primarily on discussing models of the curriculum and of curriculum change.

The authors make particular reference to the work of the French postmodern theorist, Lyotard, especially his concept of performativity, which stresses the importance of higher education in preparing students for the labour market. They present a curriculum model consisting of three domains – knowledge (i.e. subject specialism), action (i.e. competences acquired through 'doing') and self (i.e. the student's developing educational identity). They then illustrate the different domain emphases apparent in three contrasting knowledge fields: science and technology, arts and humanities, and professional subjects.

Having set up this structure, Barnett and his co-authors then discuss the changes taking place in each of the three curriculum domains. These changes include changing knowledge structures, new topics within knowledge fields, new techniques for studying knowledge fields, the use of new technologies, the greater attention paid to the development of students' skills, the closer relationship with the world of work, and the increased responsibility being placed upon students for their own development. On this basis, they distinguish between different kinds of performativity: epistemological, pedagogical, educational and self monitoring.

Though their emphasis is on curriculum change, the authors do also note two strong forms of continuity in higher education practices: the importance of lectures within the teaching/learning transaction, and the dominant relationship being between single lecturers and groups of students.

While the authors note the relative absence of recent studies of the higher education curriculum, there are at least three contemporary literatures to which their study may be related. One of these focuses on the variations in practices between different academic disciplines, and is particularly associated with the research of Tony Becher (e.g. Becher 1999, Becher and Trowler 2001, Neumann *et al.* 2002), A second, to which Barnett himself has made notable contributions, has examined the changing nature of knowledge and knowledge development in higher education (e.g. Barnett 1990, 1994, 1997, 2000, Barnett and Griffin 1997, Delanty

2001, Gibbons *et al.* 1994, Jacob and Hellstrom 2000, Nowotny *et al.* 2001). The third takes a more pragmatic approach to the issues of course design (e.g. Toohey 1999).

References

Barnett, R. (1990) *The Idea of Higher Education.* Buckingham, Open University Press.
Barnett, R. (1994) *The Limits of Competence: knowledge, higher education and society.* Buckingham, Open University Press.
Barnett, R. (1997) *Higher Education: a critical business.* Buckingham, Open University Press.
Barnett, R. (2000) *Realizing the University in an Age of Supercomplexity.* Buckingham, Open University Press.
Barnett, R. and Griffin, A. (eds) (1997) *The End of Knowledge in Higher Education.* London, Cassell.
Becher, T. (1999) *Professional Practices: commitment and capability in a changing environment.* New Brunswick, NJ, Transaction.
Becher, T. and Trowler, P. (2001) *Academic Tribes and Territories: intellectual enquiry and the culture of disciplines.* Buckingham, Open University Press, second edition.
Delanty, G. (2001) *Challenging Knowledge: the university in the knowledge society.* Buckingham, Open University Press.
Gibbons, M., Limoges, C., Nowotny, H., Schwartzman, S., Scott, P. and Trow, M. (1994) *The New Production of Knowledge: the dynamics of science and research in contemporary societies.* London, Sage.
Jacob, M. and Hellstrom, T. (eds) (2000) *The Future of Knowledge Production in the Academy.* Buckingham, Open University Press.
Neumann, R., Parry, S. and Becher, T. (2002) 'Teaching and Learning in their Disciplinary Contexts: a conceptual analysis', *Studies in Higher Education,* 27, 4, pp. 405–417.
Nowotny, H., Scott, P. and Gibbons, M. (2001) *Re-thinking Science: knowledge and the public in an age of uncertainty.* Cambridge, Polity Press.
Toohey, S. (1999) *Designing Courses for Higher Education.* Buckingham, Open University Press.

CONCEPTUALISING CURRICULUM CHANGE

Introduction

For all the discussion of the changes, often profound, that have taken place in contemporary higher education, the undergraduate curriculum has commanded rather less attention than might be expected. Yet the curriculum remains one of the most important products that higher education institutions offer to their customers. A few significant studies in the past have attempted to describe its major components and its variation between disciplines (Boys *et al.*, 1988; Squires, 1987; Silver & Brennan, 1988; Goodlad, 1997). A more recent study has clarified those components of the curriculum that impart skills (Bennett *et al.*, 2000). The curriculum as such, however, receives scant regard in current debates about teaching and learning in higher education.

In the UK, this may be about to change as the curriculum comes under scrutiny. Quality assurance mechanisms, such as Subject Review (formerly TQA) and benchmarking, are encouraging transparency and accountability in curriculum design and delivery. Furthermore, the determination (apparently receiving some support across the sector) of the Funding Councils to introduce a profiling system may prompt reflection on curriculum intentions. The HEFCE requirement for institutions to develop learning and teaching strategies may also be stimulating discussion on what was once largely a private activity undertaken by individual academics. How will the curriculum be understood in such policies and strategies?

This paper sets out to conceptualise key patterns of change in the undergraduate curriculum, and proposes models for configuring the main components of curricula as they vary between subject areas. The focus of the paper is primarily conceptual, although we illustrate its themes with observations drawn from a research project on changing patterns of undergraduate curricula.[1] The fieldwork was conducted in six universities in England and centred on five subject areas. The universities were chosen for their diversity of institutional mission and because they offered under-graduate courses in at least four of our five chosen knowledge fields: business studies, chemistry, electrical engineering, history and nursing studies. Analysis of curriculum materials and interviews with academics in these institutions and knowledge fields offered a ready basis from which to develop a conceptualisation of change in the curriculum.

Curriculum change

We begin with several general observations prompted by the literature, but buttressed by our study. First, knowledge fields continue to dominate higher education, not only as a source of academic identities, but as a means of structuring curricula. A growing number of studies on subject cultures and disciplinary identities have revealed the power of knowledge fields in shaping academic life (Huber, 1990; Gerholm, 1990; Becher, 1989; Henkel, 2000). For most academics, an institutional loyalty is secondary to a disciplinary loyalty and a working relationship within the institution is framed through the deep, underlying epistemological structures of the knowledge fields. Consequently, curricula will be shaped in significant degrees by the values and prac-tices of the different knowledge fields.

Secondly, changes are taking place in the production and application of academic knowledge. For Lyotard, the main criterion of academic knowledge is no longer 'is it true?, but 'what use is it?' (Lyotard, 1984, p. 51). However, the performative shift, associated with an increased emphasis on 'efficiency', 'outputs' and 'use-value', has played out differently across the subject areas.

Knowledge in the science fields has been altered through new technologies and their ability to improve efficiency, as 'the search for truth ... has given way to the principle of optimal performance, that is, the best possible input/output equation which characterises technology' (Gokulsing, 1997, p. 95). The professional subjects have always been orientated towards their 'use-value', as they were created in response to the needs of the world of work (Silver & Brennan, 1988). The humanities subjects may resist such trends, but are not unaltered: in history, for example, skills that were once implicitly acquired through learning to become a historian are now represented as 'transferable' and appropriate for a variety of occupations.

The principle of performativity is, therefore, associated with the relationship of higher education to the labour market. It implies doing, rather than knowing, and performance, rather than understanding. In the performative society, there is a mistrust of all things that cannot easily be quantified and measured. Those knowledge fields that were once intrinsically valued for their own sake must now demonstrate their relevance to the wider world.

Changes in the undergraduate curriculum are related to these shifts, and might be expressed in terms of traditional and emerging curricula, as follows:

Traditional Curricula	*Emerging Curricula*
Knowing that	Knowing how
Written communication	Oral communication

Personal	Interpersonal
Internal	External
Disciplinary skills	Transferable skills
Intellectual orientation	Action orientation
Problem-making	Problem-solving
Knowledge as process	Knowledge as product
Understanding	Information
Concept-based	Issue-based
Knowledge-based	Task-based
Pure	Applied
Proposition-based learning	Experiential learning

In setting out these modalities of curricula, it is not intended to make value judgements *or* to imply that there has been a wholesale movement from one type of curriculum to another. Nor do these columns represent dichotomous positions. Obviously, there are large sectors of higher education where some of the traits associated with 'traditional' curricula still retain their value. Even some newcomers to higher education (as it becomes possible to take degrees in certain professional fields) may take up the characteristics associated with traditional curricula. Rather, the intention behind this typification is to begin to suggest aspects of change and underlying patterns that help to make sense of emerging curriculum structures.

These changes can be situated within the higher education context through a few concrete examples. On a national level, policy initiatives such as the Enterprise in Higher Education initiative have attempted to inculcate skills from the world of work into the curriculum and have been associated with a 'performative' shift in higher education (Assiter, 1995; Wright, 1995). At the level of the knowledge fields, recent developments have also indicated a move towards performativity. Electrical engineering and business studies, as examples, are relatively new subject areas created in response to professional needs, rather than through the inner structure of a subject (Silver & Brennan, 1988). As such, they are knowledge fields orientated more towards their use-value to society, rather than to a disciplinary knowledge base, In addition, within these knowledge fields themselves there may be an increased emphasis on 'doing', rather than 'knowing' (Silver & Brennan, 1988, p. 180). The idea that a performative shift is emerging within curricula will be developed in the analysis that follows, but we begin with a general schema to distinguish curriculum components and relationships.

A curriculum model

We set out in this paper to identify some fundamental categories by which contemporary and emerging undergraduate curricula can be understood. However, the sheer variety of curricula render problematic any attempt to impose a set of universal categories. While recent policy may be read as an attempt to harmonise curricula, the devolved character of curriculum design in the UK suggests that each curriculum will retain its own distinctiveness, depending on the play of forces and interests at work.

In order that emerging patterns of curricula can be examined across the knowledge fields, three curriculum models under the broad categories of science/technology subjects, arts and humanities subjects, and professional subject areas will be proposed. The differences between the knowledge fields, as exemplified in the models, suggest that any attempt to develop institution-wide policies on the curriculum (for example,

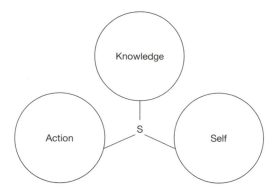

Figure 6 Curriculum: a general schema

on 'skills') should take into account the presence of such variations within the deep structures of the knowledge fields.

'Knowledge fields' in this context is a shorthand: behind this term stands a hinterland of contending interests of shifting epistemologies, academic communities, institutions, professions, the corporate world, students and state agencies. A curriculum, in other words, is a dynamic set of forces: the actual form that curricula take in particular settings represents the balance of the interplay of the separate interests.

The proposed models are based on an understanding of modern curricula as an educational project forming identities founded in three domains: those of knowledge, action and self. We can posit this general relationship as a set of moments in the student experience (Figure 6).

The 'knowledge' domain refers to those components of the curriculum that are based on discipline-specific competences and those aspects of teaching and learning that develop subject specialists, so creating, in our sample, an 'historian' or a 'nurse'. The 'action' domain includes those competences acquired through 'doing': an oral presentation in art history or the clinical practice of a student nurse. The 'self' domain develops an educational identity in relation to the subject areas: history students learn to perceive themselves as 'critical evaluators', while nurses are encouraged to become 'reflective practitioners'.

There are three generalisations to be made about the proposed general schema:

1   The weight of each of the three domains varies across curricula.
2   The domains may be integrated or held separate.
3   Patterns of curricular change are dominated by epistemological differences in the knowledge fields.

The following models exemplify these generalisations across the knowledge fields, by showing how they play out across the three curriculum domains already identified.

Science and technology

The curricula in science and technology courses are heavily weighted towards the knowledge domain. The domains are held separate (there is little or no integration between the domains). The emerging pattern within these knowledge fields is shown in Figure 7.

Figure 7 Curriculum: science and technology schema

Arts and humanities

The arts and humanities curricula are also heavily weighted by the knowledge domain, but here there is more integration with the self domain. The action domain is held apart and is a smaller component of the curricula (Figure 8).

Figure 8 Curriculum: arts and humanities schema

Professional subjects

In the professional subject areas, there is a high degree of integration across the three domains. The action domain is often more weighted than the knowledge and self domains (Figure 9).

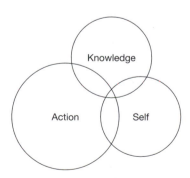

Figure 9 Curriculum: professional subjects schema

We now turn our attention to analysing *change* in each domain.

The knowledge domain

As was apparent in our informants' observations, change in the knowledge fields – and in the curriculum – took three main forms. Firstly, *the structure of the knowledge field might itself be taking new shape*. Nursing studies is a relative newcomer to higher education and is in the process of establishing its structure, and is currently divided between a science-based self-conception (or a hard, pure knowledge base), and one that is more communicative and self-reflective (soft applied Jervis, 1996). However, the established disciplines, too, have a dynamic structure that is expressing itself in the curriculum. The science-based fields are subject to a tacit responsiveness to extramural interests, especially of the global economy and also to changing instrumentation. For example, lasers and optic fibres have come into electronic engineering. The humanities, on the other hand, find a dynamic internal to knowledge as such: history, for example, has become more sociological in character.

Secondly, new topics emerge *within* knowledge fields. Women's history has emerged within history; media technology has entered electronic engineering; spectroscopy has become part of chemistry; tourism and leisure studies have entered business studies. What is striking, particularly in the science-based and technological fields, is how temporary some of these movements might be: we came across examples of quite rapid change and obsolescence. A topic introduced in 1 year might be withdrawn within 3–4 years, such as optoelectronics in electronic engineering or scientific management in business studies. In science and technology, these knowledge movements reflect changing conditions in the global economy among science- and technological-based industries: a change in the disposition of Pacific Rim economies can affect the value of knowledge expertise in particular domains. What was felt worthy of study today may be felt not to yield profitable skills and knowledge tomorrow.

Thirdly, *new techniques and new forms of realisation emerge within* knowledge fields. Computers are to be found in the developing epistemological structure of all of the knowledge fields that we looked at, but are not yet central outside of the science and technological domains. One does not yet have to use a computer in order to be a historian, although computers are evident in historical modes of inquiry.

More generally evident across our knowledge fields is an increasing fuzziness and porousness, not only in their practices, but in their theoretical base (Scott, 1997). The latter development is particularly apparent in chemistry and electronic engineering, exemplified in an incorporation of practical interests within the structuring of the intellectual field. In history, fuzziness is apparent through the appearance of topics that straddle sociology and politics, particularly in modern history and social history, in topics concerning social movements, or the use of oral history. The professional fields are constituted as fuzzy domains in any event, but show an ever broadening of approaches, whether through incorporating a wider array of fundamental disciplines and sub-disciplines (ethics, game theory, action research) or through the incorporation of professional knowledge-in-action (Schön, 1987), captured through structured forms of reflection. In short, the basic knowledge constituents of knowledge fields appear to be falling in with recent commentaries that we are seeing the end of the disciplines as discrete bodies of knowledge (Barnett & Griffin, 1997) with identifiable boundaries, conceptual frames and tests of truth.

This dynamic to the epistemology of knowledge domains refracts on curricula, but differently across the knowledge fields, Despite their increasing porousness, the basic building blocks of chemistry and electronic engineering are still a significant aspect of the curriculum. The students may have little or no optionality, but they will gain a chemistry or engineering degree that has a high degree of reliability in its knowledge content for employers of these graduates.

In other knowledge fields, there is less consensus over the basic epistemological content. In history, topics and modules could be introduced or withdrawn depending serendipitously on staff's own professional interests. In nursing, while there is something approaching a consensus over the constituents of this new field, this consensus – built around a 'reflective practitioner' model – is having to be negotiated with dominant academic interests that look to see a science-based approach to nursing studies and with managerial interests that are seeking a competency-based model of professional practice.

It follows, and it was evident in our study, that the space for personal interpretation of a knowledge field is greatest in the humanities (in our sample, in history). The humanities are marked by an increasing heterogeneity, having a culture of personal interpretation and realisation enjoyed neither by the science-based fields nor by the professional fields. The variability, therefore, in the epistemic contents of curricula is greatest there. There is far from a consensus, too, in our professional fields, but the personal space for interpretation and curricula offerings are relatively confined compared with history. In the professional fields, there is more of a collective interplay between, as it were, contending forces. These differences in the research and scholarly cultures that support the knowledge fields have their separate influences on the shaping of the undergraduate curriculum (and doubtless colour, for example, the contemporary efforts of the UK's Quality Assurance Agency in developing 'benchmarking' characteristics of competence in the different knowledge fields).

The action domain

Since the mid-1980s, 'key skills' in the undergraduate curriculum have been promoted through various government initiatives (Drew, 1998). The National Committee of Inquiry into Higher Education encouraged more systematic attention being paid to skills, and identified these as communication, numeracy, IT and learning how to learn (NCIHE, 1997). The traditional emphasis in higher education on imparting a deep understanding of a discipline has given way to more 'mechanistic' concerns (Becher, 1994, p. 233). Against this policy background, we were, therefore, keen to gain a sense of how far 'skills' as such are now part of the currency of curricula approaches in higher education. However, we were also interested in the matter from the point of view of our theoretical approach in which, crudely, we posited a possible move from a conception of knowledge as contemplation to one of knowledge-in-use (and having value only insofar as it has a use-value and/or an exchange value). The skills most valued by employers are not higher level skills, but are generic 'multi-skills', which are more integrated and simplified by new technologies. 'Flexibility' has become increasingly valued (Ainley, 1998).

Inevitably, we saw differences across our sample. The science-based fields are subject to a tacit responsiveness to extramural interests, especially of the global economy and also to changing instrumentation. As 'high tech' displaces 'low tech', the knowledge field undergoes subtle, but profound changes in which competent handling of the procedures and instrumentation becomes important in its own right. The skills internal to the knowledge fields are altered through new technologies. Being a chemist or an electrical engineer now entails not just doing different things; it calls for being a different kind of chemist or electronic engineer:

> A lot of it is really the move from circuit design to system design. When I was an undergraduate, I used to do acres and acres of courses on transistor circuit design, which we simply don't do any of now, because you just buy a chip to

do it all. If you want to make a radio receiver now, you don't design it from scratch, you buy a chip that does it . . .

(Lecturer in Engineering, University C)

These changes are partly a result of technological shifts enabling an increase in efficiency. Students now learn that being a chemist or electronic engineer requires coping with new technologies designed to increase productivity. For some, such changes refract in subtle, but significant ways upon epistemologies themselves: 'progress in knowledge is thus subordinated to technology which has become the most efficient way of achieving scientific proof' (Gokulsing, 1997, p. 95).

In history, the new technologies are entering the curriculum in a different way. Computers are increasingly used as a means of exchanging knowledge, through CD-ROMs and specialist Web sites. One of our case studies offered extensive curriculum 'packages' to their history students on the Web. Here, again, students were learning new ways of being a 'historian', through a more efficient means of storing, retrieving and analysing data.

More strikingly, in history, we came across a different kind of attention being paid to key skills internal to the discipline whereby modules or units are being injected into curricula that pay explicit attention to the skills of history as such. It was in this way, that the idea of 'transferable skills' gained its meaning in history, such skills here being those of interpretation, analysis and scholarly presentation. Accordingly, 'the main issue dividing the profession is not whether their subject should offer training in transferable skills but whether that training should be made explicit or be left implicit' [History at the Universities Defence Group (HUDG), 1997, p. 3].

The humanities have characteristically exhibited a greater self-reflexiveness than the sciences, being intrigued with their own constitution. Yet this debate also demonstrates a shift towards performativity: the new emphasis on making skills explicit is an attempt to exhibit the marketability of history graduates. Knowledge in history is no longer valuable for its own sake.

The influence of the domain of work

The higher education climate seems increasingly pressured to produce graduates ready for the labour market and 'employability' is rapidly becoming yet another 'performance indicator'. It might seem likely that the world of work would be a strong influence on the design of the curriculum. There is, however, a degree of variability across institutions and knowledge fields.

Students may be exposed directly to the domain of work by being either required or invited to experience work as such within their studies. For a professional field such as nursing, where a professional training field is being incorporated into higher education, the domain of work is an integral part of the curriculum model. The changing professional standing of the nurse is entering the curriculum through a 'reflective practitioner' model, exemplified in the keeping of reflective logs and diaries by students (Hill *et al.*, 1996). In consequence, debate over relationships between theory and practice has been particularly strong in nursing studies. As one nursing studies lecturer explained:

> For too long, nursing suffered from 'this is what they teach you in college, but never mind, this is what happens in practice'. Everything we do is related to what happens in practice. The theory-practice link is part of our philosophy of the whole curriculum.

(Lecturer in Nursing Studies, University C)

Business studies has had a history of a similar debate, particularly throughout the 1980s when degree programmes were validated by the CNAA and had a stronger vocational tendency. The dominant issues were whether business studies courses were 'for' business or 'about' business (Tolley, 1983, 1990; Macfarlane, 1997), and the necessity to blend 'relevant knowledge' with 'practical experience' (McKenna 1985, p. 7). Yet this debate has shifted, and the changing circumstances of the labour market have entered the curriculum. Although many business studies degrees are now relatively non-vocational, the business world they are 'about' is increasingly complex. The handling of multiple data and reaching decisions in the open-ended environment of the business world, for example, become reflected in the construction of business scenarios for group projects within undergraduate courses.

In chemistry and electronic engineering, the presence of employers is becoming even more evident. Employers are increasingly consulted in the development of courses; they are invited in to lead teaching sessions; they constitute advisory groups that meet with increasing frequency; and they may offer studentships. In many universities, a year's experience in industry is often built into the basic undergraduate course. While some of these links are long-established, in many institutions these relationships are widening and developing, and are becoming more systematic. Furthermore, the curricula of these subjects may incorporate units which are designed to equip students with specific skills necessary for a particular sector of the world of work. As one engineering lecturer explained:

> The applied technology programmes are more skills based. The whole programme is built around a very focused skill base. It is back to the niche market. It's what the world out there wants at the moment.
>
> (Lecturer in Engineering, University B)

The carry-over from work into the curriculum may be even more subtle and indirect. As indicated above, topics may come and go depending on current challenges within the relevant industry. However, the drivers may be much less visible, with research programmes and interests being affected by large-scale changes in the global economy, and in the unforeseen effects of new technologies. In this sense, and in these fields, epistemologies reflect their corporate and industrial character, which in a short space of time can influence the withdrawal or inclusion of large topics within curricula.

In history, direct exposure to the world of work is much less common. The history degree is largely, as several interviewees suggested, suitable for different types of employment through the development of students' capacity to be critical thinkers. Some informants in our sample suggested that it would be virtually impossible to incorporate a notion of the world of work into the history curriculum. Yet the increasing use of computers in history and the assessment of students' presentations reflect a shift towards the inclusion of skills associated with the labour market.

The knowledge fields in this study were therefore differentially influenced by the domain of work. At one end, the fields that prepare students to enter the labour market for specific jobs are, inevitably, more directly influenced by changes in the labour market. At the other end, knowledge fields that offer a general process of human or intellectual development are less likely to incorporate elements from the world of work into the curriculum. Yet in spite of these differences, there has been a general shift across all knowledge fields towards an emphasis on 'doing', rather than 'knowing'.

The self domain

The self domain is, as yet, an embryonic component of the curriculum but its emergence is clear. Not just talk of 'self-reliance', for instance, but examples presented themselves of curricula forms with this end in mind. Nursing studies presents the most striking instance, requiring students not only to keep reflective logs or diaries and, thereby, to develop self-monitoring and self-responsive capacities, but also to internalise systems of personal accountability. In the sciences, students are now required to develop their public personae by giving presentations, often in groups. It is in the humanities where the student self is, as yet, a relatively unidentifiable explicit component of the curriculum. There, the student self is relatively internal to the academic world, at most developing general critical powers: the external self is barely apparent as a curriculum feature.

Curricula in the sciences are becoming a matter of the formation of students in themselves as sets of knowledge products, carriers of technological and economic products valued for their likely global market worth. The incorporation of skills from the world of work has led to an increasing focus on 'outputs' and exchange-value:

> Our products at the end of the degree are more immediately applicable than someone who has a more academic background.
> (Lecturer in Electronic Engineering, University E)

This general pattern of change suggests that Mode 1 of academic knowledge production is taking on the characteristics of Mode 2 of knowledge created in the context of application (Gibbons *et al.*, 1994). In other words, the production of knowledge has shifted from within the epistemological development of the disciplines, to sites outside of the university where knowledge is applied.

Our overarching concept at the outset was that of performativity: that we may be witnessing an increasing emphasis in higher education on use-value, rather than knowledge for its own sake. There may be emerging notions of the student self that are formed through a principle of performativity. However, performativity takes various forms, including:

1   *Epistemological performativity*: the way in which the scientific fields are shifting, epistemologically, to take on a more practical interest.
2   *Pedagogical performativity*: the way that pedagogies themselves take on a performative character. As a result the lecture, especially through the use of technologies is, perhaps, less an engagement with knowledge so as to develop understanding.
3   *Educational performativity*: especially in the humanities, the skills internal to the discipline are re-defined in terms of their value to the world of work, rather than being left as tacit components of a disciplinary competence.
4   *Self-monitoring performativity*: especially in nursing, students are asked to develop a self-reflexivity which enables them to perform more effectively in clinical practice.

In themselves, these modes of performativities in curricula are relatively weakly developed. Some forms take on a greater dimension in some knowledge fields, notably in science and technology courses; some may be seen more prominently in the newer universities. It is, though, their collective presence that may be beginning to suggest certain curricula movements or, at least, raise some large curricula issues as to balance and integration.

The implications of these performative shifts, especially on the formation of students' educational identities, are bound to alter the traditional conception of a 'graduate'. The increasing focus on the 'outputs' of higher education has meant that students are products of this system, and their market worth will be an indication of the form of education they have received. Their own sense of self as students has changed: they may emerge from a degree with a 'portfolio' designed to market themselves to potential employers. We were therefore interested to investigate to what extent pedagogical strategies had also changed.

Changing pedagogies?

Two generalisations can be made with some confidence. First, lectures continue to dominate as the main form of teaching (Ramsden, 1992) and, so far as we can judge, the form that they take is relatively uni-directional, perhaps even more than previously:

> These days, the lectures tend to be more directed, almost school-teaching. You cannot rely on the individual to take an initiative to go and find out something. If you think that they ought to go to the library, you have to stamp it on their forehead to say go and look in the library.
>
> (Lecturer in Engineering, University F)

In spite of the performative shift in the knowledge field, there remains an underlying pedagogical tight framing (Bernstein, 1990) that encourages learning based on reproduction:

> Essentially, what students learn very rapidly is that you go to the lecture, you listen to what is said, you write it down as well as you can, and you reproduce it as well as you can, and you get good marks. In laboratory work, you go in, you have a set of instructions, you follow the instructions, you get the right answer . . . The students aren't independent, they are reproducers of fed material.
>
> (Lecturer in Chemistry, University F)

> When I was a student, the responsibility was entirely on us in terms of learning, exam results: the onus was on us. I think that the whole culture has turned around now. I find it deeply ironic that students are so much more led than they ever were.
>
> (Lecturer in History, University F)

Secondly, the dominant pedagogical transaction is that between a single lecturer and individual students. These two generalisations hold especially for the non-professional fields. There, the dominant paradigm of the teaching responsibility remains that of the authority in the field engaging with and imparting knowledge and skills to individuals. We came across, for example, several sites in these fields (science and humanities) where there is, as yet, little or no group work among students. The professional fields contain more relaxed pedagogical frames in which there is a greater openness of exchanges between teacher and taught, and in which students engage more with each other.

In the humanities, the dominant belief is that of developing 'independent learners'. In practice, this belief is reflected in students still being asked as individuals to produce in isolation written texts (essays), although, under conditions of mass higher education, the expectations have to be made more explicit:

> History is a degree you largely do on your own. I think we are selling this message more consciously, so in that sense the expectations have not changed much. It is just that the students need more leading, need it to be more spelled out.
>
> (Lecturer in History, University F)

There is, accordingly, relatively little space for the students to inject their own offerings and so construct their own voice, there being relatively limited non-timetabled time. There is some suggestion that the range of problems that students are being set is broadening to take in, for example, environmental or resourcing considerations, but this widening is at the margins. The more open-ended forms of pedagogy implied by 'problem-based learning' (Savin-Baden, 2000) were not in evidence within our sample, although some informants were beginning to experiment with these methods of teaching.

Across the different knowledge fields and institutions, we saw evidence of a performative shift in pedagogies, where the main driver of change is a concern to adapt to a larger number of diverse students. There seemed to be an increasing concern with imparting the relevant knowledge and developing the appropriate skills in the time available. Thus, students were presented with more basic documentation or information on Web pages in order to save time. Reducing face-to-face contact with students was deemed to be more 'efficient'. Innovation that increases efficiency was more valued than innovative pedagogical strategies that require time to develop. As one informant, after his time-consuming attempts to be pedagogically innovative had largely failed, said: 'there is no substitute for talk and chalk'.

Conclusions

If different curricula models of the kind proposed here are developing across knowledge fields (as a result of the varying configuration of forces at work), any attempt to implement a UK-wide curriculum policy is faced with challenges. It will be interpreted in significantly different ways across the various epistemic communities. Institutions, as yet, are not developing institutional curriculum policies that significantly counter this general picture: the institutional dimension is, at most, exerting a weak influence on curriculum patterns.

At all levels of curriculum formation – course team, department, institution, national policy – curricula should be understood as embracing the three domains of knowledge, action and self. The challenge in developing curricula is not just to ensure that these three domains are adequately represented in the curriculum, but that the moments of these three domains are, in due measure, integrated.

There is a greater need for the output-driven system of higher education to concentrate on the processes. Performance indicators, recruitment and reward structures at both national and institutional levels should pay explicit attention to staff's preparedness to take a professional interest in curricula as such and not – so far as teaching and learning are given attention – focus unduly upon individuals' teaching activities. It could be argued that, for the most part, departmental discussions about the curriculum have actually been about particular courses or programmes. We would suggest that 'curriculum' (a somewhat neglected term within higher education) is a larger concept than even that of 'course'. As such, the curriculum deserves professional attention in its own right, and such professionalism needs to be properly nurtured.

Note

1 'Changing Patterns of Undergraduate Curricula' was an ESRC-funded project directed by Professor Ronald Barnett (based at the Institute of Education, University of London) with Dr Gareth Parry, completed in June 1999. We would especially like to acknowledge the contribution of Svava Bjarnason to this project, who as the first Research Officer conducted interviews with nearly 100 academics.

References

Ainley, P. (1998) The end of expansion and the consolidation of differentiation in English higher education, *Teaching in Higher Education*, 3(2), pp. 143–156.

Assiter, A. (Ed.) (1995) *Transferable Skills in Higher Education* (London, Kogan Page).

Barnett, R. & Griffin, A. (Eds) (1997) *The End of Knowledge in Higher Education* (London, Cassell).

Becher, T. (1989) *Academic Tribes and Territories: intellectual enquiry and the cultures of disciplines* (Buckingham, SRHE/Open University Press).

Becher, T. (1994) The state and university curriculum in Britain, *European Journal of Education*, 29(3), pp. 231–245.

Bennett, B., Dunne, E. & Carre, C. (2000) *Skills Development in Higher Education* (Buckingham, Open University Press).

Bernstein, B. (1990) *The Structuring of Pedagogic Discourse, Vol 4: class, codes and control* (London, Routledge).

Boys, C., Brennan, J., Henkel, M., Kirkland, J., Kogan, M. & Youll, P.J. (1988) *Higher Education and the Preparation for Work* (London, Jessica Kingsley).

Drew, S. (1998) Students' perceptions of their learning outcomes, *Teaching in Higher Education*, 3(2), pp. 197–210.

Gerholm, T. (1990) On tacit knowledge in academia, *European Journal of Education*, 25(3), pp. 263–271.

Gibbons, M., Limoges, C., Nowotny, H., Schwartzman, S., Scott, P. & Trow, M. (1994) *The New Production of Knowledge* (London, Sage).

Goodlad, S. (1997) *The Quest for Quality: sixteen forms of heresy in higher education* (Buckingham, Open University Press).

Gokulsing, K. (1997) University education in England and the principle of performativity, in: K.M. Gokulsing & C. Dacosta (Eds) *Usable Knowledges as the Goal of University Education* (Lewiston, Edwin Mellen Press).

Henkel, M. (2000) *Academic Identities and Policy Change in Higher Education* (London, Jessica Kingsley).

Hill, Y., Dewar, D. & MacGregor, J. (1996) Orientation to higher education: the challenges and rewards, *Nurse Education Today*, 16, pp. 389–396.

History At The Universities Defence Group (1997) Submission to NCIHE, *Higher Education in a Learning Society*, Chairman Sir Ron Dearing (London, HMSO).

Huber, L. (1990) Disciplinary cultures and social reproduction, *European Journal of Education*, 25(3), pp. 241–261.

Jervis, M.L. (1996) Nursing-education in universities – a perspective from biological sciences, *Teaching in Higher Education*, 1(1) pp. 49–64.

Lyotard, J.-F. (1984) *The Postmodern Condition: a report on knowledge* (Manchester, Manchester University Press).

MacFarlane, B. (1997) The Business Studies First Degree: institutional trends and the pedagogic context, *Teaching in Higher Education*, 2(1), pp. 45–57.

McKenna, B. (1983) *Undergraduate Business Education* (London, London Chamber of Commerce and Industry).

NCIHE (1997) *Higher Education in a Learning Society*. National Committee of Inquiry into Higher Education, Chairman Sir Ron Dearing (London, HMSO).

Ramsden, P. (1992) *Learning to Teach in Higher Education* (London, Routledge).

Savin-Baden, M. (2000) *Problem-based Learning in Higher Education: untold stories* (Buckingham, Open University Press).

Schön, D. (1987) *Educating the Reflective Practitioner* (San Francisco, CA, Jossey-Bass).

Scott, P. (1997) The postmodern university, in: A. Smith & F. Webster (Eds) *The Postmodern University? Contested Visions of Higher Education in Society* (Buckingham, SRHE/Open University Press).

Silver, H. & Brennan, J. (1988) *A Liberal Vocationalism* (London, Methuen).

Squires, G. (1987) *The Curriculum Beyond School* (London, Hodder and Stoughton).

Tolley, G. (1983) Foreword, in: D. Graves (Ed.) *The Hidden Curriculum in Business Studies* (Chichester, Higher Education Foundation).

Tolley, G. (1990) Enterprise, scholars and students, in: G. Parry & C. Wake (Eds) *Access and Alternative Futures* (London, Hodder and Stoughton).

Wright, P. (1995) Learning through enterprise: the enterprise in higher education initiative, in: R. Barnett (Ed.) *Learning to Effect* (Buckingham, SRHE/Open University Press).

CHAPTER 10

COMING TO KNOW IN HIGHER EDUCATION

Theorising faculty entry to new work contexts

Paul Trowler and Peter Knight

Higher Education Research and Development, 19, 1, 27–42, 2000

EDITOR'S INTRODUCTION

This article was categorised in the introductory chapter as adopting an interview-based methodology to researching academic work. It makes use of three sets of interview data: 24 interviews conducted with new academic staff in England and Canada, 50 previous interviews in one English university, and a re-examination of data produced for three North American studies. The focus of the study is on how new academics are inducted and socialised into their roles.

The authors contextualise their study with reference to two related theoretical frameworks: activity systems theory as developed by Engestrom, and communities of practice as developed by Lave and Wenger. Becoming an academic is seen as entering and coming to know an activity system or a community of practice. They illustrate their argument with lots of illustrative quotations.

Trowler and Knight usefully contrast the rational-cognitive model of learning, which underlies most formal induction processes, with the need of new academics to learn what they refer to as 'embedded' knowledge, which includes also the informal or tacit routines by which things get done in any organisation. In these circumstances, transfer of necessary knowledge may not be easy because those who possess it may not be aware of it. There are clear implications here for academic practice, which the authors set out at the end of their article.

Trowler and Knight argue in their article that research on university culture and organisation lags behind that in other organisations, and schools (see Knight 2002) in particular. Nevertheless, there are developing higher education research literatures in these areas. They include not only the work on academic cultures, particularly associated with Tony Becher, to which Trowler has contributed (Becher and Trowler 2001, Tuire and Erno 2001, Valimaa 1998), but also research into the changing nature of academic work, both in particular countries (e.g. Askling 2001, Cuthbert 1996, Henkel 2000, Lafferty and Fleming 2000, McInnis 2000, Prichard 2000, Taylor 1999, Tight 2000, Trowler 1998) and internationally (e.g. Altbach 1996, Enders 2001, Kogan *et al.* 1994).

References

Altbach, P. (ed.) (1996) *The International Academic Profession: portraits of fourteen countries.* Princeton, NJ, Carnegie Foundation for the Advancement of Teaching.

Askling, B. (2001) 'Higher Education and Academic Staff in a period of Policy and System Change', *Higher Education*, 41, pp. 157–181.

Becher, T. and Trowler, P. (2001) *Academic Tribes and Territories: intellectual enquiry and the culture of disciplines*. Buckingham, Open University Press, second edition.

Cuthbert, R. (ed.) (1996) *Working in Higher Education*. Buckingham, Open University Press.

Enders, J. (ed.) (2001) *Academic Staff in Europe: changing contexts and conditions*. Westport, Ct, Greenwood.

Henkel, M. (2000) *Academic Identities and Policy Change in Higher Education*. London, Jessica Kingsley.

Knight, P. (2002) 'Learning from Schools', *Higher Education*, 44, pp. 283–298.

Kogan, M., Moses, I. and El-Khawas, E. (1994) *Staffing Higher Education: meeting new challenges*. London, Jessica Kingsley.

Lafferty, G. and Fleming, J. (2000) 'The Restructuring of Academic Work in Australia: power, management and gender', *British Journal of Sociology of Education*, 21, 2, pp. 257–267.

McInnis, C. (2000) 'Changing Academic Work Roles: the everyday realities challenging quality in teaching', *Quality in Higher Education*, 6, 2, pp. 143–152.

Prichard, C. (2000) *Making Managers in Universities and Colleges*. Buckingham, Open University Press.

Taylor, P. (1999) *Making Sense of Academic Life: academics, universities and change*. Buckingham, Open University Press.

Tight, M. (ed.) (2000) *Academic Work and Life: what it is to be an academic, and how this is changing*. Oxford, Elsevier Science.

Trowler, P. (1998) *Academics Responding to Change: new higher education frameworks and academic cultures*. Buckingham, Open University Press.

Tuire, P. and Erno, L. (2001) 'Exploring Invisible Scientific Communities: studying networking relations within an educational research community – a Finnish case', *Higher Education*, 42, pp. 493–513.

Valimaa, J. (1998) 'Culture and Identity in Higher Education Research', *Higher Education*, 36, pp. 119–138.

COMING TO KNOW IN HIGHER EDUCATION

Introduction

This paper is based on a study designed to explore early experiences of 24 new academic appointees (NAAs) in 10 Canadian and English universities and a re-analysis of data collected in a 5-year ethnographic study of one medium-to-large English unchartered university; a 'NewU' (i.e. post-1992) institution (Trowler, 1998a). Our purposes were to identify points that were persistently problematic and to learn about practices that made the transition into full-time academic life easier. It was expected that the work would allow us to offer advice about induction practices at a time when accelerating numbers of retirements would mean that higher education institutions would soon be in the business of recruiting, socialising and hoping to retain new academic staff. Some of these research conclusions are presented in our final section, although they are quite far removed from the helpful hints that can be found in guidebooks such as Gibson's (1992).

Associated with our aim of making a useful contribution to induction practice was the intention of developing a grounded theory of this socialisation process. As researchers, we found that we were gaining increasing insight into the nature of the relationship between the organisational context, particularly cultural characteristics, on the one side, and individual and group hermeneutics and practices on the other.

The consequence was our increasing recognition of the importance of the activity systems and communities that lie 'between' the organisational and the individual levels of analysis on which we had been focusing. Of course, theory development is intimately involved with the professional biographies of researchers (Ball, 1994), and our conceptual repertoires and previous work also influenced this theory-building work.

Our view is that practice benefits from the expansion of the range of theories that can be brought to bear in trying to understand research data since, 'without theory, experience has no meaning . . . without theory, there is no learning' (Deming, 1993, p. 105). We concluded that the data could be interpreted in terms of activity system theory (Engestrom, 1987, 1990), which could be complemented by the concept of 'communities of practice' (Lave & Wenger, 1991). Neither the idea of activity systems nor the concept of communities of practice can be exempt from criticism: Vygotsky's Marxian legacy to activity systems theory is simultaneously useful, constraining and distorting, while 'community' can mislead those who are mesmerised by the metaphor.

Our purpose here is neither to test theories nor to deconstruct these two heuristics but to show something of the way in which these borrowings from other academic territories have led to an analysis of the socialisation of NAAs that has considerable implications for practice. It indicates that if we are to understand how they 'come to know' about the rules of their new workplaces, we need to treat localised activity systems or communities of practice as important sites in the acquisition, enactment and creation of culture and knowledge ability, and to reflect upon the processes involved in identity-construction. This has led us to claim that these are heuristics or working hypotheses with potential.

The NAAs data were collected in 1997/1998 and the English unchartered university data came from 1991–1996. The North American studies were done mainly in the early 1990s, although Perry and colleagues' report presaged Menges' 1999 book, which gives a full account of the research. The studies took place at a time when conditions in the higher education work environment were, in the opinion of Australian commentators such as Everett and Entrekin (1994), Smith and Sachs (1995), and Currie (1996), giving cause for concern. In Canada, Karpiak reached similar conclusions (1996, 1997). In the U.S.A., Tompkins had commented on changes of climate in the workplace in 1992. In the U.K., Fisher (1994) explored the stressful effects of such changes. In other words, the issues we identified may become more vexing, if work conditions continue to become uncongenial.

Not universities but activity systems or communities of practice

The main conclusion we reached was that what the higher education institution does about the induction of NAAs is far less significant than what happens in activity systems and in the cultures created in communities of practice. In essence, induction is about the discourses and practices of the teams and departments that the NAA is trying to join.

The literature on university cultures tends to follow, but lag considerably behind, that in the areas of management and of organisation studies generally. It has, for example, adopted an approach to understanding the cultural life of universities, which is nomothetic and functionalist in nature, despite the sustained criticism of such approaches in management and organisation studies over the past few years. Universities as organisations are usually portrayed as fitting into one of four cultural types, with their 'culture' being portrayed as fairly static. 'Strong' and successful cultures are considered to be those where there is a widely shared set of values, a strong ethos and an organisational saga (Clark, 1972) which is communicated to and learned by new entrants (Smart & Hamm, 1993). Bergquist (1993), for example, tells us that there are 'collegial', 'managerial', 'negotiating' and 'developmental' types of universities.

Theorising in the management area has moved on (see, for example, Alvesson, 1993; Sackmann, 1997). Likewise, researchers into the years of compulsory schooling have increasingly moved away from the idea that the school is a homogeneous organisation and are now looking at activity systems (notably departments) and at the different cultures, structures and practices that are identified with differential effectiveness (Gray *et al.*, 1999).

We found that the best understanding of our data meant rejecting the functionalist view of culture as something static, to be learned and conformed with, seeing it instead 'as dynamic and unbounded, comprising a diversity of groups each with the capacity to develop unique mini cultures' (Grbich, 1998, p. 69). This echoes Alvesson's work in which universities consist of multiple cultural configurations which are dynamic in character. The lived reality in one department or service section is quite different from that in another. The group members might almost be in different organisations:

> There are strange experiences [in this department] that . . . people in other departments say wouldn't happen to them. Things that other people would be encouraged to do in other departments you are sometimes discouraged from doing because it means you wouldn't be a faithful psychologist.
>
> (Respondent 15, English unchartered university study, female, psychology)

Indeed, there is usually an antipathy expressed between the local context and the upper levels of the university:

> I mean if you talk to people at my level, at the sharp end of teaching you very quickly form the view that the people at the top from the management to the administration . . . do not know, they do not understand education, they do not understand what they are doing.
>
> (Respondent 44, English unchartered university study, male, applied physics)

Moreover, there are considerable differences between the front-of-stage aspects of culture, the public arena, back-stage, where the deals are done, and under-the-stage, where gossip is shared and opinions formed (Goffman, 1959). Under-the-stage cultural articulation usually takes place amongst close, trusted colleagues in private contexts.

The diversity and dynamism of a university's cultural configuration derives from smaller units within it. These are the cultural powerhouses of university life, places where culture is both enacted and constructed and where personal identity coalesces, is shaped and re-shaped. Following a line of literature stemming back to Soviet work, especially that of Vygotsky, we refer to these small units as activity systems. Space does not allow us to discuss the family resemblances between activity systems and communities of practice (Lave & Wenger, 1991; Wenger, 1998), nor to identify the concept's limitations. Our priority is to show something of a distinctive conceptual position that we have come to invest with heuristic value.

Entering activity systems in university life

We identify activity systems as key sites in the enactment, consolidation and construction of cultures so that different social practices, norms, values, predispositions and taken-for-granted knowledge become instantiated at different locations in the university. It is here that recurrent practices become embedded and developing meanings are shaped, as individuals work together on the issues of professional life. Hart-Landsberg and colleagues offer a succinct description of an activity system:

> An activity system [comprises] . . . a number of basic elements, including a given practitioner or subject, the object or motive of the activity, its mediating artefacts (e.g. tools, signs and symbols), the rules generally followed in carrying out the activity, the community of co-workers and colleagues involved in the activity, and the division of labour within the activity.
>
> (Hart-Landsberg *et al.*, 1992, p. 7)

To understand social practices we need to understand these crucial relationships. Engestrom (1987) has illustrated this in diagrammatic form. Figure 10 develops it by treating a degree program as an activity system.

People are usually members of several activity systems. In higher education, the academic department (or a sub-unit of it) is usually the main one for academic staff but it may also be a research, curriculum development or teaching programme team. Where activities are repeated often enough to have an institutional life, then a community of practice may be identified. It may be strengthened by physical proximity and shared space:

> In actual fact this corridor, I think, is made up of people who have worked together quite closely for a number of years and they are all in that same field. There are a lot of telecommunications people in this corridor and they have a sort of sub group in which I think they have quite a cohesive group of people there.
>
> (Respondent 6, new academics study, female, engineer, English chartered university)

The university may set the structural context for academic work, setting out some of the rules and providing resources, establishing guidelines for the division of labour and setting the task. The community of practice develops the day-to-day practices – behavioural and discursive – and develops codes of signification and sets of assumptions about what they are doing, which quickly become taken for granted (Giddens, 1984, pp. xxxi, 17). Cultural enactment and cultural construction are both taking place. Behaviour is shaped by structure, but social action is also important in shaping behaviour. In short, activity systems are the locus for structuration to occur: 'social structures are both constituted by human agency, and yet, at the same time, are the medium of this constitution' (Giddens, 1976, p. 121).

The task facing the NAAs entering an established activity system is to become engaged with the common sets of understandings and assumptions held collectively in the community of practice; that is, to establish intersubjectivity: 'Intersubjectivity exists when interlocutors share some aspect of their situation definitions. Typically this overlap may occur at several levels and hence, several levels of intersubjectivity may exist' (Wertsch, 1985, p. 159). Although the bulk of psychological work has concentrated on the formation of intersubjectivity between adults and children, the

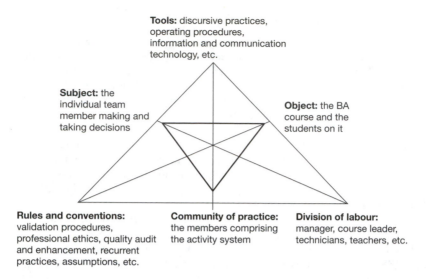

Figure 10 Engestrom's diagram of an activity system (adapted)

concept and ideas about its development are important in understanding induction as well as other areas of organisational life (for example educational policy reception and implementation). Analysis of our data indicates that intersubjectivity is not easily achieved and sometimes this 'coming to know' is impeded because neither members of the activity system nor the NAAs have come to know what they don't know – to recognise the limits of their intersubjectivity.

The key to the development of intersubjectivity is communication: 'Communication aims at transcendence of the "private" worlds of participants. It sets what we might call "states of intersubjectivity"' (Rommetveit, 1979, p. 94). These 'maps' are provisional, what Rommetveit calls 'rough drafts of contract', and they are the new entrant's constructions, rather than objective maps of a fixed and agreed reality. Furthermore, these constructs are seldom built through formal induction, being more the product of participation in the community of practice:

> In terms of initiation into the sort of central philosophy or the culture about approaches to students, well that was by osmosis, we picked that up through centre discussions really.
>
> (Respondent 8, new academics study, female, teacher
> education, English unchartered university)

This operates at the level of the dyad as well as the group:

> Angela and I spent hours ... because we were sharing a unit, she was doing the Geographical aspects and I was doing the History bit, and we spent hours just sharing our views and saying 'yes, I think that's this particular level'.
>
> (Respondent 7, new academics study, female,
> education, English unchartered university)

Many academics (and others) will be familiar with the experience of believing that a conversation was about one thing and suddenly realising that for the other party it was about something different. Meaning is notoriously slippery and even apparently unambiguous terms turn out to be interpreted in different ways. Thus, assessment criteria and departmental handbooks, which should be helpful, can turn out not to be because of the lack of intersubjectivity which needs to be achieved through the processes described above:

> It wasn't really induction. They said it was but I had to find things out I wanted to know and different people were telling me different things. So I just learned it by asking and looking at the handbook. Even then I wasn't sure what the handbook means.
>
> (Respondent 12, new academics study, female, education, English unchartered university)

The constructs formed by members of activity systems are not only somewhat subjective (within the context of intersubjectivity) but also provisional and influenced by power relations. They are not, as functionalist analyses would suggest, based upon realism that allows a shared set of norms, values and discursive practices. Instead, activity systems are multivocalic, sometimes similar, usually different, and frequently contradictory. In that contradiction and conflict lie the roots of cultural construction (Blackler, 1995). An understanding that we developed was that trying to improve induction through improving institutional routines has some value and that it is more valuable to look at the normal quality of communication and relationships within teams – a point made rather differently by Ramsden (1998) talking about departmental effectiveness in general.

Activity systems or communities may be characterised by the usual quality of communication and relationships but they are not, in other respects, static enough for us to think of NAAs entering them once and for all. There are ongoing dialogues – sometimes clashes – between individuals who may share some ideas but who adopt different positions on others. At this point differential power relations come into play as individuals use the resources at their disposal to advance their preferences. The positions adopted may derive from particular roles taken up within the system (manager, teacher, course leader) or may be the expressions of structural factors emanating from the environment. Activity systems are not closed systems, although they are often portrayed as such. They are highly permeable and all actors within them bring cultural 'currents' into the academy. These identities, values and abilities may derive, for example, from professional and gender socialisation, social class location, ethnicity, political or religious affiliation. This is illustrated by the following respondent:

> That first few weeks I just remember feeling a complete culture shock for a number of different reasons. I had come from working in a fairly small infant department with a small staff. You get to know each other, you share a staff room, you share workloads, generally we have our own subject areas but generally you share. So to come to an institution where you felt as if you were an individual, that you had a department but then we had our own offices . . . and this has actually helped our team in working, in a way, by being together, but we were all in our own offices and you were expected to, you know, 'here's your course, get it up, get it running, just get on with it, we've got enough to do'.
>
> (Respondent 8, new academics study, female, education, English unchartered university)

This cultural flow, combined with the internal dynamics of an activity system or community, frequently makes micro-politics a central feature of professional life:

> It's also part of the induction process of learning what the micro-politics are, because I was totally naive about those and I was just talking to people totally openly and honestly thinking they were the same to me. And I thought they were genuine, but it's also because they've got their own battles going on and they think by encouraging me to do something ... [it may help win them]. That's something no one really tells you about but it's part of the assimilation process, the way the academic world is; the forward agenda and the hidden agendas.
>
> (Respondent 10, new academics study, male,
> English chartered university)

The theoretical positions developed to provide the best analysis of the data with which we were working lead to the practical suggestion that the most important way to improve induction is to concentrate on the normal quality of communication and relations in teams and departments. Routine good practice is superior to special institutional induction arrangements, however good they might be.

The individual and activity systems

In this section, we shift the level of analysis down to the individual, considering the processes involved in the continuing construction of personal and professional identity and how these are embedded within the activity system.

What has been said above implies that NAAs involved in university life are engaged in considerable identity 'work', that they are establishing their position in and actively engaging with particular cultural fields, making and re-making their identities, In the process, the activity system is changed, although the impact of the NAAs on the system may not readily be observed.

Identity, then, is not fixed and singular but multiple, dynamic and provisional (Weick, 1995). In studying children, Maclean argues that individuals:

> are positioned by the actions they undertake as group members, by their relative centrality to the group's activities, by the power they wield and the restrictions placed on them as a result of group membership, and by the boundaries which separate members of a group from members of another. ... Membership of a group helps to constitute identity, but it is an identity which is restated and renegotiated with each action.
>
> (Maclean, 1996, p. 172)

Important ways in which this identity work is done within a community of practice include using the discursive resources available to the group to send messages and achieve goals, acting 'politically' to change the character of the group and one's own role in it, constructing and re-constructing relationships with others, giving messages about the 'self' through actions and so on. So, identity construction is always a social activity:

> Because you are in a competitive university world you have to actually construct yourself to be good at all three of these things [research, teaching and administration]. ... You have to present yourself as ... being good in all these three

areas and then it's actually hard to take yourself back out of that and say 'well what originally was I interested in', or 'what did I think I was good at?' . . . You have to have this very fluid identity.

(Respondent 2, new academics study, female,
women's studies, English chartered university)

Of course this accommodative identity construction, though common, is not the whole story. Identity can also be alienated or oppositional:

One of the first things that hit me was my lack of autonomy as a lecturer in the system and I . . . got a bit of a nickname when I first came here because my colleagues in sociology kept talking about disempowerment. Every time I came in they would say 'oh here she comes to talk about disempowerment' because that was my major feeling and that was what I kept saying to them. I feel really disempowered within this context.

(Respondent 31, English unchartered
university study, female, sociology)

[I asked myself] how much work does the University actually do in terms of partnership with other people? . . . I didn't come to this university as a blank slate [but] . . . when I say something . . . what I have to say isn't considered, . . . I went to the Dean and I said 'I don't want to be socialised into this system. I don't know how long I'm going to last here because there are so many things that are against who I am, in conflict with who I am as an individual' . . . [There are areas in which I] can't say the kind of things I really want to. If I really start on the meat and potatoes, the real essence, the core where some of this stuff is coming from, then it's like all of a sudden the person is gone.

(Respondent 17, new academics study, female minority ethnic
group member, teacher education, Canadian university)

While the activity system is important in this identity work, academic staff bring to it cultural characteristics from their background and discursive resources associated with them, as was noted above. Thus the identity work of female academics, for example, is not entirely located within their central community of practice but is crucially influenced by structural factors related to gender socialisation, both their own and that of those they interact with, as one respondent noted in discussing personal support for students in her department:

I do feel from talking to colleagues and students that women do get a disproportionate number . . . it is women who get caught for a lot of that. . . . I frequently get students coming to see me and I'm not their academic counsellor at all but they may have an academic counsellor . . . whom they don't know or don't get on with and so they tend to seek out women, I think, who they see as sympathetic . . . [It] takes up a huge proportion of my time and is emotionally often draining . . . but you're always left with a sense of 'I didn't do enough, I should have done more'.

(Respondent 31, English unchartered university
study, female, sociology)

Here the attitudes and assumptions of the students, as well as those of the woman herself (as illustrated in the last comment), combine to set structural parameters conditioning identity construction. Discursive repertoires are drawn on and both reflect and support this. Respondent 26 in the English unchartered university study draws on gender-related nurturing imagery in talking about 'looking after' a course on which there are 'twenty-five hungry mouths to feed. Or brains.'

However, although structural factors and discursive repertoires available are important, neither identity construction nor discursive use is structurally determined: academics are not simply 'captured by the discourse'. They are aware of the role of discourses and draw on and develop them selectively, or subvert or oppose them, just as they do important, sometimes conscious, identity work which goes beyond structural constraints:

> I am 'marketing' my modules and students 'accumulate credit'. So I think the language of the administration of higher education gives us a very clear indication of what's happening. And of course all of the business about whether to refer to the students as customers or clients, the Student Satisfaction Survey ... These things are always double edged. There is the apparent democratisation that in reality ... is commodification [linked to] fundamental movements taking place.
>
> (Respondent 50, English unchartered university study, male, English)

An implication of the understandings we reached with our data is that NAAs could benefit by appreciating that, while induction involves coming to know aspects of how things are in an intersubjective sense, it is also an invitation to identity creation and to change the community or activity system.

The individual and knowing

In this section we re-present our position by summarising the understanding of knowledge and knowing that was developed by working with data on NAAs.

The implicit theory upon which most professional practice associated with induction and professional socialisation is based is the rational-cognitive model of learning (see, for example, CVCP, 1992). In this model, learning is considered to be individual, private, cumulative, permanent, context independent, acquired and predominantly rational in nature. Such notions presumably derive from, and are reciprocated in, the assumptions embedded in the experience of schooling which most of us share. Of course, there are some forms of learning that NAAs in particular have to do that are close to the rational-cognitive model: learning health and safety rules and procedures, finding out who is responsible for what, learning to use information and communication technology systems and so on. But there is also what Blackler (1995) calls 'embedded' knowledge, which resides in systematic routines and the forms of technology used as well as the way they interrelate. It includes the rules and formal procedures but as they are located in the emergent, often tacit, routines which enable things to get done in an organisation (Wenger, 1998). Understandably, our respondents found it particularly troublesome and irritating to lack this form of knowledge:

> I'm still running around saying 'who's this?' 'who's that?' 'who do I send this to?' 'who do I send that to?'
>
> (Respondent 1, new academics study, female, women's studies, English unchartered university)

It would have been very useful to have someone explain the timetable to me because it completely foxed me.

(Respondent 8, new academics study, female, education, English unchartered university)

Nobody told me there was a pink form system: I had to go and find that out by making lots of mistakes ...

(Respondent 23, new academics study, male, Deaf Studies, English unchartered university)

How basic does it get? Where do I get a desk from? Who do we contact to get the computer plugged in?

(Respondent 24, new academics study, male, Deaf Studies, English unchartered university)

However, in talking of knowledge, there is a danger in suggesting that it has an objective character, and that it is located somewhere 'out there' to be passively acquired by the individual. We have taken a contrary view in our depiction of activity theory. There are advantages in speaking of 'knowing', reflecting the dynamic, social processes by which understandings are constructed, contested and continually changed. Consider Lave's view that:

1 Knowledge always undergoes construction and transformation in use.
2 Learning is an integral aspect of activity in and with the world at all times.
3 What is learning is always complexly problematic.
4 Acquisition of knowledge is not a simple matter of taking in knowledge; rather, things assumed to be natural categories, such as 'bodies of knowledge', 'learners', and 'cultural transmission' require reconceptualisation as cultural, social products (Lave, 1993, p. 8).

The suggestion is that much professional learning is social, provisional, situated, contingent, constructed and cultural in nature. With Lave and Wenger (1991) we argue that activities, tasks, functions and understandings are interwoven with the system of relations in which they have meaning, that is they are contextually located. As a result, social agents tend to 'compartmentalise' conceptions and abilities (Engestrom, 1990, p. 13) and to hold mutually contradictory, and often only partly formed, positions in different parts of their lives (Weick, 1995). As a volume of psychological research attests, one consequence is that people are able to operate skilfully in one context but not in another, albeit a closely related one. This phenomenon problematises the notion of 'transferable skill':

Although I'm quite competent in terms of Primary Geography ... that was a bit of a shock to the system. I suppose that the whole assumption being that if you can teach eight year olds then you can teach eighteen year olds and twenty eight year olds. I mean, there are transferable skills but there's still a lot to learn.

(Respondent 3, new academics study, female, education, English unchartered university)

In terms of activity system theory, the reason transfer is so difficult – and by implication, why 'coming to know' is so problematic – is that some forms of mental processes can be apprehended only by understanding the particular tools and signs that mediate them, and some forms of higher mental processes are rooted in contexted social processes. The task of the NAA here is essentially drawing inferences about how things work within an organisation, what is appropriate and inappropriate behaviour and what the connotative codes which infuse signs and symbols are. It also implies not just passively accepting but actively contributing to the recurrent practices and assumptions, at least after the NAA has achieved a reasonably good understanding of them. This 'coming to know' can be eased where colleagues recognise that the quality of communication and relationships in daily practice is more significant than centrally determined induction arrangements.

This approach rejects the Cartesian or rationalist outlook that locates expertise 'inside' individuals. Instead 'Expertise is socially distributed among workers, jointly constructed in close articulation with features of the work activity and environment' (Hart-Landsberg *et al.*, 1992, p. 5). To repeat: this position, that expertise is socially located, makes it difficult to endorse assumptions that learning (or expertise) is unproblematically transferable from one context to another. Socialisation, then, is not a process of 'assimilation' in which the NAA acquires the viewpoint, attitudes and definitions of other people or groups, although this is the emphasis in much of even recent American work, as Tierney (1997) points out. Rather, it is a joint enterprise to create a situation in which the NAA will become fully involved in the social constitution of work practices, values and attitudes within structural constraints.

This does not just apply to NAAs. Activity systems are not stable but are 'rocked' as the often turbulent environment and internal processes result in change over time. However, as Blackler (1993, p. 870) points out, ambiguities, uncertainties and contradictions such as these can provide key opportunities for individual and collective development. In these cases the context has effectively become 'new' for everyone involved and some form of learning is a likely outcome.

Implications for professional practice

Whilst our main aim here is to elaborate a theoretical model, as we stated in the introduction, it is worth summarising the main implications for professional practice:

*   It leads us to emphasise departmental (or other activity system) leadership as central to successful induction over and above any arrangements made centrally. Recent work on leadership has given considerable attention to the idea that leaders can affect the professional learning of all members of their activity systems through the cultures, expressed in practices and discourses, that they promote. Whilst all members of a community of practice have important effects on the success or otherwise of the integration of NAAs into the community, leadership which has helped an activity system to take itself as an open learning community provides a particularly favourable setting for the NAAs' integration and development – and hence for the development of the whole system.
*   The rational-cognitive model of learning (Blackler, 1993), which is usually tacitly adopted in the planning of induction procedures, needs to be supplemented by a situated model of learning, that is one which considers the activity system as central in conditioning what is learned and how it is learned. This firmly identifies induction as departmental or team business.
*   Whilst some forms of knowledge can be transmitted relatively straightforwardly in the learn-then-do approach, it is clear that for much important professional learning the process of 'coming to know' is not so simple. The notion of situated learning suggests that professional learning involves the negotiation of meaning

and significance and that this is done in social settings, each of which inevitably has unique characteristics. In other words, the quality of the activity system as a site for continuing learning is as important to professional development as the provision of more formal learning opportunities: indeed, it may be more important (Knight, 1998).

- At one level, issues of the sociocultural organisation of space in universities, the sociotemporal locations of the articulation of knowledge and skills and the access that NAAs have to them are important. At another level, questions about the conflicts within communities, alternative discourses, the levels of intersubjectivity that already exist, the motivations of participants, and the maintenance of, and change in, their identities are relevant. There may be coherence or antagonisms here.

- The NAA is involved in considerable inferential work. Whilst tacit knowledge cannot be simply transmitted whole, NAAs can be assisted in their constructivist task. One way in which this can be done is holding an informal induction seminar comprising members of the community of practice in which free-ranging but tightly timed discussion and activities are arranged to address a number of issues, for example:
  - What are our students like?
  - What is a good day?
  - What makes a good teaching session?
  - What is the place of research in the department?
  - What are the characteristics of a good graduate?

- Exercises such as an essay marking moderation workshop or a role-play of key issues which have affected the activity system can be used to supplement the discussion. These suggestions reflect a common view that collaborative and collegial cultures are congenial to continued individual and organisational learning.

- Other forms of induction and socialisation at the activity system level can include:
  - the opportunity for work shadowing of people occupying different roles in the community of practice;
  - the provision of a mentor who is close to the NAA, part of the community of practice and likely to be willing to help (However, Boice, 1992, has argued that there is value in having mentors who are not members of the subject's activity system: the nub of this issue appears to be whether the subject is able to see the mentor as a formative advisor [which is desirable] or as a summative arbiter of success or failure);
  - the creation of as many opportunities as possible for informal discussions and shared work ('. . . less effective academics are more likely to be members of academic departments in which their colleagues rate the department's level of co-operation, discussion and participation low . . .' Ramsden, 1998, p. 363).

- Where it is appropriate to transmit knowledge in more conventional ways this can be done through central course provision (health and safety matters), the use of handbooks (where to get flip chart paper, how to get 'wired'). However, even here these need to be delivered and written with a careful appreciation of the slipperiness of meaning and of the contextualised nature of ways of knowing.

- A comment about the wider management implications of this approach is worth adding here. A once-popular management textbook approach to organisational change through cultural manipulation (Beckhard & Pritchard, 1992) has been enthusiastically adopted by writers in the educational field searching for simple levers of institutional change: '. . . institutional leaders are encouraged to "lead by example" in order to commit others to their vision. . . . Our investigation has convinced us that strategic change is cultural change, and cultural change is related to institutional mission' (Robertson, 1994, pp. 314–315). Where this amounts to a corporate culturalism (Willmott, 1993) that imposes meanings and manipulates culture, then we have considerable reservations, not least on ethical grounds, a view developed more fully by Trowler (1998b). Besides, we have argued that induction, learning and cultural change occur at the level of the activity system, not at the organisational level. Institutional leaders may be 'leading by example' but the eyes and ears of most social agents are fixed on their community of practice locally.

- Finally the theoretical and conceptual approach to understanding professional development and life within universities has important implications for research approaches. To date, most research in higher education institutions – including our own – has adopted approaches based mainly upon methodological individualism. They have relied largely on interviews with, or questionnaires completed by, individual academics. In addition to them, we need fine-grained ethnographic studies at the local level to illuminate and exemplify the important social processes at work within communities of practice in higher education settings.

We predict that as research clarifies the operation of activity systems in higher education there will be an increasing realisation that explanations of academic work need to follow an emergent trend in accounts of school teaching (Hargreaves, 1998) and treat much more seriously the role of emotions. Our interview transcripts contain plentiful data reminding us that the faculty member is not just a cognitive or sociological construct. That realisation is pregnant with implications for the management of induction; of change processes; and of academic careers (Knight & Trowler, 2000).

References

Alvesson, M. (1993). *Cultural perspectives on organisations*. Cambridge: Cambridge University Press.

Ball, S.J. (1994). Researching inside the state: Issues in the interpretation of elite interviews. In D. Halpin & B. Troyna (Eds), *Researching education policy: Ethical and methodological issues* (pp. 107–120). London: Falmer.

Beckhard, R. & Pritchard, W. (1992). *Changing the essence: The art of creating and leading fundamental change in organisations*. San Francisco: Jossey-Bass.

Bergquist, W.H. (1993). *The four cultures of the academy*. San Francisco: Jossey-Bass.

Blackler, F. (1993). Knowledge and the theory of organisations: Organisations as activity systems and the reframing of management. *Journal of Management Studies*, 30(6), 863–884.

Blackler, F. (1995). Knowledge, knowledge work and organisations: An overview and analysis. *Organisation Studies*, 16(6), 1021–1046.

Boice, R. (1992). *The new faculty member*. San Francisco: Jossey-Bass.

Clark, B. (1972). The organisational saga in higher education. *Administrative Science Quarterly*, 17, 178–183.

Clark, J. (1996). The effects of globalisation on 1990s academics in greedy institutions. *Melbourne Studies in Education*, 37(2), 101–128.

CVCP (1992). Resourceful induction; A manual of materials for higher education. In B. Hardwick (Ed.), *CVCP Universities' Staff Development and Training Unit*. London: CVCP.

Deming, W.E. (1993). *The new economics for industry, government, education*. Cambridge, MA: MIT Centre for Advanced Engineering Studies.

Engestrom, Y. (1987). *Learning by expanding. An activity theoretical approach to developmental research*. Helsinki: Orienta-Konsultit.

Engestrom, Y. (1990). *Learning, working and imagining: Twelve studies in activity theory*, Helsinki: Orienta-Konsutit Oy.

Everett, J.E. & Entrekin, L. (1994). Changing attitudes of Australian academics. *Higher Education*, 27(2), 203–227.

Fisher, S. (1994). *Stress in academic life*. Buckingham: Open University Press.

Gibson, G.W. (1992). *Good start: A guidebook for new faculty in liberal arts colleges*. Bolton, MA: Anker Publishing.

Giddens, A. (1976). *New rules of sociological method*. London: Hutchinson.

Giddens, A. (1984). *The constitution of society*. Cambridge: Polity Press.

Goffman, E. (1959). *The presentation of self in everyday life*. New York: Doubleday.

Gray, J., Hopkins, D., Reynolds, D., Wilcox, B., Farrell, S. & Jesson, D. (1999). *Improving schools: Performance and potential*. Buckingham: Open University Press.

Grbich, C. (1998). The academic researcher: Socialisation in settings previously dominated by teaching. *Higher Education*, 36, 67–85.

Hargreaves, A. (1998). The emotional practice of teaching. *Teaching and Teacher Education*, 14(8), 835–854.

Hart-Landsberg, S., Braunger, J., Reder, S. & Cross, M. (1992). *Learning the ropes: The social construction of work-based learning*. ERIC accession number 363726.

Karpiak, I.E. (1996). Ghosts in the wilderness. *Canadian Journal of Higher Education*, 26(3), 49–78.

Karpiak, I.E. (1997). University professors at mid-life. *To Improve the Academy*, 16, 21–40.

Knight, P.T. (1998). Professional obsolescence and continuing professional development in higher education, *Innovation in Education and Training International*, 35(3), 241–248.

Knight, P.T. & Trowler, P. (2000). Editorial: academic work and quality. *Quality in Higher Education*, 6(2), 109–114.

Lave, J. (1993). The practice of learning. In S. Chaiklin & J. Lave (Eds), *Understanding practice* (pp. 3–32). Cambridge: Cambridge University Press.

Lave, J. & Wenger, F. (1991). *Situated learning: Legitimate peripheral participation*. Cambridge: Cambridge University Press.

Maclean, D. (1996). Quick! Hide! Constructing a playground identity in the early weeks of school. *Language in Education*, 10(2&3), 171–186.

Menges, R. & Associates (1999). *Faculty in new jobs*. San Francisco: Jossey-Bass.

Perry, R.P., Menec, V.H., Struthers, C.W., Hechter, F.J., Schönwetter, D.J. & Menges, R.J. (1996). *Faculty in transition: The adjustment of new hires to postsecondary institutions*. Winnipeg, MB: Centre for Higher Education Research and Development.

Ramsden, P. (1998). Managing the effective university. *Higher Education Research and Development*, 17(3), 347–370.

Robertson, D. (1994). *Choosing to change*. London: HEQC.

Rommetveit, R. (1979). On the relationship between children's mastery of Piagetian cognitive operations and their semantic competence. In R. Rommetveit & R.M. Blakar (Eds), *Studies of Language, Thought and Verbal Communication* (pp. 457–466). London: Academic Press.

Sackmann, S. (Ed.) (1997). *Cultural complexity in organisations*. London: Sage.

Smart, J.C. & Hamm, R.E. (1993). Organisational culture and effectiveness in two year colleges. *Research in Higher Education*, 34(1), 95–106.

Smith, R. & Sachs, J. (1995). Academic work intensification: Beyond postmodernism. In R. Smith & P. Wexler (Eds), *After Postmodernism: Education, politics and identity* (pp. 225–240). London: The Falmer Press.

Tierney, W. (1997). Organisational socialisaton in higher education. *Journal of Higher Education*, 68(1), 1–16.

Tompkins, J. (1992). The way we live now. *Change*, 24(6), 12–19.

Trowler, P. (1998a). *Academics responding to change: new higher education frameworks and academic cultures*. Buckingham: Open University Press.

Trowler, P. (1998b). What managerialists forget: Higher education credit frameworks and managerialist ideology. *International Studies in Sociology of Education*, 8(1), 91–109.

Weick, K. (1995). *Sensemaking in organisations*. Thousand Oaks, CA: Sage.
Wenger, B. (1998). *Communities of practice: Learning, meaning and identity*. Cambridge: Cambridge University Press.
Wertsch, J.V. (1985). *Vygotsky and the social formation of mind*. Cambridge, MA: Harvard University Press.
Willmott, H. (1993). Strength is ignorance; slavery is freedom: Managing culture in modern organisations. *Journal of Management Studies*, 30(4), 515–552.

CHAPTER 11

AGENCY, CONTEXT AND CHANGE IN ACADEMIC DEVELOPMENT

Ray Land

The International Journal for Academic Development, 6, 1, 4–20, 2001

EDITOR'S INTRODUCTION

This article was categorised in the introductory chapter as adopting a conceptual approach to the analysis of academic work. It makes use of 31 interviews with academic developers working in UK higher education institutions, a group the author describes as 'a fragmented community of practice'. While extracts from these interviews are used as illustrations, the focus of the article is, however, on identifying and explicating different models and theories of, and orientations towards, academic development. That is why I have characterised it as a conceptual piece, rather than an example of an interview-based piece of research. It is relatively uncommon, in the higher education literature, to find this level of engagement with concepts and theories.

Using his data, Land first identifies 12 orientations to academic development practice, including the managerial, entrepreneurial, romantic, reflective practitioner and vigilant opportunist. he then maps these on to a two-dimensional model of academic development, in terms of whether the focus is on the individual or the institution, and whether what he terms domesticating or liberating strategies are adopted.

The second half of the article then categorises academic developers' attitudes to change, each of which is exemplified by quotations from Land's interviewees. Nine varieties of attitude are identified, including systemic models, empirical-rational strategies, disjointed incrementalism, the 'garbage can' model, cybernetic models, diffusion models, opportunistic change, Kai Zen, and chaotic theories. Finally, links are made between orientations to academic development and change conceptions, and associated theorists are identified.

Land's study is unusual in focusing on the academic development function, an area for research which is only gradually being opened up as academic development becomes a standard and accepted part of academic life (e.g. Macdonald 2001). Publications in this area tend to take either a more theorised or more 'how to' approach (cf. Webb 1996 and 1994 respectively). However, Land contextualises his study in terms of the literature on university cultures (Becher 1989, McNay 1995: see also the article by Trowler and Knight (2000) included in this Reader; pp. 155–170).

References

Becher, T. (1989) *Academic Tribes and Territories: intellectual enquiry and the cultures of disciplines.* Buckingham, Open University Press: note a second edition, co-authored with Paul Trowler, was published in 2001.

Macdonald, I. (2001) 'The Teaching Community: recreating university teaching', *Teaching in Higher Education*, 6, 2, pp. 153–167.

McNay, I. (1995) 'From the Collegial Academy to Corporate Enterprise: the changing cultures of universities', pp. 105–115 in Schuller, T. (ed.) *The Changing University?* Buckingham, Open University Press.

Trowler, P. and Knight, P. (2000) 'Coming to Know in Higher Education: theorizing faculty entry to new work contexts', *Higher Education Research and Development*, 19, 1, pp. 27–42.

Webb, G. (1994) *Making the Most of Appraisal: career and professional development planning for lecturers*. London, Kogan Page.

Webb, G. (1996) *Understanding Staff Development*. Buckingham, Open University Press.

AGENCY, CONTEXT AND CHANGE IN ACADEMIC DEVELOPMENT

Introduction

What emerged from the analysis of data generated from 33 interviews with practising academic developers in the UK was the many-faceted aspect of their agency. They were in some respects a fragmented community of practice. Stones (1991, 1996) has spoken of 'agent conduct analysis' and 'agent context analysis' as ways of understanding practice, and the agent's 'strategic conduct' and 'strategic terrain' as means of characterizing the site of practice. We might perceive the context and strategic terrain of academic development as the organizational forms, academic cultures and sub-cultures within which they have to practise. Their strategic conduct can be characterized by what have I termed their orientation to academic development. Orientations are analytic categories which include the attitudes, knowledge, aims and action tendencies of academic developers in relation to the contexts and challenges of their practice, but they do not relate to developers' personal characteristics, and are not fixed.

'Development', suggests Webb (1996, p. 65) 'may be viewed as a site for contest: it is not a unitary concept for which, one day, we will provide a model. The very meaning of the word "development", how it is constituted, the kind of activities it implies, are all discursive, and can be interpreted according to various ontological and epistemological standpoints.' He argues that there is no 'super-standard' from which we can judge these positions, and our notions of development are 'of necessity a site for encounter and dispute'. The analysis of qualitative data in the present study should be viewed in the light of Webb's comments. Twelve distinct orientations to practice emerged, which are discussed below. The term orientation, derived from phenomenographic studies, is chosen deliberately so as not to imply innate or fixed personal attributes but a way of making sense of a given situation or set of tasks that subsequently informs and influences action. In this definition a practitioner may (and indeed does from the data available in this study) adopt differing orientations in different strategic contexts. Hence it is inappropriate to talk of an individual practitioner as say, a 'romantic developer', but rather 'a developer with a romantic orientation'. The differing orientations may alternatively be viewed as variations on practice, for, as Marton (1999) has recently argued, variation is a crucial dimension of understanding the nature of skill and expertise. These orientations, it is argued, need to be mapped against organizational cultures and the needs and expectations of differing stakeholder groups. They can also be located in terms of their tendency towards emancipatory purposes (critique) or 'domesticating' purposes (institutional policy). Practice can have a systemic direction or be directed towards the needs of individuals, and can be seen to draw on different theoretical perspectives and literatures. This analysis will culminate in a complex theoretical model demonstrating these interacting relationships and influences. It is hoped that, from the accounts discussed below, a better understanding, an illumination, of the conceptions and approaches of academic developers to their practice will emerge.

Orientations to academic development

The orientations to academic development that were identified in the study can be represented in the form of a typology, see Table 35. A fuller discussion of these orientations illustrated by the comments of practitioners may be found in Land (2000).

Organizational cultures

Such orientations, to be effective, need to be congruent with the strategic terrain – the organizational culture or cultures within which the developer practises. The most well known of these is probably Becher's (1989) examination of university culture. Becher stresses the complexity of universities as organizations and provides four main patterns or models of organizational behaviour (Table 36).

The first category in Becher's typology, *hierarchical* forms, refers to an organizational culture predicated on recognizable lines of command, predetermined bureaucratic procedures and clarity of role. However, Sawbridge (1996, p. 5), in her study of UK employment-led staff development, concluded that '. . . hierarchy, in the form that would be recognisable in the civil service, the army or in many industrial and commercial enterprises, is not evident in universities in spite of distinct trends towards a more sharply defined post-Jarratt (1985) role for vice-chancellors and immediate seniors'. What she did conclude was that hierarchical decision-making was more prevalent in the ex-polytechnic institutions, where staff developers were found by Sawbridge to refer to the Vice-Chancellor as a significant figure far more than in older universities. Smaller HEIs, or monotechnic institutions, might also be more likely to retain aspects of hierarchical culture.

'The counter-balance', she argues, '(some would argue that it is a barrier) to more centralised control systems is because of other organisational forms at work. Of most significance in academic folklore and tradition, is the question of *collegiality*, sometimes embraced in the concept of a community of scholars' (Sawbridge, 1996, p. 5). In this she draws on Becher's view that hierarchical forms tend to be compromised in academic institutions because 'there remains a fundamental value in the academic community that the trade in ideas should be free . . . the result is a strong sense of collegiality in which scholars are called upon to respect each other's intellectual independence regardless of age and position. Authority is, in this tradition, always subject to ratification from below' (Becher, 1989). However, if collegialism is a constant counterweight to hierarchy within academe, then Sawbridge recognizes that a threat to the collegial ideal may still arise from a newer *managerialism*:

> It would appear to be the case that the increased focus on employer-led initiatives in the last decade, appraisal, performance-related pay, increasing casualisation of the workforce, trends towards massification and more pro-active staff development to name but a few, is different in character than in the post-1960s. Then

the major concerns were about growth within an elitist structure and perceived problems about how to deal with staff, many with unfamiliar pedigrees and/or disruptive and unsocialised students. In this sense one can see employer initiatives, including the growth of interest in staff development, as intervening in the collegial culture because it leaves too much to chance at a time of institutional challenge.

(Sawbridge, 1996, p. 6)

However, a countervailing tendency might be observed in relation to *anarchical* forms in that academics in some respects are able to retain an arm's length independence from their employing institution. 'Because their reference group is national and international, they are more able to resist managerial pressures', suggests Sawbridge (1996, p. 7). 'In any event their subject expertise makes it difficult for managerialist interventions to succeed without their co-operation.' Becher, also, concludes that the anarchic tendency of some academic organizations, which are 'more antimanagerial than managerial, concerned with disorganisation rather than organisation ... stems from the high degree of autonomy enjoyed by academics.' However Gouldner (1979) reminds us that there remains an important difference between 'cosmopolitans', those outstanding academics whose status allows them a privileged role within managed organizations, and the less privileged, more managed and more put-upon 'locals'.

Becher's identification of *political* forms within academic organization draws attention to the personal and professional power of individuals and groups in decision-making processes. Birnbaum (1988) points out that the most powerful departments are those generating the greatest income through research or fees and in turn attracting the best students, enhancing their status and power further. But political cultures are, according to Becher (1989), usually conflictual cultures and resolution of such internecine strife usually amounts to political expediency, compromise and short-term vision. Sawbridge (1996, pp. 8–9) argues that decision-making within the institution 'will rest on the degree to which it is seen to be in the political interests of influential people in departments and faculties'. In her study such political power was also found to be a prerequisite of the effective functioning and even survival of academic development units and was dependent on how effectively developers could negotiate with senior staff and on the strength of the constituency they could gather around them.

McNay (1995) alternatively, suggests the four cultures of *collegium, bureaucracy, corporation and enterprise*. 'All four co-exist in most universities', he argues, but with different balances amongst them. These differences depend on a range of factors including 'traditions, mission, leadership style and external pressures' (McNay, 1995, pp. 105–6). He provides in Figure 11 a diagrammatic representation of how the four cultures relate to tight or loose coupling in relation to policy definition and control of implementation.

The key word for the collegium, suggests McNay, is 'freedom'. For bureaucracy it would be 'regulation', though 'This can have many positive objectives: consistency of treatment in areas such as equal opportunities or financial allocations; quality of activities by due process of consideration; propriety of behaviour by regulatory oversight; efficiency through standard operating procedures' (McNay, 1995, pp. 105–6). In the corporation culture the key word is 'power', and the enterprise culture 'my choice of keyword would be client'.

That carries with it connotations not only of the market, where customers would be more appropriate but of professionalism where the knowledge and skills of experts, and the needs and wishes of those seeking their services, come together.

Table 35 Orientations to academic development practice

Orientation		Description	Operational focus/level
1	Managerial	Concerned with developing staff towards achievement of institutional goals and mission	Institution
2	Political strategist (investor)	Principally aware of shifting power relations within organization and wider HE environment. Aligns development with agencies most likely to yield dividends	Academic development unit
3	Entrepreneurial	Fosters innovative practice related to needs of world of work and employers. Often involved in income-generating, partnership approaches	Employers, other external stakeholders
4	Romantic (ecological humanist)	An outreach approach concerned with the personal development, growth and well-being of individual practitioners within the organization	Individual practitioner
5	Vigilant opportunist	Takes advantage of topical developments and opportunities in strategic way as they arise within the institution or environment unit	Academic development unit
6	Researcher	Sees most effective way of influencing colleagues' practice as being through presentation of compelling educational research evidence	Discipline or community of practice
7	Professional competence	Brings staff up to baseline level of skill competence in aspects of teaching and learning	Service to student body
8	Reflective practitioner	Seeks to foster culture of self- or peer-evaluative, critical reflection amongst colleagues, to help them cope with uncertain and ambivalent organizational environments	Individual practitioner
9	Internal consultant	Works with departments or teams in observational/evaluative/advisory capacity, often on longer term basis	Department/course team
10	Modeller/broker	'Trojan horse' approach of working alongside colleagues to demonstrate good practice or innovation. 'Do as I do' rather than 'do as I say'	Individual practitioner/department
11	Interpretive/hermeneutic	Dialectic approach of 'intelligent conversation' with colleagues in which balancing of different views, relation of local to wider perspectives, part to whole, etc. leads to critical synthesis and production of new shared insights and practice	Individual practitioner/department
12	Discipline-specific	Predicated on notion that colleagues are driven by their subject–specific 'guild' culture, hence development only effective when going with grain of disciplinary needs. Development can be seen as 'situated learning' within a disciplinary community of practice	Departmental colleagues/wider 'guild' or discipline

Table 36 Becher's four main patterns of organization behaviour (from Sawbridge, 1996, p. 9)

Organizational pattern	Characteristic features
Hierarchical	Authority conferred from above Recognizable chains of command Pre-determined regulations and procedures Specified roles
Collegial	Authority ratified from below Equality of rights in decision-making Decisions exposed to dissent High personal discretion
Anarchical	Authority eroded by personal loyalties Emphasis on individual autonomy Ambiguous goals; pluralistic values Influence based on expertise
Political	Authority deriving from personal power Conflict as basis for decisions Policies based on compromise Influence deriving from interest groups

In organisation terms, it means that key decisions should be located close to the client, within a well-defined general policy framework, and that the good of the client should be the dominant criterion for decision-making.

(McNay, 1995, p. 107)

A model of academic development

We are now in a position to map the orientations to academic development that were identified earlier against the organizational cultures we have just discussed. We might go further and construct a tentative model which also aligns orientations to academic development with particular stakeholder groups, with bodies of procedural knowledge, and with either emancipatory tendencies or domesticating tendencies in relation, respectively, to institutional policy adoption or policy critique. Figure 12 presents a cumulative representation of practice. The usual caution would apply against reading too much prescription, closure, or foundationalism into this model. It is intended to be a useful heuristic at a given point of time, and is meant to serve only as a useful and illuminative simplification.

The orientations to academic development discussed above can first be located in relation to two axes each representing polarized tendencies. The vertical axis charts the extent to which academic development practice might be seen as focused more directly towards meeting the personal needs of individual practitioners (academic staff or students) as opposed to being oriented more towards the requirements of the institution and its functioning at a systemic level. A concern with the efficient implementation of a system of modularization, for example, might be considered as demonstrating a systems orientation whereas concern with helping a junior member

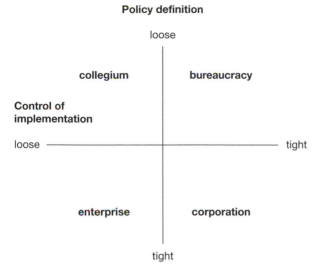

Figure 11 McNay's model of universities as organizations

of staff cope with the stress levels engendered by burdensome assessment loads might be deemed more as a person orientation.

The horizontal axis again measures polarized tendencies. A domesticating tendency indicates practice that is principally concerned with encouraging or developing behaviours both in self and others that conform with the expressed 'official' or explicit purposes or mission of the institution or its prevailing and influential normative culture(s). These may be either explicit and overt or implicit and covert. A liberating tendency on the other hand would indicate practice that ran counter to such prevailing purposes and cultures and sought to transform them.

These tendencies have been adapted from a conceptual model originally proposed by Wellington and Austen (1996) in relation to differences in orientation to reflective practice. It is suggested here that these tendencies have equal validity in relation to how orientations to academic development might be plotted against these differing values. Figure 12 elaborates their model by suggesting that a systems orientation implies the meeting of institutional needs as opposed to the meeting of individual needs through a person orientation. Similarly it is argued that Wellington and Austen's domesticating-liberating axis can be interpreted as marking a spectrum which emphasizes adherence to expressed policy at one extreme and commitment to 'emancipatory' critique at the other. The plotting of specific orientations to academic development against these tendencies can also be found (amongst other factors) in Figure 12. It might of course be argued that not all educational research activity should be construed as offering critique and that educational research can be deployed to support an existing policy stance. Such policy-oriented research would of course be plotted further towards the domesticating end of the horizontal axis. This is omitted on grounds that the model is acknowledged as demonstrating an inevitably simplified view, particularly as further contextual factors are to be added to the model in a pattern of increasing complexity.

One such further factor, superimposed in the diagram, is the organizational culture (strategic terrain) against which the academic developer conducts his or her practice. Again the choice of representative cultures is inevitably a simplification for the sake

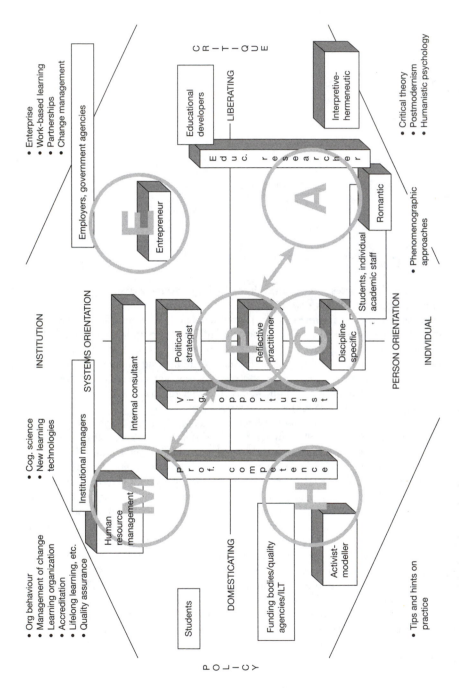

Figure 12 A model of academic development

of greater clarity, and is derived eclectically from the typologies of academic cultural forms and structures discussed earlier. In this simplified representation the letter endings have the following signification:

- A = anarchic culture
- C = collegial culture
- E = enterprise culture
- H = hierarchical culture
- M = managerial culture
- P = political culture

The diagram once more shows how the various orientations to academic development might be located in relation to these prevailing cultures. For example, an interpretive-hermeneutic or researcher orientation would, it is suggested, be a more likely feature of agent conduct, to use Stones' term (1991, 1996) when the agent context is a mainly anarchic culture, just as a human resource management orientation would be more likely to characterize agent conduct when the agent context and strategic terrain is predominantly a managerial culture.

The diagram incorporates a further factor, namely the bodies of research literature or forms of procedural knowledge from which particular orientations to academic development might be seen principally to draw. A romantic orientation, for example, might well imply a preference for the development literature associated with humanistic psychology, an educational researcher orientation with phenomenography, interpretive-hermeneutic orientation with critical theory or postmodernism and human resource management orientation with the literature.

Layered upon the representation of organizational cultures in the diagram are the various stakeholder groups within higher education whose needs the particular organizational cultures are considered principally to address. Hence within a managerial culture the needs of managers themselves, as well as the collective consumerist presence of the student body, would be valorized. Within an anarchic or collegial culture, however, greater priority, it is argued, is more likely to be given to the needs of individual students or individual academics.

In the diagram all these factors combine and interact to form a complex semantic space, the two-dimensional nature of which constrains its representation. Ideally a dynamic three-dimensional representation would serve better to render the fluid and ambiguous nature of the model and its essential tensions. Though by necessity simplified, the model is intended to provide a starting point for the examination of issues that arise from a recognition of the interplay between agent conduct and the strategic terrain within which such conduct is found.

Academic development and change

A further significant attribute of academic development practice is the practitioner's attitude to change. Though developers emerged from the study as a fragmented tribe, dwelling in many neighbourhoods of a divided village, nonetheless one feature which all would appear to have in common is an identification with the notion of change. Some developers are uncomfortable with being seen in any way to predetermine the direction of development. Nonetheless, all recognize that a process of change must be negotiated in some fashion, entered into and supported if the developer's role is not to be superfluous. Academic developers, unlike, perhaps, other professional groups within higher education, have no vested interest in maintaining the status quo. As we have seen in the analysis of other complex concepts, such as organizational culture and orientation to academic development, attempts at definition inevitably lead to understandings that are multi-faceted, inter-related, overlapping and dynamic. It is not surprising therefore to find that developers' attitudes to change are similarly variegated and complex. The following represent a range of the conceptions of change that emerged as underpinning developers' practice, either explicitly or by analogy.

Systemic models: force field analysis, the law of unintended consequences, unfreezing and refreezing

> I think a lot of it is about identifying what harriers there are around in the system that're getting in the way of changes – positive changes – that need to be happening. And that's not always easy because there are so many conflicting forces pushing things this way and that. But it's often more effective to try and remove barriers if you can identify and locate them than just banging on trying to change things and hitting a brick wall all the time. It's that notion of a force field with change forces and resistance forces all held in check, in a balance, an equilibrium, and if you move away certain of the resisting forces then you don't have to keep driving the change. It will just flow, it will free things up. Deconstipate it! (*laughs*)
>
> (Respondent 21)

An early and influential contributor to theories of organizational change was Lewin (1952) who posited the notion of a *force field* operating in a social system, and emphasized the need when contemplating organizational change to consider not just the forces at the point of change – i.e. destabilizing forces for change – but as far as is possible all the forces operating in the system.

> the system had been stable before the change, and any stable system which is disturbed in the first place tries to return to its former stability. The result is that the forces which previously ensured the stability of the system will now act so as to re-establish that stability, i.e. they will oppose the change.
>
> (Elton, 1998, p. 1)

As the reactive (stabilizing) forces oppose the original force for change this can mean that the pressure for change produces unintended effects quite dissimilar from those envisaged. This tendency was noted by Tutt (1985, p. 34) and has come to be known as Tutt's law or the 'law of unintended consequences'. There is, as Elton has pointed out, a continuously changing balance between the forces which support the change and those which oppose it. Academic developers need to concentrate as much on the barriers to innovation as on the forces supporting it.

> As the drivers of change invariably have more control over the supporting than over the opposing forces, they tend to increase the former with the inevitable consequence of the latter also increasing, which is usually a recipe for disaster. The alternative strategy, which involves the drivers of change attempting to reduce the opposing forces, over which they generally have little or no control, may be a difficult one to pursue, but it is the only one which is likely to lead to success. It certainly requires patience and time.
>
> (Elton, 1998, p. 2)

So the innovation process, according to Lewin's theory, is a *political* process taking place in a field of mutually opposing forces around an equilibrium, and has to be appreciated in the light of the state of the field as a whole. The main phases of the innovation process are *unfreezing, moving* and *refreezing*. 'Unfreezing', explain Berg and Östergren (1979, p. 267), 'signifies that the possibility for change is created. Moving denotes a continuous disequilibrium, caused by the dominance of the driving forces over the restraining forces. Refreezing means that balance is created around a new equilibrium'. The model has obvious implications for the modus operandi of developers of a political-strategic orientation.

Empirical-rational, normative-re-educative and power-coercive strategies

A different respondent introduces the notion of rationality as a mechanism for change in higher education. He speaks of colleagues 'coming on board' because 'they will see the logic' of 'a compelling idea'.

> A lot of the job . . . is really about changing attitudes and conceptions and in that sense we are being proactive. I think we should be focussing on changing attitudes, the attitude that students are at fault when they don't learn. We have to switch to organisational development, balance of forces and, I think, the power of ideas as a change mechanism. I think that that's the thing that is critical to the development process that academics will respond to the power of ideas. Sometimes their attitudes will make them not respond but if you can really marshal together a compelling idea then people will find it hard to – and some of them may still resist it – but people will come on hoard because they will see the logic of it.
>
> (Respondent 12)

Respondent 12's view is in keeping with influential perspectives originally proposed by Benne and Chin (1969). They suggested three 'general strategies for effecting changes in human systems' which were an *empirical-rational* strategy predicated on reason, a *normative-re-educative* strategy based on motivation, learning and positive affective factors, and a *power-coercive* strategy utilizing power relations. In the empirical-rational strategy the underlying assumption is that people are reasonable and, given sufficient understanding of a situation, will act in a rational fashion. Hence the primary task of the innovator is to demonstrate through the best known method the validity of a certain change in terms of increased benefits. Of course the success of this approach depends on the extent to which colleagues will respond rationally. Whereas Respondent 12's perspective was very much in line with the empirical-rational perspective – which accords well with educational researcher and consultant orientations to academic development – Respondent 1 can be seen to be working within a normative-re-educative framework in which the motivation and conviction of colleagues is seen as crucial to organizational change:

> I don't feel those sort of [managerial] pressures. Well, there probably are but I don't feel them. No, fortunately, either you are working with people who want to bring about the changes themselves, for whatever reasons . . . there are not many ostriches we have to work with. I know we ought to reach them but my feeling is given that there's two of us and life is short, it's better to help the people who want the change, than you know . . . If you go in with a rigid preconception of what . . . where they should be going, it doesn't work.
>
> (Respondent 1)

This respondent, with a background in nursing, introduces a biological distinction between growth and development, but points out that, as an academic developer she can only establish a context in which development can occur:

> Growth is an increase in size. Development is a change in function. Ha-ha! That is actually true ... biologically speaking. Change in function ...
>
> *The Interviewer: would that apply to higher education?*
>
> ... yes course it would. As well as the growth of the present methods we use. But I can't do that, I can provide opportunities for that to occur. But it's the individual who ... I can provide opportunities for people to develop. They can only develop themselves. You can't change someone. They can only change themselves. You can point out areas where they might want to explore, and having explored will decide to see things differently, but I cannot make that decision for them.
>
> (Respondent 1)

Of central importance within a normative-re-educative approach is how the client understands his or her problem. With this strategy the change agent works with the client to discover the client's attitudes, values and opinions. The change agent seeks to avoid manipulating the client by bringing the values of the client, along with his or her own values, into the open and by working through value conflict responsibly. This approach does seem to have an effect on 'hearts and minds', but the timescale involved may be unacceptably long. The normative-re-educative change strategy appears to have the greatest correspondence with romantic and reflective practitioner orientations. A power-coercive strategy, on the other hand, seems, not surprisingly, to be adopted more by those of a political orientation:

> And you work with them to engage the people who are in leadership positions. Because there's not much point in trying to work with the people that you know are going to be really hard to convert. So unfortunately – and this is where academic development needs the support of champions in order at some point or other maybe to say to some of the die-hards: 'You gotta do this guys!' So I think ... that's overtly political and I think that academic development has always been a political process.
>
> (Respondent 2)

or developers of a managerialist orientation who recognize the coercive power of external 'imperatives':

> The obvious coming imperatives are the RAE 2001 {UK Research Assessment Exercise}, and the new Quality Assurance arrangements. These are absolute coming imperatives. Everybody will focus their mind on those issues because they're up in big neon lights in front of them. (*laughs*)
>
> (Respondent 14)

In power-coercive strategies the change agent may use power to get things done to order, but colleagues may remain unpersuaded of the benefits, refuse to 'own' the innovation and harbour resentments which may surface later.

> People always see imposed change as something to be resisted but change that they have identified and chosen for themselves they get interested in and are

keen on. I quite like the model of change put forward by Hersey and Blanchard (1988), basically saying that if change is imposed then it's perceived as being that you've got to do something differently, i.e. it's about behaviour. But they point out that change is concerned with knowledge and understanding and attitude. You have to try working from both directions. It's the old idea of working *with* people not working *on* people.

(Respondent 28)

Disjointed incrementalism

A key question for developers is the extent to which change can actually be managed in complex organizations. Elton (1998) points out that organizational change has to be considered strategically as a *systemic* phenomenon, but also that *as* systems, higher education institutions tend to be very different from each other. The following respondent endorses this view of tackling organizational change systemically:

> You've got to be capable of systems thinking and of working in the political domain, I think one of the things that academic developers have to get good at is *creating the context in which change is possible*, and you need these qualities to be able to do that. I think academic developers should pay more attention to creating the context of change rather than just 'getting on with the change'.
>
> (Respondent 28)

Though a rational-deductive ideal, appearing systematic and comprehensive, might be attractive as an approach to organizational decision making, the reality is much more likely to be what Lindblom (1959) referred to, felicitously, as 'the science of muddling through'. The technical name he gave to the way he felt that decisions are actually made in organizations is disjointed incrementalism. According to Lindblom's classic model of organizational decision making, decisions tend to be:

- *incremental* – taken a bit at a time, dealing in small changes to the existing situation and therefore easier to comprehend
- *serial* – a series of attacks on problems, which are not usually solved but merely alleviated; decisions only move in the general direction of a solution
- *remedial* – the marginal changes move away from the ills of the day rather than towards defined (strategic) goals
- *means-oriented* – the means (i.e. strategies) are not adjusted to ends (i.e. goals) but often the objectives are redefined so that they can be brought within the cost of the means
- *restricted* – only a restricted number of alternatives is considered, with only a restricted number of consequences for each alternative; in this way the task remains manageable through the exclusion of imponderable possibilities that might prevent any decision being made at all
- *disjointed* – decisions are made by many people at scattered and unco-ordinated decision points

The 'garbage can' model of organizational choice

> I don't know if you're familiar with what Americans call a 'garbage can' model of how things . . .
>
> *The interviewer: Cohen and March?*

Right! Well it's not far off the mark here. This place is definitely a garbage can. There's all kinds of stuff swilling around in here, in {name of senior committee} and no-one seems ever to link up solutions to what we're meant to be solving. And then things move on and other stuff keeps coming over the horizon, every bloody day, it seems, and when stuff does get decided it's usually because the big players have lost interest or it's just got derailed by something else and things get settled ... by default I suppose.

The interviewer: organized anarchy!

Yes! Absolutely. But don't get me wrong. If you asked me whether I'd want the culture to be different I'd probably say no. In many respects it suits. There are opportunities. Gaps open up. People's eye goes off the ball and things can 'happen' (laughs). I mean I remember quietly squeezing through a module on Independent Learning. Colossal precedent! Students could design their own learning! Not a squeak. Committee were obsessed with some other daft thing about APEL that didn't matter a hoot as it turned out.

(Respondent 21)

This recalls Cohen and March's (1986) reference to 'the phenomenon in complex organisations of "important" choices that often appear to just "happen"' (Cohen and March, 1986, p. 200). Another developer notes how, as Cohen and March would put it, 'problems, choices and decision makers arrange and rearrange themselves'.

You know for all the world the senior managers and deans in this place remind me of little kids at Christmas. They've got all these projects and initiatives and corporate objectives all over the floor like toys at Christmas. And they get excited because they've just unwrapped one present but then they get another and now they're confused because they don't know which one to play with first and they keep picking them up and putting them down and then another shiny toy appears, so they chuck the others aside. It's really like that! They just don't know what they're doing. Then another kid comes in and thinks 'Ooh I like that one too, I think I'll have that!'

(Respondent 32)

These responses reflect an influential systemic view of universities which was offered by Cohen and March. They characterized their modes of governance as 'organised anarchies' (1986, p. 197) and based this assumption on three factors: the ambiguity of goals, the lack of clarity about purposes, and the transient character of many participants' involvement. This view sees correspondences between the academic freedom found in collegial cultures and the lack of centralized government, and preference for voluntary co-operation that characterizes the political version of anarchism. It similarly recognizes in the two scenarios a concern for responsible individual and collective decision-making.

They draw upon their earlier work (Cohen *et al.*, 1972) relating to 'garbage can theory'. Garbage cans can have 'streams' of problems, solutions, participants and choice opportunities, and these provide opportunities for analysis of situations. 'A solution', they suggest, 'is an answer actively looking for a problem' (1972, p. 3). Within a garbage can there is no easy causal relationship between problems and solutions, or questions and decisions. 'Despite the dictum that you cannot find the answer until you have formulated the question well, you often do not know what the question is in organisational problem-solving until you know the answer' (Cohen *et al.*, 1972, p. 3).

The interesting aspect of Cohen and March's analysis is their disengagement of problems and solutions. In their garbage can model a decision is an outcome (or an 'interpretation') of several relatively independent 'streams' within an organization. Though 'problems' affect everyone in the organization, and stem from such things as job frustration, family, lifestyle, career, relations with colleagues, money and so forth, they are, however, distinct from 'choices'. Problems 'may not be resolved when choices are made' (Cohen *et al.*, 1972, p. 3).

> University decision-making frequently does not 'resolve' problems. Choices are likely to be made by flight or oversight. University decision processes appear to be sensitive to changes in load. Active decision-makers and problems seem often to track one another through a series of choices without appreciable progress in solving problems. Important choices seem particularly likely not to solve problems.
>
> (Cohen and March, 1986, p. 201)

The authors acknowledge that their findings appear to be complex, paradoxical and capricious, yet at the same time appear to be a convincing explanation of 'how organisations survive when they do not know what they are doing' (Cohen and March, 1986, pp. 199–200). They point out that their model:

> ... does enable choices to he made and problems sometimes to be resolved even when the organisation is plagued with goal ambiguity and conflict, with poorly understood problems that wander in and out of the system, with a variable environment and with decision makers who may have other things on their minds. This is no mean achievement.
>
> (Cohen and March, 1986, p. 202)

Cybernetic models and loosely coupled systems

As a variant on or development of disjointed incrementalism and garbage can models, Birnbaum (1988, 1989) proposes a *cybernetic* model of decision-making as the most appropriate for higher education institutions. In this approach the institutional system as a whole is goal-directed, but its common purpose is not driven from the top but via 'multitudinous individual decisions' at the point of activity.

> You've heard of the bidet and the shower approach? (*laughs*). I think probably in my first couple of years here I was a bit too confident about the value of policies and guidelines and putting them through committees and then somehow thinking that would influence people. I've become much more sceptical about those although that's not to say occasionally we don't still do that.
>
> (Respondent 6)

This respondent has learned the value of not putting too much faith in top-down decision making and engages rather in something more akin to 'multitudinous individual decisions'.

> This is not the kind of institution, as I said at the beginning, which really drives things from the top. So we can't really expect, unfortunately, any strong strategic direction. So in a sense we're forced to work the bottom-up. But it isn't entirely bottom-up in the sense we're not working only with lecturers, I mean, as I've

said, we work at the Committee level, we work with Heads of Departments, with Deans . . .

(Respondent 6)

'I think change is about complexity and interconnectivity' suggests Respondent 28, whereas Respondent 1, when asked if change is a rational process, replies 'I don't think it is. Well I think it's multi-layered isn't it?' Respondent 12, similarly, recognizes that change is not 'single-faceted':

When you said where does the change come from I suppose I had something like yeah outside-inside, inside the institution, . . . the change occurs from a variety of different sources it's not single faceted, you can see the government creates lots of pressures, TQA has had a big effect so there's all these things so . . . internally there are things.

(Respondent 12)

As Birnbaum points out, universities seem to have enjoyed a remarkably stable institutional history over many centuries without resort to tightly coupled management structures. Elton (1998, p. 2) points out that such stability depends on 'constant adjustments and responses through cybernetic controls' and on 'self-correcting mechanisms at a micro level based on negative feedback' with information flowing freely in all directions throughout the organization.

it is the resulting self-correcting mechanism at a micro level which controls the large scale forces which are observable in change processes. It is therefore at this level that the large scale forces must be influenced by the change agent, if they are to be influenced successfully.

(Elton, 1998, p. 2)

Birnbaum's model accords well, as does the garbage can model, with Weick's notion of loosely coupled organizations. 'Change in *loosely coupled* systems', suggests Weick (1980, pp. 78–79), 'is continuous, rather than episodic; small scale rather than large; improvisational rather than planned, accommodative rather than constrained and local rather than cosmopolitan . . . To construct a loosely coupled system is to design a system that updates itself'. Elton (1998, p. 2) warns against the embracing by top management of misleading, deceptively transparent, 'simplistic cause and effect models' in hierarchically managed, tightly coupled systems. Cybernetic systems, he advocates, are more accommodative of innovation and do not have chaotic effects. The following respondent clearly shares such a view:

I think there's an increasing desire amongst senior officers in universities . . . to have tidy pictures. Whereas my view is the world is messy . . . It's always going to be fluid and dynamic, changing . . . So there's no point in having this lovely tidy picture because it's never going to work that way. That doesn't mean that you let it be completely senseless chaos. So what you've got to do is try and have this notion of moving in a direction, that sometimes I think is a bit like crazy-paving. It's a slightly zig-zagging course that maybe allows for wind-changes and so on. You know essentially the direction you're trying to move in and you know essentially, at least for periods of time how you're trying to move there, but the detail will change a great deal. Priorities shift about.

(Respondent 14)

Diffusion models of innovation

The classical tradition of research into change and innovation views the development of innovations as a process of *diffusion*, The work of E. Rogers (1967) and Havelock (1973) is representative of this approach. Diffusion is seen as occurring between individuals, even though the innovations take place in a geographical and social field, which has a bearing on the nature of the diffusion. One such model of diffusion is Havelock's (1973) 'stepping stones' strategy. The following respondent self-consciously models his practice of innovation on this theory, and provides a simple account of its operation:

> I don't think I'd look at it that way. I don't know if you've come across the 'stepping stones' strategy for introducing change? It's by a guy called Havelock, and he's an American author. he wrote something like *A Change Agent's Guide to Innovation in Education*, some years back now. It was quite a simple idea, and it's something that almost instinctively one tends to do. Do you want to bring about a change? First of all you contact the people you know are already on board with it, and you work with them in order to approach the people that you think are potential converts.
>
> (Respondent 2)

Respondent 14 describes 'Doing work with particular people who are interested . . . you know, departments who are interested, and just trying to drive that forward because they've become exemplars that you can attract other people to, and doing these sorts of things, and that's a deliberate strategy.' Respondent 18 reflects that 'I suppose it is a kind of accumulative osmosis'. Respondent 7, similarly, trusts to 'good contacts' and 'personal contact':

> I know how I operate and that it is that I believe that the only way that we can be successful is by personal contact. Which means that you work with people who want to work with you. You hope that they will tell other people and in that way that it will spread. And that takes a number of years. And we've made a substantial number of good contacts this way. The alternative is that we announce what we are capable of doing. What we have done and so on and spread it through the Web, through newsletters and so on, and our Director is more inclined towards that. I don't believe people take sufficient interest to actually do anything to change as a result of reading something. So I very much believe that the personal contact is in fact the only way that we can make progress.
>
> (Respondent 7)

'I think it helps to do things like identifying champions or nurturing champions', reports Respondent 10, 'thinking about incremental change and embedding that, bringing others along'.

> I think about involving key influences. Sometimes, you know, the 'not-invented-here', the champion-from-outwith-the-institution person. I think that there's a range of tactics you might want to think about, depending on the given change and what would be the most effective way to manage that and the strategic change environment.
>
> (Respondent 10)

Respondent 6, operating on a similar basis, says 'I think we work much more effectively by working with departments we know are active, then try to get some examples out to other people. They see that it works and then we try to bring them on board.' The diffusion approach would be a strategy particularly favoured by developers of an activist-modeller or discipline-specific orientation.

'Organizational cracks' and opportunistic change

An alternative model to diffusion innovation has developed which considers change not merely *within* a system but also *of* a social system (Berg and Östergren, 1979, p. 262). In this approach, described as 'a combination of a systems approach and a contingency approach', there is a greater emphasis on the behaviour of groups and organizations and on interaction within and between groups. They distinguish between *system-consistent* and *system-divergent* innovations.

> Our terminology is designed to emphasise that the innovation process is either consistent with or divergent from the main characteristics of the system. In the former case the process is one of dissemination and in the latter of a political battle.
>
> (Berg and Östergren, 1979, p. 262)

Berg and Östergren reject the efficacy of power-coercive strategies in educational settings because 'to produce new knowledge or transmit it to students is itself a creative activity at the heart of the system and closely depending on its main properties. Such innovations cannot be inserted from outside: they have to be created anew within the system, by those who are members of it' (Berg and Östergren, 1972, p. 262). If, however, as we discussed earlier, any system has a tendency to resist change, how can systemic change ever occur? Their answer lies in the notions of 'cracks'.

> How can we understand that system-divergent innovations do occur? The answer is that few systems are completely homogeneous. There may be – and this is a precondition for change – lack of concordance, for instance in membership interests or ideology. This lack of conformity gives rise to 'cracks' or conflicts in the system, and these in turn constitute a further precondition for change. Change also presupposes that the system is open, i.e. that it has contacts with its environment. One could put it that such contacts allow impulses from the outside to flow into the 'cracks' in the system and to break the system by creating a potential for moving.
>
> (Berg and Östergren, 1972, pp. 264–265)

We recall Respondent 21 stating that 'In many respects it suits . . . There are opportunities. Gaps open up.' This, of course, is predominantly the model favoured by developers of an opportunistic or entrepreneurial orientation. The following respondents, employing different metaphors, demonstrate a similar opportunistic conception of change.

> I think it's like most things in educational development. You alight on some shiny substance, raven-like, and if it's really nice you kind of fly off with it and show it to as many people as you think might be interested.
>
> (Respondent 2)

You kind of float (if we're using the watery metaphor) you hang on to the bit of old door that you can and try not to get too swept away and actually what surfaces is what you work with. It's quite a good metaphor really isn't it? But it's true, what surfaces is where you focus your attention. And that's not to say the other stuff isn't all there underneath and isn't going to pop up any minute, but we can't do the whole thing all the time.

(Respondent 3)

Kai Zen and continuous improvement

Influential though the three-stage systemic model of Lewin has been, not all developers subscribe fully to it. The following respondent considers that the refreezing stage is, given today's organizational complexity, more problematic.

Lewis Elton uses a three stage model from an author whose name I've completely forgotten, which is embarrassing, because it will come to me. But it's the model ... you unstick things, you change them and then you let them re-stick again. The author will come back to me.

The interviewer: Lewin?

Kurt Lewin. Right. That's the one. Now, I suspect that model's probably two-thirds right. I think the last bit's getting less important. I think he's wrong . I think it's more than that. These visionary management text clichés about permanent white water, and so on, I think they're probably right, by and large. It's a long time since somebody said to me, when are things going to settle down? I think it's starting to dawn that they aren't going to settle down. And part of me's quite pleased actually, because some of the patterns we settled to in the past were pretty hideous and unproductive and wrong. So it's going to keep on changing. And one of the tricks is going to be to help people come to terms with that appalling prospect. Namely that things are going to continue changing. I embrace it, I welcome it, I love it.

(Respondent 27)

The model that this developer prefers is that of 'continuous improvement', associated with the Japanese industrial approach to quality improvement of Kai Zen. The approach also has affinities with the notion of the 'learning organisation' (Senge, 1990) and the 'learning university' (Duke, 1992).

I used to think that change was about stopping things being wrong and getting them right again. But I've since abandoned the simplistic notion of getting things right. I'll settle for Kai Zen, for continued improvement. I mean I think that's what it's about. But in order to talk sensibly about continued improvement, in order to help people achieve it, first of all you've got to help them have the necessary courage, because it's bloody scary ... It's not entirely scary, I'll try and come back to that ... so you've got to give them the courage. You've got to give them the resources, by which I don't mean money, I mean things as simple as thinking space, and things as important as expert colleagues, like academic developers with whom to talk things through. Things like a culture in which it's possible to talk sensibly about these things. Things like access to ideas and materials which are published somewhere – all of those things. These are all necessary conditions for continuous change. And there are many others besides. But that's the model I want to shoot to.

(Respondent 27)

This developer does not see change as only geared to increased efficiency ('doing more with less') but also to debate about the nature of quality – 'finding out which way's up'. As he points out 'Change is not the point. Improvement is the point.' The notion of continuous improvement within a learning organization can be seen as the institutional equivalent of reflective practice within the individual – an organization talking and listening to itself, evaluating itself, seeking to improve itself. In this regard this model of change would appear to be the most obvious to be embraced by developers of a reflective practice orientation.

> Underpinning the idea of continuing change, rather than getting it right, is there's got to be some agreement on which way is up. On what you mean by improvement. And that's where I think some leadership is needed on that, possibly following debate, because I don't think there is much agreement on what's better. Change is not the point. Improvement is the point. Change must be – going back to our Physics days – must be a vector quantity not a scalar quantity. It must have dimension and direction. And it's crucial. I think we're losing it a bit on direction at the moment. I think direction is … what is it? It's … Oh God. … it's above all about doing more with less. That's about the only direction there is. And that's horrible. It's brutal. So finding out which way's up. And I hope that that's what the debates will lead to. And I hope that … Yes that's what I want to do. I want to help … I don't want to tell people which way's up partly because I don't know and partly because that's not a model of development I subscribe to. As a developer I would want to help institutions and disciplines and courses and individual teachers – different constituencies right – to work out which way's up. It's coming a bit. The Funding Council's saying take teaching more seriously. That's not exactly saying which way's up, except to say that teaching's important. It's a start! (*laughs*). It's a great start. But it's not enough. And some … just some debate about that. What would we mean by things getting better? If we can get that debate kicked off, academic development will get easier and more highly valued.
>
> (Respondent 27)

Uncertainty, non-linearity and chaotic theories of change

However, in Taylor's view (1999, p. 142) change does not always have 'dimension and direction'. It requires a disruption of familiar contexts, a discontinuity and loss of meaning. Taylor distinguishes between 'plan-driven change', which he associates with managerialism, and 'action-driven change', the flow of which most academics are willing to go along with, and, he argues, is a more effective strategy within academic cultures.

> Problem solving is focused on sources of uncertainty which are everyday yet unpredictable, even random. Uncertainty generated by organisational change is different from more 'natural' causes in at least two senses: it implies an intention; and it involves a disruption of familiar contexts. When universities change their practices, most academics tend to assume that there are good reasons underlying the decisions – that the need for the change and the processes by which it will be achieved have been considered carefully. Thus, there is a sense that change is imposed in an intentional and reasoned way. But change-focused decision making is made necessarily under conditions of uncertainty.
>
> (Taylor, 1999, pp. 142–143)

As academic managers have to grapple with uncertain external factors it is therefore inevitable that their decision-making includes 'elements of ambiguity, and the outcomes cannot be predetermined'. Academics should not therefore attribute certainty 'where uncertainty is the case'. Academics need to be wary of misrecognizing the 'best guesses' of their managers as informed 'solutions' (Taylor, 1999, pp. 142–143). Such a situation, argues Taylor, is 'an emulation of certainty, when much more tentativeness is called for ... The expectation of leadership generates both leaders and followers.' He advocates that academics adopt a practice of 'self-interested self-management' (Taylor, 1999, p. 7) based on critical reflection.

But whereas garbage can and cybernetic models were seen earlier to be highly complex but 'non-chaotic', Taylor (1999) and Fullan (1993) envisage notions of change that are non-linear and with chaotic tendencies. Fullan enumerates what he calls the 'Eight Basic Lessons of the New Paradigm of Change' which is, in effect, a chaotic non-linear view of change based on a postmodern perspective (Fullan, 1993, pp. 21–22):

1 You can't mandate what matters. (The more complex the change the less you can force it.)
2 Change is a journey, not a blueprint. (Change is non-linear, loaded with uncertainty and excitement and sometimes perverse.)
3 Problems are our friends.
4 Vision and strategic planning come later.
5 Individualism and collectivism must have equal power.
6 Neither centralization nor decentralization works. (Both top-down and bottom-up strategies are necessary.)
7 Connection with the wider environment is critical for success. (The best organizations learn externally as well as internally.)
8 Every person is a change agent. (Change is too important to leave to the experts, personal mind set and mastery are the ultimate protection.)

Respondent 21 seems well aware of the chaotic nature of change and the need for 'personal mind set and mastery'.

> I don't think my Assistant Principal would be too happy to hear this but I'm not sure that you can manage change in an institution like this. The operational environment is too complex. It's chaotic. I don't think you can be like a railway signalman pulling levers and changing the direction of things. I see it more that you have to be like one of those Hawaiian surfers. You've got one big wave behind you and another coming in from a different angle and there's a point that you can see you want to get to but the wind's blowing you away from that point so you twist and turn to try and keep going where you want to get to but then you're getting closer and closer to the those rocks! (*laughs*). It really feels more like that! I think you have to surf change these days.
>
> (Respondent 21)

This non-linear conception of change would seem to be most likely embraced by developers of opportunistic or entrepreneurial orientation on the one hand and interpretive-hermeneutic on the other.

A model of orientations to academic development and conceptions of change

There are of course further models of change which, space permitting, it would be interesting to pursue in relation to academic development practice. There are clearly managerialist developers who hold to a more linear, causal notion of management by objectives:

> Development mainly implies change, but you need to consider the term from the perspective of both its denotations and its connotations. In its denotative sense it means change towards something, but in its connotative sense it implies change for the better, that progress is being made. But I think I would define development as transition management, basically getting from where you are now to where you need to be. And that's a cycle that will need to be repeated over and over again as time goes on . . . I think institutions can also become good at institutional signalling. They can do this through contractual requirements, performance review, putting appropriate policies in place, applying resource constraints. These are all levers for change that can be used but all the levers must be pointing in the same direction, and this leads us back to the need for clear strategic direction and management.
>
> (Respondent 28)

Others, such as Webb (1996), put emphasis on the role of dialectic and *contestation*. One could employ a Foucauldian perspective of surveillance, perhaps, and interpret the development of reflective practice entirely differently, as a regime of self-regulation, intermediated by the academic developer 'therapists' (Foucault, 1979). Or one could see developers much in the mould of Lipsky's 'street level bureaucrats' (Lipsky, 1980), being afforded a high level of front line discretionary power to embed difficult policy objectives when senior management have abrogated responsibility for implementation. Developers of a Romantic orientation might be seen as working within the Rogerian conception of organic growth (Rogers, 1969).

It will suffice here to attempt to map the orientations to academic development identified earlier against the conceptions of change just discussed [see Table 37]. Again, as with the proposed model of orientations to academic development, this model is not intended to be in any way deterministic or comprehensive. Some of the interrelationships represented in the model below are closer than others and it is important not to stretch the analogies further than they can go. However, the model is intended to draw a reasonable and illuminative set of correspondences between orientation and conception.

It is worth remembering that, whatever change strategy a developer might adopt, he or she should not expect too much recognition for their effort. As Respondent 14 wryly observes:

> I am absolutely certain that we are in the business of the management of change. . . . But what we have to do is to make that change palatable as well as achievable. If we just go in as evangelicals we'll fail. If we go in as instruments of government or the management or whatever else it is, we'll fail. So the trick is actually facilitating this change without people thinking we did it. Now of course the rub about doing that is, the better you do that, the less they think you had any part in doing it. So if you're really superb at doing it they don't think you did it! (*laughs*) It's true. It's absolutely true. So if you're really, really good at it, they don't even realise that you were instrumental in that happening. They think they did it. (*laughs*)
>
> (Respondent 14)

Table 37 Academic developments and concepts of change

Orientation to academic development	Conception of change
Opportunist entrepreneurial	chaotic/complexity (Fullan, 1993) non-linear, multi-perspectival cracks' theory (Berg & Östergren, 1979) garbage can (Cohen & March, 1972) cybernetic (Birnbaum, 1989) loosely coupled systems (Weick, 1976, 1980)
Reflective practitioner	Kai Zen, continuous improvement (Senge, 1990), normative-re-educative (Benne & Chin, 1969)
Interpretive-hermeneutic	dialectical (Marx, Webb, 1996) chaotic/complexity (Fullan, 1993) cybernetic (Birnbaum, 1989) loosely coupled systems (Weick, 1976, 1980, 1995)
Romantic (outreach)	personal growth (C.R. Rogers, 1969) self-identified (Hersey & Blanchard, 1988) normative-re-educative (Benne & Chin) biological/ progressive cybernetic (Birnbaum, 1989) loosely coupled systems (Weick, 1976, 1980)
Professional competence activist-modellers	stepping stones/interconnectivity (Havelock, 1973) diffusion (E. Rogers, 1967) tightly coupled systems
Political strategist (pragmatist)	power-coercive (Benne & Chin, 1969) force field (Lewin, 1952) unfreezing/ refreezing (Lewin, 1952) street level bureaucracy (Lipsky, 1980)
Consultant researcher	rational-empirical (Benne & Chin, 1969)
Disciplinary	diffusion (E. Rogers, 1967) stepping stones (Havelock, 1973) cybernetic (Birnbaum, 1989)
Managerial/HRM	unfreezing/refreezing (Lewin, 1952) strategic leadership transition management (MBO) progressive power-coercive (Benne & Chin, 1969) linear

History, too, can be illuminative:

> It must be remembered that there is nothing more difficult to plan, more doubtful of success, nor more dangerous to manage than the creation of a new system. For the initiator has the enmity of all who would profit by the preservation of the old institution and merely lukewarm defenders in those who should gain by the new ones.
>
> Nicolo Machiavelli 1469–1527
> (Chapter IV, The Prince)

References

Becher, T. (1989). *Academic tribes and territories: Intellectual enquiry and the cultures of disciplines*. Buckingham: SRHE/Open University Press.

Benne, K. D., & Chin, R. (1969). General strategies for effecting changes in human systems. In W. G. Benne, K. D. Benne, & R. Chin (Eds), *The planning of change* (2nd ed.). New York: Holt Rinehart.

Berg, B., & Östergren, B. (1979). Innovation processes in higher education. *Studies in Higher Education*, 4, 261–268.

Birnbaum, R. (1988). *How colleges work: The cybernetics of academic organisation and leadership*. San Francisco: Jossey-Bass.

Birnbaum, R. (1989). The cybernetic institution: Toward an integration of governance theories. *Higher Education*, 18, 239–253.

Cohen, M. D., & March, J. G. (1986). Leadership and ambiguity. In O. Boyd-Barret, T. Bush, J. Goodey, I. McNay, & M. Preedy (Eds), *Approaches to post-school management: A reader*, London: Paul Chapman Publishing.

Cohen, M. D., March, J. C., & Olsen, J. P. (1972). A garbage can model of organisational choice. *Administrative Science Quarterly*, 17, 1–25.

Duke, C. (1992). *The learning university: towards a new paradigm?* Buckingham: SRHE/Open University Press.

Elton, L. (1998). Managing new ways of learning. People, problems and practicalities – Paper 2, *SRHE/CVCP/THES Seminar (Change)*, 30 April 1998.

Foucault, M. (1979). *Discipline and punish: The birth of the prison*. Harmondsworth, UK: Peregrine Books.

Fullan, M. (1993). *Change forces: Probing the depths of educational reform*. London: Falmer Press.

Gouldner, A. (1979). *The future of intellectuals and the new class*. London: Heineman.

Havelock, R. (1973). *A change agent's guide to innovation in education*. Educational Technology Publications, New Jersey: Englewood Cliffs.

Hersey, P., & Blanchard, K. H. (1988). *Management of organisational behaviour: Utilising human resources*, (6th ed.). London: Prentice-Hall International Editions.

Jarratt Report (1985). *Report of the steering committee for efficiency studies in universities*. London: Committee of Vice-Chancellors and Principals (CVCP).

Land, R. (2000). Orientations to educational development. *Educational Developments*, 1, 19–23.

Lewin, K. (1952). *Field theory in social science*. London: Tavistock.

Lindblom, C. (1959). The science of muddling through. *Public Administration Review*, 19, 78–88.

Lipsky, M. (1980). *Street-level bureaucracy: Dilemmas of the individual in public services*. New York: Russell Sage Foundation.

Marton, F. (1999). Variatio est mater studiorum, Opening address, *8th Conference for Research on Learning & Instruction (EARLI)*, Gothenburg, Sweden, August 24.

McNay, I. (1995). From the collegial academy to corporate enterprise; The changing cultures of universities. In T. Schuller (Ed.), *The Changing University?* (pp. 105–115). Buckingham: SRHE/ Open University Press.

Rogers, C. R. (1969). *Freedom to learn*. Merrill, OH: Columbus.

Rogers, E. (1967). *Diffusion of innovations*. New York: Free Press.

Sawbridge, M. (1996). The politics and organisational complexity of staff development for academics: A discussion paper, UCoSDA Occasional Green Paper No. 14, Sheffield, UK.

Senge, P. M. (1990). *The fifth dimension*. London: Random House.

Stones, R. (1991). Strategic context analysis: a new research strategy for structuration theory. *Sociology*, 25, 673–695.

Stones, R. (1996). *Sociological reasoning: Towards a post-modern sociology*. London: Macmillan.

Taylor, P. G. (1999). *Making sense of academic life: Academics, universities and change*. Buckingham: SRHE/Open University Press.

Tutt, N. (1985). The unintended consequences of integration, *Educational and Child Psychology*, 2, 30–38.

Webb, G. (1996). Theories of staff development: Development and understanding. *The International Journal for Academic Development*, 1, 63–69.

Weick, K. E. (1976). Educational organisations as loosely coupled systems. *Administrative Science Quarterly*, 21, 1–19.

Weick, K. E. (1980). Management of change amongst loosely coupled elements. In P. Goodman and Associates (Eds), *Change in organisations*, Thousand Oaks, CA: Sage Publications.

Wellington, B. & Austin, P. (1996). Orientations to reflective practice. *Educational Research*, 38, 307–316.

CHAPTER 12

MOVING WITH THE TIMES

An oral history of a geography department

Alan Jenkins and Andrew Ward

Journal of Geography in Higher Education, 25, 2, 191–208, 2001

EDITOR'S INTRODUCTION

This article was categorised in the introductory chapter as adopting a biographical approach to the study of institutional management. It stems from an unusual study and is a very unusual kind of article.

The study was a thirty-year history of a geography department at an English university (see also Jenkins *et al.* 2001), carried out by an independent consultant who interviewed many of those who had worked in the department over this period. It provides, therefore, an oral history, and one focusing on the teaching function.

The article itself is highly unusual in that, following a few introductory pages, it consists almost entirely of selected quotations from those interviewed. There is very little in the way of linking material or analysis provided by the article's authors – one of whom was also one of the interviewees. The story and the analysis is provided by carefully pasting together the quotations in a particular order. There will be varied opinions on how well this works. I think it works well, or else I would not have included it in this Reader, and it also demonstrates what can be done with focused data collection of this kind.

To a large extent, the article works because it has a clear and fairly coherent story to tell. The department in question has had, as the authors indicate, a shared pedagogic culture over the last three decades, focusing on the encouragement of active learning amongst its students. It has had a close association with the journal in which the article appeared. And the members of the department have been responsible for many publications concerned with the teaching/learning experience, a sample of which is appended to the article.

The inner life of higher education institutions, and of their component departments, has rarely been explored using the kind of biographical or life history approach adopted in this article. University vice-chancellors do occasionally end their careers by producing a volume of memoirs, but these hardly provide a rounded view of what it is like to work in a university. Some studies of academic work have focused on the institutional story (e.g. Potts 1997, Trowler 1998), or on the departmental level (e.g. Knight and Trowler 2001), but these are relatively few.

More auto/biographical research of this kind might, therefore, be encouraged, and – particularly at the departmental level – should be very 'do-able'. There are, though, risks to this kind of research. While the authors of this article can provide a generally positive account of a successful department with a shared culture, many departments and institutions are not so together.

References

Jenkins, A., Jones, L. and Ward, A. (2001) 'The Long-term Effect of a Degree on Graduate Lives', *Studies in Higher Education*, 26, 2, pp. 147–161.
Knight, P. and Trowler, P. (2001) *Departmental Leadership in Higher Education*. Buckingham, Open University Press.
Potts, A. (1997) *College Academics*. Charlestown, NSW, William Michael.
Trowler, P. (1998) *Academics Responding to Change: new higher education frameworks and academic cultures*. Buckingham, Open University Press.

MOVING WITH THE TIMES

Introduction

For over 30 years, the geography department staff at Oxford Brookes University (formerly Oxford Polytechnic) have worked hard to develop appropriate teaching strategies. What follows is an edited account of their story using the words of the staff themselves.

Our approach relies heavily on the methods of oral history (Thompson, 1988; Perks & Thomson, 1998), narrative psychology (Reissman, 1993) and ethnography (Atkinson, 1990; Coffey & Atkinson, 1996). Geographers have used such qualitative methods to study the development of their discipline (Buttimer, 1983; Billinge *et al.*, 1984; Sidaway, 1997), gender and professional identity among physical geographers (Madge & Bee, 1999) and the relationship between geographers' personal and professional lives (Monk, 2001). McDowell (1994, p. 241) argued that qualitative research is relevant to the practice of teaching geography, in that it gives space for student voices to be heard. Here we make a parallel point: qualitative research also allows staff voices to be heard.

Methodology

This paper is a by-product of a project that studied the long-term impact of the Brookes geography curriculum on graduate lives (Ward & Jenkins, 1999; Jenkins *et al.*, 2001; Ward *et al.*, 2001). The research was undertaken by an independent writer (Andrew Ward) and was commissioned and directed by Alan Jenkins, who had taught in the Brookes geography department from 1975 to 1990. The Oxford Centre for Teaching and Learning Development, where Jenkins now works, provided some funding for the study.

Interviews were conducted with staff who had held full-time permanent jobs in the department. John Willmer, now at Courtland State University, New York, was interviewed when he returned to England during the interviewing period. However, we did not interview others, such as Pyrs Gruffudd, who had a one-year appointment in 1990–91, or Anna Kilmartin, Jackie Tivers, Stephen Ward and Martyn Youngs, and those who had taught part-time in the department. No doubt they would have added something to this narrative, as would have the reflections of heads of school and other institutional managers.

The interviews were conducted between June and September 1998, so this story fails to take account of more recent developments. Peter Keene retired in 1999, Derek

Elsom was promoted to Deputy Head of School in 2000 and three young geographers with strong research backgrounds – Simon Carr, Adrian Parker and Emma Treby – were appointed. A specialist physical geography course was introduced in 1998, a significant departure from the integrated view of the curriculum that is presented here.

In the interviews, staff were asked about how they came to join the geography department, the situation when they arrived and what they saw as the department's aims. They were asked about the effects of change – in higher education, the institution and the department – and about how their teaching methods had altered over the years. We quickly realised that these staff accounts contained powerful and important stories in their own right. Hence, we have used a selection of these individual accounts to reconstruct a chronological history of the department.

The departmental history presented here is *our* interpretation. *Our* questions shaped the data and *our* editing produced the final account. The interviews, which lasted between 40 and 90 minutes, generated approximately 90,000 words of transcript material, of which less than 6 per cent is reported here. Our approach to editing was to eliminate repetition, minimise details and capture the main facets of the teaching history. In some instances we have deliberately included sharply contrasting views. The interviewees, having read the manuscript, agreed that we can use their words, but we all would stress that the final textual mosaic is that of the authors.

We decided to present this story as a *teaching* story. The staff's research – even their research on teaching issues – and the many hours they spent developing *JGHE* are rarely mentioned here. This is partly because it was their teaching that was germane to the larger project's major question – what was the impact of the department on graduate lives?

Even so, this story reveals significant features that are seldom analysed and rarely presented as directly as this. Classic oral-historians, such as George Ewart Evans, Tony Parker and Studs Terkel, used reporting techniques that favoured the words of interviewees rather than commentary or analysis. Readers have direct access to that testimony and a greater freedom to interpret it as they see fit (Taylor & Ward, 1997). Oral history is also valid because the development of teaching practice takes place in an oral culture. It is a world of departmental meetings, informal discussions and, of course, face-to-face talk with students.

Background: an innovative department

At the start of this story, in 1969, a much smaller proportion of British people attended university than today. In those days universities were well funded for teaching and research, class sizes were much smaller and geography degrees were taught in linear structures with an emphasis on assessment in the final year. University teaching had the traditional emphasis on formal lectures, seminars and unseen examinations.

In contrast, our setting is one of a number of polytechnics formed in the early 1970s in order to expand the number of students in higher education. Oxford Polytechnic was unusual, however, as it introduced a modular framework in the early 1970s, well before modularity was the norm in Britain (Watson *et al.*, 1989).

Polytechnics were established mainly as undergraduate and sub-degree institutions. They were less selective in student intake and their staff were not directly funded to conduct research. When, in the 1990s, these institutions became universities, and could seek research funds through the Research Assessment Exercise, they faced the problem of more limited resources than the traditional universities. Many polytechnic departments then sought to develop a range of postgraduate courses.

In the 1980s and 1990s, the whole UK Higher Education system faced the challenge of educating many more students – and educationally more diverse students – at lower resource levels with continued demands for efficiency gains and external accountability. This is the story of one department in this system, a small British department that has gained a national and international reputation for effective teaching innovations in the discipline.

The staff of this department have published papers on many aspects of geography teaching – see Appendix for a selected list – and the *Journal of Geography in Higher Education* was founded there (Jenkins, 1997; Pepper, 1997). John Gold, Alan Jenkins, Peter Keene and David Pepper all edited *JGHE* during its first 12 years (1977–88) and Martin Haigh is on the current editorial board. Gold and Jenkins were two of the authors of *Teaching Geography in Higher Education* (Gold *et al.*, 1991), and Pepper has been a strong exponent of curricula that effectively link physical and human geography within a strong environmental perspective (Pepper, 1987). Field-based teaching was central to the curriculum and Peter Keene founded an independent charity (Thematic Trails) to publish and promote popular understanding of landscape.[1]

In 1993, the department won the national British Petroleum Exploration Prize for curriculum innovation, with the assessors commending 'the student-centred approach to learning [which] emphasises groupwork, self and peer assessment from which students emerge with good communication and other interpersonal skills'.

Interpretations

As you read this account you will interpret it from your own national context, institutional position, personal history, professional experience and theoretical and methodological perspectives. You may see it as a case-study of (1) an innovative department (Hannan *et al.*, 1999), (2) a particular workplace culture (Crang, 1994) or (3) a departmental culture (Parlett, 1977; Ramsden, 1997). Alternatively, it might be a contribution to the history of education (Monk, 1998) or simply a good story about one small group of teachers in a geography department where field teaching was important.

The staff's story

> *David Pepper*: I came [on a temporary contract] in 1969, when it was still a college of technology, and the geography department consisted of David Irvine, who was near to retirement, and a cupboard with a couple of globes. We taught three or four students within the University of London external degree and there was a question mark over geography because there were so few students. At the end of my first year the Dean said, 'There's no geography post coming up but I'll support you if you want to apply for an economics post'. Then, at the last moment, the woman I was replacing said she wasn't coming back. After that I must have impressed the new Head of Arts & Humanities with my 'youthful exuberance'. Instead of closing us, he determined that we could get another member of staff. That was in 1972 when Denis Cosgrove came along.

Denis Cosgrove and David Pepper were in their mid-twenties. With David Irvine about to retire, it was left to them to create a framework for a geography curriculum and satisfy a new body called the Council for National Academic Awards (CNAA). This was at a time when the new polytechnic was introducing a modular course, an American credit-style degree framework.

Denis Cosgrove: One of the driving forces behind the modular degree was a biologist called David Mobbs. He argued very strongly that you shouldn't have prerequisites because a modular degree covers the whole of the institution and students should be able to join together any two modules.

We had some advice from Ted Lewis at Middlesex Polytechnic, who had worked on CNAA. I remember him saying, 'You have to show that the whole thing hangs together because the great criticism of modular courses is that they are supermarket courses – how are students going to cohere their education?' The argument, of course, was that the progression and the education goes on in the students rather than the courses.

We decided against a single-honours geography degree, partly because of staff numbers and partly because of principled objections. We felt that geography should be part of a trans-disciplinary thing.

David Pepper and I shared an office. We became close friends and spent a lot of time talking. There seemed to be more time for that then than there is in higher education now. Also, the polytechnic required us to defend our curriculum at meetings, so that meant we had to practise defences. It was very rigorous but (at first) it was all hypothetical. Once the students arrived it was very different from the beautiful flow diagrams we had been producing.

Pepper contributed the initial physical geography ideas and Cosgrove the human geography. As Pepper says, 'We knew we weren't going to teach most of the curriculum and it's dead easy to design courses that you know you're never going to teach.' But there was one course that was hard to design, because they were both involved.

Denis Cosgrove: We had a double-module environmental course which we called (in a very unpolitically correct manner) 'Man, Environment, Attitudes'.

The intellectual conception came from a disagreement that David and I had. At that time, David was very committed to the first wave of environmentalism with Blueprint to Survival (*The Ecologist*, 1972). We shared the same political vision but I had much less sympathy with this doomsday ecological view. My own interests were in the history of environment and attitudes to nature, and I said, 'Hang on, there have been Cassandras ever since the beginning of time.' We really came to blows on this – the historian and the environmental scientist – and it was a very productive exchange. One day we agreed on what we would do: 'Okay, rather than have one course or the other, why don't we have a course where we argue this out and get the students to read and think through it?' As well as being a unifying thing for a modular degree, that course captured our aims of a liberal education.

David Pepper: At that time I was sucked in by the *Limits to Growth* school (Meadows *et al.*, 1972). Denis came along and he was very much cast in the socialist mould. I knew nothing about Marxism, having been trained as a physical geographer, but my interest in environmentalism was broadened to an interest in the social and cultural sphere, and that (the exploration of physical human interactions) has been reflected in the way we have developed the programme in geography throughout the years.

When I look through various things that I've written, I see that they are rooted in the 1960s. They are about social change, and one theme that comes through is critical and questioning attitudes to the received wisdom. That's something I thought important then and I still do. It is my prime mission. I think the spirit of the 1960s was the questioning of received wisdom. There was a general feeling of 'Why should we believe this?' – from the right and the left. That came out in *Private Eye*,[2] which was launched and run by a group of right-wing public-school boys, and you see it in Lindsey Anderson's film *If*,[3] which is set in a public school. Isaiah Berlin's view of education is education as patricide. Not literally 'the killing of the father' but the critical examination and probable rejection of the values and assumptions that went before. Berlin said that unless education is doing that then society is dying. That is what has come through quite strongly, and my major vehicle has been environmental concerns.

Four new members of staff – John Gold, Peter Keene, Derek Elsom and Alan Jenkins – joined the department in the mid-1970s. The newcomers had to wrest control away from Pepper and Cosgrove, who were seen as 'a couple of parents who wouldn't let anybody touch the new baby'.

John Gold: I joined in September 1974 as a replacement for David Irvine. The modular course had already started with a science intake but not for social science, arts and humanities. The geography course was constructed around human geography having two separate strands: one was a cultural, historical look into the arts and humanities; and the other was a spatial science looking to regional economics and statistics and quantification. I was probably the wrong person because I was actually on the same [cultural] strand as Denis.

Peter Keene: I was teaching at Lady Spencer Churchill College [a nearby teaching-training college] and it was quite clear that either there was going to be an amalgamation or the place was going to close. I had been contacted by David Pepper to teach occasional lectures and I gradually built it up and transferred full time in 1976, by when Lady Spencer Churchill College was like rats leaving the sinking ship. David Pepper was switching from physical geography mode to environment mode, and I was a physical geographer so I could fit into his slot. I had the same aspirations in terms of teaching. I felt the central thing was throwing the responsibility for learning on to the students

Derek Elsom: I came in January 1975 from Manchester University, where I was a research assistant doing my PhD. I regarded myself as a science-oriented physical geographer. Through the 1970s and 1980s there was always this tension within the students about physical geography versus human geography. I began teaching a traditional climatology course, but it began to have a flavour of relevance, what I called 'Applied Climatology'. I recognised that perhaps one doesn't need to teach students the depth of science and the maths and physics of atmospheric systems at the expense of other aspects of socially relevant issues of climatology.

David Pepper: One of the things I've argued is that physical geography should be taught within a social context to illustrate the issues in society and help us understand and do something about them. Derek Elsom and Peter Keene took this on.

Peter Keene: Derek was interested in the relationship between society and climate. Those are the areas that he has subsequently written on. In many senses I was not a hard-science physical geographer so my interest in landscape surfaces fitted in very well. Having been rescued from a college of education I would have been prepared to have done all sorts of gymnastics to fit in. It was just luck that I didn't have to do that.

John Gold: The most important thing as regards teaching methods was Alan Jenkins coming. Alan had a package of ideas that were outside everybody else's experience. We still have a saying here: 'Think Jenkins'. If you've got a problem, think Jenkins. That means you have to think of a way to place the onus on the student to do the most and the teacher to do the least, and that is virtuous.

Alan Jenkins: I came in 1975. By appointing me, it was quite clear that they were confirming the focus on teaching rather than research because I had a school teaching background and at interview I made it clear that my interests were in teaching. The focus was very clearly on creating the undergraduate curriculum and getting it moving. Research was not really on the agenda although people like John Gold and Derek Elsom were saying, 'We've got to get in there'.

A team of six male lecturers were in place by the mid-1970s. But there was another key full-time member of staff. In her 25-year career in the department, Heather Jones progressed from secretary to technician to administrator.

Heather Jones: I was to be the person betwixt the students and the staff. My office was on the main corridor, so I was accessible to students. I had a few heart-to-hearts with students over the years in that room. I suppose there was an element of 'the mother' in it. I remember one particular student. On graduation day, her mum knocked on my door and introduced herself. She said, 'I just wanted to meet the woman who has taken my place for three years.'

Students would come in and talk about the weather and in the end they'd tell me why they'd come in to see me. Oh, we've had everything: the heartbreaks and the weddings and the 21st birthdays and the Christenings. I suppose the biggest change is that we had an intake of 10 or 12 [in the early-1970s] and the last intake when I was there [1997] was 70 students. I suppose it's a thing to do with age, but I think that you got to know the students better then [the 1970s and 1980s] and if something went wrong you could cope with it better.

Derek Elsom: The group dynamics were such that I think we were all keen to allow each other to experiment. Some of our experimental teaching methods have failed, and some have been pretty bad to begin with, but the most important thing is that we had a context where we could try different ways. We have ended up producing a very diverse set of approaches to teaching and learning.

John Gold: It wasn't necessarily thought through as well as we probably would wish to present it in retrospect. Much of what happened in the early days was building up the blend of people within the department and allowing them to express their own interests. What's taught in geography is not just a reflection of what things students need to know about geography. In fact that has seldom been part of our consideration. It's much more a compromise between a group of people who've been locked up in a cage together for a very long period of time who've got particular interests and wish to see those interests represented in the courses they offer.

Denis Cosgrove: Some of the ideas were on the crazier edge of things. Alan Jenkins and David Pepper, particularly, would wind each other up. Alan would come up with an idea and they would talk about it and say, 'Let's do it.' It was pretty wild. It wasn't that I disagreed with what they were doing, it was more a concern with how we could make it acceptable to the relevant committees. Everything had to have CNAA approval, even minor changes like booklists.

Alan Jenkins: It's late September 1975 and we are going to Wales for the first-year field trip. I remember the staff saying 'What are you going to do?' I said 'I'll do you a game on Saturday night.' I did a classic group game called Star Power by Gary Shirts,[4] and it really buzzed that Saturday evening. You could see staff and students jumping around and enjoying it. I remember someone coming up and saying, 'That was really good, you could see it work.' I felt more confident that I was bringing in something valuable.

A number of things were happening. It was a new polytechnic and a time of growth and change. It was the first degree that we had set up and controlled and shaped and we were doing it collectively. We were a small group of six people with a lot of autonomy. There was a sense of excitement and newness, and also conflicts about what should be taught, how it should be taught, the balance between teaching and research, and conflicts of personality. We were learning how to work together. It was rather like the beginning of a marriage and there were some pretty strong individuals, different individuals. What was important was that there was a lot of discussion, much laughter, and we were often in positions where we saw each other teach, particularly on fieldwork, and we learned from seeing different approaches.

John Gold: Alan, despite the rhetoric, does not much like teaching and never has. He was endlessly finding very creative ways of getting round that and having a great deal of fun in the process. We suddenly realised, around 1978 and 1979, 'Hey, this guy does this and it works, his courses are effective and the students are learning and having fun.' The content didn't seem to matter very much, which was a revolutionary thought then.

Alan Jenkins: When I came to Oxford Poly I was interested in issues of teaching and student learning. Donald Bligh's book, *What's the Use of Lectures?*, had first come out in 1972.[5] There was detailed research evidence showing that a typical lecture – the 50-minute standard talk-at-me approach – is not very effective at promoting high-level thought or creativity. After 15 to 20 minutes of a typical lecture, attention-span goes and very little is learned. It's even less effective for conveying information than many other methods. What Bligh suggested was breaking the lecture down so that for some of the time the teacher talked, but for other times students acted: read, thought, talked and discussed. With time I became very clear and confident that this method could work, even with large classes.

David Pepper: Quite early on I had experiences that made me aware that the students were not some sort of passive, inert mass. They had strong views on what had taken place and what might take place. I remember one experience of coming to terms with the fact that students had a perception of me, and that my perception might not be the same as theirs. I was approached after a lecture by the boyfriend of one of the other students. He told me that his girlfriend was intimidated by me. I was appalled. I had no idea.

John Gold: David Pepper thought these things through and worked out how he could teach the students. He was an awful lecturer but he took that point on board and re-created himself as a very good seminar teacher.

David Pepper: Feedback from students suggested that lecturing was not my strong point and rather than struggle with that I came round to other ideas, stimulated by Alan Jenkins and people like John Willmer, who sat in on my sessions for the best part of a term when he was over on a secondment from the US. That peer observation had a major impact on me.

John Willmer: I argue that subject-matter basically doesn't matter. What you really learn is not as important as how you learn it and what you are doing with what you've learned. David was asking questions about his teaching methods and he wanted someone to bounce ideas off. I did the old trick of getting him to talk. I would ask, 'Well, what do you think?' And one day, after about 5 weeks, he told me what he thought.

David Pepper: John Willmer didn't come in with lots of suggestions or ideas. he got me to think about my attitude towards the students and my attitudes to teaching. he helped me recognise that the students' perceptions of me as bombastic, sarcastic and iconoclastic came from my lack of confidence. Thinking about your attitude comes first and then you bring in techniques and innovations and teaching methods to suit. The most important component in what I'm trying to do is to get students in contact with the teacher in relatively small classes, or one-to-one situations, where students cannot be passive. From 1980 to 1997 I taught courses with no lecture component. I gave students written course units and talked with the students at feedback sessions or question sessions.

In 1980 Denis Cosgrove left for Loughborough University. By then Martin Haigh had joined the department.

Martin Haigh: In 1980 I was on an assistant professor contract at the University of Chicago and that was not a career position because I think about one in 20 got tenure. I had met Alan Jenkins and John Gold at the Association of American Geographers' meeting and had explained to them about my theories of teaching and they didn't seem to object to them. I used to say that if I set my students a problem, or a challenge as I called it then, the idea was that they should pull their way up to the knowledge rather than have it shoved down at them. That linked with some of the ideas that were cooking at the time. I was brought in, in the traditional manner, to teach the courses that nobody else wanted to teach. These were 'Introduction to Physical Geography' and 'Soils'.

After Martin Haigh's arrival, the six academics stayed together for 10 years, until Alan Jenkins moved to the Educational Methods Unit (now the Oxford Centre for Staff and Learning Development) in 1990.

Martin Haigh: Part of the problem is that you are never trained to teach. You are trained as a researcher. The model you get from the other colleges is lecturing: tell people things and hope it registers. You set people practical tasks in a laboratory but there is still the problem of the 'sea of faces' and students at the back could be otherwise engaged. Over the years I've developed what I think are some smart tricks for getting ideas across. I'm increasingly of the idea that the best way is to get them to tell you rather than you tell them. That's the goal I've been working towards ever since, wrapped up in fancy words like student-active learning and student-centred learning. I think you have to think of the class as a teach-itself community rather 'a teacher and a class'.

John Gold: Around 1981 or 1982 I packed up lecturing for 4 years. I taught by resource-based learning. Then I reintroduced a bit of lecturing – illustrated talks – on the basis that my public lectures were stuttering because I was out of practice at talking to groups of people. I reintroduced lectures just to retain some fluency. I started doing all manner of things that I'd never thought of before. The students ran one 'public inquiry' where I wasn't allowed to speak for three weeks.

Besides the emerging consensus over active-learning teaching methods, the geographers also agreed that all courses should be taught around relevant issues of society and environment.

Martin Haigh: In many departments there's a big line between human geography and physical geography with very little interaction between the two. If you take the society and environment idea, however, you say, 'We are not going to teach about limestone landscapes this week and transport in cities next week, we're going to pick up a big problem and get everyone to look at it.'

The problem could be, say, personal responsibility when you go shopping, or desertification. Then you try to integrate the human geography and physical geography perspectives.

Peter Keene: I taught coastal geomorphology but it was really applied coastal geomorphology and it quite quickly became coastal management. What we taught on the physical side was what they would need to know in order to make decisions. For example, when new countries were discovered in the empire-building period there were preconceptions that coloured attitudes to the people who were there, what was seen and what was extracted from what was there. We built the human geography image into the structure of physical geography courses.

John Gold: A consensus emerged by about 1982 or 1983, and we increasingly taught things that were relevant to environmental issues. Geography is a complicated discipline because it's always had distinctive themes on the human geography side – a landscape theme, a spatial theme and an environmental theme. The environmental theme really passed out of fashion in the 1960s and 1970s, when people wanted to make more of spatial science, which produced rules and laws about land space, so we were fairly unusual in wanting to go back to the relationship between society and environment. Then, as the consciousness of environment shifted in society, people became more aware of pollution issues and there was a tendency for us to present that as a socially relevant and important area rather than just something that we fancied doing. The students were very keen to accept that.

The course that pulled all this thinking together was the third-year synoptic or capstone triple module originally called 'Man, Environment, Attitudes'. In the 1980s the responsibility for the course was David Pepper's.

David Pepper: 'Man, Environment, Attitudes' had its sexist language expunged, and changed hugely, but it ran until 1997. A few students were definitely into environmental issues but the great majority weren't. When they did this course, though, they were shocked or confused or jerked out of their way of thinking. A lot of people said, 'I'm really confused' and I said, 'Great'.

In the mid-1980s another issue came on the agenda – employability and transferable skills.

Alan Jenkins: Our students of the late 1970s just wandered off and got jobs somewhere, but the students of the early 1980s were starting to realise that it wasn't going to be so easy. I have a very strong memory from about 1980 or 1981 of a field course. Some of the final-year students turned on us (or it felt like that) and said, 'What am I going to do now, what's the point of doing this geography degree?'

Derek Elsom: When I started, I automatically thought that students would go on to do research or teaching or something like that. After a while I recognised that students weren't going on to become specialised geographers. I thought, 'Yes, I want to give students sufficient grounding to go on to do a Master's degree or a PhD but not at the expense of the majority who are not going to be specialist geographers'. The skills aspect became a big part, as did students' ability to see how things fitted together. I have said many times to students, 'You're not going to remember this in two years' time but I want you to remember this particular way of looking at things'. Sometimes students will say 'What's the equation for that?' or 'What are the particular parameters?' They seem surprised when I say, 'The important thing, when you come to deal with the problem, is that you understand the basics and you can convey that understanding to other people who you in turn may influence. If you really need to know particular equations, or processes in detail, then you have the ability to know where to look and how to develop that.'

Alan Jenkins: We had got involved in groupwork and presentations because it was a way of students learning more effectively. It was exciting to us and different. We didn't see it in terms of employability. We didn't get into it for that reason. If that was part of the national agenda we weren't aware of it. We were projecting ourselves across the institution and outside in the late 1970s and early 1980s, and we were probably seen as maverick individuals, interesting people, but not really doing serious stuff. Then Bob Ross, a careers counsellor, said to me, 'Look at this report on groupwork', and we started to argue for groupwork as being a good thing because of employability. And that made it harder for the powerful senior people – in the institution or outside – to drop bricks on us.

Martin Haigh: You will find an outburst of publications about employability from that period. We started looking at what the employers claimed they wanted. They wanted people who could work in a team, people who could make spoken presentations, people who could write clearly, people who could solve problems, people who could work to deadlines. We made a deliberate decision to build these kinds of skills into the course and try to develop the skills systematically.

The geographers had also formed links with Graham Gibbs, who set up the Educational Methods Unit at Oxford Polytechnic in the early 1980s. Gibbs shared their interest in student-centred teaching methods, and he recognised the value of self-reflection and course evaluation. He and the geographers cooperated on a variety of departmental and cross-institutional projects.

Martin Haigh: Lobbying from Alan Jenkins and the others created the Educational Methods Unit and that brought in Graham Gibbs and created the political pressure that we should do course evaluation across the institution. I was part-time evaluation officer here for a couple of years [1982–84] and my work with

Graham helped to set up the system that we have. We were trying to devise a system of course evaluation that actually helped teachers teach and students learn rather than one that got in the way. We deliberately decided not to put out a template across the institution; the more you look at questionnaires, the more of a straitjacket they seem. We set up the evaluation specifically as a dialogue between the teacher and the student.

John Gold: I think the geographers pioneered evaluation at this institution. In about 1985 I introduced a cohort study where we identified a cohort of students and interviewed those students each year. It is usually very flattering. Students like to talk, but we were listening really for the silences rather than what they were actually saying. I found that quite instructive.

David Pepper: Alan Jenkins and I suggested to the Academic Board [in 1986] that the whole polytechnic should take a week where it tried to do things in different ways and report back on what they did. It became known as Alternative Teaching Week.[6] The problem was that a lot of staff felt they were being directed or coerced. For some reason staff consider the act of teaching to be as private as going to the lavatory. They don't like the element of coercion.

Martin Haigh: Another important thing was the CNAA Quinquennial Review. Every 5 years the whole programme reinvented itself and there was a cycle of students' results going up and down. Students paid for the first year of a new programme and then the middle 3 years were a time of maturity [see Gibbs *et al.*, 1995]. After the 1989 review we ended up with a programme with the compulsory modules (from year one to three) being collectively taught.

Also, in the late 1980s, more part-time staff were introduced to support the seminar-based system. Judy Chance, then a geography doctoral student at Oxford University, was one of them.

Judy Chance: The first-year course ran a number of seminar sets of about eight to 10 students. The students were learning from a series of workbooks. My job was to run a discussion of what they'd been reading and help them choose a project on the impact of economic change in Britain. Essentially I was fitting into a module that was already running. I didn't have any real contact with the Geography Unit. I didn't have an office. I came in once a week, saw my students and pedalled back down the hill.

Then one year I went to another polytechnic to run a module for second-year students on a Monday afternoon and evening. The course content was similar to what I was working on, so I assumed it was going to be very much like Oxford Poly. I had the shock of my life. At Oxford Poly I'd learned how to organise seminars and how to arrange the seating so it was friendly. At the other polytechnic I was allocated a room like a laboratory. It had solid wooden benches which were shackled to the floor with iron bolts. I'd set up a structure for a course which involved students working in small groups, going off to prepare some research material and coming back to do a presentation, and they'd never been asked to do anything like that before.

Judy Chance progressed to a permanent post, and Alan Jenkins left to work in the Educational Methods Unit.

Derek Elsom: When we [the six long-serving members of staff] were first in place, in 1980, I think we felt that we would continue to grow. Then in the 1980s, as education suffered its cuts, student numbers grew but staffing didn't. That added a tension which influenced individuals who were wanting to research and still wanting to do teaching innovation. Some of the teaching methods that were being developed needed quite a lot of resources. Our first-year groups took up a lot of time. Producing workbooks increased the time and energy that you put into it. Alan Jenkins was always coming up with innovations that supposedly saved time, like walking into a tutorial, leaving the tape-recorder and then going out and leaving the students to carry on. It didn't reduce the time. In practice you had to listen to the tape and give feedback. There was a joke at the time about getting students to mark their own essays but peer assessment didn't save time in the end. Other people thought it saved time, but it actually required more feedback, And it doesn't save student time. It adds to student demands. All these things stretch resources. Inevitably, over time, it restricts people's ability to innovate.

Judy Chance: When it became clear that staffing ratios were going to deteriorate, around 1989, we reorganised the whole of the geography course. We decided to invest a lot of time in first-year teaching, so that by the end of the first year the students would be confident, independent learners. The students are still getting a lot of time in the first year, but it's not necessarily our time. However good you are, on a part-time basis you don't necessarily know how the system works, and you haven't got an office so you're not available to students. On the other hand, if you've got to produce research work, losing the first-year teaching is the best way of doing it, because your second- and third-year teaching is much more likely to be linked to your research, and it's much harder to buy in anybody to teach that.

Around the same time the method of timetabling was changed for the whole polytechnic. Instead of the traditional one-hour lecture and seminar slots, modules were allocated one four-hour block at a fixed time each week. One of the aims of this change was to make the courses more accessible to part-time mature students, many of whom had jobs.

John Gold: The four-hour block changed everything. That was the big bang. It was assimilated reasonably easily but it meant teachers had to teach differently. That's when our own example, which was to teach non-traditionally, was taken up by other people, because they realised that you just could not occupy 4 hours any other way. Also, once the four-hour block was in place, and the scattering of teaching hours throughout the week was no longer true, then you had a system that was ready-made for students to spend whole days doing paid work. So the system connived in that change. These days students are working in restaurants such as Brown's or driving for taxi firms or whatever, It has led to a totally different relationship between us and them.

Two new members of staff – Pyrs Gruffudd (on a temporary contract) and George Revill – contributed to the development of cultural geography in the department.

George Revill: I came in September 1992 and it was very different from Loughborough and Nottingham. People talked an administrative language, a kind of Polyspeak which people from a conventional university didn't understand – all about the modular course and its rules and regulations. But I'd long believed in the idea of no lectures. My father was a schoolteacher and he was interested in alternative teaching methods. He believed that (a) people should be able to develop when they're ready and should be able to go into higher education at any age, and (b) learning should be fun and should be all about self-exploration, self-understanding and self-discipline rather than being cramped. When I came I found (a) a kind of teaching environment which suited my prejudices and (b) people who were also serious about their own research, and had a little bit of time to build a reputation in research. I stick closely to the idea that teachers are also learners. When my students say, 'I'm up half the night doing this, that and the other,' I say, 'You're not the only one, so am I, we're all in the same boat, we can all learn from each other'. This is perhaps where I may diverge from those aspects of the old Poly system which valued teaching over research. We should all be learners. We shouldn't be telling people to do things we wouldn't do ourselves.

The thing that I really liked was that even in a tiny department like this I was given a great deal of freedom in doing my own special subject. The people here said, 'It doesn't matter what people study as long as they're studying issues and developing their ideas and relating those back to a broader context'. We toe the party line, which is that we are about society and environment – relationships, attitudes and values – but as long as you were feeding into that then the subject-matter is whatever takes your fancy.

In 1992, 30 new universities were created from the polytechnics. Oxford Polytechnic became Oxford Brookes University.

Derek Elsom: Twenty years ago we couldn't have anticipated the removal of the divide between polytechnics and universities. I think that's affected me more on a personal level. It's recognition that we are actually doing things better than many traditional universities. That's been a pleasant surprise. Over the last 20 years we have been doing the research and we have also been doing the teaching innovation.

Judy Chance: The transition of status – polytechnic to university – brought two new influxes of money. One was that we had extra capital to spend, partly because the polytechnics had extra capital to try to bring their resources up, so within the unit we've become quite well equipped in terms of Information Technology. The downside of that is that we have lost our big resources room which had lots of tables where the students could come and work. That's been eaten up, partly by more staff offices and partly by space being taken up by new computers and satellite receivers.

George Revill: We also introduced a postgraduate course in 'Environmentalism and Society'. That ran for the first time in 1994–95 with a small number of students. We could see that staff at other institutions were putting on Master's courses and students had said that they wanted more of what they were doing at undergraduate level. Environmentalism was playing to the strengths of our department and was something that every member of staff could take part in. We were trying to do what we could do when there was a small intake of undergraduates: spend more time with students and discuss issues in a serious way. There was an element of staff development and it was a way to build up some postgraduate life: bringing in outside speakers and starting debates, and hearing good ideas from postgraduate students.

The postgraduate course has been a lot of hard work but it's been very positive intellectually. It has brought in some very talented and interesting people who have remained friends, and some now do teaching for us. It's hard work because it sometimes involves teaching three or four evenings a week and dissertation supervision extends the year through the summer and then gives you another round of marking in October. A Master's degree brings all sorts of issues of its own. A lot of students bring personal problems because they are doing an MA while changing their lives – marital break-up, job difficulties, etc. – and foreign students can have language problems or visa trouble. And Master's programmes are not a financial panacea. There are a few popular ones but they are not the way for departments to solve all budget problems.

Judy Chance: The other big way that money has come in is through research funding. As a result various things happened. One is that a lot of people have bought out of their first-year teaching, which means the students don't meet full-time staff very much in their first year. Most of the people who teach first-year courses are not that much older than the students because we've used postgraduate students or recent graduates still in the area. That helps in some ways but it leaves the students less familiar with the staff and maybe making less use of staff. Since I've been here the number of students has gone up, and the increases are even more marked for those people who had been there before me. I think that makes it harder to get to know students personally. Well over half the students have substantial work commitments and inevitably that impacts on what we can expect from them. There is an increasing sense that students see their degree as a commodity that we are contracted to deliver to them as clients. *Their* expectations and evaluations have shaped what *we* do.

There was a cohort of people who started teaching here more or less at the same time and have gone through together. I suspect that a lot of the very positive interaction with students was partly because there wasn't a huge age gap to begin with. Everyone has got older and that has probably changed the feel for students over time. I suspect that we are seen as much more remote than we would have been seen 15 years ago. But remoteness isn't just to do with the age gap. Obviously there are more students now and that makes it harder.

George Revill: We are now part of the School of Social Science, where research is more valued and more central, even though the amount of teaching has also gone up. The Head of School would probably not have been doing her job 7 or 8 years ago, because she came out of a research institute and is a research person. She doesn't have a teaching background.

John Gold: If you wanted to take time to try to think about new teaching courses you would be taking time out of the other things that the school thinks is more important – research and raising money. I have always had strong research interests so I'm not bothered by the implications of my last statement, whereas other people would be very bothered by it. In the 1970s I wrote and published, which was looked upon as a rather quaint thing to do. Now, if you don't do it you are in trouble. I have a friend at one university who was regarded as non-productive. He was deputed the university's fire officer and had to go on fire-brigade training courses. It was done to humiliate him. The increasing pressure is that we are about research.

George Revill: The administration doesn't get any less, teaching gets more, research is making demands on us. Yes, we may be told to economise on this, that and the other, but it doesn't work and you can't really do it, not if you want to be fair to the students. My way forward is to invest time in producing course units and workbooks which are fairly structurally robust so they can stand the test of time for a couple of years or so. We don't want to innovate just for the sake of resource depletion. We would rather fight tooth and nail to keep what we've got and stick to the educational principles we do have, rather than find some flashy way of giving the students less.

Concluding thoughts

Somewhere in these words – or behind these words – are the answers to a number of key questions concerning teaching and teaching methods. How do staff learn to teach more effectively? How do they learn to shift much of the responsibility of learning onto students? How does a departmental culture incorporate innovation? Can that innovative culture be maintained or is it a function of a particular era and a particular group of individuals? How does a department assimilate new staff and new ideas? How does a department find consensus rather than conflict, or does conflict have an essential role in creating change? When does an innovation become commonplace throughout the system? And what is the role of the institution, the community of geographers and the national education system in supporting these changes?

We do not have the final answers to these questions but we feel that our methodology is a useful one for sparking the debate. We have provided pointers to guide your answers and are encouraging you to compare this account with your own departmental history. We have offered you a story of innovative teaching and we have tried to do so in an innovative way.

Notes

1 Thematic Trails, 7 Norwood Avenue, Southmoor, Abingdon, Oxon OXl3 SAD, UK. http:// www.thematictrails.u-net.com/home.htm
2 *Private Eye* is a UK weekly satirical magazine questioning whatever and whoever is in power or authority.
3 The film *If* (1969), directed by Lindsay Anderson, tells the story of a group of students who rebel against the power structure of their boarding school. Some see it as a metaphor for class revolt.
4 *Star Power* is a classic simulation game. It is presented as a simple trading game but soon changes into a three-tier model of a society where those with power make the rules and the rest react. *Star Power* was designed by R. Carry Shirts, Western Behavioral Sciences Institute, 1150 Silverado, La Jolla, California 93027, USA. Shirts also developed *Bafa Bafa*, a simulation of cross-cultural misunderstandings. Both these games were used effectively in the introductory year-one field course, until staff grew bored with them and invented their own exercises.
5 A new edition appeared in 2000.
6 During Alternative Teaching week it was decreed that no one should give a lecture or teacher-led session. The teaching methods 'emphasised student activity and involvement' (Jenkins, 1999).

References

Atkinson, P. (1990) *The Ethnographic Imagination: textual constructions of reality* (London, Routledge).

Billinge, M., Gregory, M. & Martin, R. (Eds) (1984) *Recollections of a Revolution: geography as spatial science* (London, Macmillan).

Bligh, D.A. (1972) *What's the Use of Lectures?* (London, Penguin).

Buttimer, A. (1983) *The Practice of Geography* (London and New York, Longman).

Coffey, A. & Atkinson, P. (1996) *Making Sense of Qualitative Data* (London, Sage).

Crang, P. (1994) It's showtime: on the workplace geographies of display in a restaurant in southeast England, *Environment and Planning D*: Society and Space, 12(6), pp. 675–704.

Gibbs, G., Haigh, M. & Lucas, L. (1995) Research note: the impacts of course restructuring on student performance, *Higher Education Research and Development*, 14(2), pp. 279–282.

Gold, J.R., Jenkins, A., Lee, R., Monk, J., Riley, J., Shepherd, I. & Unwin, D. (1991) *Teaching Geography in Higher Education* (Oxford, Basil Blackwell). Web version at http://www.chelt.ac.uk/el/ philg/gdn/gold/index.htm

Hannan, A., English, S. & Silver, H. (1999) Why innovate? Some preliminary findings from a research project on innovations in teaching and learning in higher education, *Studies in Higher Education*, 24(3), pp. 279–289.

Jenkins, A. (1997) Twenty-one volumes on: is teaching valued in geography in higher education?, *Journal of Geography in Higher Education*, 21(1), pp. 5–14.

Jenkins, A. (1999) Institution-wide staff development events: Oxford Brookes University IT Term, NASD,' *Journal of the National Association for Staff Development*, 40(Jan), pp. 17–25.

Jenkins, A., Jones, L. & Ward, A. (2001) The long-term effect of a degree on graduate lives, *Studies in Higher Education*, 26(2), pp. 149–163.

Madge, C. & Bee, A. (1999) Women, science and identity: interviews with female physical geographers, *Area*, 31(4), pp. 335–348.

McDowell, L. (1994) Polyphony and pedagogic authority, *Area*, 26(3), pp. 241–248.

Meadows, D., Randers, J. & Behrens, W. (1972) *The Limits to Growth* (London, Earth Island).

Monk, J. (1998) The women were always welcome at Clark, *Economic Geography*, 74 (extra issue), pp. 14–30.

Monk, J. (2001) Many roads: the personal and professional lives of woman geographers, in: P. Moss (Ed.) *Placing Autobiography in Geography* (Syracuse, Syracuse University Press).

Parlett, M. (1977) The department as a learning milieu, *Studies in Higher Education*, 2(2), pp. 173–181.

Pepper, D.M. (1987) Physical and human integration: an educational perspective from British Higher Education, *Progress in Human Geography*, 11(3), pp. 379–404.

Pepper, D.M. (1997) JGHE: twenty-one this year, *Journal of Geography in Higher Education*, 21(1), pp. 15–16.

Perks, R. & Thomson, A. (1998) (Eds) *The Oral History Reader* (London, Routledge).

Ramsden, P. (1997) The context of learning in academic departments, in: F. Morton, D. Hounsell, & N. Entwistle (Eds) *The Experience of Learning* (Edinburgh, Scottish Academic Press).

Reissman, C.K. (1993) *Narrative Analysis* (London, Sage).

Sidaway, J.D. (1997) The production of British geography, *Transactions of the Institute of British Geographers*, 22(4), new series, pp. 428–504.

Taylor, R. & Ward, A. (1997) Kicking and screaming: broadcasting football oral histories, *Oral History*, 25(1), pp. 57–62.

The Ecologist (1972) *Blueprint to Survival* (London, The Ecologist).

Thompson, P. (1988) *The Voice of the Past* (Oxford, Oxford University Press).

Ward, A. & Jenkins, A. (1999) Collecting the life-stories of graduates: evaluating students' educational experiences, *Oral History*, 27(2), pp. 77–86.

Ward, A., Jones, L. & Jenkins, A. (2001) What use is a Degree? Life-stories of geography graduates from the modular degree at Oxford Brookes University (Cheltenham, Geography Discipline Network). Available online at http://www.chelt.ac.uk/gdn/ward

Watson, D., Brooks, J., Coghill, C., Lindsay, R. & Scurry, D. (1989) *Managing the Modular Course: Perspectives from Oxford Polytechnic* (Buckingham, Society for Research into Higher Education and Open University Press).

Appendix: selected pedagogic publications

During the period in question, the geography department staff published a large number of papers about curriculum development. This is a sample of their work.

Chance, M.J. (1994) Integrating transferable skills into geography through a compulsory core, in: A. Jenkins, & L. Walker (Eds) *Developing Student Capability Through Modular Courses*, pp. 63–69 (London, Kogan Page).

Chance, M.S. (1995) Skill-based profiling at Oxford Brookes University, in: A. Jenkins, & A. Ward (Eds) *Developing Skill-based Curricula through the Disciplines: case studies of good practice in geography*, pp. 133–140 (Birmingham, the Staff and Educational Development Association), Web version at http: //www.chelt.ac.uk /el/philg/gdn/seda/index.htm

Cosgrove, D. (1981) Teaching geographical thought through student interviews, *Journal of Geography in Higher Education*, 5(1), pp. 19–22.

Cosgrove, D. & Pepper, D.M. (1976) An answer to the problems of subject development in the smaller polytechnic geography departments, *Geography*, 61(2), pp. 89–94.

Elsom, D.M. (1987) *Taming the Rivers of Oxford: a riverside walk* (Oxford, Thematic Trails).

Elsom, D.M. & Keene, P. (1990) *Exe in Flood* (Oxford, Thematic Trails).

Gibbs, G. & Jenkins, A. (1984) Break up your lectures or Christaller sliced up, *Journal of Geography in Higher Education*, 8(1), pp. 27–39.

Gold, J.R. (1991) Why modularisation, why now, and what implications does it have for geographical teaching?, *Journal of Geography in Higher Education*, 15(2), pp. 180–187.

Gold, J.R., Revill, G. & Haigh, M.J. (1996) Interpreting the Dust Bowl: teaching environmental philosophy through film, *Journal of Geography in Higher Education*, 20(2), pp. 209–222.

Haigh, M.J. & Gold, J.R. (1993) The problems with fieldwork: a group-based approach towards integrating fieldwork into the undergraduate geography curriculum, *Journal of Geography in Higher Education*, 17(1), pp. 21–32.

Haigh, M.J. & Kilmartin, M.P. (1999) Student perceptions of the development of personal transferable skills, *Journal of Geography in Higher Education*, 23(2), pp. 195–206.

Haigh, M.I., Revill, G. & Gold, J.R. (1995) The landscape assay: exploring pluralism in environmental interpretation, *Journal of Geography in Higher Education*, 19(1), pp. 41–55.

Jenkins, A. (1985) Peace education and the geography curriculum, in: D.M. Pepper & A. Jenkins (Eds) *The Geography of Peace and War*, pp. 202–213 (Oxford, Blackwell).

Keene, P. (1982) The examination of exposures of Pleistocene sediments in the field: a self-paced exercise, *Journal of Geography in Higher Education*, 6(2), pp. 109–121.

Keene, P. (1988) Teaching physical geographers to talk, *Journal of Geography in Higher Education*, 12(1), pp. 85–94.

Pepper, D.M. (1987) Physical and human integration: an educational perspective from British Higher Education, *Progress in Human Geography*, 11(3), pp. 379–404.

Pepper, D.M. & Jenkins, A. (1988) *Enhancing Employability and Educational Experience: a manual on teaching communication and group-work skills in Geography*, Occasional Paper No. 27, Standing Conference on Educational Development, Birmingham. Web version at http: //www.chelt.ac.uk/el/ philg/gdn/pepper/index.htm

Revill, G.E., Gold, J.R. & Gold, M. (1997) Mastering the niche: the experience of taught masters programmes in British geography departments, in: P. Knight (Ed.) *Masterclass*, pp. 85–95 (London, Cassell).

CHAPTER 13

CONCEPTIONS OF RESEARCH

A phenomenographic study

Angela Brew

Studies in Higher Education, 26, 3, 271–285, 2001

EDITOR'S INTRODUCTION

This article was categorised in the introductory chapter as adopting a phenomenographical approach to researching knowledge. As I argued in that chapter, phenomenography may be seen as the only methodological approach which has been substantially, though not exclusively, developed through higher education research, particularly into the learning experience (Ashworth and Lucas 2000, Bowden and Walsh 1994, Entwistle 1997, Prosser 1993). Phenomenographic research proceeds by focusing on a particular phenomenon of interest, interviewing people to collect their own accounts of their experience of this phenomenon, 'bracketing out', in so far as possible, the researcher's own assumptions and experiences, and continuing the analysis until a full description of the phenomenon has been produced.

Brew's focus in this article is on how research is experienced by established senior researchers. For her study she interviewed 57 researchers in Australian universities, chosen so as to reflect three disciplinary groupings: sciences and technology, social sciences, and arts and humanities. The data collection had three stages, starting with a focus on one university, expanding this to cover four universities, and then discussing the initial findings in group meetings with some of the interviewees.

Brew uses her data to identify four categories of research experience, organised along two dimensions – whether there was an external product or internal process orientation, and whether the researchers themselves were in the forefront or incidental to awareness in the research. She describes these four categories as the domino (series of tasks), trading (a social phenomenon emphasizing products), layer (excavating reality) and journey (research transforms the researcher) conceptions. She then explores some of the implications of these variations for academic practices and exchange.

The article forms part of a more extensive study into the nature of research (Brew 2001). While there is no necessary and direct relationship between the categories of research experience identified and particular disciplines, the connection between Brew's research and that focusing on different disciplinary experiences is clear (e.g. Becher and Trowler 2001, Neumann *et al.* 2002). There is also a link to another literature, that examining the relationship between the teaching and research functions in higher education (e.g. Drennan 2001, Robertson and Bond 2001).

References

Ashworth, P. and Lucas, U. (2000) 'Achieving Empathy and Engagement: a practical approach to the design, conduct and reporting of phenomenographic research', *Studies in Higher Education*, 25, 3, pp. 295–308.

Becher, T. and Trowler, P. (2001) *Academic Tribes and Territories: intellectual enquiry and the culture of disciplines*. Buckingham, Open University Press, second edition.

Bowden, J. and Walsh, E. (1994) *Phenomenographic Research: variations in method*. Melbourne, Royal Melbourne Institute of Technology.

Brew, A. (2001) *The Nature of Research: inquiry in academic contexts*. London, RoutledgeFalmer.

Drennan, L. (2001) 'Quality Assessment and the Tension between Teaching and Research', *Quality in Higher Education*, 7, 3, pp. 167–178.

Entwistle, N. (1997) 'Phenomenography in Higher Education', *Higher Education Research and Development*, 16, pp. 127–134.

Neumann, R., Parry, S. and Becher, T. (2002) 'Teaching and Learning in their Disciplinary Contexts: a conceptual analysis', *Studies in Higher Education*, 27, 4, pp. 405–417.

Prosser, M. (1993) 'Phenomenography and the Principles and Practices of Learning', *Higher Education Research and Development*, 12, pp. 21–31.

Robertson, J. and Bond, C. (2001) 'Experiences of the Relation between Teaching and Research: what do academics value?' *Higher Education Research and Development*, 20, 1, pp. 5–19.

CONCEPTIONS OF RESEARCH

Introduction

Every conversation about research in universities, every research project, and every discussion in research committees rests on the underlying ideas researchers have concerning what research is and what researchers are doing when they carry it out. Researchers know what research is. This is almost a truism. Yet while many researchers are able to articulate their own ideas about the nature of research, the absence of systematic investigation into the ways research is conceptualised means that many commonly held ideas have not been examined empirically.

There are a number of widely held assumptions about the nature of research experience. One is that conceptions of research are determined by disciplinary differences. Another is that the methodology used or the kinds of research (i.e. strategic, applied or curiosity-driven) determine researchers' conceptions of research. Yet these assumptions tend to be based on researchers' personal experiences, not on empirical evidence. For, while research on conceptions of learning and teaching in higher education is now well established, conceptions of research have rarely been a subject for investigation, and empirical work on the ways in which research is experienced by those who undertake it is hard to find.

The changing context of higher education, however, provides an urgent reason for developing a systematic understanding of the nature of research as it is experienced. Questions about what counts as knowledge, and what counts as an appropriate method for generating it, are now known to be bound up with questions about the ownership and control of knowledge, including questions of power (see, for example, Lyotard, 1993; Gibbons *et al.*, 1994). Indeed, it has been suggested that knowledge itself is in crisis (Barnett & Griffin, 1997).

In this context, there are a number of practical concerns about the nature and role of research in the economy (Bazeley *et al.*, 1996), and about how research should be funded (Bourke, 1997). Changes in the role and status of some institutions – e.g.

polytechnics – mean staff previously in teaching-only positions are now being expected to engage in research, and some of the newer universities are developing specific research niches (Turpin *et al.*, 1996). So, how are these developments influencing and being influenced by academics' conceptions of the nature of research? How, for example, is critical questioning of traditional methods of inquiry, occasioned by the changing knowledge context, having an impact on how academics think about research? By identifying variation in experiences of research among senior academic researchers in different domains of inquiry and different types of university, the investigation reported here establishes a framework which can be used to explore the conceptions of research of other groups, for example, early career researchers, postgraduate students and their supervisors. The article presents an overview of the literature, outlines the findings of the study and their analysis, and discusses the implications for higher education.

Background

My assertion that experiences of research have been neglected as a subject for study has sometimes been treated with incredulity by my academic colleagues. In discussing the relevant literature, therefore, it is first important to distinguish investigations into the experience of research (such as the one discussed here) and research projects (which may be investigations of any kind in any discipline area). Among the very few studies which are examples of the former are those by Startup (1985), who researched academics' ideas about the impact of changes in higher education on how they viewed their research, and Bruce & Bahrick (1992), who looked at psychologists' perceptions of past research. More recently, Jenkins and colleagues (1998) have examined students' conceptions of their teachers' research.

Perhaps one of the reasons why it tends to be assumed that research on academics' experiences of research is commonplace is that there are a number of traditions which touch upon it. For example, research focused on the nature of academic disciplines, on forms of scholarship, on the nature and practice of science, on the relationship between teaching and research, and on the nature of knowledge all inform an understanding of how research is experienced. Yet, in foregrounding disciplines, scholarship, science and/or knowledge, none of this work specifically addresses the ways in which research is experienced by those who carry it out.

Differences in research activity are often attributed to disciplinary differences. The work of Becher (1989) is frequently quoted to support this. Indeed, Becher argues that his focus is on the ways research is perceived. However, it is inevitable, from his disciplinary starting point, that his analysis should focus on the actions and ideas of groups (academic tribes), not the ideas of individuals. What is not provided by Becher's analysis is a comprehensive map of the variation in how research is experienced. He constantly struggles with the finding that disciplines do not provide the primary way in which people think of their research. For example, he found that academics had less of a tendency to stay in one discipline than expected, and also that they differ in the extent to which the external climate or their personal concerns influence their perceptions of research. Becher's analysis suggests that individuals' conceptions of research are a function of a complex set of factors, of which disciplinary allegiance is only one.

Growing specialisation, competing methods of inquiry within disciplines, the growth of interdisciplinarity, shifting disciplinary boundaries (Gibbons *et al.*, 1994), and the fact that academics in some areas of study do not even conceptualise themselves in disciplinary terms are also likely to affect how academics conceptualise research. A framework capable of explaining how individuals experience research, not dependent upon disciplinary distinctions, is, therefore, needed.

In the USA, it has been argued that, in the changing context and climate of universities and their changed relationship to society, research has increasingly come to be viewed narrowly, in terms of publication of fundamental knowledge based on technical rationality (see, for example, Rice, 1992; Scott & Awbrey, 1993; Schön, 1995). Conceptualising research, scholarship, academic teaching and learning as all part of the same enterprise, Boyer and colleagues (Boyer, 1990), in endeavouring to redefine scholarship, suggest a fourfold definition (the scholarships of discovery, application, integration and teaching). The scholarship of discovery, Boyer suggests, comes closest to the idea of 'research'. It contributes to the 'stock of human knowledge', and also to the intellectual climate of the institution. The focus here is normative, that is, on the conceptions academics should have (Davis & Chandler, 1998). This leaves open the question of the conceptions which academics do have, which is the focus of the research discussed in this article.

Empirical studies of different frameworks for scholarship in the USA have consistently identified a wide range of teaching, research and community service activities as important elements of university scholarship (Paulsen & Feldman, 1995). Sundre (1992), for example, focusing on the characteristics of the ideal scholar, identified four dimensions: pedagogy; publication and professional recognition; intellectual characteristics of scholars; and creative and artistic attributes. Sundre's framework is helpful in mapping dimensions of scholarly work, but does not provide guidance on the ways the ideas cluster together in the minds of academics. Paulsen & Feldman relate Sundre's categories to their own four-function framework, arguing that some academics will be seen to divide their time between all four kinds of scholarship and others will specialise. This does not take into account the point that different academics may have different conceptions of scholarship, nor how these conceptions of scholarship relate to their conceptions of research. In foregrounding scholarship and using it to encompass the full range of academic work, the American literature has neglected to consider different conceptions of research held by academies.

There is also an extensive literature on the relationship between research, teaching and scholarship. Much of this focuses on the outputs of research rather than on the process of doing it, with a range of mechanistic research indicators being used, such as number of publications, citation score, membership of research societies, judgements of departmental heads and research grants received (Brew & Boud, 1995). Such research, it has been argued, would benefit from the articulation of qualitatively differentiated conceptions of research (Brew & Boud, 1995; Hattie & Marsh, 1996). Calls to make university teaching more research-like (Shore *et al.*, 1990; Barnett, 1997) also suggest that a consideration of different conceptions of research would be fruitful. By defining the different ways research is understood, it may be possible to match conceptions of research to conceptions of teaching (see, for example, Trigwell & Taylor, 1994) to open up a more sophisticated discussion of the relationship.

There are a number of areas of literature where science rather than research is foregrounded. Indeed, 'science' is frequently used as a synonym for 'research'. So, ideas about the nature of research lurk within the sociology of science literature, including historical studies of famous researchers and research institutions. In this context, the study reported in Marton *et al.* (1994), which examined Nobel prizewinners' conceptions of scientific intuition, is important to note, since it, like the investigation reported in the current article, used a phenomenographic methodology. However, once again, the focus was on scientists and how they came to understand the content of their research, that is, on how scientists go about doing research (or an aspect of it). It was not focused, like the study described here, on what researchers experience research as being.

The philosophy of science literature has also been powerful in establishing views about the nature of research practice. This also foregrounds 'science' rather than 'research', however, again privileging science and scientists' views about the nature of research. Such work leaves open to question whether researchers in other domains of inquiry share scientists' conceptions of research. Nonetheless, this work has drawn attention to the need to take into account the academic, social, political and historical contexts in which it occurs. The research reported here begins to suggest how researchers do this.

Methodology

When we experience something, we differentiate the phenomenon from its context, noticing some things and not others. Some aspects are in the foreground and others recede to the background. Different people notice and interpret different things. What individuals are aware of is related to the meaning they attach to the phenomenon. However, when they share a common language and culture, there are relationships between all of the different ways of experiencing a particular phenomenon. Phenomenographic research on a range of phenomena has established that there are limited ways in which any given phenomenon is experienced.

The task of the phenomenographic researcher is, firstly, to separate out the variation in the ways the phenomenon is experienced. Then, within each of these different ways, the relationships between their component parts have to be mapped. The meanings/interpretations which result from what is noticed/experienced have then to be identified. This is referred to in phenomenography as mapping the structural and referential relationships of the variation in the ways in which a particular phenomenon is experienced (for a fuller account of this process, see Marton & Booth, 1997). The technique of differentiating categories of description which arise from the data captures the richness of the data as a whole and renders it meaningful. Broad clusters of ideas that go consistently together are identified through sorting and re-sorting, until the interstices between the clusters of ideas are clear and unambiguous. The phenomenographic analysis thus results in a coherent framework for understanding what is presented, providing both an approach to analysing data and a theory for analysing the structure of the variation in experiences of the phenomenon being researched (Marton & Booth, 1997).

Following the seminal work of Marton and colleagues (Marton, 1981) there is now a well-established phenomenographic literature on students' conceptions of learning in higher education (see, for example, Entwistle, 1997; Marton & Booth, 1997), and on teachers' conceptions of teaching (Martin & Ramsden, 1994; Trigwell & Taylor, 1994). There is not, however, an equivalent literature on conceptions of research. Since the intention of phenomenography is to describe the variation in the ways a phenomenon is perceived, it is particularly suited to an investigation of the variation in the ways academic researchers conceptualise the phenomenon of research. However, this study did not set out to replicate the structure of the outcomes found in relation to learning and teaching. Rather, there was an attempt to set aside any preconceptions concerning what would be found.

The investigation utilised a phenomenographic approach to identify the different conceptions of 57 researchers. Thirty academics from one large 'research' university were interviewed in the first phase of the study. These were all senior researchers holding large Australian Research Council (ARC) grants. These grants are highly competitive and there is evidence that a high level of academic seniority is required to acquire them (Bazeley *et al.*, 1996). Since it was hypothesised that the variation in conceptions would mirror disciplinary differences, the researchers were chosen to represent three disciplinary groupings: sciences and technology, social sciences, and the arts and humanities. There were 10 researchers in each group. In the second phase of the study, 27 experienced researchers from four Australian universities were interviewed. Chosen to represent the same disciplinary groupings, they all had a track record in obtaining research grants and/or a substantial record of publication. In this group, 11 were in scientific and technical areas, seven were from the social sciences, and nine were from the arts and humanities.

All of the interviews consisted of nine questions, seeking information concerning the nature of the research participants were pursuing and their ideas about research. There were also some background questions to verify that the researchers were indeed in the target groups. Prior to the interviews being conducted, many potential interview questions were examined, discussed with academic colleagues and tried out with researchers in the target groups. It was important to arrive at a series of questions which would enable conceptions of research to be appropriately identified. Even so, four questions were not 'oriented to the phenomenon as and how it appears' (Sandberg, 1997, p. 210), but provided information concerning attitudes to phenomena related to research, such as personal learning, satisfaction, students' attitudes and whether and how research is changing. The responses to these questions, as well as the background questions, were excluded from the phenomenographic analysis.

Each phase of the study was analysed separately, with all of the transcribed responses being treated as one long transcript. Throughout the painstaking analysis of the data, there was an attempt to look beyond or to 'bracket out' (Lucas, 1998) ways in which research is traditionally differentiated: such as by disciplinary differences, whether the research is perceived as pure or applied, and differences in methodology. In analysing the second data set, the variation found in phase one data was also bracketed out. The robustness of the categories of description over the two data sets, even when in analysing the second data set there was a deliberate attempt to set them aside, provides strong reason to have confidence that all of the variation is accounted for.

Following the analysis of the first set of data, a document was prepared outlining the findings. This was sent to all of the interviewees with an invitation to comment and to attend a meeting to discuss the ideas. Two meetings were held and these were recorded and transcribed. Typical of their comments were the following:

> I thought these were useful, probably because I think of myself as thinking about my own research and why I do what I do, but I realised, when I read this, I never really think about why other people do what they do, and therefore it was quite interesting to see these archetypes enunciated, and I could identify other colleagues with other types of research, which is simply something I never bother to think about. I'm too busy doing my own. So from that point of view I thought it was enlightening.
>
> (01: Egyptian archaeology)

> I read the document . . . It made sense to me. I could see certain classifications that you'd adopted . . . I'm more aware of how broad the conceptions of research are among various academics, and I saw myself as . . . fitting into one of those broad conceptions.
>
> (21: financial institutions)

Findings

The study resulted, in each phase, in the identification of four categories delineating the variation in the ways in which research is understood. These have been labelled, the 'domino', 'trading', 'layer' and 'journey' conceptions. There were some minor differences in the two data sets and these are described later. However, it was impossible to avoid the four categories in each case and there were no additional or missing categories in the second phase of the study. The numbers 1–30 identify researchers in phase one, while 31–57 relate to those in phase two.

Variation 1: domino variation

In this variation, research is viewed as a series (often a list) of separate tasks, events, things, activities, problems, techniques, experiments, issues, ideas or questions, each of which is presented as distinct. The use of collecting metaphors suggests the importance of linking them, and the idea that what is being linked are quantities of things: ideas, data, techniques etc.

> Often you get important technical results out but they're not quite as meaningful as being able to connect a whole bunch of ideas together or forming a more detailed idea about something.
>
> (55: nuclear radiation)

> ... it's materials which you've gathered ... bits and pieces, for example, about the language of sport, or ... about Eliot's life and you've assembled that. So sometimes it is what another scholar has assembled, but often it's what you've assembled and bringing [it] together in some coherent form.
>
> (37: life of T. S. Eliot)

> ... there's an element of stamp-collecting about ... the ... new facts you're collecting that then ultimately lead to new insights.
>
> (35: reproduction biology)

This variation takes its name from the game of dominoes, because, just as dominoes are separate but can be combined in a number of patterns and/or meaningful ways, so too separate elements of research are conceptualised as illuminating other elements. There is an external product orientation because, in describing separate things, research is interpreted as the activity of combining them to solve practical problems, answer questions or illuminate wider areas of understanding. Solving one problem can have spin-offs in regard to other problems, as in the 'domino effect', where dominoes are lined up and when one falls it sets up a chain reaction. There may be a number of reactions in different directions and on different levels. The task may be conceived as, firstly, identifying a problem, and perhaps breaking it down into a number of sub-problems, and then working on these. Or it may be seen as applying different techniques and synthesising new information. Generally, in this conception, the primary emphasis is on synthesis.

> My interests are in industrial drying technology, but that covers quite a large number of different sub-areas and techniques. That includes the use of computational fluid dynamics techniques and also the use of process flow sheet and techniques, together with advanced optimisation techniques so there's quite a wide range of techniques ... on a range of different problems.
>
> (07: timber drying technology)

It involves synthesis, characterisation of those compounds, evaluation: once you've made them you have to decide whether they are useful or not useful . . . then going on and doing a series of tests. Now that may mean some spectroscopic tests, it may mean biological tests, not animal tests but just standard biological tests. And then it means coming back into the loop again and perhaps resynthesising something . . . it's a bit like tailoring a molecule to fit . . . or tailoring a suit to fit yourself. . . . And so you go in circuits around and around in order to find a molecule that will probe DNA well.

(40: bio-organic chemistry)

To the extent that anything I do is original it comes in that synthetic process . . . [usually] it's a matter of finding . . . some new interpretation of a philosopher that you're doing in history . . . cobbling together bits of other people's ideas and putting them into new form is a lot of what makes work original.

(34: philosophy of mind)

Variation 2: trading variation

Research in the trading variation is a social phenomenon. What is in the foreground are the products of research: publications, grants, and social networks. These are created and then exchanged in a social situation for money, prestige or simply recognition. The way in which respondents always come back to the idea of the finished product and how the researcher is going to be seen at the end of it is characteristic here. There is, thus, an external product orientation, with the researcher always present to the awareness.

You go and give papers and that sort of thing, . . . by giving papers you talk to other researchers in the field, the main body [of work] is there. You interact with others through email as well.

(11: political history of Russia)

Well it started as a small ARC grant way back in the early '90s and I did quite a lot of work then and I've got a selection of poems coming out as a book very shortly and then all the poems together will come out as a . . . major anthology.

(04: old Welsh)

Whether the research outcomes are conceived in terms of publications, research grants, the achievement of objectives or social benefits, more often than not in this variation, research is described in terms of relationships, activities or ideas of other people (e.g. research assistants, collaborators or other researchers in the field).

When I worked on the Bicentennial history of Australia . . . a really big group of about twenty people, . . . [had] very wonderful exchange meetings . . . where you'd get some feedback from other people.

(12: feminist literature)

It involves interacting with colleagues and designing experiments: both my own experiments that my students might do and then having regular meetings to . . . discuss results we might be getting or problems we might be having and implications for further experiments.

(36: biochemistry)

An aspect of the external product orientation of this variation is the idea of research being for an audience. Researchers stress the importance of being part of and valued by an international community. In the following extract, the researcher demonstrates the connection between the networks and personal recognition. This serves to explain why these elements go together in the trading variation:

> Through publishing – not just through academic journals, but other places – you get a level of recognition outside of the academic community which then connects you into other networks, so that, for example, I'm on an advisory committee to the NSW Government and I'm on there as an expert person because people know that I'm engaged in this work and I've published a lot in the area.
>
> (43: housing policy)

Consistent with the external product orientation is a strong focus on writing. As one said: 'I find the writing of it intrinsic to the doing of it' (31: News Media). In phase two data, there was also a focus on reading. Reading was also conceptualised as located in a social context, but reading to understand the ideas of other people.

> I'm with the school that believes you should always be writing while you are researching and I always tell my . . . students too, that it's fatal just to go away and read for a year. You should always be writing, . . . even if what you have written is discarded you should always be writing . . . Half the time is reading, half the time is writing.
>
> (37: life of T. S. Eliot)

Variation 3: layer variation

It is helpful to think of this variation as describing two or more layers. Data, previous theories or ideas are initially in the foreground. There is an internal orientation, where the researcher is bringing to light the ideas, explanations and truths lying in the background by illuminating or uncovering the underlying layer. The researcher is absent from the focus of awareness.

> [In research there is] . . . the satisfaction of finding an underlying pattern or simplicity in things which appear initially to be confusing or complicated.
>
> (47: communications policy)

> Historical research . . . [is] trying to get at another level of what people were doing . . ., who were perhaps the recipients of that culture but were not necessarily receiving it in the same way that we would receive it today. So . . . adding another dimension.
>
> (20: nineteenth century travel)

While these are examples of interpretive research, embodied in the layer variation are different ideas about the ontological status of findings. There may be the idea that what is lying underneath, and is found, exists; what is sought is a correct description of reality.

> For example, in our own case, . . . we appear to have identified a receptor protein molecule on the surface of a cell that wasn't previously recognised as being there.
>
> (36: biochemistry)

[Research is] searching for something that you know is there.

(22: nineteenth century art)

The task of examining the layer underneath may, alternatively, rest on the idea that what is being sought is simply a better explanation.

> I had the [idea] when I started the biography that I would find out the truth! I would know exactly what made this bloke tick and why he wrote these books and so on. And . . . the big thing I had to face about halfway through [was] I wasn't going to find any truth. There wasn't going to be any . . . magic fact, . . . brought in. . . . That was really hard for me to face because I really wanted to cling to . . . that magic stone that one day I'd overturn it and there would be the truth.
>
> (42: Australian biography)

In the layer variation, research may alternatively be described as an artistic process; meaning being created, not discovered. The theories which are created illuminate the surface reality.

> I think of it sometimes like painting where you're working with a palette knife and you're constantly touching it up, jumping back into earlier parts of what you've written, adding new data, it's just a constant . . . creative process . . . , I think . . . that good research is a very creative activity.
>
> (01: Egyptian archaeology)

Variation 4: journey variation

In the journey variation, the activities in which the researcher engages, whether or not they appear to have a direct bearing, are viewed as relevant to research because they inform the life issues which underpin the research questions. Encounters with the data are viewed holistically as transforming theoretical and experiential understandings of the issues which are the focus of interest. The researcher grows or is transformed by this. The content or topic of the investigation is less important than the issues or underlying questions posed, or the ways in which they dovetail with the researcher's life or career. The researcher is central to the focus of awareness.

> The whole fieldwork experience is a much deeper basis than simply collecting a bunch of data, it actually has major transformative effects on the personality.
>
> (09: linguistics)

> Since anthropologists are interested in groups . . . group dynamics and culture and rules, and all of those sorts of things, then anything you do – including working in a university committee . . . can be a kind of a research . . . How do committees function? Who makes the decisions? Do you have a nominal chair and then somebody else is actually pulling the strings or what? All of these sorts of things can be very interesting, so one can actually as an anthropologist write about one's own university life. And some have done that, actually produced books on that. So . . . it changes you.
>
> (38: performance)

Typically, in this variation, the story of how the researcher arrived at the particular institution in which they worked, or at being interested in the issues currently being explored, is foregrounded.

> One of the areas I'm looking at is fungi in compost and the relationship they have to some of the fungal diseases of humans. So what I'm trying to do is fit in to where I see myself trying to fit into this University, rather than trying to stick with my old background and knowledge and ... interests. ... Originally when I first came here, I made contact with some people I knew at the Botanic Gardens ... and ... said, 'Okay, what have you got in the way of things I can do up there, because I work with plants'. [Because] I thought 'well, we can't work with plants here at the moment, we don't have a glass house' ... And ... we started off by ... developing a project which was a need they had to replace peat in their potting mixes ... So we actually went for an internal grant. ... From that, I ... happened to hear on the grapevine ... [story continues]
>
> (41: plant microbiology)

> Quite apart from my change of interest, the question arises: why my interest changed? And a part of it ... was to discover the human side of science. Part of it was ... to give my science a wider context: where did the science I had done for 20–30 years ... fit in the broader picture? What role did that have in the society at large? What benefit was it to the community at large? ... But ... it had a very personal element too, and that was trying to discover where I myself fitted into the broader picture. I felt I understood myself as a scientist, I understood my personal commitment to science. I understood what role I thought I was playing in the scientific community, but then [that] became inadequate to me. I wanted a broader picture of where I sat personally in the university culture, in society at large ... So I think coming across the campus has also been part of my personal search for a wider understanding of what a university historically has been, and therefore to try and inform my views about what it should be in the future.
>
> (54: history of science)

Here, research, learning and personal transformation are viewed as different facets of the person:

> For me, research is a kind of transcendental therapy, that's the best way to express it ... a kind of tantra. It transforms one through the process of engaging in it. ... It's the most intensive form of psychotherapy you can do.
>
> (09: linguistics)

> the field worker can't expect to come back the same as they went. If they do expect that then they are not going to do very good work and even if they expect it when they go, they probably will have their minds changed when they get back. So it's a major transformation.
>
> (38: performance)

Analysis of findings

Table 38 presents the structural and referential dimensions of conceptions of research found within the data. In describing the dimensions of the ways in which a phenomenon is understood, phenomenography does not ascribe individuals to those dimensions.

Table 38 Structural and referential dimensions of conceptions of research

	Structural dimension (what is perceived and how the elements of what is perceived are related to each other)	*Referential dimension (the meaning given to what is perceived)*
	What is in the foreground is/are:	Research is interpreted as:
Domino conception	sets (lists) of atomistic things: techniques, problems etc. These separate elements are viewed as linking together in a linear fashion;	a process of synthesising separate elements so that problems are solved, questions answered or opened up;
Layer conception	data containing ideas together with (linked to) hidden meanings;	a process of discovering, uncovering or creating underlying meanings;
Trading conception	products, end points, publications, grants and social networks. These are linked together in relationships of personal recognition and reward;	a kind of social market place where the exchange of products takes place;
Journey conception	the personal existential issues and dilemmas. They are linked through an awareness of the career of the researcher and viewed as having been explored for a long time.	a personal journey of discovery, possibly leading to transformation.

While individual researchers may principally be associated with one particular category, others span two or three. No researchers demonstrated evidence of all four categories.

In specifying the relationships between different dimensions, phenomenographers typically postulate a hierarchical relationship, with some categories being viewed as less complex, less well developed or less sophisticated than others. The interviewees in the current study were all experienced senior researchers. It therefore seems presumptuous to designate some of their conceptions as less complex or less well developed, particularly since the idea that there have to be hierarchical relationships between categories does not flow from the logic of phenomenography. It is a supposition which is based on the evidence of empirical findings in studies of students'

Table 39 Relationships between conceptions of research

	External product orientation where the intention is to produce an outcome. Tends to be atomistic and synthetic	*Internal process orientation where the intention is to understand. Tends to be holistic and analytical*
Researcher is present in awareness	Trading	Journey
Researcher absent from awareness	Domino	Layer

conceptions of learning. While it may be supposed that the domino conception is less complex than, for example, the journey conception, this depends on the conception of research from which one does the looking. In other words, investigations of conceptions of research inevitably suffer from a problem of self-reference. Thus, any attempt to understand the relationships between categories is contingent. Phenomenographers debate the role and status of categories of description and their relationships, but, as Entwistle argues, 'the test is generally not its theoretical purity, but its value in producing useful insights' (Entwistle, 1997, p. 129).

Lucas (1998) warns of the danger of moving too quickly from the data to an attempt to structure the data. In the current study, setting aside prior assumptions included setting aside the assumption that categories of description would be hierarchically related. Indeed, the four categories were discussed with numerous groups of researchers over a long period of time before any attempt to delineate a structure was made. The question addressed was how to capture the richness of the data in a useful structural framework of interpretation. This entailed delineating what was the essence of the conceptions of the phenomenon and what was peripheral.

Most of the variation is captured by interpreting the categories as having either an orientation outwards, focusing on external products, or an orientation inwards, focusing on internal processes. The categories are also differentiated according to whether the researcher is in the focus of awareness or is essentially absent from it (see Table 39). Interestingly, these dimensions accord with Becher's (1989) finding that researchers are differently oriented to the external climate, and to the extent to which their personal concerns influence their conceptions of research. The domino conception, thus, is focused externally on solving problems or answering questions through a synthetic process of combining separate elements. The person doing the research is conceptually kept separated from the research, which is wholly oriented towards the ideas, techniques and/or activities. The trading variation, similarly, is focused externally on products, yet here the researcher is consistently present to awareness through the recognition or reward which follows, or the social networks in which they are engaged.

In the layer variation, the focus of attention is on the analysis of the data being researched with the intention to understand what lies beneath it. There is thus an internal focus on the process of coming to understand the phenomena being researched. The researcher is absent from the focus of awareness. The journey variation is also oriented inwards. Here the focus is on the personal interests and issues of the researcher. The presence of the researcher is the primary focus of awareness.

It was initially hypothesised that the variation identified would mirror disciplinary differences. However, this hypothesis was not supported. While scientific and technical disciplines were represented more in the domino variation, this was not exclusively so. The humanities and social science disciplines were also represented. On the other hand, while there were more examples of humanities research in the journey variation, scientific disciplines were also represented. In the trading and layer variations, there was, similarly, a spread of discipline areas. Interestingly, researchers from any one discipline could be represented in any or all categories. This is consistent with the view expressed earlier that discipline is only one factor influencing the ways research is experienced. It also supports the findings of Neumann (1993), who found that although senior academic administrators' views on research recognised disciplinary differences, their definitions of research did not.

Discussion

By demonstrating variation in how research is experienced, the framework outlined here provides a basis for understanding a number of phenomena relating to research in higher education which have hitherto been insufficiently understood. Since each variation entails different kinds of orientations in relation to research output and achievements, the framework may provide a useful tool in performance review discussions. For example, the trading variation, with its external, product orientation, may be more likely to lead to publication than, for example, the layer variation, with its internal, process orientation. Thus, it may be possible, on the basis of a knowledge of the variations, to discuss future research output.

When researchers with markedly different orientations met, it was found that they were unable to communicate effectively. They apparently shared the same language and endeavoured in meeting to find common ground, but essentially talked at cross purposes. It is possible to explain this by reference to the differences in their conceptions of research. Informal discussions with researchers have subsequently indicated that in research committees, the external product orientation is frequently dominant. Many academics on such committees have indicated difficulties in communicating with and understanding the perspectives of others round the table. The framework presented in this article provides a way of understanding different perspectives in such groups. Since academics may exhibit evidence of more than one variation, these effects may be mitigated. Nevertheless, it does provide an alternative to the conventional assumption that disciplinary differences are responsible for failures in communication.

The findings have important implications in relation to the research development of postgraduates and early career researchers, because they present a framework for understanding their primary preoccupations *vis à vis* their more experienced colleagues. Being clear about one's own way of viewing research provides a basis for making sense of others' conceptions. The variations in conceptions of research may, for example, provide a way of understanding difficulties with, or non-completion of, research degrees due to incompatible conceptions of supervisor and student. Pearson & Brew (2002) argue that an important task facing postgraduate supervisors is to develop an understanding of the different ways in which research can be conceptualised, in order to be in a position to help the research student articulate their understanding.

The variation described in this article is also important in relation to debates about how research is changing and the effects of research policies. An interesting question for higher education is the extent to which research agendas are being driven by particular conceptions of research. The focus on publication enshrined in government funding policy, for example, in the UK and in Australia, may be interpreted as emphasising the trading variation. Indeed, it would appear that the emphasis on research as a commodity within funding policies has had a more significant impact on research than the broad shifts in the intellectual climate mentioned earlier (Brew & Phillis, 1997). Such policies place conceptions of research which have an internal process orientation under threat. Attempts in the UK and in Canada to encourage what has been termed 'blue skies research' have, by and large, been unsuccessful. This is particularly worrying in some of the newer disciplines and in education, where research is often used as a vehicle for personal learning and where researchers may be endeavouring to establish new forms of inquiry.

Conclusion

The study reported here has examined variations in conceptions of research of senior Australian academic researchers in traditional areas. Further work is needed to establish if the variation is shared in other academic domains. If conceptions of experienced researchers were compared with those of inexperienced researchers, there would be further implications for the development of new researchers. Comparisons between the conceptions of males and females, and between researchers with different cultural backgrounds, would also have implications for the development of these researchers. A comparison of conceptions within research-based institutions with those of academics in new universities, or where there are not strong traditions of research, would establish whether research is experienced differently depending on differences in institutional culture, including differing levels of support for research, facilities available, promotions procedures and teaching loads.

In addition, further research is needed to elucidate how stable these variations are over time, and whether or not they are likely to change from one research project to another. Whether the way a person views research is a consequence of doing research of a particular kind and on a particular topic, or whether researchers choose the research topics they do because they have particular conceptions of research, is another area for future research. In studies of students' conceptions of learning, some students were shown to exhibit different conceptions in different circumstances (Ramsden, 1997). Further empirical work is needed to establish if this is also true of researchers' conceptions of research.

Whenever a process of inquiry is talked about or engaged in, what is said and done is dependent upon underlying conceptions about the nature of research. These influence the types of projects researchers feel comfortable in pursuing, the choice of methodology, the questions, ideas and issues pursued, and the ways in which the work is carried out. Further study is clearly needed to elucidate the relationships between conceptions and what researchers do. Work to integrate conceptions of research, conceptions of teaching and conceptions of learning is also needed. The findings reported in this article, however, have thrown light on aspects of research which are often hidden from view but which influence research at every level. They represent a first step in explaining differences in researcher orientations and practice.

Acknowledgements

I am particularly indebted to Frank Phillis for assistance with the research reported in this article, also to the 57 senior researchers who participated. The research was funded by a grant from the University of Sydney.

References

Barnett, R. (1997) *Higher Education: a critical business* (Buckingham, Open University Press and Society for Research into Higher Education).
Barnett, R. & Griffin, A. (Eds) (1997) *The end of knowledge in higher education* (London, Cassell).
Bazeley, P., Kemp, L., Stevens, K., Asmar, C., Grbich, C., Marsh, H. & Bhathal, R. (1996) *Waiting in the Wings: a study of early career academic researchers in Australia*. Commissioned Report Number 50. National Board of Employment, Education and Training (Canberra, Australian Government Publishing Service).
Becher, T. (1989) *Academic Tribes and Territories, intellectual enquiry and the cultures of disciplines* (Buckingham, Society for Research into Higher Education and the Open University Press).

Bourke, P. (1997) *Evaluating University Research: the British research assessment exercise and Australian practice*. Commissioned Report No. 56 (Canberra, Australian Government Publishing Service).

Boyer, E. (1990) *Scholarship Reconsidered, priorities for the professoriate* (Princeton, NJ, Carnegie Foundation for the Advancement of Teaching, University of Princeton).

Brew, A. & Boud, D. (1995) Teaching and research: establishing the vital link with learning, *Higher Education* 29, pp. 261–173.

Brew, A. & Phillis, F. (1997) Is research changing? Conceptions of successful researchers, *Proceedings of the Higher Education Research and Development Society of Australasia Conference*, Adelaide, pp. 131–135.

Bruce, D. & Bahrick, H.P. (1992) Perceptions of past research, *American Psychologist*, 47, pp. 319–328.

Davis, W.E. & Chandler, T.K.L. (1998) Beyond Boyer's *Scholarship Reconsidered*: fundamental change in the university and the socioeconomic systems, *Journal of Higher Education*, 69, pp. 23–64.

Entwistle, N. (1997) Introduction: phenomenography in higher education, *Research and Development in Higher Education*, 16, pp. 127–134.

Gibbons, M., Limoges, C., Nowotny, H., Schwartzman, S., Scott, P. & Trow, M. (1994) *The New Production of Knowledge: the dynamics of science and research its contemporary societies* (London, Sage).

Hattie, J. & Marsh, H.W. (1996) The relationship between research and teaching: a meta-analysis, *Review of Educational Research*, 66, pp. 507–542.

Jenkins, A., Blackman, T., Lindsay, R. & Paton-Saltzberg, R. (1998) Teaching and research: student perspectives and policy implications, *Studies in Higher Education*, 23, pp. 127–141.

Lucas, U. (1998) Beyond categories of description: a further role for phenomenographic research, in: C. Rust (Ed.) Improving students' learning outcomes, *Proceedings of the 1998 6th International Symposium on Improving Student Learning*, pp. 202–215 (Oxford, Oxford Centre for Staff and Learning Development).

Lyotard, J.-F. (1993) *The Postmodern Condition: a report on knowledge*, trans. from the French by G. Bennington & B. Massumi (Minneapolis, MN, University of Minneapolis Press).

Martin, E. & Ramsden, P. (1994) *Effectiveness and Efficiency of Courses in Teaching Methods for Recently Appointed Academic Staff* (Canberra, ACT, Australian Government Publishing Service).

Marton, F. (1981) Phenomenography: describing conceptions of the world around us, *Instructional Science*, 10, pp. 177–200.

Marton, F. & Booth, S. (1997) *Learning and Awareness* (Mahwah, NJ, Lawrence Erlbaum).

Marton, F., Fensham, P. & Chaiklin, S. (1994) A Nobel's eye view of scientific intuition: discussions with the Nobel prize-winners in physics, chemistry and medicine (1970–1986), *International Journal of Science Education*, 16, pp. 457–473.

Neumann, R. (1993) Research and scholarship: perceptions of senior academic administrators, *Higher Education*, 25, pp. 97–110.

Paulsen, M.B. & Feldman, K.A. (1995) Toward a reconceptualization of scholarship: a human action system with functional imperatives, *Journal of Higher Education*, 66, pp. 615–640.

Pearson, M. & Brew, A. (2002) Research training and supervisor development, *Studies in Higher Education*, 27, 1.

Ramsden, P. (1997) The context of learning in academic departments, in: F. Marton, D. Hounsell & N. Entwistle (1997) *The Experience of Learning: implications for teaching and studying in higher education*, 2nd edn (Edinburgh, Scottish Academic Press).

Rice, R.E. (1992) Towards a broader conception of scholarship: the American context, in: T.G. Whiston & R.L. Geiger (Eds) *Research and Higher Education: the United Kingdom and the United States*, pp. 117–129 (Buckingham, Society for Research into Higher Education and The Open University Press).

Sandberg, J. (1997) Are phenomenographic results reliable? *Research and Development in Higher Education*, 16, pp. 203–212.

Schön, D.A. (1995) The new scholarship requires a new epistemology, *Change*, 27(6), pp. 26–34.

Scott, D.K. & Awbrey, S.M. (1993) Transforming scholarship, *Change*, 25(4), pp. 38–43.
Shore, B., Pinker, S. & Bates, M. (1990) Research as a model for university teaching, *Higher Education*, 19, pp. 21–35.
Startup, R. (1985) The changing perspective of academic researchers, *Studies in Higher Education*, 10, pp. 69–78.
Sundre, D.L. (1992) The specification of the content domain of faculty scholarship, *Research in Higher Education*, 33, pp. 297–315.
Trigwell, K.P.M. & Taylor, P. (1994) Qualitative differences in approaches to teaching first year university science, *Higher Education*, 27, pp. 75–84.
Turpin, T., Garrett-Jones, S., Rankin, N. & Aylward, D. (1996) *Patterns of Research Activity in Australian Universities*. Commissioned Report No. 47, (Canberra, ACT, Australian Government Publishing Service).

CHAPTER 14

FLIGHTS OF IMAGINATION

Academic women be(com)ing writers

Barbara Grant and Sally Knowles

The International Journal for Academic Development, 5, 1, 6–19, 2000

EDITOR'S INTRODUCTION

In this article, Grant and Knowles discuss how to make writing pleasurable as well as productive for women academics. This is seen as not just a matter of making time and space for writing, but also of making imaginative space and developing one's understanding of oneself as a writer. Their analysis is set within the context of women's place within the academy as being largely subordinate and subject to the assessment and appraisal, predominantly, of men.

The authors describe two interventions which they led in different institutions in their role as academic developers. One of these took the form of a one-week writing retreat, involving seven participants from three New Zealand universities. The other was a peer mentoring group of six women at one Australian university, which met fortnightly for two hours over two semesters. The accounts are illustrated by feedback comments from the women involved. They demonstrate the motivational and supportive elements which such interventions can provide to stimulate writing.

This article was categorised in the introductory chapter as adopting a biographical approach to the study of academic work. With its feminist concerns, it might also have been described as taking a critical approach, but has been classified as biographical because of its focus on the experiences of the women concerned (including the authors themselves).

The article may be related to two kinds of higher education literatures. One of these deals specifically with academic writing, and how it may be developed (e.g. Morss and Murray 2001). There are links here, of course, to the literature on student writing, represented in this Reader by the article by Maclellan (2001). The second literature of relevance is that focusing on the position of women within higher education institutions (e.g. Asmar 1999, Brooks 1997, Brooks and Mackinnon 2001, Eggins 1997, Howie and Tauchert 2002).

References

Asmar, C. (1999) 'Is there a Gendered Agenda in Academia? The research experience of female and male PhD graduates in Australian universities', *Higher Education*, 38, pp. 255–273.

Brooks, A. (1997) *Academic Women*. Buckingham, Open University Press.

Brooks, A. and Mackinnon, A. (eds) (2001) *Gender and the Restructured University*. Buckingham, Open University Press.

Eggins, H. (ed.) (1997) *Women as Leaders and Managers in Higher Education*. Buckingham, Open University Press.

Howie, G. and Tauchert, A. (eds) (2002) *Gender, Teaching and Research in Higher Education: challenges for the 21st century.* Aldershot, Ashgate.

Maclellan, E. (2001) 'Assessment for Learning: the differing perceptions of tutors and students', *Assessment and Evaluation in Higher Education*, 26, 4, pp. 307–318.

Morss, K. and Murray, R. (2001) 'Researching Academic Writing within a Structured Programme: insights and outcomes', *Studies in Higher Education*, 26, 1, pp. 35–52.

FLIGHTS OF IMAGINATION

Introduction

> In changing [writing] habits, you will find yourself getting your results far more quickly and with less 'backwash' if you *engage your imagination* in the process instead of calling out the biggest gun of your character equipment first.
>
> (Brande, 1934/1983, 58, emphasis added)

For Virginia Woolf (1929/1977), a room of one's own and money were necessary for a woman to write. Yet although academic women have both – in a way that Woolf could only imagine – we often struggle to write, finding frustration and self-doubt where there could better be accomplishment and joy. As academic women who are also academic developers, we share this struggle. We suggest here that, in academic development, we follow Dorothea Brande's advice to bring flights of imagination, as well as the weight of our wills, to the task, helping ourselves and other academic women to become writers who write productively and with pleasure.

In the first half of what follows, we briefly sketch the position of women in academic life early in the twenty-first century and outline some of the dilemmas we face with respect to our professional writing. In the second half, we give a description of two academic development projects that focus on how individual women, through collaborating in small groups, can change ourselves and our circumstances to write more. We close with some reflections on the role of academic developers in supporting this process of change.

Before going any further we want to point out some of the dangers for academic women attendant upon such projects. One is that they may serve to constitute women as a 'problem' group (Ferres, 1995) in need of remediation. However we do not see the projects as remedial but as subversive: as long as being an academic means also being a writer in a competitive individualistic culture, the need for them will continue. At the same time, we acknowledge the necessity for structural and cultural change in universities to ensure women can recognize themselves in the rewarded meanings of teacher, scholar, researcher and writer. For example, changes are needed in promotion criteria and procedures, and in more flexible definitions of what constitutes quality research and research competence (Park, 1996), even perhaps in the very hierarchical structure of the academy itself (Baldwin, 1990). We understand that some academic men struggle to write and to enjoy writing – the projects described here clearly have relevance for them too.

Another danger lies in talking about 'women' as if we are a homogenous group. Simple figures for representation of women in the academy hide the within-group differences based on ethnicity, class and sexual orientation, for example – differences which are socially constructed and in asymmetrical power relations. Thus women from some social groups (for instance Aboriginal and Torres Strait Islanders, Maori, rural and/or poor women) are largely excluded from the academy in Australasia and, when they participate as students or staff, they face a range of obstacles that are not faced by women from privileged groups. Where women have to traverse a greater gap between their cultural ways of talking and writing and those demanded in academic discourse (Aronson & Swanson, 1991), the struggle to write is likely to be even greater. In such cases it is crucial for effective academic development interventions that there are academic developers who either belong to or have rapport with such social groups.

Overall, we assert the importance of finding ways to enhance the experience and productivity of academic women as writers in part to give us access to the extrinsic rewards the academy offers, but also to open the door to a powerful personal and interpersonal pleasure.

The modern scene of women and academic writing

In the early twenty-first-century university, while the position of academic women has improved from the days of which Woolf writes, there are still some searching questions that need to be asked about the position of women in the academy. For instance, in terms of student representation, undergraduate women show significantly increased participation in many disciplines over the last 20 years (Martin, 1996). What is more, academically they are outshining men in many areas. Yet at the level of doctoral programmes, their numbers are proportionally fewer (Brooks, 1997). This trend is even more evident when we consider the profile of women academics. Many studies show we are drastically under-represented towards the top of the institutional hierarchy and heavily over-represented at the bottom among the part-time teaching staff (Acker, 1993; Brooks, 1997; Martin, 1996). It appears that 'it is what the university stands for, and what it rewards and what it ignores, that is at issue' (Acker & Feuerverger, 1996, p. 14). What the university rewards is research productivity – measured by grants won and prestigious publications listed. Here the habit of writing – or not – is crucial.

Some surveys have shown that women academics, except those few who are in senior positions, do not appear to write as much as men, particularly in the more prestigious forms: books, book chapters, and articles in internationally refereed journals (Brooks, 1997; Lie & O'Leary, 1990; Wilson, 1986). However, because of the way in which academic publishing is counted, it is difficult to know whether women, on the whole, do not literally write as much as men. For there is research indicating that even when they do write as much, widely used peer-review systems are nepotistic, favouring men over equally productive women (Wenneras & Wold, 1997). As well, the political economies of grant funding and academic publishing marginalize not only their preferred disciplines but also some of the kinds of research and writing that women do more frequently (Kim, Ricks, & Fuller, 1996).

If, overall, women do indeed write as much as men, only to have their work refused or unrecognized, it is unsurprising that many experience ambivalence about and resistance to writing. What we, as academic developers, want to achieve with our colleagues through the interventions described here is not only the access to power and prestige that published academic writing brings, but also the sense of a self who has something to say, who takes up the mantle of writer to actively contribute as an intellectual to her discipline and to the public community that supports her.

Writing dilemmas

From the stories told, the difficulties for academic women in writing for publication are often about making space in their lives. Here we understand space in two ways: one is the literal sense of finding the time and place for writing, the other is the metaphorical sense of making imaginative spaces to occupy as writers. In this dual sense, the struggle is not just with the material day-to-day realities of our gendered positions within a normatively masculine academy, but also with our own sense of self. While these struggles are also real for many academic men, as they too negotiate the conflicted subject position of 'academic', the struggles to make literal and metaphorical space are likely to be more difficult for women for many of the reasons explained below.

Finding/making time and space

The problem of finding/making uninterrupted time and space is both a systemic and an individual one. It is the problem most likely to be consciously struggled with by a woman. It can be seen in the endless re-decisions to mark out time for writing, to put a 'busy' sign on our office doors, to get up a little or a lot earlier each morning. We have made these attempts to discipline ourselves – our nights and days – since we were students so that we could write first our essays, then theses, later conference papers, journal articles, film scripts and books. This ongoing struggle reflects:

> the fractured nature of academic life, with its conflicting demands of quality teaching, up-to-date scholarship, the pursuit of original research and the cultivation of substantial partnerships with external communities.
>
> (Deane, Johnson, Jones & Lengkeek, 1996, p. xvii)

It also reflects the gendered responsibilities to care for others that many women carry outside their work as academics, which often conflict with the requirements of academic life (Acker, 1993). Moreover, this sense of responsibility at times spills over into our work with students and colleagues (Acker & Feuerverger, 1996): thus women often bear the brunt of the unrecorded and unrecognized pastoral care within universities. Alison Jones (1997, p. 4) has this to say of such 'academic housework':

> Although [the academic woman] is horribly aware that her mode of teaching involves her in invisible, 'non-productive' housework she is unable to alter it – and nor does she want to. Because to do so would make her somehow less human and would take away some of the very best relationships and insights of academic life, and substantially reduce its quality for her, as well as her students . . . She is torn, knowing that she 'needs' to get to research and writing and reading more than she does. But she just does not seem to get the time.

Not only do many women want to do this work, but students often expect it from them in ways they do not from male academics (Fullerton, 1993; Stasiulis, 1995). For instance, Deborah Tannen (1991) tells the story of a graduate student who called her at home on a Sunday because she did not want to bother her male dissertation director at his home!

Further, women from particular social groups may carry more responsibilities both within the university (towards students from their group) and outside (to their communities). In 'Ko taku ko ta te Maori: The dilemma of a Maori academic', Linda Smith (1993, p. 9) writes:

We write submissions to government rather than theoretical discussions in international journals, we become ordinary participants in Maori organic educational movements and are seen as ideologically bound apologists of folklore, we carry out research to get our land back and it is classified as a 'report' rather than a refereed article, we speak to our own people at hui and gatherings all over the country but we do not connect with our discipline at an international level. We build supports around our students and try to incorporate our own pedagogical practices and then discover that teaching skills are not as important as publications. But all of this counts as the work of Maori academics.

Since these immensely practical aspects of the struggle are the most obvious, they are also likely to be the focus of interventions such as academic development workshops or individual counselling. Yet in our experiences as writers and academic developers we have found complex resistances to such interventions, some reasons for which may be found in another more elusive aspect of the struggle.

Making imaginative space

> The problem is indeed to 'become' a writer.
>
> (Bradbury's foreword in Brantle, 1934/1983, p. 16)

This other struggle has to do with the kinds of imaginative spaces women can find for themselves in their subject positions as academics. More than simply a talent or caprice of the individual, imagining is understood here to be a socially constructed capacity to be a form of subjectivity which hails us and offers us a way to act. To be able to imagine ourselves as a writer (in our mind's eye), and to find pleasure in and attachment to being this writer, is crucial to 'be(com)ing' a writer. Marking the word in this way underscores the potentially transformative relationship between what we do and how we understand ourselves. In being a writer, by regularly doing the practice of writing, we may also come to think of ourselves as writers, that is we become writers in our own and each other's imaginations. In this sense, the act of writing has significance far greater than putting words on paper or on to the computer screen. It is a way of transforming ourselves into writers: 'Transformation, or writing the body, implies that "change" is a change in way of meaning *and* way of *being* – a becoming' (Game, 1991, p. 189). Yet there are many obstacles that may stand between an academic woman and the imaginary spaces required to do writing.

One obstacle is a culturally enduring yet romantic idea of what it means to be a writer:

> When I picture writing, I often see a solitary writer alone in a cold garret working into the small hours of the morning by the thin light of a candle. It seems a curious image to conjure, for I am absent from this scene in which the writer is an Author and the writing is Literature.
>
> (Brodkey, 1996, p. 59)

This scene of the writer remote in the attic room, wealthy in time and inspiration, is perhaps the most pervasive. Watch the words flow effortlessly on to the page. But where are the children, the essays to mark, the committee agendas, the elderly parents, the toilets to clean, the friends to enjoy and support? This is a deeply gendered image – the individual outside of relationships and careless of physical needs, the implication being that someone else will provide for them. Linda Brodkey argues that a destructive implication of this image is the belief 'that writing costs writers their lives' (1996, p. 61), a price we are mostly unwilling or unable to pay.

Another obstacle to some women's pleasure in writing is their resistance to the academic voice with its curious absence of the writing subject and a notorious tendency towards obfuscation. In her thesis, *Hysteria and women's resistant voices in academic writing*, Christy Hartlage (1996, p. 71) points out how academic writing, based as it is on conflict and competition, is in some senses violent, both in what it suppresses and in what it attempts to achieve: 'The power of the academic argument is produced through the mastery of its form; he who is most skilful at the rational defeat of his opponent is the Master'. Women's resistance against thinking and writing like that runs deep, deeper than it may be possible to understand through individual introspection:

> 'Like Scheherazade in the Arabian Nights, life in the academy is prolonged with the production of words that please predominantly male assessors, confusing whether women academics write from anxiety or from desire.'
> (Morley, cited in Acker & Feuerverger, 1996, p. 14)

The anxiety and self-doubt generated by the struggle to take up the phallogocentric voice may be enough to silence an emerging voice.

In spite of the fact that women often excel in the academy and that we have interesting and important things to say, many of us feel ourselves to be 'temporary tenants rather than legitimate residents of the academic community' (Acker & Feuerverger, 1996, p. 13) and suffer crippling anxieties of authorship (Broughton, 1994). Often exacerbated by 'broken' career paths as a result of childbearing and rearing, that sense of temporariness may be linked to anxiety about being discovered as frauds. In this fraught zone of risk, writing becomes a process of exposing the inadequate self to the critical glare of peers, rather than an impulse borne out of some 'deep connections between one's intellectual preoccupations and one's human experience' (Brett, 1991, p. 521). The rituals of humiliation in academic life, which we first experienced as students, have made their mark on the reluctant writing body. In writing groups, when women are asked to share their writing with each other, the anxiety is often palpable. 'It is not ready', we claim, protectively holding our papers to our bodies. The strong reluctance to show the imperfect body of the text bespeaks feelings of shame towards our texts, reminiscent of dominant Western cultural attitudes towards viewing the physical body of a woman – if it's not perfect, then it's not good enough to show.

Such deep reluctance points to a strong attachment between our writing and our deeper, in part unconscious, sense of self, which has been formed through earlier experiences. It can be seen in students' responses to grades awarded to essays (which were nearly always written in isolation): elation for 'good' grades and despair for 'bad' ones. There is a sense in which the grade seems to point to the truth of ourselves. As students, men and women, we were subjected – and subjected ourselves – to various disciplinary technologies (Grant, 1997) with their abundant pleasures and pains, one of which was learning to write academic texts. Brodkey talks about how the teaching and assessment of writing, which often focuses on the regulation of correct use of language and mode of argumentation, threatens to 'extinguish altogether the desire to write' (1996, p. 149). And yet, she argues, the desire for a hearing is the *raison d'être* for being a writer.

Judith Brett (1991, p. 521) argues that '[a]cademic writing is writing that never leaves school'. In this sense, the disciplinary technologies experienced as students continue to operate into academic maturity. Their effects are diffuse yet pervasive, and rarely occur in a conscious way. One such effect is that many academic writers, instead of being driven by the desire to be heard or having a strong sense of 'Listen to me, I have something to tell you' (p. 521), mostly fear exposure of their imperfections or lack of having something interesting to say. Peter Elbow adds:

> Frankly, I think there are problems with what it means to be an academic. If academics were more like writers – wrote more, turned to writing more, enjoyed it more – I think the academic world would be better.
>
> (Elbow, 1995, pp. 81–82)

Unsurprisingly, then, many academic women experience feelings of deep ambivalence about writing. Some will go to extraordinary lengths to avoid it, while along the way rationalizing these avoidances as out of their control. Yet interventions based simply on problem-solving issues of time and space do not account for the powerful unconscious dimension of writing. For example, Tristine Rainer (1980) describes specific unconscious forces – the internal critic and the internal censor – that act more or less powerfully in particular people and at different times to block us from writing through an ongoing internal self-critical monologue.

But while the unconscious is undoubtedly a source of trouble, Dorothea Brande (1934/1983) reminds us that it is also the source of creativity and inspiration. Even though she is writing with fiction writers in mind, this is true for academic writers as well, While '[t]he unconscious is shy, elusive and unwieldy', says Brande (p. 45), its desires and energies can be harnessed to the task of writing. Her suggestion is to rise half to one hour earlier than usual each day and write whatever comes into your head: 'what you are actually doing is training yourself, in the twilight zone between sleep and the full waking state, simply to *write*' (p. 66, author's italics). In so doing, she argues, you will begin to write more effortlessly and 'you will find that you are more truly a *writer* than you ever were before' (p. 69, author's italics). Yet Brande gives the following 'solemnest word of warning' to the prospective fiction writer: '*If you fail repeatedly at this exercise, give up writing. Your resistance is actually greater than your desire to write, and you may as well find some other outlet for your energy early as late*' (p. 73, author's emphasis).

Unfortunately giving up writing is no solution for the academic woman who must write for reasons beyond any immediate desire to be a writer. When deep ambivalences towards writing combine with a heavy load of academic housework, we don't write as much as we need to and, in spite of our professed desire to write more, we find many creative ways of avoiding it.

How does this understanding infuse our interventions with academic women?

Given the complexity of the relationship of attraction and repulsion between many academic women and their writing, and the necessity to write, an interesting question arises. How might we get a fundamental shift towards be(com)ing a writer that will ease the path for the work of writing? How might we acquire the 'aura of writing' of which Brodkey (1996, p. ix) writes?

> Many people who like the way I write presume that words come easily to me. They do not. It is true that I write often and that sometimes I write well. It is

even true that I cannot imagine not writing. I like to believe I am most myself on the days I write. Certainly the self I like the best writes. I probably owe my patience as a writer and teacher to the fact that while my prose falls apart far more often than it comes together, the pleasures of writing are unlike the other pleasures of my life. It's not that others are any more or less pleasurable, but that the unexpected moments in writing when time becomes space literally and figuratively move me. For the duration of the convergence of time and space, I am in my body, and the body of my text.

Malcolm Bradbury claims that '[w]riting is, to some extent at least, a writer's acquired habit; the rhythms of it, the particular styles we each possess in doing it, are practices we each teach ourselves in order to write continuously, and with a hope of doing ever better' (Foreword to Brande, 1934/1983, p. 15). This suggests that, while there is no single right way for everyone to be a writer, the practice of writing regularly is important. It is not uncommon for fiction writers to set regular daily goals to structure their writing lives and to assist them through the arid times.

In addition, while the act of writing is most often performed in private (hence perhaps the unrealistic ideas about how others write), it may usefully he rethought as a social act. Brodkey for instance argues we need to engage in 'an act of imaginative resistance' (1996, p. 78) in which we see ourselves as a member of a community of writers. This means vacating the solitude of the garret (read office) and moving into the house with many rooms (that Woolf described in 1942 in *Professions for women*), so that you can 'imagine yourself in the company of others even as (you} sit alone writing' (Brodkey, 1996, p. 79). Part of what makes such imaginative resistance possible is the experience of reading about the writing lives of others. Yet another way is through the lived experience of being a member of a community of writers. In this different, social, scene of writing, the production of text is experienced as a messy process of engagement with the word and the world, and is integrally tied up with revision and response. The risk of ultimate exposure, which may prevent us from ever starting to write, is pre-empted by multiple exposures to others in the community along the way.

There is an emergent literature on 'experiments' with writing groups for academic staff (sometimes men and women, sometimes only women) in universities and on the outcomes for the participants. Positive effects are documented in terms of shifting attitudes to writing, learning new ways to write, and increased productivity (Aronson & Swanson, 1991; Boice, 1987, 1993; Lucas & Harrington, 1990; Moore, 1995; Murray, 1996; O'Leary & Mitchell, 1990). Aronson and Swanson (1991, p. 169) sum up the value of these groups thus:

> Creating writing and research groups allows us to step outside this illusionary individualistic framework. By recognising and discussing the contexts of our writing and sharing ideas and methods, we transform the scene of writing to make room for the woman writer and to reflect the writer as in society, indebted to others. Writing becomes not the disembodied transcription Brodkey describes . . . but the work of a person interacting with others in a world of [deadlines], laundry, bills and conversations over lunch.

Both authors have been part of intervention projects that offer women opportunities to explore and develop their writing lives along the parallel paths of making imaginative and literal spaces for becoming academic writers. By participating in groups, we have also developed a language with which to articulate our writing experiences and share them with each other. Both our projects have involved relatively inexperienced academic women, from a range of sometimes but not always related disciplinary backgrounds. Other kinds of groups that could be organized include women from within a particular theoretical or disciplinary framework, or people who share some identity category. Groups organized around such categories may offer their participants additional strengths, although one of the features of the mixed-discipline groups is the unexpected connections between work and the ensuing cross-fertilization of ideas. Most importantly, writing interventions must be usable, that is they must fit into the busy and conflicted fabric of women's imaginations and then into the similarly busy and conflicted fabric of their daily lives.

Barbara's project: the writing retreat for academic women

'Women Writing Away' was a five-day live-in writing retreat attended by a small group of women from three different universities. The goal of the retreat was to produce an article for publication or, in some cases, another chapter of a PhD thesis. I had responsibility for the overall organization, and for planning and facilitating workshops, although the idea was developed jointly with Sue Watson (whom I had met at a writing workshop about 18 months earlier). The retreat was informed in some ways by the understandings about the struggle to write already discussed here, but it has also contributed to these understandings. As the facilitator (and an often frustrated writer) I anticipated the participants' needs for a substantial amount of dedicated writing time, and for an atmosphere of trust and safety that would allow (but not coerce) talk about writing fears and self-doubts. The non-negotiable goal was to give a clear message that this was going to be a productive working experience and that we were actually going to write, not just talk about it. For busy academic women, with much to arrange to clear a week for writing, not to mention the financial cost, this was essential.

The seven participants, most of whom were strangers to one another, arrived at the rural Tauhara Retreat Centre on a Sunday evening. After a shared meal and introductions, we negotiated the retreat programme, which comprised a mixture of workshops (one each day, after lunch, on topics agreed by the group), seminars of work-in-progress (two each evening), and a large amount of quiet writing time. The process of negotiating the programme was important and not without compromise: 'I think we all felt comfortable and we all "owned" the enterprise ... I think the structure we settled on was great. It was the result of an "almost consensus".'

We agreed that while most of each day would be individual writing time, we would come together for the workshops and seminars to share experiences and learn from each other. By the time the retreat ended over lunch on the Friday, we had formed warm bonds, finding kinship, support and fun in sharing the struggle to write, but also some useful and unexpected connections between each other's work. In their letters of feedback to me, written within three weeks of the event, the participants commented on many aspects of the retreat which had worked particularly well for them (and some that had not!). Below I have included some comments that illustrate their experience of the retreat in terms of literal and imaginative space, as well as what they had to say about experiencing writing as a social act.

About the experience of dedicating an entire week to write at a place removed from everyday life, they commented:

> So what do I think that unique experience [of the retreat] did for my writing? Firstly, the mundane – it got me sitting at the computer for hours *doing* it,

'doing writing'. Not being the most disciplined of people and having a reasonable degree of anxiety about whether or not I have anything to say, that was an achievement in itself.

While having some concerns about the size of the room I was to work in – it seemed so big – all was resolved with the fantastic fire which kept us comfortably warm all day with the added bonus of overlooking the Tauhara gardens. Having a desk of my own and plenty of room for my gear was a real plus for me.

I felt empowered to find my own space for writing and for sharing ideas. The flexibility of the arrangements for the morning meant that I was very much able to find a working pattern that functioned for me.

I think it was great that we immediately agreed that writing time, silence during that time, and respecting other people's peace in that time were important.

I think the danger of 'retreating' is the expectation that writing can only occur in a place that is physically (and emotionally?) removed from 'everyday life'. However I do think there is value in making a space for critical reflection, provided the emphasis is on developing skills that can be used when making such a space for writing is not a possibility.

On making imaginative space, an issue we talked about frequently:

I have . . . gradually found an image of myself as a writer. I have moved from believing that I have something valuable to say in my writing and a sort of pious hope that I would some day do something about putting things into writing, to knowing that this is a task I will gradually achieve.

Take seriously that emerging identity as a writer in yourself. Give it a chance to develop. Create the preconditions for it to grow.

As is evident in the last quotation, and in the literature on writing, there are strong links between making literal and imaginative spaces to be a writer. Many comments made by the women illustrate these links:

The time apart was . . . a time to open up new possibilities for change – in this case changing my actions and habits as a writer. In relation to the latter, until this week I have always said 'I am not a writer, I'm an action person'. Yet at an academic and practical level, this has bothered me because I teach action/reflection, expecting my students to do both. For me change often happens when I have time and space to experience the full force of such contradictions. This week did that for me.

[A] really important thing I took away with me came up in one of our discussions . . . S talked about 'feeding the writer' within us, in the way we feed our bodies a regular and varied diet of nourishing 'food'. You could extend it to things like sitting down to meals – making sure you have time and space to write . . . She also talked about valuing our identity as writers – 'being writer' – I guess to make sure we get time 'doing writer'. It's too easy, for women especially, I think, to forget that it's important to look after ourselves, even in these professional, work-related spheres of our lives. These phrases and metaphors are really powerful and will stay with me – great reminders to do exactly as S said.

I guess one of the main achievements was that for the first time I considered the idea that maybe I could be a writer and not just a thesis writer – I started to take myself seriously. The week was a delicious indulgence and a much needed break to write uninterrupted in a peaceful environment and it might just give me the inspiration and boost I need to finish my thesis. It also gave me the impetus to claim more space at home instead of just grumbling.

Experiencing writing as a social act was pleasurable for all the participants even though, as one commented, not everyone defined themselves as 'a very group-oriented "sharing" person':

The small number of women from a range of academic disciplines added rich-ness to the time away and the relationships we formed provided a safe environment in which to critically appraise each other's work. This critical yet supportive environment is something I have found difficult to establish at the university; mainly I think because of the extensive demands on women academics' time which makes it difficult for writing groups to meet regularly.

The love and support of the group, getting to know each other and our different areas of expertise was a really important part of the process for me. Laughter was also very important in making the joy of writing more than hollow rhetoric.

The norm to be present during workshops was important, because it meant support for the person presenting or contributing one's thoughts and experiences to others.

[T]here was also pleasure in the shared enterprise of it all. Having made the commitment to being there it was a good feeling to sit down knowing six other women were doing the same thing at the same time and that we were going to get together later in the day and talk about it.

The pleasure of writing with others was joined by other pleasures mentioned in the feedback – the pleasures of playing with our own and other's texts (in editing), of shar-ing good food and wine, of sitting by the fire and talking in the evening, of walking in the countryside, and the swim we shared in some nearby warm springs. In the end, these all no doubt contributed to the decision to meet again as a group for a further retreat in a year's time. Further, the ongoing contact (reporting on and exchanging writing) between some women since the retreat (mostly by email) appears to demon-strate Brodkey's point that the lived experience of writing socially provides the existen-tial ground for feeling part of a community even when writing alone. Subsequent retreats have had the character of reunions although the number of women who participate has grown to 10 to 12, with new women being added each time.

In terms of the specified goal, to produce a paper for publication, no one actually achieved it during the retreat. Some people came very close, and everyone felt that they had made significant progress on the piece of writing they brought with them. Importantly, however, the goal functioned to attract some women: '[B]ecause it was such a desirable goal for me, it was probably the single most significant [factor] in changing my mind from deciding not to come, to coming.'

Several participants said they had learned that to achieve that particular goal they would need to do a lot more advance preparation, and as we prepare to set a date for the next retreat this is an issue people have come back to. However, feedback ten months after the retreat indicated that most people had finished their papers and some had been published. An overall outcome of the retreat was to establish a writing community that continues to function in some ways as a community despite geographical separation. But it also had some other outcomes. One participant reported:

> Our discussion about needing support in academia has led me to ask the famous American professor [X] to be my mentrix. Imagine my anxiety! Yet she accepted and we have agreed upon the arrangement that I can send her three papers a year on which she will give feedback ... Without the Taupo talk on the need for a mentor/mentrix I would never have dared to do this.

The writing community formed at the initial retreat continues to meet for a week-long writing retreat twice a year, and is gradually expanding. It has been a source of enriched understanding for all of us, and especially for the writing of this paper. Being privy to intense conversations with the group and with individuals about what writing means to them and their struggles to write has immeasurably helped my thinking as an academic developer and a writer.

Sally's project: the peer-mentoring programme

The 1997 peer-mentoring programme was funded through a Commonwealth Staff Development Fund grant, and focused on developing higher research profiles for junior-level academic women. Its aim was to provide a structure to make it easier for junior academic women to produce a piece (or several pieces) of writing such as a research proposal, thesis chapter, conference paper and presentation, research grant application, book chapter or book proposal. From 25 women, five writing groups were formed based on both discipline area and the category of writing in which they were most interested.

In our group there were six women from six different divisions: Education, History, Sociology, Humanities, Women's Studies and the Teaching and Learning Centre, Meetings were held fortnightly in the campus coffee shop for one to two hours over two semesters. In line with the stated project aim, which was firmly product oriented as well as concerned with process, the peer writers provided each other with support and constructive feedback on work in progress and exchanged information on research and writing interests.

In the first meeting, information was exchanged about each member's professional background and interests, expectations about how the group would operate were clarified and ground rules were negotiated. The project coordinator joined each initial meeting to provide any information needed and to get a clearer idea of the interests of group members so they could be placed in a different group if necessary. A few weeks after the first meeting, a session for all groups was organized by the coordinator so that peer writers in different groups could all meet to pick up tips about group processes from each other and clarify aspects of the project. Each person was sent a copy of *Just do it: Academic writing on the run! A guide to writing research grants and academic articles* and received a stipend of $500 to purchase books, buy out teaching time, or to obtain assistance that directly supported the person's writing in the group.

In the ongoing meetings of our group we used different strategies, according to needs, based on the goals established in the first meeting. Generally, we planned the next meeting at the end of each session. Sometimes we focused on someone's work that had been circulated and read beforehand. At other times we read brief excerpts of each other's work during the meeting, or gave equal time to two or three participants. Usually we read and critiqued each other's work to varying degrees, giving feedback that included global comments, specific comments, and editorial comments. Sometimes one of the participants tested out a key issue, a dilemma or a brilliant idea with the group.

In our meetings we talked about wide-ranging topics and, when not working with someone's writing, we often reflected on the process of writing itself. For example, to prepare for this paper I asked the peer writers about the pleasures (or not) of writing, as well as questions about their sense of themselves as writers, where this came from and so on. A strength of our group was the frequent discussions about the culture of the university, producing the need to problematize the contexts/constructs within which we are working. Topics have included the politics of publishing, performance criteria, fear of not measuring up, instability of work and its impact on teaching and writing. The quotations below illustrate the ways in which the peer writers believe they have been able to increase productivity and satisfaction with writing, stay motivated, get published and reflect on their identities as writers:

> I felt part of an academic network, instead of a tired teacher working on her research in isolation!

> As a new member of staff, the group gave me people to contact about all types of issues.

> [The group] allowed us to discuss issues related to research and publishing. If the group did not meet, a lot of time would have been wasted trying to find out information.

> I am a writer. Thank You! This has been so helpful.

The final quotation captures how this particular woman understands herself as a writer. At the beginning of the group's conversation, she said she did not consider herself to be a writer but as a teacher who dreamed secretly of being a writer. Others in the group said they did not consider themselves as writers either, with one commenting that she had been good at writing at school but had forgotten this. It seems that the insecurity of being an academic and telling herself that she was not as good as other academics had erased this memory. In discussing the researcher/teacher disjunction, we found that most of us spend our time on teaching, which is more pleasurable, and that although we are successful teachers of writing, we are not necessarily successful writers ourselves. In other words we readily help our students and colleagues, but we do not seem to construct ourselves as writers. Returning to the writer's acknowledgement above, by the end of our discussion this group member became very animated, made the comment above, and left with a big smile on her face. What remains to be seen is how enduring this revelation will be and what effects it will produce.

In terms of immediate outcomes for the participants, many have achieved the stated goal of the project and produced one or more pieces of writing, such as an article for a book, a thesis chapter, journal article or seminar paper. What I believe has contributed to increased productivity has been the validation participants have received from the group that their work is ready and good enough. Five other types of benefits (see O'Leary & Mitchell, 1990) have been gained. One is the exchange of information about many matters, including bibliographic references, contacts, intellectual property and teaching materials. The second is the collaboration that has occurred. Our conversations provided us with a source of ideas and inspiration, and sharing of research interests. Indeed, there was often agreement that our experiences should be documented in a book. Some of the peers were invited as guest speakers to others' seminars/classes, and this sort of networking among peers provided a level of emotional support for those in similar positions. The accounts of experiences of other members helped group members realize that what we had assumed to be idiosyncratic was often shared. The third kind of benefit was career planning and strategizing. Information on policies and actual requirements not found in formal publications was exchanged, as well as strategies that provided avenues for integration of new staff into academic departments and the institution as a whole. Valuable networks were developed to support each other. The other two kinds of benefits were professional support and encouragement – in the form of suggesting publication outlets and acknowledging our writing identities – and access to becoming more visible, through giving conference and seminar papers and being invited to collaborate in classes and course development.

The following comments from three of the group members highlight the positive outcomes such a programme can provide. They include benefits such as contacts with a variety of colleagues for the purpose of encouragement, information sharing, evaluation, friendship and a sense of belonging:

> I thoroughly enjoyed the peer writing group. I particularly like its interdisciplinary nature as I've met women I wouldn't have otherwise. Not only that, I felt less isolated and thoroughly supported by the other women. On a personal level I enjoyed being part of the group. Plus I learnt a lot about writing and academic life for us as we joyfully struggle at the bottom of the ladder.

> I felt that I wasn't alone and that other people were having similar difficulties with writing and that it was worth persevering. The group gave me a sense of enrichment because it fed my soul more than mainstream culture can. Meeting with other people gave me the conviction that we have a legitimate voice.

> An important benefit for me has been the externally enforced deadlines for production of a draft for circulation, and then getting some helpful and constructive feedback on that draft and the encouragement to let go of it. I particularly value the friendships which have developed and the general networking and collaboration that goes on.

As the reflections of these writers illustrate, the project allowed us to derive greater pleasures from writing. They show that co-operative arrangements of this kind can ease this path when women belong to a community of writers. In the final section of this paper, these insights are combined with our research to illuminate why interventions that address the conscious and unconscious dimensions of the writing process are more likely to succeed.

The role of academic development in enhancing the experience of writing

It seems clear that money and Woolf's room of one's own are not in themselves sufficient conditions for an academic woman to write. Instead we find varying and complex relationships between individual women and their writing. Academic developers have a role in assisting women in negotiating those relationships so that they come to write more productively and with more pleasure. A key role is to devise academic development opportunities that address the issue in a searching and ongoing way, rather than glossing over its complexities. Because for many women the deepest level of struggle with writing involves elements of our unconscious, it is crucial that any interventions address the somewhat elusive issue of be(com)ing a writer. Without that, says Brande, advice on 'what to do' is a waste of time. If through collectively imagining ourselves as writers we can overcome some of our deep resistances, then it is possible that we will have the will to overcome other more pragmatic obstacles. But this involves acknowledging the transformative nature of the process of be(com)ing a writer, the danger of stepping outside normative subject positions, and the strength of the resistance we will sometimes experience from within ourselves, consciously and unconsciously. This kind of change is only likely in certain kinds of contexts, notably ones where there is time and circumstance for intimacy and trust to be established.

The other roles of the academic developer in the kinds of projects described here include much that is recognizable from our everyday practices This includes planning and organizing the writing events, consulting with individuals about their writing lives, facilitating workshops, setting up networks, giving feedback on writing, searching out and providing varied and stimulating resources about writing (of which there are many), gathering evaluative data, finding funding and so on. This work is crucial to the existence and continuation of such projects.

In the projects described here we found that when groups of women talk about be(com)ing writers, several good things happen in terms of academic (or professional) development, none of which depends on the academic developer alone. (Indeed because Barbara could not attend the most recent retreat, two past participants took over the facilitation.) First, we become more motivated to write, and can effectively assist each other in negotiating our writing lives. In conducive conditions, writing can be very pleasurable, such that we leave our writing spaces desiring to return. (Hence the discussion during the closing moments of the retreat about doing it again – there have now been four subsequent retreats.) Second, we found that talking about aspects of the writing process while in the midst of writing feeds the process. Third, through sharing work in progress we became more robust in the face of questions and criticism, more willing to show unfinished work. These social aspects of writing do not remove the necessity for the solitude and immobility of writing but can nourish the writer so she can more easily enter that state, and more often derive pleasure from it. Fourth was the emergent sense of community and the discussions around be(com)ing a writer, Both the experience of social writing and the talking we shared actualized the preconditions of Brodkey's notion of imaginative resistance, that is of coming to see ourselves as members of a community of writers. Thus we found the experience resonated beyond itself, so that when we sat alone later to write there was still sometimes a sense of being with the group. In this way, while our interventions in themselves do not alter daily lives, they do interrupt the very 'individual' lives academic women live because of the culture we work in, separated from colleagues in many ways, especially as writers. Finally, by sharing our personal struggles in a community of writers, by listening to, provoking, affirming and challenging each other, we gave each other the courage it takes to write in the competitive individualistic world of the academy.

Fundamentally, however, the role of the academic developer in these kinds of projects is to participate as a colleague because, built into the project design, is the assumption that academic women can help each other in the task of be(com)ing writers. This is one of the most effective forms of academic development because it is one that does not depend on an expert but can be ongoing in women's daily lives. Our role is to provide all the skills and support described above but, as Graham Webb (1996) describes, it is also to share in an open-ended and ongoing conversation with others so that we too are changed. In practice this means we must bring to this work a reflexive interest in our own writing selves and a willingness to share in the struggle to actually write (that is, to fully participate in the event). In this process, there is never a closure, a final be(com)ing, and all are 'developers' in the sense of provoking others to change their beliefs and practices. As colleagues, we can stimulate in each other a passion to write by sharing stories of vision, diligence, pleasure, success and determination.

This kind of work raises various tensions for academic developers. For one, it is possible that our role could consist of simply explaining academic culture and uncritically endorsing both that culture and the dominant discourse of femininity which positions women as Other to rationality and authority. This is not the position we take. Understanding academic culture to be changeable, we take a critical insider's stance, in which we collaboratively exchange insights into existing norms, the pros and cons of adapting to them, transgressing them, or just gently pushing at them. As academic developers, we share the struggle to be successful in the academic culture of which we are so critical. Traces of that struggle are evident in the unstable voice that we write with here – actually two voices, separate yet in sympathy with each other, trying to be academic and publishable but also interesting and alive. Indeed these sorts of issues are the subject of many discussions among the women writers that are the focus of this paper. One outcome has been the production of a list of journals that will publish more experimental and/or explicitly feminist academic writing.

Other tensions arise when we position ourselves as both facilitators and participants. This can lead to a sense of relinquishing some of our expert authority which, for academic developers who often occupy marginal places in the academy, can feel risky. There may also be a sense of walking a line between the different expectations that those positions raise. For instance, sometimes a writer might want the academic developer to pronounce on the worth of her writing in an unfamiliar field, or solve problems that the writer needs to work through herself.

Another tension arises when criticisms of the norms of academic writing are taken to imply that they should be abandoned entirely. To advocate this 'solution' is both risky for the individual and naive. Academic writing, like any cultural form, involves both 'regulation and exploitation and a potential mode of resistance, celebration and solidarity' (Batsleer, Davis, O'Rourke, & Weedon, cited in Kramer-Dahl 1995, p. 22). There is no innocent form of writing out there waiting for us to take up – every form enables and constrains us simultaneously. Understanding the dominant form, being able to use it adroitly, to subvert and transform it, are powerful positions to take. Yet, as academic developers and colleagues, we must respect the right of each woman to forge her own academic voice and resolve the dilemma about adapting to or rebelling against current norms in her own way.

A final tension is one that arises when we are challenged (not by participants) about why these projects are for women only. Many of the obstacles to writing outlined in the first section of this paper arise in the context of a gendered culture where the experiences and expectations that men and women face are systematically different. In our projects we wish to address those issues and their impact on women's experiences as academics. This would be much more difficult to do in mixed gender groups where what often happens is that women are positioned as either having to educate their male colleagues or, worse, defend themselves. This deflects time and energy for both participants and facilitators from the task at hand. This is not to say that individual men do not experience similar obstacles to writing, nor that they would not benefit from such projects. Until, however, the position of women in the academy is more equitable with men, further justification for women-only academic development opportunities seems unnecessary.

Conclusions

For all academics, women and men, the processes of practising writing and be(com)ing a writer are inextricably entangled. If we discipline ourselves to write regularly, 'doing writer' as a daily event, we may contribute to producing ourselves as writers who, finding pleasure in the act, seek more opportunities for it. While academic writing is different from fiction writing in some important ways (although perhaps the boundaries are fruitfully blurring), there is much that can be learned from the way productive fiction writers go about their business and live out their writer selves. Contrary, then, to the romantic image of the lonely figure bent over the candlelit table in the shadowy garret, or its Antipodean version of sitting 'in your high/small room, a view of mangroves at your back' (from *The Perfect Text*, a poem by Anne French), for the academic woman the solutions to be(com)ing a writer are likely to be much more prosaic, although the possibilities for them being highly pleasurable remain. Some solutions will be found in leisurely sweeps of time but, more commonly, others will simply have to be perched in the interstices of our working days. The work of the academic developer is to address this struggle in her own life as creatively as possible while using her energy and skills to work alongside others who likewise want to take up the mantle of writer.

Acknowledgements

Thanks to many critical readers who assisted us with this paper (especially Rian Voet and Janet Mae Stratford), to Sue Watson for the productive term 'doing writer', to Frances Rowland the 1996–97 project coordinator in the Teaching and Learning Centre at Murdoch University, to Trish Harris and Edwin Oroyo for reminding us of the struggles of some academic men, to the three anonymous reviewers, and to the 12 women who gave us permission to cite their responses to the projects.

References

Acker, S. (1993). Contradiction in terms: Women academics in British universities. In M. Arnot & K. Weiler (Eds), *Feminism and social justice in education: International perspectives* (pp. 146–166). London: The Falmer Press.

Acker, S. & Feuerverger, C. (1996). Doing good and feeling bad: The work of women university teachers. *Cambridge Journal of Education*, 26, 401–422.

Aronson, A. L. & Swanson, D. L. (1991). Graduate women on the brink: Writing as outsiders within'. *Women's Studies Quarterly*, 19 (3 & 4), 156–173.

Baldwin, G. (1990). The pursuit of the PhD: Women in postgraduate study. In D. R. Jones & S. L. Davies (Eds), *Women in higher education: An agenda for the decade* (pp. 127–140). Armidale, Australia: University of New England, Department of Administrative, Higher and Adult Education Studies.

Bell, J. (1996). *Just do it: Academic writing on the run! A guide to writing research grants and academic articles*. Murdoch, Australia: Murdoch University.

Boice, R. (1987). A program for facilitating scholarly writing. *Higher Education Research and Development*, 6, 9–20.

Boice, R. (1993). Writing blocks and tacit knowledge. *Journals of Higher Education*, 64, 19–54.

Brande, D. (1934/1983). *Becoming a writer*. London: Macmillan.

Brett, J. (1991). The bureaucratisation of writing. *Meanjin*, 50, 513–522.

Brodkey, L. (1996). *Writing permitted in designated areas only*. Minneapolis: University of Minnesota Press.

Brooks, A. (1997). *Academic women*. Buckingham, England: Open University Press.

Broughton, T. (1994). Life lines: Writing and writer's block in the context of women's studies. In S. Davies, C. Lubelska, & J. Quinn (Eds), *Changing the subject: Women in higher education* (pp. 111–123). London: Taylor & Francis.

Deane, E., Johnson, L., Jones, G., & Lengkeek, N. (1996). *Women, research and research productivity in the post-1987 universities: Opportunities and constraints*. Canberra: Department of Employment, Education, Training and Youth and Australian Government Publishing Service.

Elbow, P. (1995). Being a writer vs being an academic: A conflict in goals. *College Composition and Communication*, 46 (1), 72–83.

Ferres, K. (1995). Tactical response: Equity from the bottom up. In A. M. Payne & L. Shoemark (Eds), *Women, culture and universities: A chilly climate* (pp. 147–150). Sydney: University of Technology, Sydney, Women's Forum.

Fullerton, H. (1993). The role of women staff developers in developing teaching skills through teaching observations. In G. Wisker (Ed.), *What's so special about women in higher education?* (pp. 15–18). Birmingham, England: Standing Conference on Educational Development.

Game, A. (1991). *Undoing the social: Towards a deconstructive sociology*. Milton Keynes, England: Open University Press.

Grant, B. (1997). Disciplining students: The construction of student subjectivities. *British Journal of Social Education*, 18, 101–114.

Hartlage, C. (1996). *Hysteria and women's resistant voices in academic writing*. Unpublished master's thesis, University of Auckland, Auckland, New Zealand.

Jones, A. (1997). *Submission to the Review on Promotion*. Auckland, New Zealand: University of Auckland.

Kim, J., Ricks, C. D., & Fuller, C. M. (1996, August). *Women in academia: Strategies for success*. Paper presented at the American Psychological Association Conference, Toronto.

Kramer-Dahl, A. (1995). Reading and writing against the grain of academic discourse. *Discourse: Studies in the Cultural Politics of Education*, 16 (1), 21–38.

Lie, S. S. & O'Leary, V. E. (1990). The juggling act: Work and family in Norway. In S. S. Lie & V. E. O'Leary (Eds), *Storming the tower: Women in the academic world* (pp. 108–128). London: Kogan Page.

Lucas, R. A. & Harrington, M. K. (1990). Workshops on writing blocks increase proposal activity. In L. Hilsen (Ed.), *To improve the academy: Resources for student, faculty, and institutional development*, 9, 139–146.

Martin, L. M. (1996). Women's access to continuing employment in higher education, *Journal Higher Education Policy and Management*, 18, 175–188.

Moore, S. (1995). Intensive writing program, *Progress Reports 1995* (pp. 39–47). Melbourne: Victoria University of Technology Collaborative Research Group Scheme.

Murry, R. (1996). Writers' support group. *The Jordanhill Researcher*, 12, 1.

O'Leary, V. E. & Mitchell, J. M. (1990). Women connecting with women: Networks and mentors. In S. S. Lie & V. E. O'Leary (Eds), *Storming the tower, Women in the academic world* (pp. 58–73). London: Kogan Page.

Park, S. M. (1996). Research, teaching and service: Why shouldn't women's work count? *Journal of Higher Education*, 67, 46–84.

Rainer, T. (1980). *The new diary*. North Ryde: Angus and Robertson.

Smith, L. T. (1993). Ko taku ko ta te Maori: The dilemma of a Maori academic. In G. H. Smith & M. K. Hohepa (Eds), *Creating space in institutional settings for Maori*. Auckland: The University of Auckland, Research Unit for Mann Education.

Stasiulis, D. K. (1995). Diversity, power, and voice: The antinomies of progressive education. In S. Richer & L. Weir (Eds), *Beyond political correctness: Toward the inclusive university* (pp. 165–193). Toronto: University of Toronto Press.

Tannen, D. (1991). *You just don't understand*. London: Virago.

Webb, C. (1996). Theories of staff development: Development and understanding. *The International Journal of Academic Development*, 1 (1), 63–69.

Wenneras, C., & Wold, A. (1997, May 22). Nepotism and sexism in peer review. *Nature*, 387, 341–343.

Wilson, M. A. (1986). *Report on the status of academic women in New Zealand*. Wellington: Association of University Teachers of New Zealand.

Woolf, V. (1929/1977). *A room of one's own*. St Alban's: Triad/Panther Books.

CHAPTER 15

KEEPING UP PERFORMANCES

An international survey of performance-based funding in higher education[1]

Ben Jongbloed and Hans Vossensteyn

Journal of Higher Education Policy and Management, 23, 2, 127–145, 2001

EDITOR'S INTRODUCTION

This article was categorised in the introductory chapter as adopting a comparative approach to researching system policy. While the methodological approach is clear, the actual methods used are not explicitly spelt out. The bibliography, however, indicates that the study was essentially a documentary analysis, analysing reports produced by government departments and agencies in the systems studied. It also clearly makes use of the knowledge built up over recent years by the research centre in which the authors are based.

The two authors provide an analysis and comparison of the university funding policies practised by 11 members of the Organisation for Economic Co-operation and Development (OECD). These countries include Australia, Japan, New Zealand and the United States, as well as seven western European countries. Separate descriptions of the policies pursued in each country are provided along with a comparative analysis.

The article is contextualised in terms of performance indicators and alternative models of performance-based funding, and of input- and output-based funding systems. An expectation here is that, with the growth of mass higher education systems in developed countries, and the increased public expenditure which that implies, governments might be interested in rewarding better performing institutions.

Jongbloed and Vossensteyn's study, however, suggests that this is not happening in most systems. The funding of university teaching remains largely based on enrolments, that is, on inputs. In the case of research, however, output-based funding is more common. The authors conclude by speculating on why input-based funding should be so popular, and on how it can be made to function more effectively.

Comparative studies of this kind are not that common, largely because they are relatively expensive and time-consuming, and also, as the authors of this article make clear, difficult to do (see also the article by Teichler (2000) included in this Reader). Comparative studies also frequently take the form of a series of national case studies produced by national experts to a common format, rather than a genuinely comparative and analytic overview. There are, however, some interesting examples of comparative higher education studies (e.g. Braun and Merrien 1999, Brennan and Shah 2000, Enders 2001, Goedegebuure *et al.* 1993, Harman 2000, Meek *et al.* 1996, Smeby and Stensaker 1999; and also the article by McBurnie and Ziguras (2001) included in this Reader).

The other literature of relevance to this article, though it is not explicitly located within it, is that devoted to the quality assurance and evaluation of higher education institutions (e.g. Bowden 2000, Drennan 2001, Gibbs *et al.* 2000, Harvey 2002, Tam 2001).

References

Bowden, R. (2000) 'Fantasy Higher Education: university and college league tables', *Quality in Higher Education*, 6, 1, pp. 41–60.
Braun, D. and Merrien, F.-X. (eds) (1999) *Towards a New Model of Governance for Universities? A comparative view*. London, Jessica Kingsley.
Brennan, J. and Shah, T. (2000) 'Quality Assessment and Institutional Change: experiences from 14 countries', *Higher Education*, 40, pp. 331–349.
Drennan, L. (2001) 'Quality Assessment and the Tension between Teaching and Research', *Quality in Higher Education*, 7, 3, pp. 167–178.
Enders, J. (ed.) (2001) *Academic Staff in Europe: changing contexts and conditions*. Westport, CT, Greenwood.
Gibbs, G., Habeshaw, T. and Yorke, M. (2000) 'Institutional Learning and Teaching Strategies in English Higher Education', *Higher Education*, 40, pp. 351–372.
Goedegebuure, L., Kaiser, F., Maassen, P., Meek, L., van Vught, F. and de Weert, E. (1993) *Higher Education Policy: an international comparative perspective*. Oxford, Pergamon.
Harman, G. (2000) 'Allocating Research Infrastructure Grants in Post-binary Higher Education Systems: British and Australian approaches', *Journal of Higher Education Policy and Management*, 22, 2, pp. 111–126.
Harvey, L. (2002) 'Evaluation for What?' *Teaching in Higher Education*, 7, 3, pp. 245–263.
McBurnie, G., and Ziguras, C. (2001) 'The Regulation of Transnational Higher Education in Southeast Asia: case studies of Hong Kong, Malaysia and Australia', *Higher Education*, 42, pp. 85–105.
Meek, L., Goedegebuure, L., Kivinen, O. and Rinne, R. (eds) (1996) *The Mockers and Mocked: comparative perspectives on differentiation, convergence and diversity in higher education*. Oxford, Pergamon.
Smeby, J.-C. and Stensaker, B. (1999) 'National Quality Assessment Systems in the Nordic Countries: developing a balance between external and internal needs?' *Higher Education Policy*, 12, pp. 3–14.
Tam, M. (2001) 'Measuring Quality and Performance in Higher Education', *Quality in Higher Education*, 7, 1, pp. 47–54.
Teichler, U. (2000) 'Graduate Employment and Work in Selected European Countries', *European Journal of Education*, 35, 2, pp. 141–156.

KEEPING UP PERFORMANCES

Introduction

This paper is about funding mechanisms for higher education. The central question is: do the funding authorities that decide on the universities' teaching and research grants base the size of the grant on measures of institutional performance? This question is triggered by the idea that the public interest in issues like value for money, quality and accountability will show up in the way public funds are provided to a nation's higher education institutions. One would expect that the funds supplied out of the public purse are dependent on institutional performance, because this would be in line with ideologies that stress a more market-like approach to management and budgeting throughout the whole of the public sector. This article, therefore, takes a look at the mechanisms used for funding universities in a number of OECD countries. It describes the situation at the end of the 1990s, and indicates to what extent the national governments employ performance-based funding (PBF) approaches or performance orientation in the funding mechanisms.

The study is restricted to *universities*; it does not address other higher education providers, and we will look at how the publicly supported universities receive their core funding for teaching as well as research. Along the way, the following research questions will be answered:

1   Do public authorities (i.e. ministries and funding councils) use a *formula* when distributing the core funds (i.e. base operating grant) for teaching and research among universities?
2   What is the relative share of competitive *research council funding* in the budget of the university sector?
3   Do the higher education systems in a number of OECD countries differ in the extent to which the main national funding bodies incorporate information on institutional *performance* in their allocation decisions?

In addressing these questions this article provides an overview of the state of the art with respect to performance orientation in university funding in 11 countries: Australia, Belgium (the Flanders community), Denmark, France, Germany, Japan, The Netherlands, New Zealand, Sweden, the United Kingdom, and the United States.

In the second section, funding models will be briefly classified, and PBF in particular. The third section goes on to address the above questions for the selected OECD countries. It describes in detail the funding of the two main functions of higher education institutions, i.e. education and research. In the fourth section, 11 national funding mechanisms are compared. The emphasis placed on performance in the various national allocation systems is illustrated by means of a diagram in which the position of a country reflects its degree of performance orientation *vis-à-vis* that of other countries. The paper concludes with some speculations on the popularity of student-based (i.e. input-oriented) funding approaches.

Some remarks on funding mechanisms

For the allocation of the basic (or core) funds supplied by the government to higher education institutions, many approaches are in use. Sometimes governments use a negotiations-based approach, in which a budget request drawn up by an institution is decided upon after negotiations between the budget authorities and the higher education institution. A part of the negotiations (or budget) sometimes is left to inter-mediary (or buffer) organisations, such as funding councils or research councils. In other countries formula-based mechanisms for the allocation of funds between the different institutions and different disciplinary areas can be found. In many countries, budget authorities make use of a combination of formulas and negotiations.

The central question of this article is to what extent the public subsidy allocated to a higher education institution is based on *input* elements (i.e. indicators that refer to the resources used and/or the activities carried out by the higher education institutions) or *output* elements (i.e. indicators that refer to the institution's performance in terms of teaching and research). In a 'production process approach' to higher education institutions – distinguishing between inputs, throughputs and outputs – performance-based funding (PBF) mechanisms are focusing on the output-side of universities and colleges. Funding then is tied to the 'products' of the teaching and research activities of higher education institutions.

In a performance-oriented university funding mechanism, examples of output indicators incorporated in the formula or the budget negotiations are: the number of credits accumulated by students, the number of degrees awarded, the number of research publications, or the patents and licences issued. These are the outputs that universities are able to control – at least to a large extent. Other output indicators, which lie a bit further away from the sphere of control of universities, would be: the relative success of graduates on the labour market, the number of graduates working in jobs related to their training ('graduate placement'), or the success of universities in generating additional funding from contract activities (in the fields of teaching as well as research).[2] Although some may argue that the number of enrolled students be viewed as an indicator of teaching output, student numbers are regarded as an input variable here – it is the 'raw material' that is transformed into 'products'.

The choice of output indicators in PBF approaches often will be a controversial issue. If one agrees on the idea that the ultimate mission of a university is to generate value added in terms of human capital, the correct way of measuring *education* performance would be some indication of the increase in knowledge and skills incorporated in students. It will be clear that such an ideal measure does not exist (Dill, 1997). What's more, for teaching, part of the increase in human capital cannot even be attributed to the university's efforts alone, but has to be attributed to the innate abilities and efforts of the students themselves (Barr, 1998). In looking for adequate research output indicators, one encounters similar problems. For instance, a straightforward indicator such as the number of research publications cannot express the impact, originality or even magnitude of the research performance of a university researcher or a research group. This is even more problematic if one tries to measure research outputs in different disciplinary areas.

Every output indicator therefore will have its shortcomings. The main reason for this is that the services of a university are not sold in a kind of market where supply is meeting demand and prices reflect costs, quality and scarcity. In fact, the market in which universities operate is very much an imperfect market. Therefore, instead of a single, one-dimensional measure, a number of different indicators will be used for approximating the many dimensions of the output in terms of quantity as well as quality. However, in practical situations, and to prevent injustices being done to higher education institutions (HEIs), the funding agencies often will use a number of input indicators next to output indicators when deciding on the budgets to be allocated.

In any case, the mix of input and output elements in the funding mechanism will be a political decision, since the indicators will directly relate to the objectives of the funding authorities and how they feel these objectives can be met in the best way. Objectives often are volatile and depend on political agendas and priorities.

Although the supposed advantages of PBF revolve around promotion of accountability and performance, the use of performance indicators for funding purposes can also have undesired side effects. It may lead to risk-avoiding behaviour among institutional administrators and academic personnel. That is, only outputs that are easily attainable are produced. Second, PBF may lead to academics operating in a way that would not be optimal. If, for instance, research *volume* is stressed by the funding formula, academics may be tempted to turn out large numbers of mediocre journal publications instead of releasing fewer, more original ones. As such, universities will underinvest in academic advancement in the long run. On the same note, if universities are funded on the basis of the number of degrees they award, some institutions may be tempted to lower the standards in order to improve their funding. So, again, quality is at risk and quality assurance mechanisms may have to be in place next to the funding mechanisms.

With regard to performance-based funding, Burke and Serban (1998) make a distinction between performance-based funding (PBF) and performance-based budgeting

(PB2). They define PBF as 'special state funding tied directly to the achievements of public colleges and universities on specific performance indicators'. In PBF, the relationship between funding and performance is automatic and formulaic. The funding authorities (ministries, or intermediary bodies such as funding councils and research councils) explicitly include quantified teaching and research output data in the formulas they use for distributing public funds among institutions. Burke and Serban comment about performance-based budgeting: 'state governments or co-ordinating boards are using reports of institutional achievements on performance indicators in an indirect way'. In PB2, performance information (i.e. a quite long list of performance indicators) is used in a loose, and indirect way to shape the total budgets for public colleges or universities. Whereas the link between performance and funding is clear in PBF, it is much less clear in PB2, because it is discretionary and undeclared. Unlike for PBF, no formulas are used in PB2 approaches.

Though the use of funding formulas is often the first step in developing a system of PBF, their use is critically debated in the literature (McKeown, 1996). The major advantage of funding formulas is that, because they use objective criteria, they provide a clear insight into the distribution of funds among higher education institutions. Therefore, they facilitate comparisons between institutions, thus reducing lobbying by institutions. However, a counter-argument held against funding formulas is the belief that they might lead to a common level of mediocrity, because units (university, college, department, etc.) are funded on the same quantitative grounds rather than on the basis of qualitative assessments. In addition, formulas may reduce the incentive to seek outside funding and may perpetuate funding inequities, because the units tend to become fixated on the parameters driving the formula. Formulas may prove inadequate in situations where changing needs and client bases are to be tackled; they may be inadequate for dealing with differentiation among institutions. To come close to a situation that is the best of both worlds, one would expect that in practice many funding authorities will use funding formulas for part of their funding decisions, and non-formulaic approaches for other parts. Performance information can be included in both.

One of the main cases in which budgets are not determined on the basis of formulas but on the basis of qualitative assessments can be found in the approaches used by research councils for allocating budgets to researchers or research groups. Research councils, being intermediary agencies between universities and government, supply monetary support for research projects. The funds generally are awarded on the basis of project proposals submitted by researchers or research groups. In a competitive process knowledgeable experts (peers) judge the submitted proposals. The quality of the proposal and the requested budget are important elements in this process. Often, the expertise of the researchers and their past performance are used in the selection process. Although the budget requests often will be based on a set of rules that prescribe how specific budget items (e.g. staff costs) should be calculated, the decisive factor in determining the budget in the end is qualitative judgement. Again, performance, or rather expected performance, is an important criterion in arriving at the funding decision. Therefore, the relative share of research council funding will be included as an important indicator of the degree of performance orientation in the (research) funding of the universities in the countries under study.

Addressing the research questions[3]

In determining the rate of performance orientation in the national university funding mechanisms, we distinguish two issues. First, the share of research council funding.

Table 40 University revenues obtained from research
councils, 1998–1999

Country	Research council income (% of all public revenues)
Australia	8
Belgium (Flanders)	17
Denmark	20
France	15–20[a]
Germany	10
Japan	21
The Netherlands	7
New Zealand	9
Sweden	13
United Kingdom	9
United States	*c.* 30[b]

Source: Own calculations, based on respective countries' official
documents

Notes: Figures mostly relate to the year 1999 (the US figure is for
1996–1997).
[a] The French percentage is a rough estimate, because total universities' income (including compensation for personnel) is difficult to
determine.
[b] The US percentage is an estimate based on the share of 'restricted
federal grants and contracts' revenue for research universities (I and
II) and doctoral universities (thus excluding community colleges and
other degree-granting post-secondary education institutions).

The reason, explained above, is that research councils fund specific projects and pay
a great deal of attention to the (expected) research outputs that result from these
projects. Second, the mechanisms of the funding authorities for allocating the core
funds supplied to universities will be analysed with a special focus on the extent of
performance orientation. All of this is described for 11 OECD countries. Based on
the information collected, the fourth section will indicate the extent to which performance is taken into account in the public financing of universities.

The share of research council funding

The relative share of public funds for basic research provided through intermediary
bodies such as research councils is used as a first indicator of the relative role of
academic achievements in allocating public funds to universities. This is because
research councils allocate funds to researchers (or teams of researchers) not just on
the basis of the contents of the project proposals submitted for funding, but also on
the basis of the demonstrated quality and capacity of the applicants. As such, research
council funding provides an indication to what extent funding authorities pay attention to the quality and output of academic research. Table 40 shows the relative
share of university revenues derived from research councils.

One of the conclusions that can be drawn from the table is that two groups of
countries can be distinguished. One group contains countries where research council
funds represent only a relatively small amount of university revenues (Australia, The
Netherlands, New Zealand, the UK, and – to a lesser extent – Germany). The other

group includes countries in which research councils account for more than 10% of the universities' revenues from public sources. The US is exceptional in the sense that the public universities receive most of their research funds on the basis of contracts with federal agencies and a relatively small part from their state governments. The largest share of federal research supports originates from the National Science Foundation (NSF) and the National Institutes of Health (NIH). This is somewhat similar to the French case, where research units within universities receive research funds on the basis of contracts with national research organisations like the Centre National de la Recherche Scientifique (CNRS) and the Institut National de la Santé et de la Recherche Medicale (INSERM).

In addition to funding temporary *projects*, the research councils in Belgium and France largely finance top research *institutes* attached to universities. This points to the fact that national figures are difficult to compare, because part of the difference between countries results from differences in national research infrastructures. In some countries – such as Belgium, France and Japan – the major research institutes are integrated in the university system, whereas in others – such as Germany, The Netherlands and the UK – similar institutes operate independently from the university sector.

Funding formulas and funding mechanisms in 11 countries

In discussing the funding mechanisms for allocating the core public funds for teaching and research, the questions whether the funding authorities actually make use of a funding formula and whether the funds for teaching and research are integrated or not are taken as a starting point. When describing the funding mechanisms[4] for the university sector, it is a fact that in some countries separate mechanisms or formulas are in place for the funding of teaching and the funding of research. Whether these mechanisms actually lead to separate, designated budgets – that is, budgets to be used exclusively for teaching or research respectively – is another question altogether. However, the funding authorities in all countries (except Germany[5]) analysed will allow the institutions the freedom to use the combined core budgets for teaching and research in any way they see fit. This is known as 'lump sum' funding. In many cases, the universities' base operating grant for teaching is supposed to be used for research as well, certainly for the research and scholarship that underpins teaching.

In four of the 11 countries surveyed – Belgium, Germany, Japan, and New Zealand – the base operating fund flowing from the funding mechanism is meant explicitly for teaching as well as research. In Belgium, the operating budget allocated to a university consists of a component for teaching and for teaching-related research. In Germany, total basic funds (*Grundmittel*) for teaching and research combined are allocated as a budget that is mainly based on last year's budget, allowing for price changes and policy-based adjustments. In Japan, integrated budgets are allocated on the basis of student numbers, the number of staff and academic units. And in New Zealand, a key reason for the fact that some research funds are included in the student-based operating grants for teaching and research is that people who teach in degree programmes should be involved in research. The latter is also the case for Australia. The funding of research in US universities takes place primarily through federal research councils and foundations. On the state level, however, some legislatures include an allowance for research in the funding rate per student which underlies the universities' teaching grants.

However, the interweaving of teaching and research is not so explicit in the other countries. There the core funds for teaching and research follow from separate funding formulas. In Denmark, for instance, teaching and research funds are allocated through two different ministries. In France, the core funds for research and teaching are supplied through two separate streams, with public institutions negotiating and signing two separate contracts with the Ministry of Education: one for the whole institution (stressing teaching) and one for research. In the UK, Sweden, and The Netherlands, the core funds for teaching and the core funds for research are based on separate formulas.

If we look more closely at the formulas and mechanisms in use in the countries under study, a first conclusion is that the use of funding formulas is widespread among the countries, in particular where the funding of teaching is concerned (see Table 41).

Of the countries surveyed here, Germany is the only one where no funding formulas are used for determining the university budgets. However, there is reason to believe that current trends towards more decentralisation and lump sum budgeting will encourage their development and use in many of the German *Länder*.

As far as research is concerned, a greater variety in the use of formulas can be detected. If the core funds for research to a large extent depend on previous years' funding, the question whether a formula underlies the research budget is answered 'No' in Table 41. One may refer to this as 'incremental' funding. This is the case for Denmark, Germany and Sweden. For France and the US, we also listed a 'No', because most of the core funding for research is allocated on the basis of contracts signed between universities and the funding authorities responsible for research (ministries, research organisations/councils).

In other countries, at least a part of the operating grants for research is allocated on the basis of a formula. In The Netherlands, almost 13% of the universities' research funds is related to the relative number of PhD degrees awarded. However, the major part (some 80% of the research budget), so far has been a component that has remained largely unaltered and that has its roots in history. In Australia, a formula known as the 'research quantum' is in place for calculating a small part of the universities' allocation for research on the basis of a weighting of input and output indicators.[6] In 2001, a new formula-based scheme was introduced to distribute funds for the research training of postgraduate students. The scheme takes into account input as well as output indicators.

Belgium, New Zealand and the UK are examples of countries where the core funds for research are mainly distributed on the basis of a formula. In Belgium and New Zealand, the amounts are driven by student numbers (the funding of teaching

Table 41 The use or funding formulas for determining the university's core funds

Country	Do formulas underlie the teaching budget?	Do formulas underlie the research budget?
Australia	Yes	Partly
Belgium (Flanders)	Yes	Yes
Denmark	Yes	No
France	Yes	No
Germany	No	No
Japan	Yes	Yes
The Netherlands	Yes	Partly
New Zealand	Yes	Yes
Sweden	Yes	No
United Kingdom	Yes	Yes
United States	Yes	No

Table 42 Performance orientation in the funding mechanisms for universities

Country	Degree of performance orientation in the allocation of core funds	
	Teaching	Research
Australia	–	–/+
Belgium (Flanders)	–	–
Denmark	+	–/+
France	–	–/+
Germany	– to –/+	–
Japan	–	–/+
The Netherlands	+/–	–/+
New Zealand	–	–
Sweden	+/–	–
United Kingdom	–	+
United States	– to –/+	– to –/+

Legend: +, fully output-oriented; +/–, mix of output and input orientation, but primarily output oriented; –/+, mix of output and input orientation, but primarily input oriented; –, fully input oriented.

and research is an integrated affair). The UK is the only country in our sample where the allocations for research are fully determined on the basis of a funding formula that takes into account the quality and the volume of research, but does not consider either historical allocations or student load. Overlooking the 11 countries it can be concluded that the funding of teaching and research includes a mix of formulas, history and negotiation. For the teaching part, often the emphasis lies on formulas, whereas for the research part most countries use multiple funding approaches.

The degree of performance orientation in university funding

The central issue of this paper concerns the question of to what extent the funding authorities in the 11 countries have oriented their funding towards the institutions' performance in teaching and/or research. As far as research is concerned, both core funds (supplied directly) and research council funds (see above) are taken into account. A relatively high share of research council funding indicates a strong performance orientation. This would be the case for countries like the US, Japan, France, Denmark, and Belgium. This performance orientation may be even stronger if the universities' core funds from the public purse are determined on the basis of output indicators. For this, a closer look at the funding mechanisms in place for distributing public funds for teaching and research to universities is required.[7] Table 42 provides an overview of the role of performance information in the funding mechanisms that underlie the core budgets for teaching and research (excluding research council funds). The performance information can take several forms. The choice of output indicators that are currently in use in the countries included in our survey is as follows:

• number of credits accumulated by students
• number of graduates (i.e. degrees awarded)
• research publications (number and/or quality)
• number of doctoral theses

Even more important is the issue of the proportion of the budget which is determined by direct reference to performance indicators. However, this proportion and, therefore, any quantitative measure of the degree of performance orientation are difficult to determine. So, for comparing the different countries' funding mechanisms, one has to resort to a qualitative judgement. An explanation of the scores is given below Table 42.

One of the main conclusions to be drawn from this table is that, with a few exceptions, one cannot speak of a high degree of performance orientation in the countries surveyed here. This is a fact for teaching as well as research. This may come as a bit of a surprise, given the attention paid to accountability and quality issues in public debates on university funding. With respect to the core budgets for teaching, Denmark seems to be the only country in our sample which employs an example of output-oriented funding of teaching. As regards the funding for research, the UK shows the strongest performance orientation. However, one should also include the relative importance of research councils (see Table 40) before drawing any firm conclusions on performance orientation in research funding. Below, the funding mechanisms of the countries under consideration are further discussed, explaining the respective country scores in Table 42.

Australia

In Australia, the base funding for teaching to undergraduates mainly depends on the number of student places negotiated between the individual institutions and the department for education in the so-called 'profiles negotiations'. Changes in the number of funded places have been relatively small over the years. As far as research is concerned, only a limited part of the universities' public funds is dependent on institutional performance. Through a formula known as the 'composite index', some 4.5% of the universities' operating and related grants – the research quantum – is allocated on the basis of research performance. The index is based on the relative success of universities in obtaining competitive research grants and other research income from public and private (i.e. industry) sources, as well as on the number of research publications and the number of higher (i.e. PhD and master's) degrees awarded. The weightings attached to the research income (i.e. input) indicators and the combined publications and completions (i.e. output) indicators are 0.8 and 0.2, respectively. From 2002, the research quantum will be replaced by an Institutional Grants Scheme, which will distribute funds on the basis of a modified formula that takes into account research income (60%), research student load (30%) and publications (10%). Recently, the Australian government introduced the Research Training Scheme, which distributes 10% of the operational and related grants on the basis of a similar formula with slightly different weights.

Belgium

In the Flanders community of Belgium, the core funds for teaching and teaching-related research are enrolment based, since student numbers (split into three different categories) and previous years' allocations produce the universities' core budgets. The universities receive most of their research income through projects funded by federal research federations and action programmes (IWT, NFWO, IOW and IUAP) after a process of competition and peer review.

Denmark

Denmark is the only country where teaching budgets are determined solely on the basis of output. This funding mechanism is known as the 'taximeter' model. Funding is based on the number of credits obtained by students during each year. The tariff per credit paid out to the institution varies according to the field of study. The basic research grant has a historical underpinning. By far the largest part of the grant is allocated according to the previous year's amount. Changes are incremental. Only a small part of the grant is related to the university's income from teaching activities (that is, the number of credits accumulated) and the institution's income from external funds (i.e. grants from the research councils, the Research Foundation, the European Union, and so forth). Over the past few years, the national authorities have also put forward proposals to use qualitative criteria in allocating the basic research budgets to institutions. In recent years, the introduction of performance contracts – with the Research Ministry and the individual institutions negotiating on the mission, goals, management and autonomy of the institutions – was debated. However, the new system is still not clear and far from the implementation stage.

France

The French system of supplying teaching funds to universities is based on the number of students enrolled. All programmes are categorised in a grid that serves as a weighting device to determine the standard costs per student. The level and type of the programme determine the weighting, taking into account issues like required floorspace and support staff for each programme (presently, there are 18 cost categories). This is known as the SANREMO (Système Analathique de Réparation des Moyens) model. The formula does not include any fixed costs, but is adjusted in line with the scale of the institution (as measured by the number of students). However, one should realise that staffing issues primarily belong to the authority of the central government. The Ministry of Education is the employer of nearly all staff. It allocates posts to the institutions, recruits staff to fill these posts, and determines salaries. So, educational staff are funded separately. Furthermore, institutions may receive some additional funds for specific projects, which are specified in additional contracts. Research is funded in a 'dual' way. On the one hand, universities receive personnel and grants from the central ministry, which also pays the staff. This is laid down in contracts, which are not legal contracts but regarded as a set of mutual, explicit and formalised engagements between public authorities and universities. The allocations are based on four-year development plans and research evaluations, implying some degree of performance orientation. On the other hand, the research units of the universities receive resources on the basis of (mostly four-year) contracts with the major national research organisations, the Centre National de la Recherche Scientifique and the Institut National de la Santé et de la Recherche Médicale. The first stream of research funds mainly concerns the funding of doctorate programmes, research schools, and the research institutes recognised by CNRS and INSERM. Of the resources for research teams and laboratories, universities may spend only 15% for carrying out their own research programme. Also most research is centrally appointed, paid and allocated across universities' units.

Germany

In the case of Germany, the integrated core funds for teaching and research are negotiated between the state legislatures (the governments of the *Länder*) and the university sector. In the majority of cases, the resulting budgets are based on historical consid-erations and not so much on factors such as enrolments or performance. An important aspect of German higher education is the fact that university staff are formally appointed and paid for by the state government. Staff salaries therefore do not show up in the institutions' financial accounts and institutions have only limited freedom to reallocate staff across the different departments in the university. Lump sum funding (*Globalhaushalt*) is heavily debated in Germany, but little progress has been made so far. Some states, however, do experiment with funding formulas and some even allocate a small part of the (non-personnel) resources on the basis of output indica-tors like the number of graduates, the number of doctorates, and the volume of research grants from the research foundations. The most important research council in this respect is the Deutsche Forschungsgemeinschaft (DFG). Some private research foundations, like the Stiftung Volkswagenwerk, or the Stifterverband für die Deutsche Wissenschaft, are also regarded as prestigious bodies. However, these supply only moderate amounts of research money.

Japan

The public universities in Japan receive their funds for teaching activities mainly on the basis of the number of student places, the number of teachers and the number of educational units. As far as research is concerned, again an input-based formula is applied which takes into consideration staff posts, type of research, and number of graduate students. Part of the core funds is allocated for quality improvement and setting up 'centres of excellence'. Research funding, however, in particular is depen-dent on money distributed by the Science Council. This council acts like a research council, although it is less independent from the government than research councils in other countries. From Table 40, it is clear that the volume of competitive research money that is distributed by the Science Council is considerable.

The Netherlands

Since the early 1990s, the Dutch funding mechanism has made use of performance indicators in the funding formulas for teaching and research. From the year 2000 on, a performance-based funding model (PBM) has been in use, which distributes 50% of the core teaching funds on the basis of the number of master's degrees,[8] 13% on the basis of new entrants, and the remainder as a fixed (historically based) allocation. For funding reasons, students and diplomas are grouped into two cost categories (roughly: social sciences, arts and humanities versus the other disciplines). As part of their research budget, Dutch universities receive a premium for each post-graduate degree (PhD, designer certificates in engineering) awarded. However, the bulk of research funding (the so-called 'strategic research component') is based on historical reasons, in spite of the government's original plans and more recent attempts to have this part based on research assessments and societal value added criteria. From the early 1990s onwards, the establishment of so-called 'research schools', consisting of researchers and PhD students from different universities but working in the same field, has been used as an instrument for the integration, concentration and proliferation of research. Research allocations to accredited research schools and a small number of high-quality research schools have recently led to a small reduc-tion of the funds distributed on historical grounds.

New Zealand

In New Zealand, the government's core funding for teaching and accompanying research in universities takes the form of tuition subsidies that are paid out to higher education providers on the basis of the number of equivalent full-time students (EFTS). In the funding formula used, 1.0 EFTS is defined as the student workload that would normally be carried out by a full-time student in a single academic year. Funding rates are differentiated by subject content and qualification type (e.g. non-degree, degree, etc.). There is no separate funding formula, or indeed allocation, for research as far as the core funding of universities is concerned. The remainder of the research funds from government sources comes from the research councils, which provide project funds out of three separate contestable pools: the Public Good Science Fund (PGSF),[9] the Marsden Fund, and the Health Research Council.

Sweden

The Swedish funding formula includes input and output indicators for calculating the universities' allocations for teaching. The Ministry of Education and each individual institution agree a contract that covers education and research. This resembles the French system to some extent. Institutions of higher education receive an 'educational assignment' for each new three-year period. The allocation of resources depends on results measured in terms of students (calculated in terms of full-time equivalent students) and study achievements (calculated in terms of annual performance equivalents) at the institutions. The weightings are, respectively, 40% (for student numbers) and 60% (for accumulated credits). The funding rates differ for broadly defined subject areas. In the educational assignments, minimum numbers of (certain) degrees taken are stipulated per institution. Objectives with respect to the minimum number of students as a whole and for the lowest number of students in science and technology areas are set out for each fiscal year. The assignment may also stipulate that the number of students must increase or decrease in certain subject areas compared with the preceding three-year period. There is a ceiling, which constitutes the maximum compensation for FTE students and annual performance equivalents permitted for the fiscal year.

Research and postgraduate training are funded by way of special grants to the universities in question. Up to 1992, the respective institutions' allocations were mainly adjusted incrementally from year to year. However, as of 1999, resources are no longer allocated by faculty but are distributed to four areas of research. The research activities are – again – covered in a contract, which, for instance, specifies that a minimum percentage of the grant is to be used to fund postgraduate training. The remaining portion of the research grants comprises project funding provided by research councils and sectoral agencies, together with local authorities and county councils.

United Kingdom

For their teaching activities the UK universities were, until recently, primarily rewarded by the Higher Education Funding Councils on the basis of their relative efficiency in instruction. However, this has recently been changed into a system of 'equitable funding', meaning that similar activities are funded at similar rates for all institutions. Projected number of full-time students is the basic variable that determines the teaching grant. The student numbers are adjusted for subject-related factors (there are four broad groups of subjects), student-related factors (e.g. different forms of enrolment), and institution related factors (e.g. institutional scale, location, age of buildings). Total weighted (FTE) student numbers are multiplied by a base price, which leads to the university's standard resource. If the difference between the standard resource and the institution's actual resource (i.e. the previous year's resource adjusted for various factors such as inflation) is no more than 5%, then the funding council will carry forward the grant from one year to the next. For institutions outside of this tolerance band, the funding council will adjust their grant and/or student numbers so that they move to within the tolerance band over an agreed period. Some variation around the standard resource therefore is allowed in order to recognise the differing circumstances and historical funding patterns of different institutions. The resulting budget forms part of a funding agreement drawn up each year between an institution and the funding council. This contract is constructed in broad terms and states the weighted student load that is being funded as well as the maximum student numbers that the institution is permitted to recruit before a financial penalty is imposed.

Public research funds are provided under a dual support system, with funds coming from the funding councils as well as the research councils. The research funds allocated by the funding councils are intended to provide the underlying infrastructure upon which funds provided by the research councils can rest. The funding councils represent the biggest source of research funds. Their research funds are distributed largely on the basis of the quality ratings of the universities' departments across some 70 academic disciplines and by a measure of the volume of research. The quality of research is assessed in a Research Assessment Exercise (RAE) conducted every four or five years. In the RAE, each academic unit that subjects itself to an assessment by a team of peers is awarded a rating, on a seven-point scale, for the quality of research in each unit of assessment in which it was active.[10] 'Low ratings (1 and 2) attract no funding, whereas the top 5* rating (five star) attracts approximately four times as much funding as the second to lowest rating (3b) for the same volume of research activity. The number of research-active academic staff in the individual departments is the most important measure of the volume of research activity. It accounts for almost two-thirds of the total. Other volume indicators are research income from private research foundations ('charities') and the number of research assistants and postgraduate research students. The RAE score is translated into budgetary allocations within three broad groups of subjects in order to reflect the relative costs of research in different subjects. Universities are not expected to model their internal allocations on the model of the funding council. They are free to allocate their block grants according to their own priorities within broad guidelines.

United States

In the United States, accountability has always been high on the political agenda. Therefore, one would expect to come across many examples of PBF approaches in the different states. Indeed, in a study carried out in 1996 by the State Higher Education Executive Officers (SHEEO), it was concluded that 'performance-based budgeting is the most significant trend in state budgeting'. In a more recent study by the SHEEO (Burke & Serban, 1998) it was shown that PBF and PB2 approaches are gaining in popularity in the different states of the US (see Table 43). In 1998, of the 50 states covered, half use a type of either PBF or PB2, or a combination of the two. However, with the exception of Tennessee, where from 1981 a PBF has

Table 43 Performance-based budgeting and performance-based funding in the US

Year	Number of states (% of all states)	States
Performance-based budgeting		
1997	16 states (32%)	Colorado, Florida, Georgia, Hawaii, Idaho, Illinois, Indiana, Iowa, Kansas, Mississippi, Nebraska, North Carolina, Oklahoma, Rhode Island, Texas, West Virginia
1998	21 states (42%)	All states mentioned in 1997, plus Louisiana, Maine, Oregon, South Dakota, Washington
Performance-based funding		
1997	10 states (20%)	Colorado, Connecticut, Florida, Kentucky, Minnesota, Missouri, Ohio, South Carolina, Tennessee, Washington
1998	13 states (26%)	Colorado, Connecticut, Florida, Illinois, Indiana, Louisiana, Missouri, Ohio, Oklahoma, South Carolina, South Dakota, Tennessee, Washington

Source: Burke and Serban (1998)

been in use (see Banta *et al.*, 1996), the other states (such as Florida, Missouri, Minnesota) have experimented with PBF or PB2 for at most five years. Earlier, we noted that the US research funding method is the most obvious example of a highly competitive and performance-oriented system. Federal agencies like the NSF, the National Institutes of Health, and the Department of Defence award the bulk of fundamental research funds for American universities and colleges. In fact, unlike their European counterparts, the American universities do not receive substantial amounts of funds as core funding for basic research from their legislatures. However, some states incorporate an allowance for research in the funding rates applied to student numbers in the enrolment-based formulas that frequently underlie the basic grants to the universities. The universities in the US therefore have to compete for the bulk of their research funding, whereas many European universities often receive historically based allocations for research from their governments or funding councils. Although there are many states that use PBF or PB2 approaches, the amount of funds that is tied (directly or indirectly) to results is relatively small, and usually does not exceed 5% of the institutional allowance. South Carolina is the only state where the legislature has expressed the intention to allocate 100% of state higher education funding on the basis of institutional performance on 37 (!) specific indicators. In the year 2000, 35% of state funding in South Carolina was based on a large number of performance indicators, in nine categories. Most US states, however, adopt performance measures primarily for accountability purposes or informing students about higher education; they do not (yet) use them for funding decisions.

Comparison and discussion

Figure 13 presents the major conclusions with respect to the degree of output orientation in university funding. It provides a tentative indication of the relative positions

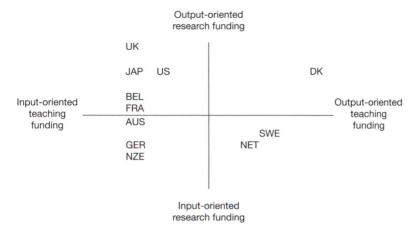

Figure 13 The relative performance orientation in the university funding mechanisms

of the 11 countries with regard to their performance orientation in the funding of teaching (the horizontal axis) and the funding of research (vertical axis). Along the vertical axis we integrate the relative importance of research council funding (see Table 40) and the role of outputs in the supply of the core research funds (see Table 42, right-hand column).

All in all, it can be concluded that most of the countries show more output orientation in regard to research than to teaching. This is due in particular to the share of research council funding, which varies between 7% and 30% of the universities' grants. The UK is exceptional in the sense that all core funding for research is highly selective and quality oriented. The funding of teaching is performance based in only three countries. In Denmark and, to a lesser extent, The Netherlands and Sweden, universities are funded on the basis of awarded degrees or accumulated credits.

The role of output indicators in the funding mechanisms is still relatively small for the 11 countries, despite increased attention to issues of accountability and value for (public) money. It seems to be the case that many governments prefer to apply a somewhat soft approach to performance enhancement, relying on other mechanisms instead. In many cases this approach is characterised by having universities generate an increasing amount of data on different aspects of their activities. This information allows the university's various stakeholders to form an opinion on the university's performance and, for instance, allows (prospective) students to make better-informed choices.

In the United States, for instance, the use of performance indicators (PIs) is mainly for accountability reasons. However, in an increasing number of states, funding decisions are informed by PIs, and incentive funds are set aside in the higher education budget to promote the achievement of specific targets. These incentive funds, however, are relatively small.

The French, Danish and Swedish cases, however, also teach us that instead of a one-sided, formulaic approach directly tying resources to results, the funding authorities may strive to engage universities in a kind of 'social contract'. This contract policy may be worthwhile if differences between institutions are relatively large. The contracts allow some freedom to manoeuvre and engage the contract partners in discussion. In short, contracts may be worthwhile if there is a need to build understanding and trust between funding authorities and higher education providers.

Concerning the funding of teaching, it was shown above that enrolment-based formulas are still widely used. Why are governments so reluctant to link resources to results in this area? The reason may lie in the belief that, if performance is to be understood in terms of increasing diversity and responsiveness in the system to the needs of students, enrolment-based formulas may be worthwhile. If an individual university's grant depends on the number of students that have chosen to enrol for its courses, it is actually the students voting with their feet which determines the university's resources. In other words, 'money follows the student'. This will probably give the universities an incentive to look after their customers and the content and quality of the programme offerings. The performance concept in a student-based funding system like this relies on the idea of quality as 'fitness for purpose', rather than quality as 'academic excellence'. A student-centred perception of quality in particular becomes relevant in times when consumer tastes are increasingly diverse.

Enrolments-based funding systems, however, can function properly only when a number of conditions are fulfilled:

- First, there should be no restrictions on the numbers of students the university is allowed to enrol, As soon as there are government-imposed limits on the number of funded student places (e.g. Australia, UK, Denmark, Sweden), the intended effects of students voting with their feet will be diminished.
- Second, in order to be able to make well-informed choices, students have to have easy access to reliable information on the programmes and courses provided by higher education institutions. This consumer information can be made available by government agencies as well as private and non-profit agencies.
- Third, national authorities and education providers should not be allowed to create unjustified obstacles that prevent students from taking parts of their degree or programmes in different universities. Barriers like this may be caused by the fact that universities fear losing part of their subsidy when students leave for other education providers. On the same note, universities may be tempted to frustrate the portability of credits and courses and the recognition of prior learning. Governments, on their part, will have to look critically at arrangements for funding and selection in the different sectors of the education sector which prevent seamless course provision.
- Fourth, student support systems need to be flexible in enabling students to do parts of their education and training at different locations and points in time. Again, like the prevention of entrance barriers, this is supportive of the idea of lifelong learning.
- Fifth and finally, the students' private contributions to the cost of their training have to be sufficiently real for them to make a wise choice of programme. Therefore, non-marginal tuition fees will have to be charged to students.

The funding of the universities' teaching activities does not need to be transformed into either a performance-based system or a vouchers-type system if work is done on fulfilling the above conditions. Governments may continue to rely on enrolment-based allocations instead of advocating PBF approaches and may feel it is wiser to make greater efforts in the areas of improving student choice and assessing the quality of teaching and research.

This observation would correspond to the low weightings attached to performance indicators in the funding formulas used by many OECD countries.

Notes

1 A preliminary version of this article was presented at the 12th annual Consortium of Higher Education Researchers (CHER) conference in Oslo, 7–19 June 1999. Comments from the participants in this conference and some valuable remarks made by Jonathan Boston (Victoria University Wellington (VUW), New Zealand) are greatly appreciated. Financial support for finalising this paper was received from the Netherlands School of Government (NIG).
2 Contract income strongly depends on a university's reputation and past achievements in specific areas. However, it also depends on the economic climate in a country (or region) and indirectly on major trends in world industry (e.g. firms investing in, or cutting back on, research and development expenditure).
3 The bibliography of each funding system described is given per country at the end of this paper.
4 Excluding research council funds and special budgets for investments or facilities for students.
5 In Germany, the states (the *Bundesländer*) generally have some restrictions on the expenditure categories (e.g. specific categories of personnel versus material and capital goods) in which public resources may be spent.
6 From 2002, a modified formula (known as the Institutional Grants Scheme) will be used, based on similar indicators but distributing a larger amount of funds.
7 One could argue that the relative share of revenues generated from non-public sources also says something about the relative performance orientation of higher education, However, the criteria for allocating public funds are the major focus of this article.
8 Officially, Dutch universities do not issue bachelor's degrees. However, in a few years' time these will be introduced in all Dutch higher education institutions, according to the Bologna declaration, which was signed by all Western European countries.
9 The PGSF has recently been abolished, and replaced by the New Economy Research Fund.
10 There is also a teaching quality assessment (TQA). However, instead of determining funding, the TQA outcomes are intended rather to *inform* funding.

References

Banta, T. W., Rudolph, L. B., Van Dyke, J. & Fisher, H. S. (1996) Performance funding comes of age in Tennessee, *Journal of Higher Education*, 67(1), pp. 23–25.
Barr, N. (1998) *The Economics of the Welfare State*, 3rd edn. Oxford: Oxford University Press.
Burke, J. C. & Serban, A. M. (1998) *Current Status and Future Prospects of Performance Funding and Performance Budgeting for Public Higher Education: the second survey*. New York: Nelson A. Rockefeller Institute of Government.
Dill, D. D. (1997) Higher education markets and public policy, *Higher Education Policy*, 10(3/4), pp. 167–185.
McKeown, M. P. (1996) *State Funding Formulas for Public Four-Year Institutions*. Denver, CO: State Higher Education Executive Officers.

Bibliography

Australia

DEETYA (1998) *Learning for Life: review of higher education financing and policy*. Canberra: Commonwealth of Australia, Department of Employment, Education, Training and Youth Affairs.
DETYA (1998) *The Characteristics and Performance of Higher Education Institutions*. Canberra: Department of Education, Training and Youth Affairs, Higher Education Division.
Kemp, D. (1998) *Higher Education Funding Report for the 2001 to 2003 Triennium*. Canberra: Department of Education, Training and Youth Affairs.

Belgium (Flanders)

Grenzüberschreitendes Netzwerk Bildungsforschung, Flandern, Niederlande, Niedersachsen und Nordrhein-Westfalen (1997) *Die Hochschulfinanzierung in der Grenzregion, Ein Länderverleich*. Düsseldorf, Ministerium für Wissenschaft und Forschung des Landes Nordrhein-Westfalen.

Ministerie van de Vlaamse Gemeenschap, Departement Onderwijs, Administratie Algemene Onderwijsdiesten en Voorlichting (1991) *12 juni 1991 Decreet betreffende de Universiteiten in de Vlaamse Gemeenschap, Verzaneling van documenten*. Brussels: Centrun voor Informatie en Documentatie.

Ministerie van de Vlaamse Cemeenschap (1991) *Onderwijsdecreet 1X inzake de financiering van de Universiteiten (inclusief hal amendement van 1996)*. Brussels: Ministerie van de Vlaamse Gemenschap.

Verstraete, L. (1998) De evolutie van de universitaire basisfinanciering 1993–1998, *Universiteit & Beleid*, 12(4).

Denmark

Ministry of Research and Information Technology (1998) *Governing and Management of Universities in Denmark*. Copenhagen.

Ministry of Research and Information Technology (1998) *Funding of Higher Education*. Copenhagen.

Ministry of Research and Information Technology (1999) *University Performance Contracts: greater autonomy, stronger universities*. Copenhagen.

Rasmussen, J. (1995) *Finance Education*. Aalborg: TACIS/EDRUS Project.

Skjodt, K. (1995) Financing higher education in Denmark, *Higher Education Management*, 8(1), pp. 41–49.

Straarup, R. (1993) *Formula Funding in Higher Education in Denmark*. Mimeo, Copenhagen: Ministry of Education.

France

Kaiser, F. (2001) *Higher Education in France: country report*. CHEPS Higher Education Monitor, Enschede, The Netherlands: CHEPS.

Germany

Grenzüberschreitendes Netzwerk Bildungsforschung, Flandern, Niederlande, Niedersachsen und Nordrhein-Westfalen (1997) *Die Hochschulfinanzierung in der Grenzregion, Ein Ländervergleich*. Düsseldorf, Ministerium für Wissenschaft und Forschung des Landes Nordrhein-Westfalen.

Hochschullehrerbundes Landesverband Nordrhein-Westfalen (1998) *Leistungsanreize in der Hochschule. Möglichkeiten und Grenzen*. Bad Honnef, Germany.

Hochschulrektorenkonferenz (1996) *The Financing of Higher Education*. Bonn.

Jongbloed, B. W. A. & J. B. J. Koelman (1996) *Universiteiten en hogescholen vergeleken*. The Hague: SDU.

Ministerium für Wissenschaft und Forschung des Landes Nordrhein-Westfalen (1998) Finanzautonomie, Kostenrechnung und erfolgsorientierte Mittelverteilung. Düsseldorf.

Statistisches Bundesamt (1998) Finanzen der Hochschulen 1996. Wiesbaden.

Ziegele, F. (1998) *Financial Autonomy of Higher Education Institutions: the necessity and design of an institutional framework*. Gütersloh, Germany: CHE (Zentrum für Hochschulentwicklung).

Japan

Arimoto, A. (1997) Massification of higher education and academic reforms in Japan, in: *Academic Reforms in the World: situation and perspective in the massification stage of higher education*. Hiroshima: Research Institute for Higher Education, International Seminar Reports.

Ministry of Education, Science, Sports and Culture (1995) *Japanese Government Policies in Education, Science, Sports and Culture, Remaking Universities: continuing reform of higher education*. White Paper. Monbusho, Japan.
Ministry of Education, Science, Sports and Culture (1997) *Statistical Abstract of Education, Science, Sports and Culture 1997 Edition*. Monbusho, Japan: Research and Statistics Planning Division.
University Council (1990) *A Vision for Universities in the 21st Century and Reform Measures: to be distinctive universities in a competitive environment*. Monbusho, Japan: Ministry of Education, Science, Sports and Culture.

The Netherlands

Ministerie van Onderwijs, Cultuur en Wetenschappen (1999) *Education Culture and Science in the Netherlands, Facts and Figures 1999*. www.minocw.nl.
Ministerie van Onderwijs, Cultuur en Wetenschappen (2000) Financiële Schema's 2000–2003. The Hague: SDU.

New Zealand

Boston, J. (n.d.) The Funding of Research in the Tertiary Sector. Wellington: Victoria University of Wellington.
Ministry of Education (1999) *New Zealand's Tertiary Education Sector: Profile & trends 1999*. www.minedu.govt.nz.

Sweden

Högskoleverket (2000) *Arsrapport för universitet och högskolor* 1999. Stockholm: National Agency for Higher Education.
Klemperer, A. (1999) *Higher Education in Sweden: country report*. CHEPS Higher Education Monitor. Enschede, The Netherlands: CHEPS.
National Agency for Higher Education (2000) *Swedish Universities & University Colleges 1999: short version of annual report*. Stockholm.

United Kingdom

HEFCE (2000) *Funding Higher Education in England, How the HEFCE Allocates its Funds*. Bristol: Higher Education Funding Council For England.
HESA (1998) *Resources of Higher Education Institutions 1996/97*. Cheltenham.
London Economics (2000) *Review of Funding Options for Higher Education in the UK: a report for universities UK*. www.universitiesuk.ac.uk

United States

Ashworth, K. H. (1994) The Texas Case Study. Performance-based funding in higher education, *Change*, November/December, pp. 8–15.
U.S. Department of Education (2001) *Digest of Education Statistics 2000*. Washington, DC.

CHAPTER 16

THE REGULATION OF TRANSNATIONAL HIGHER EDUCATION IN SOUTHEAST ASIA

Case studies of Hong Kong, Malaysia and Australia

Grant McBurnie and Christopher Ziguras

Higher Education, 42, 85–105, 2001

EDITOR'S INTRODUCTION

This article was categorised in the introductory chapter as adopting a comparative approach to researching system policy. As with the preceding article by Jongbloed and Vossensteyn (2001), while the comparative methodology is clear, the methods used to collect and analyse the data are not so explicit. Again, however, the research presented evidently rests upon the analysis of documents produced by governments and agencies in the systems compared.

McBurnie and Ziguras focus on transnational higher education, that is, higher education provided by institutions based in one country through satellite operations in other countries. They locate their analysis within the general context provided by globalisation, the World Trade Organisation (WTO) and the General Agreement on Trade in Services (GATS). In terms of the WTO's categorisation of modes of international service delivery, their focus is on 'commercial presence'.

The region in which they base their analysis is an interesting one, both for the substantial growth in the demand for higher education, and for the varied approach towards transnational higher education taken by the governments concerned, which vary from relatively laissez-faire to highly regulatory. Quality and standards issues are clearly to the fore in their consideration.

The authors provide case studies of three systems – Hong Kong, Malaysia and Australia – in each case discussing the degree of regulation applied, how it operates and the rationale for it. They show that consumer protection is of key importance in Hong Kong, together with transparency in regulations. In Malaysia, by comparison, the chief rationale appears to be the advancement of specific national goals, while in Australia the concern is to protect the local system from recent pressures from overseas institutions.

The literature on transnational higher education is relatively limited (e.g. Knight and de Wit 1997), but growing as the phenomenon itself grows in importance. It has connections with the literature on international study, represented in this Reader by the article by Kember (2000).

References

Jongbloed, B. and Vossensteyn, H. (2001) 'Keeping up Performances: an international survey of performance-based funding in higher education', *Journal of Higher Education Policy and Management*, 23, 2, 127–145.

Kember, D. (2000) 'Misconceptions about the Learning Approaches, Motivation and Study Practices of Asian Students', *Higher Education*, 40, pp. 99–121.

Knight, J. and de Wit, H. (eds) (1997) *Internationalisation of Higher Education in Asia Pacific Countries.* Amsterdam, European Association for International Education.

THE REGULATION OF TRANSNATIONAL HIGHER EDUCATION IN SOUTHEAST ASIA

Introduction

Higher education is part of the increasing globalisation of the trade in goods and services. The World Trade Organisation (WTO) estimates that in 1995 the global market for education represented US$27 billion (WTO 1998a, p. 6). Using projections based upon 25 selected countries, IDP Education Australia estimates that the number of international students seeking education in or from a foreign country will reach 1.4 million in 2010 and rise to 3.1 million in 2025 (Blight 1995).

An important subset of international students are those engaged in transnational education (TNE). We use the term 'transnational education' to denote education 'in which the learners are located in a country different from the one where the awarding institution is based' (UNESCO/Council of Europe 2000; see also Global Alliance for Transnational Education 1997; Adams 1998; McBurnie and Pollock 1998). Blight and West (1999) estimate that demand for TNE by a sample of Asian countries (excluding China) will rise to more than 480,000 students by 2020. Demand is high and exporters are eager to supply. In 2000, an estimated 31,500 students were enrolled in Australian higher education institutions' transnational programmes, predominantly located in Singapore, Hong Kong, Malaysia and China (Australian Education International 2000; IDP Education Australia 2000). It should be noted that transnational higher education includes significant numbers of students at both university level and in post-secondary vocational training.

TNE is attractive to providers as it offers opportunities for increased market expansion, and for raising their international profile. For students, transnational programmes offer the possibility of obtaining a foreign qualification at a considerably reduced cost, compared with travelling abroad. In the host country, fees are usually lower than for the same programme offered in the foreign institution's home country and living expenses are also lower. For mature age students, studying in their home country means being able to stay with one's family and continue to work while studying part-time. Students receive an education that is often geared more to international rather than local forms of knowledge and practice, meaning that they may be able to work in different countries more easily, and have better developed cross-cultural skills. Governments are often in favour of the establishment of transnational higher education in their countries in order to cater to some of the demand for higher education that is unable to be met by local universities. Foreign providers build the capacity of the higher education system within the country. Increasing the capacity of the local higher education system can have the effect of reducing the number of students who go abroad to study, thus reducing the net currency outflow.

The fact that education is an internationally tradeable service raises issues of appropriate regulation. In this context it is important to note that education is both a private good and a public good. As a private good, education provides economic benefits and personal satisfaction for the student/graduate. As a public good, education plays a role in enhancing the national economy, and promoting non-market social benefits including health and social cohesion, fostering community values, reducing crime and welfare dependency (for example, see the literature survey by Wolfe and Haveman 2000). Education is not unique in combining attributes of private and public good. Other examples include health care, water supply and telecommunications. The WTO (1998a) provides a useful broad typology for modes of international service delivery. The four WTO categories and their incarnations in higher education are outlined below:

> *Consumption abroad* is trade in which the consumer travels abroad to the country where the supplier is located, such as tourism. Historically, the largest proportion of international education has been delivered in this way, by students traveling abroad to live and study in another country for a number of months or years.

> *Cross-border delivery* is trade in which the provider and recipient of a service remain in their own countries, and the service is delivered through communications. In education, remotely-supported international distance education falls into this category. When there is also local support (in the form of persons providing academic or administrative services), delivery moves into the category of commercial presence.

> *Commercial presence* describes trade in which a foreign provider delivers services in the consumer's country. In education, this typically involves a foreign course that is taught in the student's country, through either a local campus of a foreign university or a private college that acts as a local partner. These arrangements are generally referred to as transnational or offshore programmes.

> *The movement of natural persons* refers to the ability of people (as opposed to organisations) to move across national borders to deliver services. In the context of TNE, the movement of persons (for example to present seminars or do block teaching for a week or so) would be a subset of the service provided through commercial presence.

In this paper, we are concerned with the category of commercial presence and the related movement of natural persons. There are two key reasons for such a focus. This is the chief type of transnational education provided in the region, and the form that governments address through regulation. Like regulation of the Internet in general, the regulation of purely online delivery presents different challenges from education supported locally.

The World Trade Organisation is leading efforts to lessen restrictions on trade in services through the General Agreement on Trade in Services (GATS). This is the first multilateral agreement to provide member countries with legally enforceable rights to trade in services. Countries that join the GATS process make a commitment to ongoing liberalisation of trade through periodic negotiations. At its most basic level, GATS attempts to enable greater international trade in services by preventing two forms of discrimination (Snape 1998). Firstly, governments should not discriminate between incumbents and new entrants into a market (be they domestic or foreign). That is, they should ensure market access. Secondly, governments should not discriminate between domestic and foreign service providers. This is referred to as the national treatment principle.

The WTO promotes free trade and the operation of market mechanisms. Such neoliberal approaches promise that competition will result in improved service, as those providers best able to efficiently and effectively satisfy the requirements of clients will be most successful. Promoters of free trade in educational services maintain that undue interference with the operation of the market (such as restrictive or discriminatory legislation) hinders competition and protects less capable providers (Self 2000). Regulation of foreign providers through such measures as qualifications authorities, customs regulations, telecommunications laws, foreign currency controls and limitations on foreign ownership are thus cast as a series of barriers to trade in transnational education services (e.g. Global Alliance for Transnational Education 1999; Moll 1999, pp. 7–8).

Critics of neoliberal education policies raise a number of cautionary points: local education systems may be damaged by the incursion of foreign providers (who may draw away large numbers of students); national values and priorities of the host country may be undermined by the presence of foreign providers not sharing such values; local academics may be exploited by foreign providers (that may pay them casual wages, and not allow time for research or staff development); local students may be exploited or misled by foreign providers offering substandard courses; the presence of foreign providers reduces the control which the host government has over higher education in the country. In regulating TNE, governments respond to these concerns to varying degrees, in some cases subjecting foreign operators to strict conditions and supervision, and in other cases requiring only that information be freely available to consumers.

Southeast Asia is something of a laboratory in the development and regulation of transnational education. As noted above, the region combines high demand from students, and keen competition among providers. Further, host country regulatory regimes range from relatively laissez faire to strongly interventionist. We examine below how the governments of Hong Kong, Malaysia and Australia have attempted to balance competing pressures through the regulation of transnational higher education. These three countries were chosen because they have all recently introduced legislation to regulate transnational education and all have considerable experience in transnational higher education, the former two chiefly as importers and the latter as an exporting nation. In their examination of global business regulation, Braithwaite and Drahos (2000, Ch. 4 and passim) suggest that trade in goods and services is best understood in terms of the interaction between actors (such as national governments, international organisations, corporations and interest groups), mechanisms (including legislation, economic rewards or sanctions, and military coercion) and principles (such as national sovereignty, liberalisation/deregulation and rule compliance), In this context we examine the role of three national governments (actors), their use of legislation (mechanisms), and their rationales (principles) for regulating trade in transnational education.

Hong Kong

There are ten government-recognised degree-awarding institutions and one stautory post-secondary college in Hong Kong as at 2000. In addition to local awards, a large number of foreign awards (575 as at April 2000) are offered, either through local private colleges, distance education centres, or in conjunction with local universities. Over half of all these courses are British, a third are Australian and there are much smaller numbers of courses from other countries, including the United States and mainland China (Hong Kong Special Administrative Region Government 2000a, 2000b). While there are currently no private universities in Hong Kong, the government is considering their introduction (Chief Executive, Hong Kong Special Administrative Region Government 2000, paragraph 68).

Hong Kong has always been a relatively unregulated market in most respects. It was a founding member of the WTO, and has continued its separate membership since 1 July 1997, using the name 'Hong Kong, China' (Hong Kong Special Administrative Region Government 1999, reference under 'Trade'). Until 1993 there were no regulations governing transnational higher education. In 1986, the Hong Kong Education Commission expressed concerns about the proliferation of foreign courses (Hong Kong Education Commission 1986). Such concerns led to implementation of the Non-local Higher and Professional Education (Regulation) Ordinance, which was legislated in July 1996 and came into force in December 1997 (French 1999).

How regulation operates

The Ordinance requires foreign providers partnered with one of the 11 government-recognised Hong Kong higher and post-secondary institutions to apply for 'exemption from registration'; other providers must apply for registration. In either case, successful applicants are provided with an official registration or exemption number for each course, which must be quoted in all advertising and correspondence. Under the exemption process, the head of the local university 'signs off' his or her endorsement of the application. Under the registration process, the application is closely vetted under the direction of the Registrar. From the viewpoint of the foreign provider, the latter process may be far more involved and require several iterations in response to questions from the Registrar's office.

The information required from foreign providers is essentially the same for both registration (partnerships with local private colleges) and exemption (partnerships with local universities). Operators are required to provide a suite of information concerning:

- Course content (aims and objectives, structure and content, and any adaptation for Hong Kong)
- Delivery methods
- Requirements of the student (admission standards including language proficiency, course assessment tasks and weightings, and details of who carries out the assessment)
- Staff involved (qualifications and relevant experience)
- Facilities and support offered in Hong Kong (classrooms, library, computer laboratories)

The type (publicly funded, private or other) and bona fides of the provider in its home country must be established, usually by reference to the relevant governmental or accrediting authority. The role of the local partner must also be clearly spelled out under the Ordinance. The proforma asks the provider to indicate which among 19 listed tasks will be carried out by the local agency. The tasks range from advertising and marketing, recruitment of local tutors, administration of examinations, through to graduation arrangements.

Foreign providers must provide details on their quality assurance procedures in relation to:

- Course design
- Student admissions
- Course delivery (including teaching and administrative staff, learning support and facilities)
- Assessment arrangements
- Management of local arrangements (including communication with local students and local personnel)

In addition to providing consumer information, the burden of the Ordinance is to satisfy the Registrar that the foreign provider is a bona fide operator in its home country, and that the course will be of a similar standard to the provider's equivalent domestic course (Hong Kong Education Department 1999).

Rationales

The Hong Kong government declares that the purpose of the Ordinance is 'to protect Hong Kong consumers by guarding against the marketing of substandard non-local courses conducted in Hong Kong' (Hong Kong Education Department 1999). Shortly after the implementation of the Ordinance, the then Secretary-General of the Hong Kong University Grants Committee, Nigel French, stressed that the government was not seeking to hinder free trade in education services:

> It would clearly be contrary to what Hong Kong stands for in other areas of trade in goods and services for us to seek to impose such invisible trade barriers. Legitimate competition on the basis of equivalent standards of provision is welcomed. However, we also wish to protect our consumers from 'cowboy' operations and 'diploma mills'.
>
> (French 1999, p. 222)

A key function of the Ordinance is to obtain detailed information from providers about their offerings, and to make this information publicly available to assist students and other stakeholders so they can make informed choices. The government therefore advises students to consider only those courses that have an exemption or registration number (these numbers must appear in all advertisements and promotional materials), and to carefully examine the paperwork held on each course in the Registry office. Basic information about foreign courses and local partners is available on the Non-local Courses Registry website. This comprehensive database of transnational higher education allows for a transparency that is not found in most countries.

The Ordinance gathers descriptive information on courses and, in the registration process, there may be several iterations of questions as well as provision for audit. Overall, however, the Ordinance does not indicate any guidelines or principles on what would constitute 'good practice' in educational provision. Rather, it relies on the domestic bona fides of the foreign provider and the implicit assumption that the institution's home country has appropriate quality assurance procedures in place. There is a further assumption that domestic approvals processes are relevant to the course being offered transnationally. In this context, French notes that Hong Kong and other major Asian 'importer' countries 'are grateful for the measures taken by the former United Kingdom Higher Education Quality Council and certain of the

United States regional accreditation agencies which require institutions in their juris-dictions to have their overseas offerings validated in the same way as their local courses (French 1999, p. 222). One may note that the other major provider to Hong Kong, Australia, will not implement such local quality assurance requirements until 2001 (see below).

Just as Hong Kong does not attempt to directly regulate the quality of trans-national higher education, it also does not try to shape the content, level or cost of courses offered by foreign providers. The legislation leaves these decisions to the market, and the state's role is confined to ensuring that all participants in the market have provided information that would enable informed choices to be made by consumers.

Malaysia

The Malaysian government takes a stronger role in shaping international trade than does free-market oriented Hong Kong. In 1995, the Malaysian government reversed its opposition to private universities and encouraged private sector investment in higher education, however the private sector, including foreign providers, is strictly regulated. Malaysia instead legislated to maintain governmental control over the emerging private higher education sector in order to make it meet what the govern-ment sees as the cultural and economic needs of the nation. While Malaysia is a member of the WTO and has made commitments under GATS in financial and other services, it has not made an offer on educational services (Ministry of International Trade and Industry 2000). However, Malaysia seems to comply with the national treatment principle, in that no substantial distinction is made in the legislation between local and foreign private educational institutions.

By 2000, there were 11 public higher educational institutions, 7 private universi-ties, 3 foreign university branch campuses, and more than 400 private colleges approved by the Malaysian government (Challenger Concept 2000, pp. 203–204, 218–224). Most of the private institutions offer their own diplomas as well as foreign-linked degree programmes, some of which require students to complete one or more years of study overseas while others can be completed entirely in Malaysia. Some of these colleges, such as Taylor's College, are foreign-owned.

How regulation operates

Private higher education institutions must go through four steps:

- They must firstly apply to the Ministry of Education for approval to establish a private higher educational institution. Intending private universities and branch campuses of foreign universities must first be invited to apply by the Minister.
- Foreign providers must then incorporate a company locally, 'subject to such terms and conditions with respect to equity participation and composition of the board of directors, as may be determined by the Minister' (Private Higher Educational Institutions Act 1996).
- After being granted approval to establish, the institution must apply for regis-tration from the Department of Private Education.
- Once the institution is registered, it must apply to the Ministry of Education for permission to conduct each course of study or training programme. These appli-cations are assessed by the Lembaga Akreditasi Negara (LAN) to determine whether courses meet minimum standards. Institutions must provide separate

documentation for each course of study, including detailed information concerning teachers, subjects, facilities, management system and rationale for providing the course (Kementerian Pendidikan Malaysia 1997a, p. 10; Challenger Concept 2000, pp. 226–227).

Once this level of approval has been granted, institutions may award degrees and their students may apply for loans from the National Higher Education Fund if they are pursuing their first degree (*The Australian* 14 June 2000, p. 43). However, these courses are not recognised as a basis for employment in the public sector. In order to obtain full recognition and be eligible for these benefits, the institution must apply to LAN for accreditation of courses. This is a more detailed appraisal of the quality of the courses carried out by a panel of assessors who are experts in the relevant field, who check documentation, visit the institution, interview management, staff and students.

Rationales

Malaysia is seeking to reduce its level of importing of education through transnational education (Ismail 1997). In 1985, Malaysian authorities estimated that the education of Malaysian students abroad was costing US$1.2 billion annually (Dhanarajan 1987). Malaysia now seeks to be a net exporter of higher education by 2020, and hopes that the expansion of private higher education will reduce the amount spent on education abroad (Mahathir 1991). Already, there has been a rapid growth in the number of international students studying in Malaysia, jumping from 5,635 in 1997 to 11,733 in 1998. Most of these students are enrolled in transnational courses or at the new private universities (Lee 1999).

Before the mid-1990s, the Malaysian government was opposed to private universities, fearing that the private sector would undermine the nation-building efforts of the public sector. Even with the establishment of a private higher education sector, the government of Malaysia has not been willing to completely hand over power of cultural reproduction to the market, amid concerns that the type of education offered by foreign providers may not meet national objectives. The preamble to the Malaysian Education Act 1996 states that 'education plays a vital role in achieving the country's vision of attaining the status of a fully developed nation in terms of economic development, social justice, and spiritual, moral and ethical strength'. In order to ensure that these objectives are met, three areas of concern have been addressed in the Private Higher Educational Institutions Act (Ismail 1997; Leigh 1997):

- English language instruction may exacerbate social divisions.
- The vocational focus of private education may not meet the country's need for graduates with high moral and ethical values.
- The curriculum offered by foreign providers may not meet the nation's needs.

The language issue is in part a feature of the substantial ethnic divide between public and private higher education in Malaysia. A quota system in public universities exists to ensure that the composition of Bumiputera (Malay and indigenous), Chinese, Indian and other students in universities reflects the overall ethnic composition of the country (Selvaratnam 1988). However, there is a high level of demand for higher education in the Chinese and Indian communities, who consequently make up around 90 per cent of enrolments in private institutions, while there is a majority of Bumiputera students in public higher education institutions. As a result, there are significant differences between Bumiputera graduates, the majority of whom have studied at local public universities and tend to be more comfortable with the Malay language, and non-Bumiputera graduates, the majority of whom have studied at local private colleges and/or foreign universities and arc comfortable with English (Lee 1999).

In order to overcome the linguistic dimension of this divide, the *Private Higher Educational Institutions Act 1996* states that 'All private higher educational institutions shall conduct its courses of study in the national language [Bahasa Malaysia]' (Section 41.1). With the approval of the Minister of Education, private colleges may teach courses in English or teach Islamic religion in Arabic. If a course is taught in English or Arabic, students must also study Bahasa Malaysia. Malaysian citizens in such courses must reach a specified level of proficiency in the national language before they can graduate. According to the Act, the Minister may at any time revoke approval to teach in English or Arabic and require that all existing students that are Malaysian citizens and all new students be taught in the national language.

In practice, English is the primary language of instruction in the private higher education sector for three reasons:

- The large numbers of foreign-linked programmes are almost exclusively linked to universities in English-speaking countries and must be taught in English.
- Private colleges, the new private universities and the government are all seeking students from outside Malaysia and there is little demand from international students for courses offered in Bahasa Malaysia.
- Ethnic Chinese and Indian students who make up the vast majority of students in the private higher education system prefer English, both for cultural reasons and because English proficiency is sought after by private sector and international employers.

The Private Higher Educational Institutions Act also requires that several compulsory subjects be taught – Malaysian studies, Bahasa Malaysia, Islamic studies (for Muslim students) and moral education (for non-Muslim students). Students who are Malaysian citizens are required to pass these subjects in order to graduate.

The Act also requires private higher educational institutions to include a provision in their constitution prohibiting students from becoming involved with any political organisations or 'expressing support or sympathy with or opposition to any political party or trade union'. Institutions are obliged to expel students that breach these conditions (Kementerian Pendidikan Malaysia 1997b).

Australia

Australia has traditionally been considered an exporter of higher education. Recently, however, the government has had to consider closely the country's position as an importer of transnational education.

The Australian higher education system in 1999 comprised 36 public universities, two of which (Deakin University and the University of Melbourne) have established private arms for education delivery. There are two private universities, both with foreign origins: Bond University, established in connection with a Japanese consortium; and the University of Notre Dame, founded through its North American counterpart. There are 84 other private providers of higher education, in the categories of professional/industry associations, theological colleges and niche market operators (Watson 2000). Universities must be established under acts of state or federal parliament, and thereafter become self-accrediting in line with procedures overseen by each university's council or senate. Prior to 2000, there has been no nationally agreed set of criteria for what constitutes a university, an absence of uniformity between state approaches to the establishment of universities, and no clear rules governing foreign providers. Most States and Territories in Australia have legislation that prevents a person or company from operating as a university unless specifically authorised to do so. Because each state has different procedures for accreditation of new providers, Australia has had no clear regulations governing transnational higher education.

The claim of Greenwich University to be recognised as the third Australian private university has been under review by the federal government for more than a year at the time of writing (Donaghy 1999, p. 11; Osmond 2000, p. 3). Greenwich University hails from the USA and has been approved by the legislative assembly of Norfolk Island, an Australian territory. By seeking accreditation from a small territorial council rather than through a state or the federal government, Greenwich could be said to be operating according to the word but not the spirit of the law. Debate surrounding the accreditation of Greenwich, which was seen by some to be a disreputable institution, underlined the lack of consistent requirements for the establishment and recognition of universities in Australia. At the same time, in the face of the protracted review of its bona fides, Greenwich was able to claim that it was the victim of discrimination, and ad hoc regulation. The controversy contributed to the federal government's decision, announced in late 1999, to create a national quality assurance system for higher education, and to develop a national accreditation framework for new universities (Osmond 2000, pp. 1, 3).

How regulation operates

In March 2000 the Australian government's Ministerial Council on Education, Employment, Training and Youth Affairs (MCEETYA) endorsed a set of 'National Protocols for Higher Education Approval Processes', including criteria and processes for recognition of universities and protocols for dealing with foreign higher education institutions wishing to operate in Australia (MCEETYA 2000).

MCEETYA noted that '[u]ntil recently, it was taken for granted that a university in Australia was an institution established by specific legislation', but that '[r]ecently some organisations have sought to use the title in a business name without seeking such formal authorisation' (MCEETYA 2000, 2.1, 2.2). Acknowledging the shortcomings of existing arrangements, MCEETYA argued that a new nationally agreed approach is 'particularly desirable to protect the standing of Australian universities nationally and internationally' (MCEETYA 2000, 1.6).

In order to comply with the broad criteria for recognition as a university in terms of the MCEETYA protocols, an institution must demonstrate that it has legal authority and sufficient resources to 'award higher education qualifications across a range of fields' (MCEETYA 2000, 2.14). In addition to legal and financial requirements, the guidelines also stipulate a number of less readily measurable characteristics, including a 'culture of sustained scholarship', 'original creative endeavour', 'free inquiry', commitment of faculty to these values, and organisation structures and processes 'sufficient to ensure the integrity of the institution's academic programmes' (MCEETYA 2000, 2.14).

To gain approval to operate in Australia, a foreign provider will additionally need to demonstrate that: it is a bona fide institution in its own country, in terms of legal and accreditation requirements; it has academic standards comparable to Australian institutions; and that '[a]ppropriate financial and other arrangements exist to permit the successful delivery of the course in the Australian jurisdiction' (MCEETYA 2000,

3.9). The guidelines also reserve the right for the Australian 'decision-maker' to 'require the proposed courses to be subject to a full accreditation process' (MCEETYA 2000, 3.9).

MCEETYA recommended that the protocols be implemented no later than 30 June 2001 (MCEETYA 2000).

Rationales

The rationales for the introduction of approvals guidelines and quality assurance requirements both for local and foreign providers may be best understood in the context of a marketist approach. Australian higher education is perceived by the government as an export industry, both in terms of attracting international students to Australia, and in delivering transnationally to other countries. In these activities, it competes with a range of other countries, most notably the USA and the UK. On the domestic front, successive federal governments have reduced funding to universities, and encouraged them to increasingly obtain external income from market-related activities (such as servicing fee-paying students, and carrying out contract and commercial research). At the same time, there has been greater pressure for universities to account for the use of taxpayers' money (see for example Meek and Wood 1997; Marginson 1997). In 1998, the government-commissioned *Review of Higher Education Financing and Policy* had criticised the system as uncompetitive, with inefficient use of resources, and protectionist barriers against new providers (DEETYA 1998, pp. 17–24, 107–112). The government's interest in competition and market issues is clearly demonstrated in the range of studies it commissioned at the close of the decade. These include two studies on options for a quality assurance system for higher education (Harman and Meek 2000; Anderson, Johnson and Milligan 2000), a survey on private providers in Australia (Watson 2000), a study on corporate, for profit and virtual universities (Cunningham *et al*. 2000) and a benchmarking manual including measures for financial management and commercialisation (McKinnon, Walker and Davis 2000).

The controversy surrounding Greenwich provided the government with an opportunity to introduce measures that could: regularise entry requirements for new providers (thereby protecting the local system, and refuting charges of protectionism); maintain the credibility of Australian education in the competitive international market; and – because the regulations apply variously to local public and private, and foreign providers – furnish a lever for greater accountability of higher education in Australia. These rationales are discussed below.

The arrival of Greenwich highlighted the lack of transparent requirements for newcomers to the Australian system. This opened the way for local critics to argue that the country was vulnerable to dubious entrants. Debate in the Australian Senate concerning Greenwich University focussed on the need to 'protect' and 'defend' the Australian system. There was frequent recourse to military metaphors:

> Australia does face a foreign invasion in its higher education sector. This foreign invasion has been intent on exploiting our international reputation for excellence and our particularly lax regulatory environment in higher education. . . . We talk a great deal about defence in this country, and so we ought to. We ought to also be discussing the defence of this country's international reputation in regard to its higher education. . . . Let us keep the invading cuckoo universities from fouling our nest in higher education.

> (Carr 1999, p. 4847)

Greenwich (and implicitly the activity of other foreign providers) was cast as at least potentially suspect, and referred to by some speakers contemptuously as 'invaders', 'interlopers' and 'freeloaders'. On a more sober note, the head of the government's Higher Education Division noted that 'it is possible that new suppliers with new products are emerging to threaten the present and prospective markets of Australian tertiary institutions both on-shore and offshore' (Gallagher 2000, p. 3).

At the same time as some decried the lack of protection for the Australian system, Australia – a major education exporter and GATS signatory – was open to the charge of protectionism in that it unfairly blocked legitimate providers (and consumer free-choice) by the use of ad hoc, inconsistent and discriminatory measures. The introduction of the MCEETYA guidelines addressed both criticisms: lack of protection and protectionism!

Consistent with the marketist outlook, the introduction of entry guidelines and a national quality assurance system also served to strengthen Australia's international market profile. This view is confirmed in speeches by the Minister. In December 1999, the Minister announced the establishment of a national quality assurance framework for higher education in order to 'uphold the international credibility of Australian higher education' (Kemp 1999a, p. 9). Australian institutions operating internationally were not able to point to quality assurance procedures in their home country. In recent years both the United Kingdom and New Zealand had established national quality assurance systems that also applied to those countries' universities' transnational operations. In the USA, several regional accreditation boards examine universities' transnational activities. Without a national QA system, Australia was at a competitive disadvantage. As the Minister for Education explained: 'To maintain market position we need to be able to advertise that we have quality assurance mechanisms in place, that they are being applied and that they are having a positive effect on outcomes' (Kemp 1999a, p. 4).

Conclusion

Legislation is clearly a powerful tool for regulating transnational higher education in cases where providers have a physical presence, partners or assets in the host country. (However, when there is no such local presence – in the case of purely online delivery, for example – legislation may have little or no effect.) Governments routinely regulate the marketing of courses, for example by putting conditions on the advertising of transnational courses, requiring that compulsory elements be included in the curriculum and by determining which foreign providers and courses may enter the country. In the cases considered above, three principles can be discerned as rationales for specific types of regulation in each country.

Consumer protection is avowedly the key goal of the Hong Kong legislation. (This is understandable in the context of a society with a historically strong commercial and consumer orientation.) To some extent the goal is achieved by requiring providers to supply detailed information about their services, and making this information publicly available. Beyond that, however, there is an onus of caveat emptor (buyer beware) on the prospective student. While there are consumer protection aspects in the cases of Malaysia and Australia, these are secondary to other principles. In the case of Malaysia, the key rationale is the *advancement of specific national(ist) goals* (including building the local education infrastructure, reducing the outflow of students, and preserving particular values by requiring the teaching of Islamic, Malaysian and moral studies). The government has a clear nation-building agenda, seeking to benefit from international trade while also maintaining its own distinct character. In this regard, Malaysia is the only country studied in which government legislation directly specifies aspects of compulsory curriculum content. One may note, however, that it is normal international practice for professional associations to specify curricular requirements for professional recognition. The key motivations in the case of Australia are *protection of the local system* and by extension the reputation of Australian higher education (including as an exporter) in the competitive global marketplace. Having made a commitment through GATS to free trade, Australia found itself lacking national standards for accreditation of new entrants to the Australian education market, such as Greenwich University. The principle of *transparency of regulations* is most clearly demonstrated in the case of Hong Kong. Malaysia also has a suite of national requirements set out in publicly available legislation, although elements of their implementation (such as the operation of LAN) are still in a developmental phase. Recognising its own shortcomings in this regard, Australia has moved to create a set of nationally consistent broad requirements for providers of higher education.

In each case, any evidence of quality relies chiefly on the bona fides of the provider in its home country. This begs the question in two ways: does the home country have rigorous quality requirements in place, and are domestic provisions applicable and appropriate to courses offered transnationally? Concerns about the quality of transnational programmes have led exporters (including the USA, UK and Australia) to devise ethical guidelines, while international organisations (such as UNESCO-CEPES and the Global Alliance for Transnational Education) have also drafted their own principles of good practice (McBurnie 2000). In recent years, the United Kingdom Quality Assurance Agency for Higher Education has initiated an overseas audit programme. These audits evaluate overseas partnerships with reference to the *Code of Practice for the Assurance of Academic Quality and Standards in Higher Education*: *Collaborative Provision* (Quality Assurance Agency for Higher Education 2000a) and the earlier *Code of Practice for Overseas Collaborative Provision in Higher Education* (Higher Education Quality Council 1996). Quality assurance reviews are primarily designed 'to help provide enhanced confidence in the work of British universities and colleges operating outside the UK' (Quality Assurance Agency for Higher Education 2000b). Participation by institutions is voluntary but many universities and local partners are participating and the resulting reports are generating considerable publicity (Education Quarterly 2000, pp. 34–38). Such scrutiny has been welcomed by the Hong Kong government (French 1999, p. 222). American offshore operations are subject to a similar level of quality control. As part of institutional accreditation requirements, various United States regional accrediting agencies carry out documentary audits and sometimes site visits in cases where a US institution has entered into an agreement with an overseas provider. However, the other major transnational provider in Hong Kong, Australia, has hitherto had no such quality assurance requirements for either local or offshore offerings. The Australian policy changes described above are intended to monitor the quality both of transnational offerings by foreign institutions in Australia and by Australian institutions abroad. These will be implemented in 2001, and, as discussed above, have been motivated in part by the Australian government's desire to be seen to be ensuring that Australian courses offered abroad are of a standard equal to other exporting countries.

There has recently been much discussion of the possible establishment of an internationally recognised system of quality assurance for transnational education (see French 1999, p. 222; van der Wende 1999; Woodhouse 1999; Van Damme 1999, 2000). Such a global system would simplify the regulatory environment for institutions operating in numerous nations. The Global Alliance for Transnational Education was established in 1995 in an attempt to pioneer such an approach, with supporters including UNESCO and the OECD. In mid-2000, however, GATE privatised and shifted its focus to quality assurance of online delivery. The trend in the late 1990s has been in the direction of national regulation of transnational education both by exporting and importing nation states. The three case studies discussed above illustrate some of the diversity of concerns of host governments. Given the range of national and international interests, and cultural variety in the field of higher education, developing internationally acceptable approaches to transnational education will be an ambitious task. It is clear that, in order to be successful, an internationally recognised system of quality assurance must address the myriad priorities of host governments.

References

Adams, T. (1998). 'The operation of transnational degree and diploma programs: The Australian case', *Journal of Studies in International Education* 2(1), 3–22.

Anderson, D., Johnson, R. and Milligan, B. (2000). *Quality Assurance and Accreditation in Australian Higher Education: An Assessment of Australian and International Practice.* Canberra: DEETYA. Also available at: http://www.detya.gov.au/highered/eippubs/eip00_1/fullcopy00_1.pdf

Australian Education International (2000). *2000 Preliminary International Student Numbers.* Canberra: Commonwealth Department of Education, Training and Youth Affairs. Available at: http://aei.detya.gov.au/industry/news/psnumbers/psn2000.htm

Australian Vice-Chancellors' Committee (1995). *Code of Ethical Practice in the Offshore Provision of Education and Educational Services by Australian Higher Education Institutions.* Canberra: AV-CC.

Blight, D. (1995). *International Education. Australia's Potential Demand and Supply.* Canberra: IDP Education Australia.

Blight, D. and West, L. (1999). 'Demand for transnational higher education in the Asia Pacific'. *Paper presented at the Global Alliance for Transnational Education Conference, Access or Exclusion? Trade in Transnational Education Services*, Melbourne, October.

Braithwaite, J. and Drahos, P. (2000). *Global Business Regulation.* Cambridge: Cambridge University Press.

Carr, K. (1999). *Mental Health: Greenwich University, Senate Hansard,* 12 May, p. 4847. Available at: http://search.aph.gov.au/search/

Challenger Concept (2000). *Education Guide Malaysia*, 6th edn. Petaling Jaya: Challenger Concept.

Chief Executive, Hong Kong Special Administrative Region Government (2000). *The Policy Address 2000.* Hong Kong: Information Services Department. Also available at: http://www.info.gov.hk/pa00/pa00_e.htm

Cunningham, S., Ryan, Y., Stedman, L., Tapsall, S., Bagdon, K., Flew, T. and Coaldrake, P. (2000). *The Business of Borderless Education.* Canberra: DEETYA. Also available at: http://www.detya.gov.au/highered/eippubs/eip00_3/bbe.pdf

Department of Employment, Education, Training and Youth Affairs (1998). *Review of Higher Education Financing and Policy.* Canberra: DEETYA.

Dhanarajan, G. (1987). 'Offshore distance education: A Malaysian perspective', *Australian Universities Review* 30(2), 39–2.

Donaghy, B. (1999). 'Greenwich's mean time ticks on', *Campus Review* (August 25–31), ii.

Education International and Public Services International (2000). *The WTO and the Millennium Round: What is at Stake for Public Education?* Brussels: Education International. Available at: http://www.ei-ie.org/pnh/english/epbeipsiwto.html

Education Quarterly (2000). 'Testing time for UK engineering', *Education Quarterly* (Jan–Feb) (8), 34–38.

French, N.J. (1999). 'Transnational education – competition or complementarity: The case of Hong Kong', *Higher Education in Europe* 24(2), 219–223.

Gallagher, M. (2000). 'Corporate universities, higher education and the future: Emerging policy issues'. *Presentation at Corporate University Week*, Sydney, 14 June. Available at: http://www.detya.gov.au/highered/otherpub/corp_uni.htm

Global Alliance for Transnational Education (1999). *Barriers to Trade in Transnational Education Services: A Report by the Global Alliance for Transnational Education.* Washington, DC: GATE.

Global Alliance for Transnational Education (1997). *Certification Manual.* Washington, DC: GATE.

Harman, G. and Meek, V.L. (2000). *Repositioning Quality Assurance and Accreditation in Australian Higher Education.* Canberra: DEETYA. Also available at: http://www.detya.gov.au/highered/eippubs/eip00_2/fullcopy00_2.pdf

Higher Education Quality Council (1996). *Code of Practice for Overseas Collaborative Provision in Higher Education,* 2nd edn. London: Higher Education Quality Council. Available at: http://www.niss.ac.uk/education/heqc/pubs96/overseas_cop.html

Holmes, L. and Hardin, A. (1997). *Service Trade and Foreign Direct Investment.* Canberra: Productivity Commission. Available at: http://www.pc.gov.au/research/other/servtrad/index.html

Hong Kong Education Commission (1986). *Report No. 2.* Hong Kong: Hong Kong Education Commission. Also available at: http://www.e-c.edu.hk/eng/on1.html

Hong Kong Education Department (1999). *Implementation of the Non-Local Higher and Professional Education (Regulation) Ordinance.* Available at: http://www.info.gov.hk/ed/english/teacher/non_local/ncr_ordinance.htm

Hong Kong Government (1997a). *Implementation of the Non-Local Higher And Professional Education (Regulation) Ordinance.* Available at: http://www.info.gov.hk/ed/english/teacher/non_local/ncr_ordinance.htm

Hong Kong Government (1997b). *Non-Local Higher and Professional Education (Regulation) Ordinance.* Available at: http://www.justice.gov.hk/

Hong Kong Special Administrative Region Government (1999). *Hong Kong: The Facts.* Hong Kong: Information Services Department. Also available at: http://www.info.gov.hk/hkfacts/facts_e.htrn

Hong Kong Special Administrative Region Government (2000a). *Non-Local Higher and Professional Education (Regulation) Ordinance List – of Registered Courses* (as at 1st April 2000). Available at: http://www.info.gov.hk/emb/eng/prog_high/high/

Hong Kong Special Administrative Region Government (2000b). *Non-Local Higher and Professional Education (Regulation) Ordinance – List of Exempted Courses* (as at 1st April 2000). Available at: http://www.info.gov.hk/emb/eng/prog_high/

IDP Education Australia (2000). *International Student Growth: Aggregate Trends.* Canberra: IDP Education Australia. Available at: http://www.idp.edu.au/research/international_student_data/snapshot.htm

Immigration Department of Malaysia (2000). *Immigration Requirements to Enter Malaysia for Study and Social/Business Visit.* Available at: http://www.studymalaysia.com/immigration/

Ismail, R. (1997). 'The role of the private sector in Malaysian education', in Marshallsay, Z. (ed.), *Educational Challenges in Malaysia: Advances and Prospects.* Clayton: Monash Asia Institute, pp. 135–152.

Kandasamy, M. and Santhiram, R. (2000). 'From national interest to globalization: The education system of Malaysia', in Mazurek, K., Winzer, M.A. and Majorek, C. (eds), *Education in a Global Society: A Comparative Perspective.* Boston: Allyn and Bacon, pp. 385–397.

Kelsey, J. (1997). 'The globalisation of tertiary education: Implications of GATS', in Peters, M. (ed.), *Cultural Politics and the University.* Palmerston North, NZ: Dunmore Press, pp. 66–88.

Kementerian Pendidikan (Ministry of Education) Malaysia (1996). *Statistik IPTS mengikut Negeri.* Kuala Lumpur: Jabatan Pendidikan Swasta, Kementerian Pendidikan Malaysia.

Kementerian Pendidikan (Ministry of Education) Malaysia (1997a). *Private Higher Educational Institutions (Conducting Courses of Study) Regulations 1997.* Kuala Lumpur: Jabatan Pendidikan Swasta, Kementerian Pendidikan Malaysia.

Kementerian Pendidikan (Ministry of Education) Malaysia (1997b). *Private Higher Educational Institutions (Expulsion of Students) Regulations 1997.* Kuala Lumpur: Jabatan Pendidikan Swasta, Kementerian Pendidikan Malaysia.

Kemp, D. (1999a). *Quality Assured: A New Australian Quality Assurance Framework for University Education.* Canberra: Department of Education, Training and Youth Affairs. Available at: http://www.detya.gov.au/ministers/kemp/dec99/ks 101299.htm

Kemp, D. (1999b). *Higher Education: report for the 2000 to 2002 triennium*. Canberra: Department of Education, Training and Youth Affairs. Available at: http://www.deetya. gov.au/highered/he_eportl2000_2002/

Lee, M.N.N. (1999). *Private Higher Education in Malaysia*. Penang, Malaysia: University Sains Malaysia School of Educational Studies.

Leigh, M. (1997). 'The privatisation of Malaysian higher education: A cost benefit analysis', in Marshallsay, Z. (ed.), *Educational Challenges in Malaysia. Advances and Prospects*. Clayton: Monash Asia Institute, pp. 119–134.

Leong, Y.C. (1997). 'Internationalisation of higher education in Malaysia', in Knight, J. and de Wit, H. (eds), *Internationalisation of Higher Education in Asia Pacific Countries*. Amsterdam: European Association for International Education, pp. 105–119.

Mahathir, M. (1991). *The Way Forward – Vision 2020*, Kuala Lumpur, Malaysia: Prime Minister's Office. Available at: http://www.smpke.jpm.my/vision.htm

Marginson, S. (1997). 'Imagining ivy: Pitfalls in the privatization of higher education in Australia', *Comparative Education Review* 41(4), 460–480.

McBurnie, G. (2000). 'Quality matters in transnational education: Undergoing the GATE review process – An Australian-Asian case study', *Journal of Studies in International Education* 4(1), 23–38.

McBurnie, G. and Pollock, A. (1998). '*Transnational education: An Australian example'*, *International Higher Education* 10, 12–14. Available at: http://www.bc.edu/bc_org/avp/ soe/cihe/direct1/Newsl0/text7.html

MCEETYA (2000). *National Protocols for Higher Education Approval Processes*. Canberra: Department of Education, Training and Youth Affairs. Available at: http://www.detya.gov.au/highered/mceetya_cop.httn

McKinnon, K.R., Walker, S.H. and Davis, D. (2000). *Benchmarking: A Manual for Australian Universities*. Canberra: Department of Education, Training and Youth Affairs, Higher Education Division.

Meek, V.L. and Wood, F.Q. (1997). *Higher Education Governance and Management: An Australian Study*. Canberra: DETYA. Also available at: http://www.detya.gov.au/ highered/eippubs/eip9701/front.htm

Ministry of International Trade and Industry (2000). *Malaysia's Obligations and Potential Benefits Under the Uruguay Round*. Available at: http://www.miti.gov.my/trade/ wtol.htm

Ministry of International Trade and Industry (1999). *Malaysia's Individual Action Plan Highlights*. Available at: http://www.miti.gov.my/apecdoc4.htm

Moll, J.R. (1999). 'The global market for higher education and training'. *Presented at World Services Congress*, Atlanta, November 1–3.

Mollis, M. and Marginson, S. (2000). 'The assessment of universities in Argentina and Australia: Between autonomy and heteronomy'. *Paper presented to the Conference of the Comparative and International Education Society*, San Antonio, Texas, 7–12 March.

Multimedia Development Corporation (1999). *Getting MSC Status: Higher Education*. Available at: http://www/.mdc.com.my/status/higher/chapl/index.html

Osmond, W. (2000). 'Greenwich University may set dangerous precedent', *Campus Review* (July 5–11), 5.

Quality Assurance Agency for Higher Education (2000a). *Code of Practice for the Assurance of Academic Quality and Standards in Higher Education: Collaborative Provision*. Available at: http://www.qaa.ac.uk/public/cop/cprovis/contents.htm

Quality Assurance Agency for Higher Education (2000b). *Overseas Collaboration Provision Reports: Introduction*. London: Quality Assurance Agency for Higher Education. Available at: http://www.qaa.ac.uk/revreps/oseas/overseas.htm

Self, P. (2000). *Rolling Back the Market: Economic Dogma and Political Choice*. London: Macmillan.

Selvaratnam, V. (1988). 'Ethnicity, inequality and higher education in Malaysia', *Comparative Education Review* 32(2), 173–196.

Snape, R. (1998). 'Reaching effective agreements covering services', in Krueger, A. (ed.), *The WTO as an International Organization*. Chicago and London: University of Chicago Press.

UNESCO/Council of Europe (2000), *Code of Good Practice in the Provision of Transnational Education*, Bucharest: UNESCO-CEPES. Available at: http://wwwcepes.ro/hed/ recogn/groups/transnat/code.htm

Van Damme, D. (1999). 'Internationalization and quality assurance: towards worldwide accreditation?'. *Paper commissioned for the IAUP XIIth Triennial Conference*, Brussels, 11–14 July.

Van Damme, D. (2000). 'Accreditation in global higher education. The need for international information and cooperation. Outline of an IAUP approach'. Memo for the Commission on Global Accreditation of the International Association of University Presidents.

Van der Wende, M. (1999). 'Quality assurance of internationalisation and internationalisation of quality assurance', in Knight, J. and de Wit, H. (eds), *Quality and Internationalisation in Higher Education*. Paris: OECD.

Warren, T. and Findlay, C. (1999). 'How significant are the barriers? Measuring impediments to trade in services'. *Paper presented to the World Services Congress,* Atlanta, GA, 1–3 November. Available at: http://www.worldservicescongress.com/

Watson, L. (2000). *Survey of Private Providers in Australian Higher Education 1999.* Canberra: DETYA. Also available at: http://www.detya.gov.au/highered/eippubs/eip00_4/survey.pdf

Wencom Career Consultancy (1997). *Private Education in Malaysia.* Available at: http://www.jaring.my/wencom/mal_priv.htm

Wolfe, B. and Haveman, R. (2000). 'Accounting for the social and non-market benefits of education'. *Presented at International Symposium on The Contribution of Human and Social Capital to Sustained Economic Growth and Well-Being* in Canada on 19–21 March, at Château Frontenac, Québec City. Available at: http://www.oecd.org/els/pdfs/Ceri/docs/Quebec/Wolfehav.pdf

Woodhouse, D. (1999). 'Quality and quality assurance', in Knight, J. and de Wit, H. (eds), *Quality and Internationalisation in Higher Education*. Paris: OECD.

World Trade Organization (1998a). *Education Services: Background Note by the Secretariat.* WTO Council for Trade in Services.

World Trade Organization (1998b). *Communication from the United States: Education Services.* WTO Council for Trade in Services.

World Trade Organization (1999). *General Agreement on Trade in Services – The Design and Underlying Principles of the GATS.* Available at: http://www.wto.org/wto/services/services.htm

Young, E. and Cribbin, J. (1999). 'Servicing the service economy: Lifelong learning in human capital development in Hong Kong'. *Presented at World Services Congress,* Atlanta, November 1–3.

CHAPTER 17

■■■■■■■■

GLOBALISATION, NEW MANAGERIALISM, ACADEMIC CAPITALISM AND ENTREPRENEURIALISM IN UNIVERSITIES

Is the local dimension still important?

Rosemary Deem

Comparative Education, 37, 1, 7–20, 2001

EDITOR'S INTRODUCTION

This article was categorised in the introductory chapter as adopting documentary analysis to analyse system policy. It has a comparative element, in that it discusses two analyses of universities in Europe and North America, and was published in a comparative education journal. It is, in essence, though, a review article, critiquing two recently published books, which is why I have characterised it as documentary analysis.

Deem locates her analysis within a discussion of the related concepts of globalisation, new managerialism, academic capitalism and entrepreneurialism. In comparing the experiences of universities in Europe and North America, she argues that the importance of the local dimension may have been overlooked in the focus on global changes, and also suggests that there are important linkages between the global and the local.

Deem's analysis centres on two recent, and fairly influential books – Clark (1998) on *Creating Entrepreneurial Universities* and Slaughter and Leslie (1997) on *Academic Capitalism*. She argues that the authors have over-emphasised the degree of convergence between the case study universities examined, and that their methodological approaches lack critique and robustness. She emphasises the need to adopt robust methodologies and less constraining frameworks in undertaking comparative research into higher education.

This article may, of course, be related to both the comparative literature and that dealing with the analysis of key concepts – such as globalisation and modernisation – particularly as they are applied within national systems (e.g. Kwiek 2001, McBurnie 2001, Meek 2000, Middleton 2000, Scott 1998). For me, though, as indicated, it is a good example of a synoptic, and critical, review article. This is something that a developing field of research, such as higher education, needs more of (e.g. McInnis 2001).

References

Clark, B. (1998) *Creating Entrepreneurial Universities: organisational pathways of transformation*. New York, Elsevier.
Kwiek, M. (2001) 'Globalization and Higher Education', *Higher Education in Europe*, 26, 1, pp. 27–38.

McBurnie, G. (2001) 'Globalization: a new paradigm for higher education policy', *Higher Education in Europe*, 26, 1, pp. 11–26.

McInnis, C. (2001) 'Researching the First Year Experience: where to from here?' *Higher Education Research and Development*, 20, 2, pp. 105–114.

Meek, L. (2000) 'Diversity and Marketisation of Higher Education: incompatible concepts?' *Higher Education Policy*, 13, pp. 23–39.

Middleton, C. (2000) 'Models of State and Market in the "Modernisation" of Higher Education', *British Journal of Sociology of Education*, 21, 4, pp. 537–554.

Scott, P. (ed.) (1998) *The Globalisation of Higher Education*. Buckingham, Open University Press.

Slaughter, S. and Leslie, G. (1997) *Academic Capitalism*. Baltimore, MD, Johns Hopkins University Press.

GLOBALISATION, NEW MANAGERIALISM, ACADEMIC CAPITALISM AND ENTREPRENEURIALISM IN UNIVERSITIES

Introduction

This paper explores some recent analyses of changes in universities in Western countries undertaken by scholars using case-study materials about different institutions. These analyses draw, either explicitly or implicitly, on four main concepts. The first of these is globalisation (that is, the global spread of business and services as well as key economic, social and cultural practices to a world market, often through multi-national companies and the internet). The second concept is that of internationalisation (the sharing of ideas, knowledge and ways of doing things in similar ways across different countries). The third concept is the ideology of new managerialism, that is, the extent to which contemporary business practices and private sector ideas or values have permeated publicly funded institutions and work practices. The fourth concept is that of entrepreneurialism in higher education, where academics and administrators explicitly seek out new ways of raising private sector funds through enterprising activities such as consultancies and applied research.

It is argued here that some comparative analyses of changes in Western universities, by stressing the similarities between universities and academic work practices across different Western countries and emphasising the extent to which values and practices from the private sector have permeated higher education, may cause us to pay less attention to more localised dimensions and features of higher education institutions. It is also suggested that the underlying research methodologies of comparative investigations of global changes in higher education need careful attention, if the claims made are to be consistent with the kinds of data collected.

Current changes in Western universities which are attributed to global and other international economic, social and cultural developments are variously referred to in a number of different ways, including new managerialism, academic capitalism and academic entrepreneurialism. New managerialism, a concept that purports to explain (and also describe) new discourses of management derived from the for-profit sector, whose introduction into publicly funded institutions has been encouraged by governments seeking to reduce public spending costs (Deem, 1998a), is examined first. Theoretical and empirical work on this concept appears in a variety of guises, not all of them easily applicable to higher education. Often the phenomenon has been explored in local or national locations rather than in cross-national contexts. Evidence of its organisational impact may be easier to find than firm indications of its cultural effects.

The article considers two particular comparative studies of change in Western universities which have been widely cited by Western academics and policy makers, The first of these is Slaughter & Leslie's *Academic Capitalism*, a study of the changing context of academic work in the United States, Australia, the UK and Canada (Slaughter & Leslie, 1997). The second is Burton R. Clark's investigation *Creating Entrepreneurial Universities*, a multi-site case-study of five enterprising universities located respectively in England, the Netherlands, Scotland, Sweden and Finland (Clark, 1998). These two studies do provide both local and global explanations of why academic work and the organisational characteristics of universities across the Western world may be converging. Nevertheless, the reader can be left with a sense of uncertainty about how the local and the global are linked. Furthermore, reading these analyses can convey the distinct impression that globalisation alone (world-wide economic and political changes in business and labour markets, as well as the social and cultural effects of these and the search by politicians for ways of cutting public expenditure) is causing the social, economic and cultural convergence of universities in different countries.

The local–global axis is an important concept both for those interested in the cross-cultural development of higher education and for those more concerned with researching the organisational characteristics of universities in one country only. The question of whether globalisation and internationalisation of universities lead to greater diversity in higher education, or greater convergence, is still unresolved. Indeed, globalisation is an extremely contested concept in the social sciences as a whole, Some writers see it as a set of economic and political processes with definite outcomes, whose existence can straightforwardly be supported or refuted (Hirst & Thompson, 1996). Others regard it as no more than a plausible hypothesis, focusing at least as much on cultural and environmental processes and discourses, as on economic and social factors (Urry, 1998).

Globalisation is a topical and contentious issue not just for academics but also for politicians. Indeed, some academics have specifically targeted politicians in their analyses of the ways in which globalising forces have led to new political approaches such as the Third Way, which is supposed to replace social democracy (where the main form of distribution of goods and services is through the state, and social welfare has a high priority as a means of addressing inequities) and neo-liberalism (where the market replaces the state as the main mechanism of distributing goods and services, and social welfare is reduced to a safety net) as the predominant political discourse (Giddens, 1998, 2000). The Third Way is intended to offer a combination of democracy and public welfare services with private sector partnerships and the modernisation of public institutions to make them less bureaucratic and more responsive to consumers. Politicians, journalists and social critics are currently much involved in speculating about the likely effects of globalisation on various aspects of Western societies. The more common-sense arguments use elements of the academic debates but ask fewer questions and make more unexamined assumptions. This is apparent, for example, in the quite frequent suggestion that the idea of independent nation-states is outmoded and has been superseded by transnational bodies such as G7 (a group consisting of the seven leading industrialised countries) and the Organisation for Economic Co-operation and Development. It is sometimes assumed that this shift from national to transnational has been brought about by the development of a global economy. The latter, in turn, is claimed to have been facilitated by financial deregulation and the deregulation of labour (such as the abolition of minimum wage agreements). As the global economy has grown, it is contended, nation-states have become relatively powerless and are forced to pursue policies that facilitate the operation of the global market. On the whole, as one might expect, the proponents of more academic contributions to the globalisation debate have shown more awareness of the subtleties needed to comprehend and explain possible globalising forces and their effects.

Nevertheless, academics as well as politicians have suggested that changes to the power of nation-states, particularly in respect of economic deregulation, can and do lead to radical changes in, and the restructuring of, social policy and welfare provision (Hill, 1996). The policies of nation-states operating in a newly globalised world appear to affect education and other public services in Western countries in two particular ways. First, there appears to be a greater reluctance to use public money for public services than at any time since the Second World War. This is so even in countries like Sweden which, traditionally, have had a very high commitment to public welfare services. This reduction in public spending can lead to quite dramatic changes in the services offered, their organisational forms and cultures, and their management practices (Hill, 1993a, 1993b; Clarke *et al.*, 1994; Cutler & Waine, 1994; Pollit *et al.*, 1998). Secondly, publicly funded institutions are themselves expected to enter or create a marketplace, adopting the practices and values of the private sector in so doing. This affects not only the financial and management strategies of public service institutions but also their organisational cultures, whom they regard as their clients/consumers and the nature and extent of the services (Le Grand & Bartlett, 1993). It is therefore possible to see how some writers arrive at the view that there are strong associations between the restructuring of welfare states and globalisation.

However, as Pierson (1998) notes, even if the existence of the globalising phenomena themselves can be established, the supposed effects of these connections need to be viewed somewhat cautiously. Both proponents of globalisation theories (Held, 1995) and those more sceptical of such theories (Hirst & Thompson, 1996) have pointed out that some claims for globalisation, and its supposed effects, are either much exaggerated or not empirically well substantiated. Moreover, divisions exist between those who see economic forces as the determining instance of globalisation, those who argue that the economic, the political and the cultural levels are all important but structurally independent (Waters, 1995) and those who suggest that the cultural, non-human and environmental dimensions of globalisation are the most salient (Urry, 1998).

Despite the prominence given to debates about globalisation and the collapse of social welfare in the social sciences as a whole, when we look at the field of educational research, rather less attention has been paid to globalisation. Rather, with a few exceptions (Brown & Lauder, 1996; Ball, 1998; Blackmore, 1998; Mason, 1998; Jarvis, 1999), social theories about globalisation have been largely omitted from a great deal of recent investigations into educational policy and analysis of educational organisations. This may reflect the extent to which educational research sees itself as distinct from the social sciences as a whole (Deem, 1998b). It may also reflect a concern with immediate practicalities rather than with theory, something typical of many analyses of school management, for example Gunter (1999). Yet theoretical debates about what comprises globalisation, especially whether it is largely economic and political, mainly environmental and cultural or a mixture of both, are not simply second order concerns for the social scientist. Theoretical analyses of globalisation indicate the existence of a multi-faceted set of changes in institutions. Thus in higher education, this might refer to changes in funding regimes, organisational and cultural changes, new forms of educational provision through the internet or the bringing in of new groups of students (Etzkowitz & Leydesdorff, 1997; Prichard, 1998).

Research into the effects of UK healthcare reforms has suggested that, whilst it is not too difficult to find evidence of radical changes to organisational forms and mechanisms, key activities and the services available, finding evidence of permanent cultural shifts is more difficult (Ferlie *et al.*, 1996). As Gewirtz *et al.*, (1995) have noted for headteachers in secondary schools in England, there may be a tendency for people in public sector institutions to operate on the basis of more than one discourse or language, contingent on the context and audience, This 'bi-lingualism', as Gewirtz *et al.*, term it, may eventually become a form of hybridisation, as bilingualism is superseded by a single new language or discourse. Nevertheless, before this stage is reached, it may not be easy to discern whether there is actually a value change and new cognitive mindset in operation or just a recognition that different audiences demand the use of different discourses. Public service workers may thus retain their existing values about the importance of the services they provide, whilst accepting the necessity of talking about markets, performance indicators and other business metaphors in certain settings.

New managerialism, entrepreneurialism and academic capitalism

New managerialism is a concept used to refer to ideas about changes in the way that publicly funded institutions are managed, following the widespread restructuring of welfare services in Western societies (Ferlie *et al.*, 1996). The concept refers both to *ideologies* about the application of techniques, values and practices derived from the private sector of the economy to the management of organisations concerned with the provision of public services, and to the *actual use* of those techniques and practices in publicly funded organisations (Clarke *et al.*, 1994; Ferlie *et al.*, 1996; Clarke & Newman, 1997; Exworthy & Halford, 1999; Reed, 1999; Whitehead & Moodley, 1999). On the whole, those analysing new managerialism have not made claims that the effects or extent of it are global but have merely suggested that global and economic changes have led Western governments to question the funding, management and organisation of public services.

Those promoting new managerialist discourses, whether politicians, management gurus or managers themselves, frequently claim that the ideas of new managerialism are based purely on an objective search for efficiency, effectiveness and excellence, with assumptions about continuous improvement of organisations often a further underlying theme. New managerialism is used to refer to the desirability of a variety of organisational changes. These include the use of internal cost centres within a single organisation, an emphasis on competition between cost centres and on the formation of internal markets (for example, academic cost centres might be asked to pay for internally provided laboratory space or information technology services), the encouragement of team working, the introduction of targets and the (sometimes) intrusive monitoring of efficiency and effectiveness. The last may be accomplished through staff appraisal, overt measurement of employee performance and outcomes (e.g. exam results, employment destinations of graduates) and more subtle self and peer-regulation. Other features of new managerialism may involve explicit attempts to alter the regimes and cultures of organisations and the values of staff, so that they more closely resemble those found in the private for-profit sector.

The search for new sources of finance to replace declining government funding of higher education may have been one of the strong imperatives for adopting new managerialism in a number of Western economies (Prichard & Wilmott, 1997; Prichard, 1998). Just how widely believed and practised this ideology about new forms of management is, in higher education, awaits further research.[1] It is also likely that attempts to introduce new organisational and management practices in universities have been superimposed on older managerial practices (for example, heads of academic departments once concerned mainly with academic leadership have now become heads of budget cost centres). However, finance may not have been the only driver of changes in the management and organisation of higher education institutions (Coffield, 1995). The move to a mass higher education system in most Western countries has also been important, since it has meant finding effective ways of dealing with larger student numbers and running more complex organisations. New forms of academic audit – of teaching, or research – may also have been important in some cases, such as in the UK, though increasingly peer-review measures around quality of teaching and research are being adopted in other European countries too (Brennan *et al.*, 1994).

Teaching and research audits may be introduced for a variety of reasons. Audits may be largely finance-driven. For example, they may arise as a means of sharing out inadequate public research funds or trying to reassure the public that university academic standards remain high, despite more students and less public money. Alternatively, they may emerge from the desire of politicians to control and regulate the public sector professions. Local and national concerns often shape the establishment of auditing practices and bodies of this kind. For example, in the UK, the Quality Assurance Agency (QAA), which deals with teaching quality and institutional systems review (and is supposedly 'owned' by the higher education sector, whose member universities are obliged to pay subscriptions to it), has been promoted to Vice Chancellors on the basis that the alternative is to hand control over to the Office for Standards in Education, which inspects schools and further education colleges and seemingly has a more rigid regime of inspection than the QAA.

Local factors may also be important in changing managerial practices. Thus in the English further education sector (which deals mostly with sub-degree work and vocational training), some recent research suggests that there has been a shift away at the lower levels of management from management practices and values infused by masculinities, to a more feminised approach drawing particularly on people-management skills, partly as a result of radical restructuring of jobs, funding and activities (Prichard & Deem, 1999). However, at more senior levels, it is suggested by other researchers that there has been a remasculinisation of management as declining resources and more intercollege competition demand a more overtly aggressive approach rather than a 'gentlemanly' one (Whitehead, 1996, 1998).

Localised factors may also be important in changing management practices in higher education (Deem & Ozga, 1997; Clark *et al.*, 1998; Deem, 1998a). The search for multiple causes of the adoption of new managerialism ideologies reveals a very complex set of factors. These include cultural factors (new ideas about knowledge) and social factors (new and more diverse student groups) as well as economic factors (the declining unit of public funding) at work in universities. Furthermore, changes in the environment of higher education may also have played a role in shaping higher education in different ways in every Western country, even if the sensitising factors are more universal. Thus natural disasters (earthquakes, typhoons, etc.), economic recession and new technologies – the extensive use of e-mail and the World Wide Web – those phenomena which Urry (1998) refers to as inhuman objects closely related to human discourses and activities, may well be of global and international importance (though natural disasters are hardly new). However, the response to these events and technologies is likely to be considerably affected by different local circumstances.

The concept of academic capitalism, as used by Slaughter & Leslie (1997) appears initially to refer to quite different kinds of changes in higher education than new managerialism, namely changes to the work done by academics in general. Although some attempts have been made to link changes in the academic labour process to welfare restructuring and new managerialism (Smyth, 1995; Cuthbert, 1996; Trowler, 1998), changes in work practices for academics in general are obviously different from changes in organisational forms and management practices. However, the rationale for changes in academic work given by Slaughter & Leslie (1997) concerns changing patterns of resource dependency in universities, which force academics to search out new sources of money. This might mean, for example, undertaking commissioned applied research for industry rather than doing 'pure' research for government-funded research councils, an issue which also affects the work of scientists employed by government in research laboratories run independently of universities (Cohen *et al.*, 1999; McAuley *et al.*, 2000).

The possible connections of the arguments about the concept of academic capitalism to new managerialism debates become more apparent when we see that finance-driven concerns, social and cultural changes (for example, in technology and in knowledge production) and intensified competition for students and resources are also to the fore in the theory of academic capitalism. New forms of academic work require new ways of managing and organising that work, for instance in the form of inter-disciplinary and entrepreneurial research centres which are given considerable autonomy *vis-à-vis* their parent university. In addition, Slaughter & Leslie (1997) note attempts to transmit new values to academics, values more usually found in the for-profit sector. Indeed, these authors also claim to have found examples of cultural change in the (Australian) academic scientists to whom they spoke. However, Ferlie *et al.*, (1996) found, in their study of changes to the National Health Service in England, that evidence of cultural changes was much more difficult to ascertain than that of changes to organisational forms and the services offered. This may signify a genuine difference between health and education, a consequence of inter-country differences or a product of the research methodology used in each case.

The idea of the entrepreneurial university is a concept used by Clark (1998) to describe the way in which higher education institutions are 'Pushed and pulled by enlarging, interacting streams of demand, [and] universities are pressured to change their curricula, alter their faculties, and modernize their increasingly expensive physical plant and equipment – and to do so more rapidly than ever' (Clark, 1998, p. xiii). Clark (1998) takes his examples of such universities from five European countries but one can see in each of the case-study descriptions many of the features of new managerialism, even though this is not the terminology he employs. These features include the search for new, more effective and efficient ways of doing things (e.g. teaching larger numbers of students through distance and flexible learning) and the setting up of new organisational forms (e.g. inter-disciplinary research centres which work closely with industry). They also include emphasis on the heightened importance of managers (e.g. by having departmental and research centre heads responsible for managing their budgets). Like new managerialism, entrepreneurialism is not seen by Clark (1998) to be a completely new departure in higher education. It builds on or supplements the existing cultures, organisational forms and practices but also introduces new elements. Thus, academic departments continue but new cross-departmental research centres are set up.

Although the three concepts of new managerialism, academic capitalism and entreprenuerial universities are distinguished from each other in the processes of intellectual formation, there is evidently some degree of overlap. All seem to be concerned in some way with changes to academic institutions and practices, and all identify the origins of these in various largely external factors, directly or indirectly linked to international developments and/or globalisation. However, what Slaughter & Leslie's (1997) and Clark's (1998) work suggests implicitly is that new managerialism ideologies are now rather well established and helping to reconceptualise universities as income-generating units in local and global contexts of the growth of knowledge industries.[2]

On the other hand, new managerialism as a concept is mainly identified in specific countries (and not just found in higher education), whereas the other two concepts, entrepreneurial universities and academic capitalism, are seen as more universally applicable to Western higher education. There are two important points to note here. First, we must not forget the continued importance of local as well as international and global factors in higher education. Secondly, diversity in the forms, practices and cultures of higher education can be overlooked if the data on which we base our analysis are too narrowly drawn. The notion of hybridisation of a range of organisational forms, practices and cultures (Ferlie *et al.*, 1996; Clarke & Newman, 1997) may actually represent a more useful account of what is happening to higher education, than attempts to document convergence across different countries. However, before returning to this question, let us next turn to a more detailed exploration of the work of Slaughter & Leslie (1997) and Clark (1998).

Academic capitalism and globalisation

Slaughter & Leslie (1997) see globalisation as a set of political and economic changes and argue that 'These changes are putting pressure on national higher education policy makers to change the way tertiary education does business' (p. 31). They display some scepticism about concepts of globalisation, not least because they see problems with all the variants of its definition. Neo-liberal approaches, which emphasise market forces and deregulation of industry and give nation-states only a policing role in their own national development, are criticised because some of the most rapidly developing economies, far from having no state intervention, actually have a great deal. The neo-Keynesian model emphasises the role of the state in supporting and stimulating the economy but also stresses the importance of industrial organisations themselves, which, assisted by state support, then help create more jobs and higher standards of living. Slaughter & Leslie (1997), however, note that increased productivity does not necessarily lead to higher wages and rises in standards of living. Finally, the post-Marxist model sees the private sector working through nation-states and international trade organisations to enable multi-national corporations to dominate the global economy and move to those countries where wages are lowest and state incentives to private industry at their highest. The authors note in their critique that the level of technological development may be more important than the labour costs in predicting an economy's productivity.

Somewhat disappointingly, after these critiques, the authors then move into a more uncritical acceptance of globalisation as a phenomenon and focus on what is happening to higher education in Canada, the USA, Australia and the UK. Globalisation, for the authors, has at least four far-reaching implications for higher education:

First is the constriction of money available for discretionary activities . . . Second is the growing centrality of technoscience and fields closely involved with markets . . . Third is the tightening relationships between multinational corporations and state agencies concerned with product development and innovation. Fourth is the increased focus of multinationals and established industrial countries on global intellectual property strategies.

(Slaughter & Leslie, 1997, pp. 36–37)

Academic capitalism is defined as a situation in which the academic staff of publicly funded universities operate in an increasingly competitive environment, deploying their academic capital, which may comprise teaching, research, consultancy skills or other applications of forms of academic knowledge. Though still technically public employees, academics who pursue private sector funding using market-like behaviour may start to distance themselves from the idea that they are public employees. Slaughter & Leslie (1997) say of this group: 'they are academics who act as capitalists from within the public sectors; they are state-subsidized entrepreneurs' (p. 9). This group also includes academics moving from curiosity-driven research towards conducting more applied research for industry.

Slaughter & Leslie (1997) explore the extent of the spread of academic capitalism by looking at global markets for knowledge, analysing national policies on higher education in the four countries chosen, examining the decline of block grant funding from the state in numeric data about all four countries and investigating the extent to which academics are engaged in the market in each. It is suggested that there is considerable convergence in three of the four countries, though Canada apparently remains somewhat different because it has a more decentralised education policy system. The authors use figures on public and private funding of universities, policy documentation and a small amount of data gleaned from interviewing 47 scientists and administrators in eight research centres based in three Australian universities. Only the last named data-set actually fully addresses many of the questions the researchers are seeking to answer, yet this aspect of the investigation relates only to one country.

Though in many ways the Slaughter & Leslie (1997) arguments are persuasive, the evidential base for their claims of convergence is not substantial in respect of several of the changes that they discuss. Thus, widespread changes in the values and practices of academics are not as convincingly argued and empirically substantiated as are the data about the resource dependency of universities. First, the researchers choose a best-case scenario in order to test out the former proposition. In other words, they claim that, if research scientists and social scientists in potentially highly applied subject disciplines are not engaging in academic capitalism, then no one else is likely to be doing so. This in itself is not a problem. Secondly, however, their interview data relate only to academic scientists in a single country, which is a pity. There is no parallel investigation of the work of academics in other countries, including Canada, which, with its absence of overall national policies for higher education, might lead to further questions about the universal effects of globalising tendencies on higher education. Thirdly, there is little sense of the permanence or fluidity of the views of the Australian academics interviewed by Slaughter & Leslie (1997).

Of course, it might well not have been feasible for the authors to collect more longitudinal material. Nevertheless, snapshot interviews can be misleading, if longer-term effects are being claimed on the basis of such data. Research on medical personnel subjected to radical changes in the organisation of their work and funding regimes shows a variety of responses over a somewhat longer period of research, with some adapting easily to the changes, others resisting and a number using the opportunities to develop new forms of autonomy and specialisms (Ferlie *et al.*, 1996). Ferlie *et al.*'s conclusions about complex and multiple responses to changes in funding and other arrangements for publicly funded services are confirmed by recent research on UK scientists working in government research laboratories (Cohen *et al.*, 1999; McAuley *et al.*, 2000). Though other research on Australian universities gives some support to Slaughter & Leslie's (1997) arguments (Mahony, 1996; Meadmore, 1998), the snapshot character of the former's interview data is in sharp contrast to the historical and contemporary detail of their secondary data analysis. We do not know whether those who have taken on the mantle of academic capitalism are actually bilingual academics comparable to Gewirtz *et al.*'s (1995) headteachers or whether these academics have become completely captured by new discourses. Slaughter & Leslie (1997) say that 'The central argument of our book is that the structure of academic work is changing in response to the emergence of global markets' (p. 209). Yet their focus is largely on research rather than teaching, whilst the latter remains the larger component of many academics' workloads. Also, much of their data are on actual changes to the organisation of universities as institutions, rather than on the academic labour process itself. The nature of the academic work investigated is based on interviews with a small number of academics, working in a narrow range of academic disciplines in three universities in a single country. It is fashionable, especially in the UK, to argue that methodological concerns in educational research are unimportant or time-wasting (Hillage *et al.*, 1998; Tooley & Darby, 1998; Woodhead, 1998), but in case-study research such as that of Slaughter & Leslie (1997), the relationship between the means of collecting and organising the data and the claims made for that data is rather crucial (Wolcott, 1994; Stake, 1995; Deem, 1998c).

Creating entrepreneurial universities

Clark's (1998) book explores five universities in Europe that he regards as displaying enterprising and entrepreneurial forms of organisation. Globalisation is not discussed in the overt and explicit manner that it is in Slaughter & Leslie's (1997) work. Indeed, in his explanation about why universities need to become more enterprising and take more risks, Clark (1998) emphasises national factors. These include more diverse students, an expanding professional labour market based on knowledge, and new fields of knowledge, though the latter are argued to be somewhat similar in all five countries and hence to be traceable ultimately to factors beyond the national level. Thus it is an implicit assumption in Clark's (1998) book that forces him to look beyond the national level. By contrast with Clark himself, Neave's (1998) introduction to the series *Issues in Education*, in which Clark's book appears, emphasises the internationalisation of higher education. This is not least in relation to transnational education policies, and the development of higher education institutions in some of the new economies outside the West.

Even if Clark (1998) does not explicitly mention globalisation and internationalisation except in rather vague terms – 'If multitudes of universities need to engage in the hard work of entrepreneurially led change, then the interrelated elements brought forward in the five-case analysis may be seen as *answers to a global problem* [emphasis added] of growing university insufficiency' (p. 129) – they are undoubtedly an undercurrent of his analysis. That analysis uses a common conceptual structure to examine the five institutions whose stories form the basis of the book. Five features of the universities under examination are considered. These are: a strengthened steering core (utilising speed and flexibility); an expanded developmental periphery (the growth of new non-departmental units such as inter-disciplinary research centres); a diversified funding base; a stimulated academic heartland in which academics accept the need for transformation; and the taking on of entrepreneurial activity and an integrated entrepreneurial culture. The last feature is characterised by 'a work culture that embraces change' (p. 7) and a transformation of beliefs.

The five case-studies of universities used by Clark (1998) – Warwick in England, Twente in the Netherlands, Strathclyde in Scotland, Chalmers in Sweden and Joensuu in Finland – are not sophisticated multi-layered or embedded case-studies. They appear to rely heavily on interviews with a small number of senior manager-academics and administrators and hence provide a rather one-dimensional picture of the institutions concerned. There is little or no attempt to subject the claims made by the universities concerned to any critical scrutiny. Hence the heroic narratives are left to speak for themselves, except insofar as it is explained that all of them fit Clark's (1998) emerging theoretical framework. Just how much this was an *a priori* framework, and how far it emerged from the use of grounded theory (Glaser & Strauss, 1967; Denzin & Lincoln, 1998) in the process of analysing case-study data, is not made entirely clear.

Though the case-study analyses provide interesting material about how the five universities examined have changed their organisational practices, teaching and research, and either attracted more students or appealed to new groups of students, there are still quite a lot of differences between them. These differences lie not just in their size, location and curriculum mix but also in their current strategies and organisational forms. Thus Warwick has highly centralised decision making and resource allocation, whilst Joensuu has a rather decentralised system. At Chalmers and at Strathclyde the faculty deans appear to be key players, whereas at Warwick they are not. Chalmers and Twente have a lot of international collaborative research – this is not so for all five institutions. Chalmers has an extensive matrix organisational structure but the others do not. Clark (1998) himself notes that academics from different disciplines may respond differently to entrepreneurial pressures and thus implicitly recognises that local factors may constrain or support entrepreneurial activities.

Though some of the claims made about individual institutions – for example, about the rising amounts of research money raised or the number of students on roll – can be easily substantiated, either in the book or independently of it, others cannot. The longer-term effectiveness of the five organisational structures cannot be derived from a single set of snapshot case-studies reliant on a narrow range of interviewees and limited interrogation of their statements. Some claims – e.g. about the supposed considerable impact of the innovatory Warwick Research Fellowship scheme on the research of the departments into which the appointees went – are not fully examined but are assumed to have occurred because the institution says so. This may be correct. However, the holders of the fellowships and their departments were seemingly not asked their opinions.

The overall message of Clark's (1998) book is presented with missionary zeal: 'The entrepreneurial response to the growing imbalance in the environment–university relationship gives universities a better chance to control their own destinies ... The new autonomy is different from the old' (p. 146). However, what we actually learn from the data in the book about the impact of global pressures, and the interaction between economic, social, cultural and material cultural factors and higher education institutions, is actually rather less extensive and less impressive. Clark (1998) claims that local conditions remain significant but is not able to show how this works, any more than he can substantiate his claims that the local factors can actually be fully understood by a common conceptual framework. Nevertheless, overall the book seems to reinforce the message that international and global forces are pushing all universities down a similar road to the five studied, albeit that some of them have not yet travelled far down that road, whilst others (like the ones featured) are almost at the junction of that road and other superhighways already.

Methodology and local–global analyses

So far, it appears that it is easier to make claims about the effects of globalisation (especially economic globalisation) and internationalisation (particularly the internationalisation of certain knowledge areas, such as bio-science or management) on higher education than it is to demonstrate empirically, except rather superficially, how these effects operate at the level of individual universities. It is also easy to forget about the importance of local and regional differences or to see these as largely subordinate to more global factors. The methods used to investigate claims for global influences on higher education perhaps need to pay more attention rather than less to the subleties of cross-cultural analysis (Hantrais & Mangen, 1996), to ethnographic techniques of research (Thomas, 1993; Hammersley & Atkinson, 1995; Carspecken, 1996; Wolcott, 1999; Skeggs, 2001) and to case-study strategies for the presentation and organisation of qualitative data (Hamel *et al.*, 1993, Yin, 1993; Stake, 1995).

Thus Slaughter & Leslie (1997) provide lots of local financial and policy detail about their cases but then do not supplement three of the cases with the same qualitative interview data of the kind they collected in Australia. Nor do they add any other ethnographic material or details about academic labour in the other three countries. Though what they do is to conduct either a multi-site case-study or a multiple set of cases (Burgess *et al.*, 1994; Deem & Brehony, 1994), the depth of their comparison and contrast across cases is limited. The odd case out, Canada, is disappointingly not subjected to further analysis beyond the level undertaken for all three countries, when actually it cries out for this.

Clark's (1998) book also does not seem to have heeded many of the conventions about case-study or qualitative research in general. In particular, issues about validity and empirical generalisations (Hammersley, 1992; Maxwell, 1992; Altheide & Johnson, 1998) do not seem to have been addressed when making claims for the generalisability of the data offered. The cases are not set up as embedded case-studies (Yin, 1989) and hence do not pay sufficient heed to the different levels of the organisations involved, or the complexities of different cultures within the same institution (Alvesson, 1993). The case analyses pay little attention to how case-study data can be used in local–global analyses (Hamel *et al.*, 1993; Deem, 1998c) and rely heavily on one form of data collection (interviews). Little attention seems to have been paid to the selection of interviewees who would enable contentious or debatable statements to be interrogated and cross-checked. Thus the claims to empirical generalisability of the data are not sustainable.

The absence of detailed and rigorous qualitative studies of all the cases proffered in both books means that important questions, both empirical and conceptual, are not asked. Thus, for instance, how do 'academic capitalist' scientists get on with humanities scholars and do the latter embrace the same ideas about their academic work? How much do changes to academic work depend on other aspects of the cultures of particular institutions? Are male university academics and managers more likely to embrace entrepreneurialism than women in the same jobs and under what conditions? In theoretical terms, Clark (1998) has an apparently tight framework of analysis and Slaughter & Leslie (1997) a looser one, but Clark's (1998) data look as though they are squeezed into the framework and exceptions are not always picked up. Slaughter & Leslie's (1997) overall theoretical frame is rather too loose and hence does not enable them to move easily from local to global levels of analysis and back again. More attention to methodological issues around case-study and validity, to the collection of more detailed and cross-sectional qualitative data and to matching the kinds of claims made for generalisability against the data collected, would have strengthened both studies considerably. In the absence of this, the two studies do not allow us to test the local–global or national–international hypotheses as well as they might have done.

Conclusion

At the beginning of the paper it was suggested that concepts of academic capitalism, entrepreneurial universities and new managerialism had something in common. All of these concepts are used by researchers to suggest that higher education institutions face common problems which can be addressed using similar strategies. It is perhaps significant that both Slaughter & Leslie (1997) and Clark (1998) draw mainly on economic versions of globalisation. Furthermore, whereas some of the new managerialist literature explicitly addresses hybridisation, neither academic capitalism nor ideas about entrepreneurial universities seem to ask about this process. Yet the major proponents of the latter two concepts do claim that the local dimension can make a difference to how universities respond to global forces, because local conditions or a lack of overall national policies can affect the extent to which academic capitalism or entrepreneurialism develop.

It is interesting to contrast the arguments of Slaughter & Leslie (1997) and Clark (1998), about globalised universities following similar paths with regard to academic labour processes and organisational forms, practices and cultures, with those of Gibbons (1998) about universities in a globalised world. He suggests that universities are primarily national or regional rather than international. He argues that the market in international students is not as great as sometimes supposed, since it is expensive for students to travel and since, as countries become richer, they tend to develop their own provision. He contends that it is in knowledge production *per se* rather than in teaching that globalisation has the most effects, but observes that, whereas knowledge production can take place anywhere, the use of that knowledge in innovation tends to take place locally. Hence universities already in established networks can use those to exploit distributed knowledge systems, not necessarily globally but regionally. Here, though hybridisation is not mentioned explicitly, it is accepted that it is likely to take place, with different institutions responding in a variety of ways.

It may well be the case, as Urry (1998) argues, that certain factors in what he calls the globalisation hypothesis, such as material culture and environment, are becoming more important than economic and social relations or the realm of the purely human. However, it seems likely that social relations and human culture will continue to have an impact on how different universities respond to the challenges of material culture and environment. It is therefore important that these dimensions are fully encompassed by the theoretical frameworks and methodologies used by those who investigate the ways in which universities in different countries respond to international and global pressures. Until this is done, it is certainly premature to talk of convergence either in the ways academic work is organised or in the framework for the enterprising universities of the future.

Acknowledgements

An earlier version of this paper was presented at the Society for Research in Higher Education conference, Lancaster University, 15–17 December 1998; thanks to the audience for a very useful discussion on that occasion. Thanks also to Ralph Hazell, Rachel Johnson, Kevin Brehony and Craig Prichard for helpful comments on the first draft.

Notes

1   A project entitled New managerialism and the management of UK universities', ESRC grant R000237661, based at Lancaster University and directed by the author, explored the sources of ideas about (and practices of) new managerialism in UK universities. The other members of the project team are Heidi Edmundson, Oliver Fulton, Sam Hillyard, Rachel Johnson, Mike Reed and Stephen Watson.
2   I am grateful to Craig Prichard for his observations on the establishment of new managerialism as rather older than its name implies.

References

Altheide, D.L. & Johnson, J.M. (1998) Criteria for assessing interpretive validity in qualitative research, in: N.K. Denzin & Y.S. Lincoln (Eds) *Collecting and Interpreting Qualitative Materials 3*, pp. 275–282 (Thousand Oaks, CA, Sage).
Alvesson, M. (1993) *Cultural Perspectives on Organizations* (Cambridge, Cambridge University Press).
Ball, S. (1999) Big policies/small world: an introduction to international perspectives in education policy, *Comparative Education*, 34(2), pp. 119–130.
Blackmore, J. (1998) Localization/globalization and the midwife state: strategic dilemmas for state feminism in education, *Journal of Education Policy*, 14(1), pp. 33–54.
Brennan, J., El-Khawas, P. & Shah, T. (1994) *Peer Review and the Assessment of Higher Education Quality: an international perspective* (Twente, Centre for Higher Education Research).
Brown, P. & Lauder, H. (1996) Education, globalization and economic development, *Journal of Education Policy*, 11(1), pp. 1–24.
Burgess, B., Pole, C., Evans, K. & Priestly, C. (1994) Four cases from one or one study from four? Multi-site case study research, in: A. Bryman & B. Burgess (Eds) *Analyzing Qualitative Data*, pp. 129–145 (London, Routledge).
Carspecken, P.P. (1996) *Critical Ethnography in Educational Research* (New York, Routledge).
Clark, B.R. (1998) *Creative Entrepreneurial Universities: organisational pathways of transformation* (New York, Elsevier).
Clark, H., Chandler, J. & Barry, J. (1998) Scholarly relations: gender, trust and control in the life of organisations, paper presented at the European Group for Organisational Studies, Maastricht University, the Netherlands.
Clarke, J., Cochrane, A., McLaughlin, P. (Eds) (1994) *Managing Social Policy* (London, Sage).
Clarke, J. & Newman, J. (1997) *The Managerial State: power, politics and ideology in the remaking of social welfare* (London, Sage).
Coffield, F. (Ed.) (1995) *Higher Education in a Learning Society* (Durham, University of Durham, Higher Education Funding Council for England, Economic and Social Research Council & Department for Education and Employment).
Cohen, L., Duberly, J. & McAuley, J. (1999) Fuelling discovery of monitoring productivity: research scientists' changing perceptions of management, *Organization*, 6(3), pp. 473–498.
Cuthbert, R. (Ed.) (1996) *Working in Higher Education* (Buckingham, Open University Press).

Cutler, T. & Waine, B. (1994) *Managing the Welfare State* (Oxford, Berg).

Deem, R. (1998a) New managerialism in higher education – the management of perform-ances and cultures in universities, *International Studies in the Sociology of Education*, 8(1), pp. 47–70.

Deem, R. (1998b) Educational research past, present and future: a feminist social science perspective, in: D. McIntyre & J. Ruddock (Eds) *The Future of Educational Research*, pp. 169–187 (London, Paul Chapman).

Deem, R. (1998c) From local to global: the role of case study in policy-relevant research, plenary address presented to conference on Case Study Research in Education, Centre for Educational Development, Appraisal and Research, University of Warwick, April.

Deem, R. & Brehony, K.J. (1994) Why didn't you use a survey so you could generalise your findings? Methodological issues in a multiple site case study of school governing bodies after the Education Reform Act, in: D. Halpin & B. Troyna (Eds) *Researching Educational Policy: ethical and methodological issues*, pp. 154–169 (London, Palmer).

Deem, R. & Ozga, J. (1997) Women managing for diversity in a post modern world, in: C. Marshall (Ed.) *Feminist Critical Policy Analyst's: a perspective from post secondary education*, pp. 25–40 (London, Palmer).

Denzin, N.K. & Lincoln, Y.S. (Eds) (1998) *Strategies of Qualitative Inquiry* (Thousand Oaks, CA, Sage).

Etzkowitz, H. & Leydesdorff, L. (1997) *Universities in the Global Knowledge Economy* (London, Pinter Press).

Exworthy, M. & Halford, S. (Eds) (1999) *Professionals and the New Managerialism in the Public Sector* (Buckingham, Open University Press).

Ferlie, E., Ashburner, L., Fitzgerald, L. & Pettigrew, A. (1996) *The New Public Management in Action* (Oxford, Oxford University Press).

Gewirtz, S., Ball., S. & Bowe, R. (1995) *Markets, Choice and Equity in Education* (Buckingham, Open University Press).

Gibbons, M. (1998) A Commonwealth perspective on the globalisation of higher educa-tion, in: P. Scott (Ed.) *The Globalisation of Higher Education*, pp. 70–87 (Buckingham, Open University Press).

Giddens, A. (1998) *The Third Way. The Renewal of Social Democracy* (Cambridge, Polity Press).

Giddens, A. (2000) *The Third Way and its Critics* (Cambridge, Polity Press).

Glaser, B. & Strauss, A. (1967) *The Discovery of Grounded Theory* (Chicago, IL, Aldine).

Gunter, H. (1999) The development of the intellectual field of education management in the UK from 1960 until the present day, unpublished Ph.D. thesis, University of Keele.

Hamel, J., Dufour, S. & Fortin, D. (1993) *Case Study Methods* (Newbury Park, CA Sage).

Hammersley, M. (1992) Some reflections on ethnography and validity, *International Journal of Qualitative Studies in Education*, 5(3), pp. 195–203.

Hammersley, M. & Atkinson, P. (1995) *Ethnography: principles in practice* (London, Routledge).

Hantrais, L. & Mangen, S. (1996) *Cross-national Research Methods in the Social Sciences* (London, Cassell).

Held, D. (1995) *Democracy and the Global Order* (Cambridge, Polity Press).

Hill, M. (Ed.) (1993a) *The Policy Process: a reader* (London, Harvester Wheatsheaf).

Hill, M. (Ed.) (1993b) *New Agendas in the Study of the Policy Process* (London, Harvester Wheatsheaf).

Hill, M. (1996) *Social Policy – a comparative analysis* (Hemel Hempstead, Prentice-Hall/Harvester Wheatsheaf).

Hillage, J., Pearson, R., Anderson, A. & Tamkin, P. (1998) *Excellence in Research on Schools* (Brighton, University of Sussex, Institute for Employment Studies).

Hirst, P. & Thompson, G. (1996) *Globalisation in Question* (Cambridge, Polity Press).

Jarvis, P. (1999) Global trends in life long learning and the response of universities, *Comparative Education*, 35(2), pp. 249–257.

Le Grand, J. & Bartlett, W. (Eds) (1993) *Quasi-markets and Social Policy* (London, Macmillan).

Mahony, D. (1995) Academics in an era of structural change: Australia and Britain, *Higher Education Review*, 28(3), pp. 33–59.

Mason, R. (1998) *Globalising Education: trends and applications* (London, Routledge).

Maxwell, J. (1992) Understanding and validity in qualitative research, *Harvard Educational Review*, 62(3), pp. 279–300.

McAuley, J., Duberly, J. & Cohen, L. (2000) The meaning professionals give to management and strategy, *Human Relations*, 53(1), pp. 87–116.

Meadmore, D. (1998) Changing the culture: the governance of the Australian pre-millenial university, *International Studies in the Sociology of Education*, 8(1), pp. 27–46.

Neave, G. (1998) Introduction, in B.R. Clarke, *Creating Entrepreneurial Universities: organisational pathways of transformation* (New York and Amsterdam, Elsevier).

Pierson, C. (1998) *Beyond the Welfare Stare* (Cambridge, Polity).

Pollit, C., Birchall, J. & Putman, K. (1998) *Decentralising Public Service Management* (London, Basingstoke).

Prichard, C. (1998) 'It's intelligent life Jim but not as we know it'. Rewording and reworking tertiary education in the age of the global knowledge economy, unpublished paper presented at the Annual Meeting of the New Zealand Association for Research in Education, University of Otago.

Prichard, C. & Deem, R. (1999) Wo-managing further education; gender and the construction of the manager in the corporate colleges of England, *Gender and Education*, 11(3), pp. 323–342.

Prichard, C. & Wilmott, H. (1997) Just how managed is the McUniversity?, *Organisation Studies*, 18(2), pp. 287–316.

Reed, M. (1999) From the 'cage' to the 'gaze': the dynamics of organisational control in late modernity, in: G. Morgan & L. Engwall (Eds) *Refutation, Risks and the Rules for Corporate Action*, pp. 17–49 (London, Routledge).

Skeggs, B. (2001) Feminist ethnography, in: P. Atkinson, A. Coffey & S. Delamont (Eds) *Encyclopaedia of Ethnography* (London, Sage).

Slaughter, S. & Leslie, G. (1997) *Academic Capitalism* (Baltimore, MD, Johns Hopkins University Press).

Smyth, J. (1995) *Academic Work* (Buckingham, Open University Press).

Stake, R. (1995) *The Art of Case Study Research* (London, Sage).

Thomas, J. (1993) *Doing Critical Ethnography* (London, Sage).

Tooley, J. & Darby, D. (1998) *Educational Research: a critique* (London, Office for Standards in Education).

Trowler, P. (1998) *Academics, Work and Change* (Buckingham, Open University Press).

Urry, J. (1998) Contemporary transformations of time and space, in: P. Scott (Ed.) *The Globalisation of Higher Education*, pp. 1–17 (Buckingham, Open University Press).

Waters, M. (1995) *Globalization* (London, Routledge).

Whitehead, S. (1996) 'Men/managers and the shifting discourses of post-compulsory education, *Research in Post Compulsory Education*, 1(2); pp. 151–168.

Whitehead, S. (1998) Disrupted selves: resistance and identity work in the managerial area, *Gender and Education*, 10(2), pp. 199–216.

Whitehead, S. & Moodley, R. (Eds) (1999) *Transforming Managers: engendering change in the public sector* (London, Falmer Press).

Wolcott, H. (1994) *Transforming Qualitative Data: description, analysis and interpretation* (Thousand Oaks, CA, Sage).

Wolcott, H. (1999) *Ethnography: a way of seeing* (Walnut Creek, CA & London, Altamira Press & Sage).

Woodhead, C. (1998) Academia gone to seed, *New Statesman*, 20 March, pp. 51–52.

Yin, R. (1989) *Case Study Research* (London, Sage).

Yin, R. (1993) *Applications of Case Study Research* (London, Sage).

CHAPTER 18

INNOVATION AND ISOMORPHISM

A case-study of university identity struggle
1969–1999

Bjørn Stensaker and Jorunn Dahl Norgård

Higher Education, 42, 473–492, 2001

EDITOR'S INTRODUCTION

This article was categorised in the introductory chapter as adopting documentary analysis to analyse institutional management. Like the article by Jenkins and Ward (2001), also included in this Reader, it is somewhat unusual in focusing on the organizational experience of higher education, though in this case at the institutional rather than the departmental level. It is also, like that article, historical in approach, though the emphasis is again on recent history.

Stensaker and Norgård present an analysis of the experience of one Norwegian university, the University of Tromsø, from its foundation in 1969 up until 1999. For data, they make use of institutional documents, two previous external studies, and interviews with 32 staff and students. The emphasis, however, in the article is on the documents rather than the interview data, which is why I have categorised the article in the way that I have.

The authors contextualise their study in terms of the struggle for organisational identity faced by the university. It started life intending to be an innovative organisation – in terms, for example, of its structure and governance, and in the use of new teaching and learning methods – making a significant contribution to the life and economy of the northern Norwegian region. Over the thirty-year period studied, however, the university had to adapt to survive against pressures to standardise and stabilise its work.

Within the history of higher education literature, one can find many histories of individual universities and colleges, and even more contemporary analyses (e.g. Warner and Palfreyman 2001), usually published at the time of some significant anniversary. Understandably, particularly when they are authored by members of staff of the institutions concerned, these tend to be relatively measured in tone and uncontroversial (recent examples include, for example, Aldrich 2002, Ives *et al.* 2000). Stensaker and Norgård, being external to the institution – though not the system concerned – have been able to take a more analytical stance.

Other significant areas of research in recent years within the literature on higher education institutions have been concerned with the effects of institutional mergers (e.g. Harman 2002), the organisation of higher education institutions (e.g. Becher and Kogan 1992), and institutional leadership (e.g. Bargh *et al.* 2000, Middlehurst 1993).

References

Aldrich, R. (2002) *The Institute of Education 1902–2002: a centenary history*. London, Institute of Education.

Bargh, C., Bocock, J., Scott, P. and Smith, D. (2000) *University Leadership: the role of the chief executive*. Buckingham, Open University Press.

Becher, T. and Kogan, M. (1992) *Process and Structure in Higher Education*. London, Routledge, second edition.

Harman, K. (2002) 'Merging Diverse Campus Cultures into Coherent Educational Communities: challenges for higher education leaders', *Higher Education*, 44, pp. 91–114.

Ives, E., Drummond, D. and Schwarz, L. (2000) The First Civic University: *Birmingham 1880–1980: an introductory history*. Birmingham, University of Birmingham Press.

Jenkins, A. and Ward, A. (2001) 'Moving with the Times: an oral history of a geography department', *Journal of Geography in Higher Education*, 25, 2, pp. 191–208.

Middlehurst, R. (1993) *Leading Academics*. Buckingham, Open University Press.

Warner, D. and Palfreyman, D. (eds) (2001) *The State of UK Higher Education: managing change and diversity*. Buckingham, Open University Press.

INNOVATION AND ISOMORPHISM

1 Introduction

University change during the last decade has been at the very forefront of the higher education policy agenda as universities have faced numerous challenges arising from a tight financial situation, a large influx of students coupled with growing demands for quality, effectiveness and efficiency in the services provided by universities. In this situation strategic change and a strengthened institutional leadership have been a response sought by many universities in an effort to stimulate innovation and entrepreneurialism (Clark 1998).

However, external pressure to innovate is also accompanied by pressure to adjust to other institutions and to the demands of the society at large, where innovations must relate to internal and external political, economic and human factors. Hence, universities are increasingly facing a double-sided pressure: to be innovative with a specific organisational mission while at the same time being an integrated part of a growing, and highly interconnected, internationalised and standardised higher education 'industry'. This dilemma has both theoretical and practical interest, and is explored in this paper through an empirical study of how one university has dealt with these challenges of innovation and standardisation over a thirty-year period.

2 Theoretical background

The dilemma between innovation and standardisation can also be illustrated in theoretical terms. Even if both the concepts of innovation and standardisation point to the need to adapt to the external environments surrounding an organisation, the concepts are linked with two rather different conceptualisations of adaptation. The first interprets organisational adaptation as determined by external forces where organisations have to adapt to economic, societal and cultural demands for reasons of legitimacy and survival. A representative theory here is the sociological version of neo-institutionalism, where a central thesis is that due to external political pressure, increased professionalisation within a societal sector, or organisational uncertainty, organisations will become increasingly similar. In other words, organisational adaptation is a change towards standardisation within a given organisational sector, e.g. higher education. DiMaggio and Powell (1983, p. 150) refer to this standardisation as a form of isomorphism, or structural homogeneity.

The second perspective also assumes that organisations are dependent on external forces, but argues that each organisation still has certain discretion left when it comes to how they should respond to external pressures. The concepts of strategic choice or critical decisions are important in this perspective, along with a view that organisations must find their environmental niche in order to successfully compete for customers, students or market shares, improve financial support or relations with society at large (e.g., Selznick 1957; Clark 1998; Sporn 1999). In this perspective innovation rather than standardisation is seen as the necessary condition for organisational survival.

Our aim here is not to give a detailed review of these perspectives, but to point to some theoretical possibilities to integrate them when studying organisational change processes. The reason is obvious: If organisations handle pressure for innovation and standardisation simultaneously, how can this be explained theoretically?

There are several views on which the perspectives could be integrated. Meyer and Rowan (1977) claim that organisations are active in 'window dressing', i.e. develop 'double-standards' to deal with these mixed expectations (see also Larsen and Gornitzka 1995). However, in a higher education setting, a counter argument would be that due to increased external evaluation activity and various forms of external reporting, such symbolic actions are difficult to maintain in the long run. The notion that organisations deliberately try to cheat and always maintain a symbolic side also establishes a quite negative view on organisations (Røvik 1998).

Another integration attempt has been launched by Tolbert (1985, p. 2), who suggested that the institutional environment of organisations is differentiated, triggering institutionalisation (isomorphism) in some cases, while organisations have more room for 'innovative' manoeuvring in others. Oliver (1991) has later developed this line of thinking further, describing a broad range of strategic responses the individual organisation may pursue when facing various external conditions. However, due to the characteristics of higher education institutions, where one in general can identify low innovation resistance (Levine 1980, p. 173), and where innovation is almost a constant activity (Clark 1983, p. 234), one could argue that the problem in higher education is not to innovate *per se*, but to 'make innovations stick' when facing pressure for standardisation. Levine (1980, pp. 14–15) has suggested that a cultural 'match' between the innovation and existing values in the organisation is important in such situations (compatibility). The alternative explanation is that an innovation may also 'stick' if it satisfies the adopters' needs better than existing solutions (profitability) (see also Van Vught 1989, p. 66).

However, we will argue that one could interpret these adaptation processes as a unified process closely related to the continuous struggle for identity in organisations, and not as two separate processes (i.e., compatibility relates to a cultural explanation whereas profitability relates to a rational choice explanation). This article will discuss the way in which institutional handling of the pressures for innovation and standardisation may be understood as an identity formation process. Our starting point is an interpretation of neo-institutionalism in which change and stability are not seen as opposing elements (Czarniavska-Joerges and Sevón 1996; Brunsson and Olsen 1997). Pressure for innovation or isomorphism is in this perspective handled as a matter of routine, where the important aspect is to attach meaning to them through a process of translation (Czarniavska-Joerges and Sevón 1996). The emphasis on a cultural 'match' where external pressure for change must fit internal values (organisational identity) is important also in our perspective (Stensaker 1998), and puts in our view severe limitations on the possibility for revolutionary 'profitability' changes. We regard the latter point as vital in understanding the incremental nature of higher education adaptation so often reported (see e.g., Clark 1983; Van Vught 1989). The important point is, however, that organisational identity should not be treated as a purely symbolic entity or a static one. We follow Scott (1995, p. 129) in that symbolism, the mechanism by which meanings are shaped, exerts great social power – power that may be used to change organisations. Furthermore, one should also be aware that the meanings attached to given identity labels could change. In this way organisational identity could become a rather dynamic concept where identity labels may last, but where the meanings attached to them are transformed over time (Gioia *et al.* 2000, p. 75). Innovations adopted for reasons of profitability may, in other words, contribute to change organisations through a process where they give new meaning to the existing identity labels. A reason is that values and traditions are difficult to maintain if they are challenged by profitability arguments, but that the concept of organisational identity still is essential when creating meaning to organisational life (Røvik 1998, p. 143). The latter process is, not least, demanding for the institutional leadership having the formal responsibility of 'keeping the organisation together' (Gioia *et al.* 2000, p. 77).

3 Historical and political context

The University of Tromsø was established in Northern Norway in 1969, after a heated debate in Norway on whether the country should establish a fourth university at that time, and especially in the region it was located. Arguments against the establishment included, among others, that the region neither had the academic manpower, nor the student base required for such an institution, and that quality as a consequence would be poor. Those in favour of establishing a university north of the polar circle claimed that this might boost regional development. At that time, the three northern counties of Norway lagged behind the rest of the country in many critical areas; including for example the provision of medical services, a general shortage of trained personnel and a lower educational level. Furthermore, those in favour argued that the establishment of the northern-most university in the world would encourage non-traditional research in fields related to regional needs, as well as academic innovation in other areas.

In other words, the University of Tromsø was aimed at being a quite unique, innovative and 'different' university for that time (Hjort 1973), but faced during the 1970s strong tensions between established university traditions in Norway and the new societal demands related to relevance, innovation and quality.[1] This tension can also be identified in the objectives for the new university construction. On the one hand the university was expected to develop into a standard 'full-size' university, including inter alia studies in medicine and humanities (Rommetveit 1976; Fulsås 1993). On the other hand the innovative profile of the university was manifested through formal objectives of the institution (Bie 1981, p. 159). These were: 1) *that research and teaching at the University of Tromsø should be of particular relevance to the region in which it was situated*, 2) *that the university should have a decentralised and democratic system of governance* and 3) *that the university should experiment with new teaching and learning methods, exemplified by an interdisciplinary approach in research and teaching, accompanied by new examination procedures and teaching approaches.*

The university commenced with strong intentions to adjust to the expectations placed upon it, where a unique, flat and multi-disciplined organisational structure was developed, and where the relations to the outside world, and especially to the region were it was situated, were given high priority. Regarding the development in students and staff in the 1970s and 1980s the situation may be defined as steady state, with only an incremental increase in number of students and staff. This picture did, however, change radically towards the end of the 1980s and in the 1990s when a major growth in number of students took place. This expansion was a result of increased demands among youth for higher education, a demand the university met with an open admission policy. Since the funding formula was linked to the number of students, this also had positive economic effects. Furthermore, in the 1990s the university changed its organisational structure and functions more in line with other Norwegian universities, even though the image and institutional identity of being 'modern' and 'innovative' still seem to be maintained (Bie 1981; Cerych 1981; Cerych and Sabatier 1986; Dahl and Stensaker 1999; Leijonhufvud *et al.* 1999). Hence, as a particular case, this university is a good example of an organisation that has handled the mixed expectations that are so present in higher education.

Today, the university is organised in 6 faculties: faculty of humanities, faculty of law, faculty of social sciences, faculty of medicine, faculty of sciences and the Norwegian college of fishery science. The university has also established four research centres whose functions are to co-ordinate and strengthen educational research in arctic research; environmental and developmental studies; Sami, indigenous and minority questions; and women's perspective in research. In addition, both the Tromsø University Museum and The University's Centre for Teacher and Further Education (UNIKOM) are important contributors in the fields of teaching, research and dissemination. In 1999 the university had approx. 6200 students, whereas the number of scientific personnel in 1999 were approx. 950.

4 Data and methods

Due to the controversy surrounding its establishment, the university has been followed with particular interest both nationally and internationally during the last decades, leading to several evaluations and studies of the institution over the years. Together with biographical material from staff affiliated with the university, this article builds to a large extent on this historical material, and where extensive triangulation of data and methods is sought to increase validity and reliability of the analysis (Kirk and Miller 1986; Hammersley 1992). A study focusing on organisational identity and change needs to be open to various parts of this huge material, but must also look for some structuring elements in the data – in what areas has the dilemma between innovation and isomorphism been particularly important? We have chosen to take the formal objectives of the institution as our point of departure. These objectives (see above) were, at that time and compared to other universities, quite unique and innovative, and must be said to make up an important part of the identity of the institution (cf. Selznick 1957). Our approach has, therefore, been to search the data to find events or developments that represent a 'test' of the sustainability of these objectives.

The data used to analyse the university can be grouped into three categories. First, internal documents like strategic plans, budget proposals and other documents of specific interest in the period have been analysed in order to understand the formal framework of the change processes during the thirty-year period more closely.

Second, historical and biographical contributions on the establishment and functioning of the university have been taken into account to both deepen and broaden the findings of the document analysis (Hjort 1973; Rommetveit 1976; Fulsås 1993; Bull and Vorren 1998; Løchen 1998; Bull and Salvesen 1999). As a part of this process, thirty-two individual and group interviews with staff and students from the University of Tromsø have been conducted (Dahl and Stensaker 1999).

Third, two large external studies of the university have been incorporated in the study to test our perspectives and interpretations of the change processes that have taken place at the institution. The first of these was an international study in the 1980s of European implementation policy where the University of Tromsø was one of the case studies (Bie 1981; Cerych 1981; Cerych and Sabatier 1986). The second was a recent institutional evaluation conducted by an international review panel (Leijonhufvud *et al.* 1999). Put together, this material constitutes a solid documentation of the University of Tromsø and its development in the period from 1969 to 1999.

5 Regional relevance of teaching and research

The regional importance attached to the establishment of the university may be considered as a primary goal for the institution during the 1970s: the university was expected to be a major contributor to the economic, social and cultural development in the region. Teaching and research, for example, should be oriented towards improved medical services, educating more secondary school teachers and stimulate overall improvements in the knowledge base necessary to the region's welfare (Bie 1981).

By 1980, this regional aspect was clearly visible in both teaching and research. The six-year study in medicine, a course in fisheries, and the development of studies in Sami (an ethnic language in the region), Finnish and Russian languages are all example of subjects which were closely connected to regional aspects. Also in the social sciences, biological sciences and geology emphasis was placed on topics and material relating to Northern Norway. At the same time, the university tried to link these subjects to more general scientific models. Furthermore, there were many examples of regionally relevant research projects within the university (Bie 1981). Both regional relevance and regional needs have continued to be an important element in the development of the university. Actually, in the late 1980s and during the 1990s, the regional focus has been extended. The 'region' is now defined beyond national borders and includes the whole Arctic area, accompanied by an extensive research portfolio both in the sciences and in the social sciences. However, to be regarded as a full member of the Norwegian University system, university priorities have also been directed towards academic expansion including a national as well as an international dimension. The need to recruit qualified personnel and students has been an important driving force behind this strategy. Thus, both in teaching and research the core activities today include a broad base of subjects, which are regionally, nationally and internationally oriented.

The dilemma between regional specialisation and a broad academic expansion has been and still is a fundamental challenge for the university. One question for future development is, therefore, whether to consolidate or expand the academic scope. Strategic plans illustrate that the regional aspect will continue to be important in the future, i.e. research in the northern and arctic area, fisheries and issues related to the Sami language and culture, are stated as prioritised fields in profiling the university. Thus, a strengthening and further development of already existing disciplines seems to be an important goal. Another goal is, however, a certain extension into new disciplines and fields. The main argument here, advocated by the university leadership, is that the university is still under 'construction' and that further academic expansion is needed, especially compared to the portfolio of disciplines at other Norwegian universities. The university, therefore, seems to deliberately choose a double-sided strategy (Bull and Salvesen 1999, Dahl and Stensaker 1999).

However, in spite of the regional emphasis on research, the degree to which regionally relevant topics are integrated in teaching on a daily basis seems to vary. Some students clearly want a stronger focus on these topics. On the other hand, the maintenance of the potential for student exchange and mobility with other higher education institutions in the country is an important consideration constraining the degree of local specialisation.

Such considerations are of particular importance in recruitment of students. In the stated objectives of the university, regional relevance includes questions related to the recruitment of students. The official objective, when established, was that most of the students should come from, or remain, in the north. In 1980, 72 per cent were recruited from the northern region. This tendency for students to seek education at their local university also applies to other universities in Norway (Bie 1981). The university actively seeks to give priority to students from Northern Norway. For example, a certain number of the available places in medicine and law is allocated to students from the region.

Recruitment of students has, despite this, been a major challenge to the university. A goal of 2,100 students by 1980 was not reached until the mid 1980s. In the following 10 year period, both new courses and an enormous increase in students seeking higher education resulted in a tripling of the number of students in Tromsø by 1995, and in 1996 the number of students reached its all time high of 6,795 students. As mentioned earlier, this extensive growth was not only a result of given demographic factors, but also a result of a deliberate 'open admission strategy' from the university. While other Norwegian universities restricted admission to their different studies and courses, the University in Tromsø gained distinction as an open and 'different' institution. In addition to attracting more students, this strategy had in fact also a positive effect on the number of scientific positions. By the turn of the millennium however, the situation is showing change. The number of students is stabilising and, as a consequence, so is the grant from the Ministry of Education. Furthermore, the university no longer attracts the same volume of students from the region. More and more, it seems, they prefer other Norwegian universities, while only a minor part of the students from the southern part of Norway choose the University in Tromsø.

This situation is challenging. On the one hand, the university may choose a strategy of being unique and innovative in order to recruit students; on the other hand, there are strong demands on the transferability of courses and studies. The hard fact is, however, that few students generally result in fewer new scientific posts and reduced grants. Furthermore, scarce resources create competition among the established disciplines within the institution, units that also need to be extended and strengthened. Existing disciplines and units at the university are, therefore, in general opposed to the introduction of new disciplines and subjects (Dahl and Stensaker 1999). At the same time, a university with few disciplines or specialities within disciplines is less attractive to both students and staff. Considering the fact that the university in meetings with the Ministry of Education has been told that the university has lost the status of being under 'construction' (Bull and Salvesen 1999), increased funding to a large extent depends upon an increased number of students. Whatever strategy is chosen in the future, it is most likely that a further expansion must take place within the existing resource base. However, in its approach to the Ministry of Education, the university still maintains the argument that the university is under 'construction' and therefore has special (resource) needs (Bull and Salvesen 1999).

6 Governance, management and organisational structure

As a 'different' and 'modern' university, founded on the 'Spirit of 1968', a decentralised, democratic system of governance became another important issue in the goal-formulating period at the end of the 1960s and in the 1970s. By providing stronger participation for students and for lower ranked scientific staff than in traditional institutions, the aim was to make university governance more democratic. The university was to be organised in 'megadepartments' with overall campus governance in the hands of an academically elected senate and an executive board. Thus, a two-level structure was implemented, lacking the traditional faculty level. The governance system did, however, not function quite as intended; not least because small research 'sections', formed already in the 1970s, acting as normal university institutes, enjoyed relative high autonomy, and contributed to the establishment of an informal three-level governance structure. By 1980 the democratic aspects of the structure was, in addition, weakened because the power of the democratically elected 'senate', the highest level of governance, over the years had gravitated to the executive board. The students were also far less active than expected when the governance system was being planned (Bie 1981; Fulsås 1993).

The design of the governance structure was not only related to democratic aspects, but was in addition closely connected to the organisation of the academic activities, and the will to create an 'inter-disciplinary and integrated' institution (Løchen 1998). Thus, some of the 'mega-departments' represented a break with traditional discipline boundaries. As the most striking example, the 'Institute of Social Science' also incorporated subjects normally included in the faculty of arts at the other universities, such as history, archaeology and philosophy. Furthermore, disciplines traditionally grouped within the social sciences were organised in research groups with emphasis on subject integration. Also, some disciplines in the sciences were incorporated in different organisational units. This especially affected the biologists. In spite of this, the degree of academic integration has, however, not been as extensive as intended.

Throughout the 1970s and 1980s, the governance structure caused several problems and discussions within the university. In spite of the 'megadepartment' model intended to promote co-operation among disciplines, individual 'sections' with groups of researchers who took care of teaching and research in their academic fields developed within the arts, the sciences and the social sciences, which on the whole seemed to function as separate units. There was also a growing recognition that the 'megadepartment', in reality, was equivalent to a faculty level, and that some 'sections' functioned much in the same way as institutes did at the other universities. Furthermore, dividing of traditional disciplines with the aim of developing cross- or interdisiplinarity made it difficult to create a well-functioning co-operation within a discipline.

The governance structure at the university was considered as a pilot project in university organisation in Norway at the time of establishment. However, in 1978 the Ministry of Education claimed that the system was both time-consuming and without ability to grasp the institution as a whole. Still, the pilot period was extended for five years and the system was maintained until 1983, mainly as a result of the institution's own choice. This strategy might be understood as one of trying to maintain the image as an innovative and different institution. In 1983, the Ministry was once more eager to change the system. They accepted that the university could keep the executive board and the 'senate', but placed, among others, restrictions on both the size and composition of these organs, which meant that the system would be less representative and democratic. Again, the outcome was a compromise between national and local level. The Ministry claimed that a clearer distinction between the responsibilities and tasks of the two organs were drawn. Despite this, the university kept its 'senate' with only a minor reduction in the number of board members (Fulsås 1993). However, during the late 1980s and the 1990s, the university's governance structure has gradually become identical with those used at other universities and colleges in Norway. One essential mechanism in this movement towards organisational homogenisation is the national Higher Education Acts in 1989 and 1996, which, inter alia demanded a certain institutional structure of governance. Another important development is a much more disciplinary orientation over time, where the academic staff at the university has 'drifted' toward more standard disciplinary boundaries and profiles due to the needs for academic recognition and research co-operation. In spite of this, the two-level structure, with a central administration and 'mega-departments', was maintained until 1997.

In 1997, a faculty level was formally implemented and disciplines were organised in faculties based on the more traditional disciplinary structure. The formal argument launched was that the structure no longer fitted the daily activity and that different levels of governance had developed across the institution. The situation made the appropriate delegation of responsibility and authority difficult. Today's structure can be considered a compromise between local and national considerations, between the unique and the traditional. In terminology and in governance the university has become more similar to other universities. However, the organisation of the arts still remains unchanged, and the biologists are still divided into separate units (Dahl and Stensaker 1999). The latter situation must be understood both as a result of what was considered a possible solution without the consequences being too large, and a result of well-established local traditions regarding the organisation of disciplines.

The opinions about the effects of the reorganisation in 1997 are divided. The academic staff tends to claim that the new structure has had few effects worth mentioning, and that the process in general has resulted in only minor changes (Dahl and Stensaker 1999; Leijonhufvud *et al.* 1999). Furthermore, the opinion is that external conditions and the relations towards other universities have become more important than a local need or wish for structural changes. Some claim that the structure in some respect interferes with established networks of co-operation. This might, however, also be understood as a result of institutional expansion, which makes the university more complex and less characterised by tight and personal relations. Among the administrative staff there is a clear tendency to claim that the distance between ground and central levels is increasing. Again, this is a possible effect of both the new faculty structure and the fact that the university increased in size throughout the 1990s.

7 Experimenting with new teaching and learning methods

The official objective related to experimenting with new teaching and learning methods included both interdisciplinary approaches as vital links between research and teaching and new examination procedures and teaching methods.

By 1980, the degree to which traditional disciplinary boundaries in research had been overcome, and influenced teaching, varied widely within the institution. There were several examples of interdisciplinary research and establishment of research groups across disciplinary borders, but these affected teaching only to a lesser extent (Bie 1981; Løchen 1998). Cooperation across departmental boundaries proved difficult, for example between medicine and the social sciences. The dilemma facing the university was, therefore, one of having institutional objectives that did not seem to quite fit the needs of the academic staff.

Still, in the first 10-year period the university initiated several projects intended to tear down the fences between disciplines. Both medicine and a professional course in fisheries were examples of innovative multidisciplinary efforts, which emphasised a common goal in the teaching of different subjects. This emphasis was maintained during the 1980s and 1990s. Also in the social sciences an attempt at integration of the various disciplines succeeded. However, the 'Institute of Social Science' was obliged to revise its four-year degree to provide a more disciplinary orientation so that its graduates might pursue courses at other institutions. This development towards more traditional boundaries in both teaching and organisation of the courses in social sciences is still proceeding today (Fulsås 1993; Løchen 1998). There are, however, still examples of special and unique courses which combine elements from several major disciplines, such as 'Planning and community studies'.

New examination procedures and teaching methods were other goals related to the idea of development and improvement of educational methods. One idea was to abolish grades; another, an extended use of smaller groups and seminars. Still, during the first 10-year period, such reforms were far less extensive than originally intended. Except in medicine, all 'megadepartments' followed the same grading and examination procedures as other institutions. Seminars and teaching in small groups were used, but these were a result of favourable student/teacher ratios as much as a deliberate educational strategy (Bie 1981). However, the six-year study in medicine is rather unique compared to the education given at the other Norwegian universities. Both inter-disciplinarity, early contact with patients and the absence of grades are integrated in the study labelled as 'the Tromsø-model'. In spite of criticism, especially during the first years, and in spite of problems with, for example, a lack of textbooks focusing on integrated topics and teaching, the model is considered to have been a formidable success. The tendency here is that other universities, both nationally and internationally, have approached 'the Tromsø-model', more so than the other way around (Fulsås 1993). Other innovative teaching and learning projects have been launched in the faculty of law and within teacher training (Dahl and Stensaker 1999).

In other disciplines, there is a strong desire to use smaller groups and seminars as the preferred teaching method. However, the opinion among the staff seems to be that because of the increasing number of students, it is difficult to maintain the tight relation/contact needed for this kind of training. In general, the large increase in the number of students seems to result in a stronger focus on carrying out planned activities and obtaining scheduled results, rather than reflecting upon how well the existing study and teaching methods function (Dahl and Stensaker 1999).

One could also find external constraints when it comes to innovation in examination and curricula. Not least are demands regarding student mobility among universities and colleges in Norway an important factor. In this respect the students have been a group arguing for the development of a compatible system of grades and curricula to make easy transfer of grades to other institutions possible. This clearly illustrates the difficulties of being innovative and unique while being a part of a national and international higher education system. Despite this movement toward standardisation, several faculties at the university in Tromsø still seem to maintain a special emphasis on inter-disciplinarity and innovation regarding teaching and learning.

This emphasis has also affected the university policy for quality assurance and improvement. In the 1990s, quality in teaching and learning has been a politically important topic in all Norwegian universities. Among these, the University of Tromsø has tried to stay in the lead. Several projects indicate this ambition. The university follow-up of several national policy initiatives in the quality area, and the report 'The student in focus' advocated that the social and academic life of students had to be more closely integrated. This ambition was partly realised in the VISAM-project implemented in 1992, after a local initiative and with some funding from the Ministry of Education (KUF). The intention with this project was to plan and co-ordinate initiatives within the field of pedagogy and learning in all university teaching. Thus, projects within the area of essay writing, attempts to integrate social and academic activities more closely and increased teacher back up were initiated (Stensaker 2000).

In 1994, a special committee responsible for the quality work at the university (FUS) replaced the VISAM project. The aim of this establishment was to create a more consistent quality assurance policy within the institution. One could say that this goal was realised when an ambitious strategy labelled 'Knowledge for a new age' emerged in 1995. The intention that was stated in this document was that problem-based teaching and learning should infuse every discipline and study offered at the university. As such, the university re-interpreted the objectives of the establishment period in the 1960s and 1970s, where this kind of teaching strategy was mentioned as a possible way forward towards innovation in educational methods. Today, this strategy has been adopted as the university's special profile in the Norwegian higher education system.

Nevertheless, the results of all these efforts are quite mixed. Neither VISAM nor FUS managed to systematically increase the focus on these issues at the local level, and the university struggles with how to organise the responsibility and follow-up of quality assurance activities. FUS was closed down in 1997 and the responsibility for quality assurance was transferred to the various faculties to obtain a more direct responsibility for this kind of work. Quality assurance is, at present, an integrated part of daily activities at some faculties and institutes (Dahl and Stensaker 1999), but the lack of an institutional 'system' to deal specifically with these issues does not provide optimal local integration. In addition, strategies such as 'The student in focus'and 'Knowledge for a new age' were initiated and authored by individuals with a special interest in these issues. Thus, the organisational involvement in developing these strategies was not optimal. University leadership is, however, quick to pick up such initiatives and relate them to existing activities and traditions. The initiatives taken in the 1990s remain, therefore, very much characterised by 'the innovative and modern project' on which the university was founded during the establishment in the late 1960s.

8 Creating meaning to organisational change

The three basic objectives related to the establishment of the University of Tromsø, i.e. regional relevance, democratic governance structure and experimental teaching and learning, still influence the development of the institution today. How the university handles the pressure to be innovative on the one hand, and to be a part of the national and international higher education industry demanding compatibility and standardisation on the other, could still be interpreted quite differently. Not least could some events described above clearly indicate the relevance of applying a symbolic perspective in the analysis of the development of the university. Still, the past

30 years show a remarkable development where the basic values and identity labels attached to the institution were integrated to the forces of change affecting the university.

[. . .] [T]rying to prioritise regional relevance was, at least at the time of the establishment, an objective which hardly was relevant for other universities in Norway – they were mostly considered as 'national' institutions. Trying to establish strong regional ties was, therefore, a quite unique objective at that time. At the same time, the university was under severe pressure to adjust to national standards, both in degree transferability and student mobility, but also in matters of research and academic development. Not least were national faculty meetings an important factor pushing the institution towards isomorphism (cf. DiMaggio and Powell 1983). A way out of this dilemma seems to have been to re-define 'region'. While the region during the establishment phase only included the city where the university was located and the northern parts of Norway, the University of Tromsø has over the years adopted a definition of region that includes northern parts of Sweden, Finland and Russia as well as the whole Arctic area. By doing this, the university complies with the demand to adjust to 'standards' of national origin while keeping a focus on the regional aspect.

'Redefining' region is also important when one consider the 'need' to adjust to international standards. Thus, it may be claimed that the redefinition process also is a strategy towards internationalisation. A look at the present international activity of the University of Tromsø strongly confirms this assumption. The university has developed agreements of co-operation with several universities within their expanded 'region' and seems to prioritise these strongly (Olsen 1999).

Another example of integration between innovation and pressure towards isomorphism can be related to the objective of having a decentralised and democratic governance structure. Again, one could view the decision to skip the faculty level as a unique innovation at the time of the establishment, especially since all other Norwegian universities had a faculty level. However, the abolishment of the faculty structure at the university could also be viewed as a necessity due to problems in establishing large and strong enough disciplinary communities during the build-up phase of the university. During the establishment phase, there was a strong message given from other universities in Norway that the University of Tromsø would not keep up to the university level of quality standards due to a general lack of qualified academic personnel.

The decision to then abolish the faculty level and develop a more interdisciplinary structure in this situation was a perfect response to external (academic) demands the university could not match, and to the stated institutional objectives of creating a democratic governance structure. The problem of recruiting enough qualified personnel to create large enough disciplinary units was solved by increasing the scope and blurring the organisational boundaries of the disciplines, creating new inter- and multidisciplinary units. Skipping the middle management level at the university could at the same time be interpreted as an attempt to develop a more democratic governing structure, i.e. closer links between the decision-making powers at the top and those that are affected by such decisions at the bottom.

During the rapid expansion period of the university in the 1990s, it became more difficult to maintain this two-level structure. The growth meant that the governance of these large units became more difficult, not least due to an increase in the academic staff. The academic staff were also orienting themselves more towards 'normal' disciplines for promotion and research co-operation. Thus, the university faced a situation where it needed to adjust to 'normal' university structures. Still, the transformation did not result in a complete adjustment to other universities. As mentioned earlier, in some areas the university kept the inter- and multidisciplinary structure (Dahl and Stensaker 1999). In other words, the innovation created in the establishment phase of the university has, within some units, been so 'infused with value' that it is difficult to change it 'back' to a more standard university structure (Selznick 1957).

Also, when it comes to the objective of creating innovative practise in teaching and learning can one find examples of attempts to integrate institutional identity with external forces of change. At the time of the establishment, no other Norwegian universities were interested in experimenting with new teaching and learning methods. However, during the late 1980s and early 1990s, the attention given to quality assurance in teaching and learning, both in Norway and internationally, challenged the whole university sector in Norway to take new action within this field. Other universities were suddenly trying to develop their own quality policies, and the special position held by the University of Tromsø in this area was threatened. Not least, because the empirical data clearly illustrated that attempts to innovate in the area of teaching and learning were very fragmented until the early 1990s. It may thus be claimed that the effort the university made in this area up until this point was more of a symbolic character, even if there can be found examples of well-functioning and innovative study programmes in some disciplines, e.g. in medicine and law.

However, the response from the University of Tromsø when facing increased competition came quite quickly, and the 'sleeping' innovation was somewhat re-invented, now formulated in separate strategic documents that again resulted in several institutional projects within the quality area. The focus of these projects was, as originally stated in the late 1960s, on the more systematic use of problem-based learning, teaching and learning within small groups of staff and students, and inter- and multi-disciplinary academic perspectives. A problem the university faced when re-stating these objectives in the 1990s was that due to the growth in the number of students and tighter university budgets, these objectives had become more difficult to implement. Still, because the University of Tromsø is considerably smaller than the other Norwegian universities, the institution continued to have a comparative advantage when trying to put these objectives into practice. Currently, it seems that the University of Tromsø, in some areas, is in the forefront of the development in this area in Norway: since the mid 1990s students in teacher training keep, e.g., a 'logbook', in which experiences and reflections on the teaching given must be written down. This logbook is part of the documentation that is necessary in order to pass the course, and as a consequence evaluation becomes an integrated part of teaching. Another example is the faculty of medicine, which among others has kept its focus on inter-disciplinarity in teaching, practical training and early contact with patients. Also, in the faculty of law obligatory practical training and problem-based teaching and learning has been introduced. Still, these initiatives depend to a too large extent on individuals, whereas the central level at the university struggles with integrating quality assurance policies in a total and systematic way (Stensaker 2000; Leijonhufvud *et al.* 1999).

9 Conclusion

The examples given disclose an interesting dynamic between innovation and isomorphism, of trying to develop and fulfil innovative institutional objectives while at the same time trying to adapt to external pressure and demands for standardisation. What can be observed is an institution that struggles with, but also to a large extent has succeeded in, integrating these two dimensions (Bie 1981; Cerych and Sabatier

1986; Dahl and Stensaker 1999). It is our view that the University of Tromsø has managed this by 'translating', re-interpreting and 'editing' institutional identity labels to attach meaning to and providing a feeling of coherence when facing organisational change.

Looking back over the thirty-year period since the establishment of the university, one may claim that the direction of change is towards 'standardisation', where one can see the 'innovative' university slowly but steadily adjusting to external demands resulting in isomorphism in, for example, governance and management systems, and in disciplinary structures. This development is following the logic of neo-institutional theory to a great extent (DiMaggio and Powell 1983). However, an interesting point is that forces of isomorphism sometimes seem to interact and sometimes counteract each other in a rather dynamic way. Regarding the governance structure of the university, there were initially two forces in action at the same time. On the one hand there was political pressure specifying important objectives (a democratic and decentralised governance structure) for the university. On the other one could find strong academic pressure to develop large and solid academic units. At the time of the establishment, one could claim that it was the coercive forces that overshadowed the academic (professional) ones. As time went by, it was the continuing academic pressure towards a more 'academic standardised' governance and disciplinary structure that seemed to be the most powerful force.

The fact that isomorphic pressure is multifaceted may be an important reason why the university has managed to keep some discretion when it comes to the adaptation processes (Tolbert 1985). However, the important point is in our view that pressure for adjustments favoured by different interest groups inside and outside the university for reasons of profitability (e.g., the need to redefine 'region' and the development of the new governance structure which partly were initiated due to academic pressure from inside), has been accomplished through a process where compatibility (organisational identity) arguments have played an essential role. This process is not that of unconscious adaptation or pure opportunism; rather it is a process with strong strategic and long-term emphasis (cf. Røvik 1998, p. 142).

A look at the transformation of the University of Tromsø over the years supports this view. Changes have not been radical or revolutionary, characterised by short term motivation, but could rather be characterised as piecemeal, somewhat experimental, yet with a strong historic link (cf. Clark 1998, p. 145). This seems to be a deliberate strategy by the university. To quote the strategic plan for the university from 1987:

> *It is important to remember the old when one changes to something new. Evolution is better than revolution in this respect. Many changes in processes have failed due to beliefs in radical change, where old structures are taken away without having new structures to replace them. The old must be administered at the same time as new things evolve*

(authors' translation)

The quotation illustrates a willingness to change according to new demands and changes in the university environment. However, it also states an interest in developing and nurturing the institutional identity. Our case study indicates that maintaining and developing the institutional identity is not only about 'impression management', but an important process during organisational change (cf. Røvik 1998, p. 142). To make only symbolic adjustments as a response to external demands may convince the environment to some degree, but is hardly a tool for convincing those who work at the institution. To be able to create 'entrepreneurial cultures' and 'stimulating academic heartlands' (cf. Clark 1998; Sporn 1999), requires that those who constitute these entities also trust and believe in the organisation they belong to. It is to support such processes that nurturing the institutional identity could play an important role.

Acknowledgement

We would like to thank Dr. Peter Maassen and three anonymous reviewers for their valuable comments.

Note

1   Even if these objectives must be regarded as 'innovations' at that time, they are at present more common objectives in the Norwegian University sector.

References

Bie, K.N. (1981). *Creating a New University. The Establishment and Development of the University of Tromsø*. Oslo: Institute for Studies in Research and Higher Education.
Brunsson, N. and Olsen J.R. (1997). *The Reforming Organisation*. Bergen: Fagbokforlaget.
Bull, T. and Vorren Red, T.O. (1998). *Universitetet i Tromsø. Glint fra de første 30 år*. Ravnetrykk nr.l7. Tromsø: Universitetet i Tromsø.
Bull, T. and Salvesen, I.B. (1999). 'Utviklinga av Universitetet i Tromsø inn i det neste tusenåret. I Arnzten, A., J-I. Nergård og Ø. Norderval red', *Sin neste sam seg selv. Ole Mjøs 60 år*. Ravnetrykk, Tromsø: Universitetet i Tromsø.
Cerych, L. (1981). 'Introduction', in Bie, K.N. (ed.), *Creating a New University. The Establishment and Development of the University of Tromsø*. Oslo: Institute for Studies in Research and Higher Education.
Cerych, L. and Sabatier, P. (1986). *Great Expectations and Mixed Performance. The Implementation of Higher Education Reforms in Europe*. Stoke-on-Trent: European Institute of Education and Social Policy/Trentham Books.
Clark, B.R. (1983). *The Higher Education System*. Berkeley: University of California Press.
Clark, B.R. (1998). *Creating Entrepreneurial Universities: Organizational Pathways of Transformation*. New York: International Association of Universities Press/Pergamon – Elsevier Science.
Czarniawska-Joerges, B. and Sevón, G. (eds) (1996). *Translating Organizational Change*. New York: Walter de Gruyter.
Dahl, J. and Stensaker, B. (1999). *Fra mnodernitet til tradisjon? Slyring og organisering av virksomheten ved Universitetet i Tromsø*, Oslo: NIFU 4/99.
DiMaggio, P. and Powell, W.W. (1983). 'The iron cage revisited: institutional isomorphism and collective rationality in organizational fields', *American Sociological Review* 48, 147–160.
Fulsås, N. (1993). *Universitetet i Tromsø 25 år*. Tromsø: Universitetet i Tromsø.
Goia, D.A., Schultz, M. and Corley, K.G. (2000). 'Organizational identity, image, and adaptive instability', *Academy of Management Review* 25(1), 63–81.
Hammersley, M. (1992). 'Some reflections on ethnography and validity', *International Journal of Qualitative Studies in Education* 5, 195–203.
Hjort, P.F. (1973). *Universitetet i Tromsø: Hvomfor; hvordan og hvorhen*. Oslo: Polyteknisk forening.
Kirk, J. and Miller, M.L. (1986). *Reliability and Validity in Qualitative Research*. Sage, London: Qualitative Research Methods Series, No. 1.
Leijonhufvud, M., Larsen, P.O., Barlindhaug, J.P., Flatin, K.A. and Lindquist, O.X. (1999). *Evaluering av Universitetet i Tronsø. Rapport fra ekstern komité*. Oslo: Network Norway Council 3/1999.
Levine, A. (1980). *Why innovations fail*. Albany: State University of New York Press.

Løchen, Y. (1998). Etterlengtede, krevende universitetsreformer. I Bull, T. and Vorren Red, T.O. (1998) *Universitetet i Tromsø. Glimt fra de første 30 år.* Ravnetrykk nr.17. Tromsø: Universitetet i Tromsø.

Meyer, J. and Rowan, B. (1977). 'Institutionalized organizations: formal structure as myth and ceremony', *American Journal of Sociology* 83, 340–363.

Oliver, C. (1991). 'Strategic responses to institutional processes', *Academy of Management Review* 16(1), 145–179.

Olsen, H. (1999). *Internasjonalisering ved de norske høyere utdanningsinstitusjonene. Omfang og organisering av formaliserte institusjonelle aktiviteter.* Oslo: NIFU 1/99.

Rommetveit, K. (1976). 'Decision making under changing norms', in March, J.O. and Olsen, J.P. (eds), *Ambiguity and Choice in Organizations.* Oslo: Universitetsforlaget.

Røvik, K.A. (1998). *Moderne organisasjoner. Trender i organisasjonstenkningen ved tusenårsskiftet,* Bergen: Fagbokforlaget.

Scott, W.R. (1995). *Institutions and Organizations.* London: Sage Publications.

Selznick, P. (1957). *Leadership in Administration.* New York: Harper and Row.

Sporn, B. (1999). *Adaptive University Structures. An Analysis of Adaptation to Socio-economic Environments of US and European Universities.* London: Jessica Kingsley Publishers.

Stensaker, B. (1998). 'Culture and fashion in reform implementation: perceptions and adaptation of management reforms in higher education', *Journal of Higher Education Policy and Management* 20, 129–138.

Stensaker, B. (2000). *Høyere utdanning i endring. Dokumentasjon og drøfting av kvalitetsutviklingstiltak ved seks norske universiteter og høgskoler.* Oslo: NIFU 6/2000.

Tolbert, P.S. (1985). 'Institutional environments and resource dependence: sources of administrative structure in institutions of higher education', *Administrative Science Quarterly* 30(1), 1–13.

Van Vught, P.A. (ed.) (1989). *Governmental Strategies and Innovation in Higher Education.* London: Jessica Kingsley Publishers.

Studies in Higher Education

EDITOR
Malcolm Tight, *University of Warwick, UK*

Supported by an International Editorial Board and Advisory Board.

Studies in Higher Education welcomes contributions on most aspects of higher education. The Editor especially wishes to encourage two kinds of paper:

- those which illuminate teaching and learning by bringing to bear particular disciplinary perspectives (such as those of sociology, philosophy, psychology, economics and history, and cultural and policy studies)

- those in which teachers in higher education engage in systematic reflection on their own practices.

A key criterion for publication is that papers should be written in an accessible while rigorous style, which communicates to non-specialists.

Studies in Higher Education is published on behalf of the Society for Research into Higher Education.

This journal is also available online. Please connect to www.tandf.co.uk/online.html for further information.

To request a sample copy please visit: **www.tandf.co.uk/journals**

SUBSCRIPTION RATES
2003 – Volume 28 (4 issues)
Print ISSN 0307-5079
Online ISSN 1470-174X
Institutional rate: US$1041; £463 (includes free online access)
Personal rate: US$217; £129 (print only)

Carfax Publishing
Taylor & Francis Group

For further information, please contact Customer Services at either:
Taylor & Francis Ltd, Rankine Road, Basingstoke, Hants RG24 8PR, UK
Tel: +44 (0)1256 813002   Fax: +44 (0)1256 330245 Email: enquiry@tandf.co.uk
Website: www.tandf.co.uk
Taylor & Francis Inc, 325 Chestnut Street, 8th Floor, Philadelphia, PA 19106, USA
Tel: +1 215 6258900 Fax: +1 215 6258914 Email: info@taylorandfrancis.com
Website: www.taylorandfrancis.com

cshe

Research into Higher Education Abstracts

EDITOR
Ian McNay, *University of Greenwich, UK*

Research into Higher Education Abstracts exists to propagate knowledge about, and encourage discussion of significant research into higher education. Published on behalf of the *Society for Research into Higher Education*, it provides a regular survey of international periodicals relevant to the theory and practice of higher education and also offers a selective coverage of books and monographs.

More than 600 abstracts are produced each year. They are grouped under eight headings: national systems and comparative studies, institutional management, curriculum (including subject studies with wider relevance), research, students, staff, finance and physical resources and contributory studies (including research design and methodologies). A key word subject index in each volume allows easy reference to those which cross category boundaries. An author index and a list of journals, with addresses, from which abstracts are drawn are also included in each issue. A cumulative index is published annually.

This journal is also available online. Please connect to www.tandf.co.uk/online.html for further information.

SUBSCRIPTION RATES
2003 - Volume 36 (3 issues)
Print ISSN 0034-5326
Online ISSN 1467-5862
Institutional rate: US$761; £417 (includes online access)
Personal rate: US$304; £149 (print only)

Carfax Publishing
Taylor & Francis Group

crhe

For further information, please contact Customer Services at either:
Taylor & Francis Ltd, Rankine Road, Basingstoke, Hants RG24 8PR, UK
Tel: +44 (0)1256 813002   Fax: +44 (0)1256 330245   Email: enquiry@tandf.co.uk
Website: www.tandf.co.uk
Taylor & Francis Inc, 325 Chestnut Street, 8th Floor, Philadelphia, PA 19106, USA
Tel: +1 215 6258900 Fax: +1 215 6258914   Email: info@taylorandfrancis.com
Website: www.taylorandfrancis.com